Women and the Law

Women and the Law

A Social Historical Perspective

Volume II

Property, Family and the
Legal Profession

edited by

D. Kelly Weisberg

SCHENKMAN PUBLISHING COMPANY, INC.
Cambridge, Massachusetts

"Historical Background of 'Protective'
Labor Legislation: *Muller* v. *Oregon*,"
© 1982 by Nancy S. Erickson.
"Women's Entry into Corporate Law
Firms," © 1982 by Cynthia Fuchs
Epstein.

Library of Congress Cataloging in Publication Data

Main entry under title:

Women and the law.

Contents: v. 1. Criminal law—v. 2. Property,
family, and legal profession.
1. Women—Legal status, laws, etc.—United
States—History—Addresses, essays, lectures.
I. Weisberg, D. Kelly.
KF478.A5W65   346.7301'34   82-843
ISBN 0-87073-592-6   347.306134   AACR2
ISBN 0-87073-593-4 (pbk.)

CONTENTS

PART III
Property Rights and the Legal Status of Women

The focus of Part III is women and property rights. Recent texts on sex-based discrimination devote some attention to this topic,[1] but tend to emphasize contemporary marital property law.[2] Essays in this section attempt to give broader coverage from a historical perspective.

Legal texts uniformly point out that until the late nineteenth century, a woman's legal identity upon marriage merged with her husband's.[3] In addition, the married woman also acquired certain civil disabilities, such as limitations on her ability to own, administer, and control property. Underlying woman's status was a concept of woman as a man's "property"—a concept applicable not only to the married woman but to the single woman as well who was subject to her father's control preceding her marriage.[4]

With the exception of research on married women's property acts,[5] little has been written about women's property rights from a historical perspective. Two classic social historical works have been long consigned to oblivion. Mary Beard's *Women as Force in History*,[6] written in 1946 and only recently "rediscovered,"[7] explores the background of the Anglo-American juristic doctrine of marital unity. Beard examines the status of women and women's property rights in medieval English law as well as the subsequent legal status of women and their property rights. Beard argues that, although the common-law doctrine submerged the married woman's legal identity, a vast body of law (composed primarily of equity) gave the married woman juristic recognition.

Richard Morris also addresses women's property rights for another historical epoch.[8] Morris explores the legal status of women in colonial America. He suggests that the proprietary capacity of the colonial wife was measurably enlarged in comparison with that of her English counterpart. The basis for her enhanced legal status was the economic and social conditions of colonial America. The commercial revolution stamped its mark more speedily upon colonial America than upon England. Because of colonial economic conditions, American women acted on behalf of their husbands in conducting mercantile establishments, supervising landed estates, and representing their husbands' economic interests. These factors contributed to an amelioration of women's legal status.

Essays in Part III attempt to redress the longstanding scholarly neglect of the topic of women and property. They focus on the dual aspects of women's property rights and women as property. The concept of women as property is reflected in the two initial essays dealing with the special regulations applicable to slave women in ancient Rome, and again with the custom of *merchet* in medieval England. Subsequent essays focus on women's property rights. Specifically, these essays touch on the rights of women to control their own earnings, administer and control property and contract regarding that property, and to inherit property and dispose of that property by will.

The essays explore women's property rights in diverse historical periods. Based on juristic and epigraphic evidence, Susan Treggiari examines the lives of slave women and freedwomen in Rome during the Principate (c. 27 B.C. to A.D. 235). Jurists' commentary on the purchase and sale of women slaves illuminate the different Roman views of women as property. Thus, the breeding potential and proven fertility of women slaves enhanced their economic value; also, sterile women might be returned to the vendor. Upward mobility existed too for slave women who might be freed for marriage or for bearing four children.

Another aspect of women as property is revealed in Treggiari's examination of the sexual exploitation of slave women. Sexual relationships with men of the household were regarded as a necessary feature of slave life. Only limited protection was offered to these women by the law. Specifically, the law sanctioned the owner's prostituting a slave without prior agreement with the vendor, and also penalized the seduction of other people's slaves.

In medieval England, we witness another aspect of women as property. Eleanor Searle in "*Merchet* and Women's Property Rights in Medieval England," examines a common medieval custom. *Merchet* signified the payment given to a manorial lord by a young woman's family to secure his permission for her marriage. Searle's research, based on jurists' works and the records of medieval disputes over this payment, explores the origins and operation of the custom and contributes a new view to the debate among historians as to the custom's significance.

The fine of *merchet*, many historians have argued, implies male control over the licit sexual activity of peasant girls. However, Searle suggests an alternative explanation: *merchet* was a form of taxation on a property transaction. Thereby, a medieval girl was taxed by her lord on both her dowry (her marriage gift from her family) and on the dower rights to her husband's estate which she acquired by virtue of her marriage. This suggests that the custom did not symbolize control over women as property, as much as a recognition of women's limited property rights.

The essay by Theodore Rivers examines a long neglected group of women—widows. Rivers suggests in "Widows' Rights in Anglo-Saxon Law" that the most favored women in England were not single women or married women, but rather widows. He explores the legal status of widows through an examination of Anglo-Saxon legal codes from the time of Aethelberht (ante 597) to Cnut (1034).

Rivers's central thesis is that the legal status of women, and widows in particular, was transformed by late Anglo-Saxon times. At first, women were under the protection of men who were fathers, husbands, or other male guardians. Payment for any injustice to women was owed to their kindred. However, by late Anglo-Saxon times, widows had obtained new guardians—the church and state. Widows were placed under the protection of the church and state against social and sexual exploitation. These new guardians constituted a more distant source of social control. This distant form of supervision enabled women's legal status to improve.

No discussion of women and property law is complete without reference to the married women's property acts. Linda Speth in "The Married Woman's Property Acts, 1839–1865: Reform, Reaction, or Revolution?" explores the significance of this legislation.

The legislation was enacted in several states during the nineteenth century to eliminate many of the civil disabilities of married women.

Speth begins with a review of prior scholarly treatment of the legislative reforms. She discusses the conflicting historical interpretations of the legislation, explaining that the acts signify something different to the bench, bar, historian, legal historian, and feminist. Speth then presents an overview of the married women's property acts from a comparative perspective. She examines the origins and nature of the legislation in several states, including Mississippi, Maryland, Vermont, New York, and Ohio. She contends that the legislation resulted from diverse origins but had a similar limited impact. Speth contends that the antebellum legislation initially did not signal a dramatic improvement in women's legal status. Rather, the significance of the legislation was in providing the groundwork for future reforms which would subsequently enhance women's legal status.

NOTES

1. Neither of the two leading sex-based discrimination texts includes a chapter on discrimination in property law. Both texts focus their primary coverage on discrimination in family law, employment, education, and criminal law. However, some discussion of property law is interspersed in textual material and cases in the preceding areas, especially in terms of employment discrimination and the family. See generally, Herma Hill Kay, *Text, Cases and Materials on Sex-Based Discrimination*, 2d ed. (St. Paul, Minn.: West Publishing Co., 1981), and Barbara Allen Babcock et al., *Sex Discrimination and the Law: Causes and Remedies* (Boston: Little, Brown & Co., 1975).

2. See Kay, pp. 200–219 on marital property regimes, and pp. 257–278 on financial provisions of dissolutions. Also see Babcock et al., pp. 737–819, on the influence of governmental programs on family structure, and pp. 595–619 on marital property law.

3. See, for example, Babcock et al., pp. 561–563; Kay, pp. 163–165; and Leo Kanowitz, *Sex Roles in Law and Society* (Albuquerque: University of Mexico Press, 1973), pp. 183–185.

4. This concept of women as property may still be witnessed in twentieth-century case law. See, for example, Tinker v. Colwell, 193 U.S. 473 (1904).

5. See, for example, Norma Basch, "Invisible Women: The Legal Fic-

tion of Marital Unity in Nineteenth Century America," 5 Feminist Stud. 346 (1979), and Peggy A. Rabkin, "The Origins of Law Reform: The Social Significance of the Nineteenth Century Codification Movement and its Contribution to the Passage of the Early Married Women's Property Acts," 24 Buffalo L. Rev. 683 (1974–75).

6. Mary R. Beard, *Woman as Force in History: A Study in Traditions and Realities* (New York: Macmillan Co., 1962).

7. For a discussion of the "rediscovery," and a contemporary critique of Beard's work, see Berenice A. Carroll, "Mary Beard's Woman as Force in History: A Critique," in *Liberating Women's History: Theoretical and Critical Essays*, ed. Berenice A. Carroll, (Urbana, Ill.: University of Illinois Press, 1976), pp. 26–41.

8. Richard B. Morris, *Studies in the History of American Law with Specific Reference to the Seventeenth and Eighteenth Centuries* (New York: Columbia University Press, 1930), chapter 3, "Women's Rights in Early American Law," pp. 135–173.

WOMEN AS PROPERTY IN THE EARLY ROMAN EMPIRE

Susan Treggiari

Shortage of evidence is a handicap in an investigation of the lower classes in the ancient world in general, and especially in studies of women. Latin literature is almost entirely written by upper-class men, or men who identified with the upper class. Inscriptions give us information about the humbler population—tradesmen, artisans, freedmen and members of slave households who could afford some form of monument. But women were more selectively commemorated than men[1] and even when women are named, we are often not given much information about them. In addition, in legal writings women may become invisible because of the rules of grammar. The masculine often includes the feminine. Not only wills, but edicts and laws might use the masculine and be interpreted as encompassing both sexes.[2]

Literary sources from the Roman period introduce us to a notable assortment of men who were or had been slaves. These include scholars such as Cicero's secretary, Marcus Tullius Tiro; authors such as Publilius the Syrian or Phaedrus; philosophers such as Epictetus; confidential agents of the great such as Pompeius Demetrius of Gadara; imperial ministers such as Pallas and Narcissus. Also included are the more typical and less successful domestics, from stewards to letter-carriers, named by their owners or their owners' friends—small men mentioned by orators in the courts or the Senate; faithful servants immortalized by moralists rehearsing *exempla*; Onesimus whose flight from his master called forth a vivid and tactful letter from St. Paul.

This richness shrinks if we search for women. Our surviving authors are upper-class with rare exceptions (such as the fabulist

The author gratefully acknowledges the support of the Social Sciences and Humanities Research Council of Canada.

7

Phaedrus; Epictetus, mediated by Arrian, and the fragmentary mime-writer Publilius) and with one exception (the poet Sulpicia), men. In their private lives they would not be closely acquainted with more than a few slave women (partly because women servants waited mostly on women and children). Thus, even in private letters or collections of anecdotes or intimate biography (such as Nepos's life of Atticus) or overtly autobiographical satire (like Horace's), women slaves and freedwomen are conspicuously absent.

Literary genres of a loftier type, such as history, concerned as it is with politics and war, gave few opportunities for women of humble class to appear. There are, nevertheless, some women of slave status or origin, including: (1) Volumnia Cytheris, the mime-actress and mistress of Mark Antony, whose presence at a dinner party added spice even for Cicero, although he claimed never to have been interested in such women and was certainly in the habit of saying cutting things about how Antony flaunted her all over Italy; (2) a freed servant called Phoebe, who hanged herself when her mistress Julia was banished for adultery, so that Julia's father Augustus wished that he had been Phoebe's father instead; (3) Antonia Caenis, secretary of Antonia (Augustus's niece and mother of the emperor Claudius) who became the concubine of the emperor Vespasian; (4) Epicharis, who, though a courtesan, an ex-slave and a woman, behaved more like a gentleman than any of the other conspirators who had tried to get rid of Nero, stood up to torture, incriminated no one, and managed to kill herself.[3] Just as freeborn Roman women sporadically make headlines in our sources because of their private lives, their marriages and adulteries, so male writers, when they focus on slave and ex-slave women at all, tend to mention courtesans (but not prostitutes of a humbler type) and concubines.[4]

For factual information on the lives of slave and ex-slave women, however, we must turn to the jurists and the inscriptions. The former may be expected to present the view of the ruling class and of the richer strata of the population. The inscriptions are funerary monuments erected by slaves and freed persons themselves. They may be relied on to present factual information on the legal status of the people commemorated at a certain point of their careers (not always at the time of death, since some inscriptions predated death).

An attempt will be made here to sketch the lives of slave women and freedwomen chiefly from the juristic and epigraphic evidence, giving more detailed treatment to the topics of work and family life. The period under consideration is the Principate (c. 27 B.C. to A.D. 235) and the geographical focus is Italy, particularly the City of Rome and the large slave households (familiae urbanae) of the upper class. In this period, it is generally held that the influx of foreign slaves, enslaved prisoners of war and free persons kidnapped by pirates or slave traders, was much reduced. Although the capital of the empire continued to absorb new slaves from provincial slave populations and from outside the empire, a high proportion of slaves in Rome were probably homebred (vernae).[5]

ENTRANCE INTO SLAVERY

A woman would enter a Roman household, like a male slave, by birth, gift or inheritance, or purchase. If by purchase, she might have been born a slave inside or outside the empire, or she might have been enslaved as a war-prisoner or as the victim of pirates, brigands or kidnappers, or sold by herself or her parents because of poverty.[6] All of these things were unacceptable inside the empire, but they happened. Perhaps if a family had to sell a child, they would tend to choose a daughter, but I have so far found no evidence on this in the jurists. A free person illegally kept in slavery, bona fide or not, often a foundling, might as easily be a woman as a man—and daughters were perhaps more often abandoned. Alumni of both sexes, that is, foundlings who were (it seems) not brought up as slaves, are frequently mentioned in the Digest, especially as beneficiaries under wills.[7]

The jurists' comments on the sale and purchase of women slaves yield interesting data. For instance, there must be no mistake about the sex of the slave. If I sell you a girl who you think is a boy, the sale is void. But if I think I am buying a virgin and she is in fact iam mulier, the sale is perfectly valid, since there was no mistake about her sex (18. 1. 11. 1) but if you know that I am buying under a misapprehension, I can sue you (19. 1. 11. 5). In addition, the slave must be guaranteed healthy. In the discussion of the illnesses and disabilities which might affect women slaves, there is naturally a preoccupation with gynaecological disorders.[8]

The childbearing capacity of the ancilla was expected to interest the buyer. Sterile women might be returned to the vendor. A woman who was congenitally sterile, however, was regarded by Trebatius as healthy.[9] A woman who is pregnant or has just had a child is healthy, indeed the pregnant slave is the healthiest of all, doing just what nature intended: *Si mulier praegnas venierit, inter omnes convenit sanam eam esse: maximum enim ac praecipuum munus feminarum est accipere ac tueri conceptum. . . .* (21. 1. 14. 1). The breeding potential and the proven fertility of women slaves clearly enhanced their value.

It was also possible, incidentally, to sell the future *partus* of a woman without selling her.[10] Paulus mentions the possibility of a man selling the *partus* of a woman whom he knew to be sterile or over 50—naturally such a fraud was actionable (19. 1. 21 pr.).[11] A seller might also arrange when selling a pregnant slave that the *partus* be returned to him (21. 2. 42).

Finally, a passage of Ulpian[12] makes a general statement about the purchase of women. The children of *ancillae* who form part of an inheritance must be handed over to the heir, even though such children are not proceeds or fruits *(fructus)* as the young of farm animals are.[13] The reasons for this apparently anomalous legal view of slave babies were and are controversial;[14] Ulpian's is idiosyncratic and seems to be drawn from his own observation. *Ancillarum etiam partus et partuum partus quamquam fructus esse non existimantur, quia non temere ancillae eius rei causa comparantur ut pariant, augent tamen hereditatem . . .* "Although the children and grandchildren of slave women are not considered to be fruits, because only after carefully weighing the possibilities do people buy slave women specifically for breeding . . ."[15] That is, Ulpian at least did not perceive breeding as the *main* function of women slaves.

Non temere might be translated in various ways, but the context and the run of the sentence lead to paraphrase "only after carefully weighing the possibilities do people buy slavewomen specifically for breeding . . ." That is, breeding was not the *main* function of women slaves.

POSITION OF SLAVE WOMEN IN THE HOUSEHOLD

The city staff of an upper-class Roman (a member of the emperor's family, a senator or a wealthy knight [*eques*] was large and complex. This is indicated even by the parodies and preachings of satirists and philosophers. Modern scholars have exhaustively documented the situation from the inscriptions. Staff range from the essential cleaners and caterers, including the valets and personal attendants whom Romans regarded as equally *necessarii*, to the luxury staff such as musicians and readers and those who secured the desired autarky of the very rich—maintenance-workers, doctors, infirmarians. Numbers might easily run into the hundreds. Since space was restricted even in some of the imperial residences, it is likely that many domestics lived out and only attended when their work was required. Others had makeshift accommodation—sleeping at the foot of the master's bed, outside a door, or in a corridor, on pallets or mats.[16] There were supervisory staff in many departments particularly on the emperor's staff, for instance head cooks, dining-room supervisors, head chamberlains, head doctors. These often seem to have been freedmen, who continued to work after manumission and whose freed status as well as their supervisory position ensured that their status was superior to that of their subordinates. In the wealthiest households a freed steward, who could act as his patron's agent *(procurator)* had overall control. Less grand houses, from the late Republic on, were run by *dispensatores* (literally, "disbursers"); in the imperial period these seem generally to have been slaves, although often wealthy ones. In the emperor's service at least, it seems that they were freed later than other administrators, but compensated in other ways for the delay.[17]

How do women fit into this structure?[18] It is striking that they hardly ever had a supervisory role. Rich households had no housekeeper: the substitute for the mistress of the house is a male steward and the people who give orders to female staff are either the owners themselves (especially the women) or male supervisors. As in the nineteenth century, the more elegant the household, the less women servants appeared before visitors. Meals were served by men and boys; waitresses *(ministrae)* were for humbler establishments. In the emperor's household and probably among the most ostentatious of the upper class, even the job of supervising the spinning of wool by women slaves was given to male supervisors; in ordinary households this supervisory job went to women. For other categories of women servants, however, there seems to be no department-head, male or female.

The chief urban jobs which women filled were those of clerks and personal secretaries (the latter working, as far as we know, only for women); ladies' maids, dressers and hairdressers, who are often mentioned in literature and are well represented in inscriptions; "clothers-folders," who again probably worked for women: both men and women owners might have male "clothes-folders" and in luxurious households these were under a "wardrobe master" (a veste); masseuses (again, for women); attendants (pedisequae, only for women); spinners, weavers and wool-weighers who supervised the spinners; clothes-makers and menders; doctors (rare) and midwives; nurses and child-minders; readers and various kinds of entertainers. These jobs are paralleled by men clerks and secretaries, valets (cubicularii), clothes-folders, masseurs, attendants, weavers, wool-weighers, clothes-makers and menders, doctors, child-minders, readers and entertainers. Women are entirely absent from outdoor work in town, such as gardening or attending to horses, and attested as cooks, cleaners, waitresses only in smaller households or in the country. They are most prominent as personal servants to women, as specialists in certain areas where they exclude men (particularly wetnurses and midwives), as entertainers and in clothes production, where they outnumber men approximately three to one.

There were certain jobs which a male slave could not with propriety perform for the mistress of the house or her daughters. Besides midwives,[19] female dressers and masseuses were essential. Such servants and her personal attendants would be at the immediate orders of the mistress. Although a good deal of the theoretical responsibility for the order of the household might also be in the mistress's hands (symbolized by her control of the keys, which on divorce she was supposed to surrender), it seems likely that she was thought to have a particular responsibility for the production of woollen cloth. This was central to the stereotype of the good wife: "she kept house, she made wool," as an early epitaph says.[20]

Both the husband and wife in the household would own slaves. The jurists note that both husband and wife were allowed to use each other's slaves, without it constituting a gift, since they were not enriched by it (24.1.18, h.t. 28.2). The husband might, for instance, provide his wife with a team of litter-bearers for her sole use, or long-haired girls (considered ornamental and therefore luxury attendants) or even men slaves for her particular use, as Ulpian tells us (32.49 pr.-2). It seems possible from the sketchy epigraphic sources that provision of outdoor servants for town houses was chiefly the husband's province: Augustus's wife, Livia, for instance, who had a large and well-attested staff, seems to have relied on her husband and on her son, his successor Tiberius, for the services of litter-bearers, grooms, gardeners and couriers. On the other hand, female slaves could perform only a limited range of services for the master, so it was natural that he should lend them to his wife.

Other slaves might work for both husband and wife, for instance, they might be provided initially for the wife but work for the husband on occasion, or vice versa, or work for both indiscriminately. They were *promiscui usus*, "for indiscriminate employment by both" (32. 49. 2). In addition, the wife's dowry would often include slaves: these belonged to the husband for the duration of the marriage.

Husband and wife might also own slaves jointly, in equal or unequal shares. They might have been bought or inherited. There is a classic example of jointly owned slaves *(servi communes)*. When Augustus died he left one-third of his property to his widow Livia and two-thirds to her son, his adoptive son, Tiberius. This meant that each individual jointly owned slave belonged two-thirds to Tiberius and one-third to Livia. There are a few examples in the inscriptions: the freedwoman Prima, who had nursed Julia the daughter of Livia's grandson Germanicus (*CIL* 6. 4352) and Pelops, a freed surveyor (*CIL* 6. 8913). *Servi communes* shared by husband and wife also show up especially as freedmen/women, identified as Gai (or Publi or Marci etc.) et Gaiae liberti/ae. For instance, from the republican period there is Larcia P.Ɔ.l. Horaea, freed by P. Larcius Neicia, himself a freedman, and his wife Saufeia Thalea, also an ex-slave.[21]

Besides husband and wife, children in the household might have their own slaves, such as nurses, tutors, or playmates.[22] Finally, freedmen residing in the household and forming part of the staff might have slaves of their own. Even slaves could own slave-deputies *(vicarii).*[23]

Upward mobility did exist for slave women. As P.R.C. Weaver has pointed out,[24] they might be freed in order to be married *(matrimonii causa)*. Weaver has found that women slaves belonging to the emperor were likely to be freed at a younger age than were men, who could be employed as "civil servants" as well as in domestic posts.[25] It seems possible that elsewhere too, women, after they had served a certain time, would be freed. Columella, when setting himself up as the model for an economical farmer, tells us that if a country slave woman bore three children he let her off work and that if she bore four he freed her.[26] (Three and four are magic numbers for free women too in the eyes of the emperor.) As freedwomen, they might continue to perform services *(operae)* for their patroness or patron (unless they were married with his consent).[27] These services would often be a continuation of work they had done as slaves. Now let us turn to the subject of the sexual and family life of women slaves and freedwomen.

CONTUBERNIUM

We begin with a sexual relationship which is quasi-marital. The "marriage" of a slave with a slave was extralegal and the institution is therefore formally ignored by jurists, although slaves who lived in a quasi-marital relationship are mentioned. The word for this quasi marriage was *contubernium*. It also covered the union of a free person and a slave, and this is mentioned by lawyers: "Between slaves and free persons marriage cannot be contracted but *contubernium* can."[28] The relationship of *contubernium*, although not a legal marriage, was, it is clear, recognized not only by the parties to it, but by their fellow slaves and by the *domini*, who probably approved or authorized it.

References to *contubernium* between slave and slave are rare in the literary sources; unions between slave and free occasionally impinged on the official mind and produced measures such as a senatorial decree in the time of Claudius *(senatusconsultum Claudianum)* and, in the early third century, a controversial decision by Pope Callistus. But a good deal of the evidence comes from the epitaphs of *contubernales* themselves.[29]

In a recent study,[30] the author examines the documentation of *contubernales* in the inscriptions from the City of Rome during the period of the Principate, roughly 27 B.C. to A.D. 235 (inscriptions dated to the last half-century of the Principate, from the year 200 on, are rare). The total number of inscriptions from the city is

39,340 and they occupy a series of tomes numbered vol. 6 of the *Corpus inscriptionum latinarum.* (I have not added the later documentation, which could be found in *L'Année Epigraphique.*) After fragmentary and incomplete inscriptions have been discarded, 260 couples of *contubernales* remain.

In sixty-eight of the 260 couples, both partners were certainly or probably slaves at the time of commemoration. Some of these might have been freed had they lived longer.[31] Ninety-six couples in the sample are mixed, with one partner a slave and one free. These unions consist of two types: either a freeborn citizen has entered upon *contubernium* with a slave, or a freed person is *contubernalis* of a slave, with whom he or she may have been already living before manumission.

Where one partner is of freed status at the time of commemoration, there is no one example which clearly shows that *contubernium* predated the manumission, but this is probably what happened.[32] Where one partner is of undefined free status, we cannot tell whether he or she was born free or had been freed from slavery.

Women united with a slave man seem likely to have included a high proportion of women of free birth but slave ancestry. This category is well represented: thus, for instance, in thirty-seven couples the "husband" is definitely a slave and the "wife" free (and we may add thirty-five where the "husband" is probably a slave). Two of these wives are definitely of free birth. A high proportion of the men in these mixed unions were imperial civil servants or belonged to women of the imperial family or dependents of the emperor. P.R.C. Weaver[33] has shown that 83 percent of "married" slave civil servants in Rome had wives of free status. These he takes to be mostly of free birth. Many of those in my collection bear imperial names, which suggest that these women are daughters or descendants of imperial freedmen of an earlier generation:[34] their background, despite the superior legal status given by their position as free citizens, was the same as that of their slave "husbands."

Here we come to one of the most striking paradoxes in the Roman slave system: the slave civil servant could attain a position of considerable emolument and influence, so that he was an attractive match for a free woman. The assumption was that he would attain his freedom (at about age thirty, or forty for financial officers) and that the union would then become a valid Roman marriage. For the "wives" in the sample under consideration, death intervened before the *contubernalis* had been freed. For instance, *CIL* 6.8839:

"To Primus, *dispensator* of Tiberius Claudius Caesar Augustus, lived 37 years: Julia Themis to her *contubernalis*."

In the above example, Primus is a financial officer who belongs to the emperor Claudius or his adoptive son Nero (who bore the same name). His *contubernalis* has a name which suggests a connection with one of the three previous emperors, who all bore the name Julius (Augustus, Tiberius or Gaius). It seems likely that her father (or mother) was an ex-slave of one of these emperors.

While women united with a slave man seem to have included a high proportion of women of free birth but slave ancestry, the evidence for the converse type of union, between women of slave status and men of free status, seems to reflect a different situation. Whereas (unless the *senatusconsultum Claudianum* was called in to redress the balance)[35] a free woman living in extralegal union with a slave man would bear free (although illegitimate) children, the children borne by a slave woman to a free man would be slave.[36] It is therefore highly unlikely that a free man would choose *contubernium* with another man's slave. The couples which consist of a free man and a slave woman probably represent unions of two slaves, in which the man had advanced to freedom and the woman's status had lagged behind. It is even possible that a freedman when he had saved enough money might commemorate a slave "wife" who had died years before, when he himself was still a slave. In this case the apparent "mixed marriage" had never in fact existed.

The largest single category consists of husbands and wives who are both free, but of undefined origin, that is, they could theoretically be freeborn or ex-slave. Fifty-seven couples of the 260 are of this type. It appears that at least one member of each pair must have been a slave during the union, for otherwise there is no reason for them to use the word *contubernalis*, instead of a word appropriate to valid Roman marriage (*maritus, coniunx, uxor*). What we see is either the final stage of a relationship that originally involved two slaves, or a relationship which started as *contubernium* between a slave and a freed or freeborn person (the latter usually the woman). When both partners achieved freedom and citizenship, the union, if they continued it, *constante coniunctione*, (23.3.39 pr., Ulpian) automatically became a valid marriage. One of the points of particular interest is the importance of *vicariae*. Slaves in theory owned nothing: anything which they acquired (wages, business income, legacies) went to enrich their owner. In practice, however, it was accepted that owners allowed their slaves, as fathers allowed sons in *patria potestate*, to accumulate property (a *peculium*), which was often left with the slave when he was bequeathed or freed, or which he could use to buy his freedom. As has been mentioned, this *peculium* often included other slaves, *vicarii*. (The slaveowning slave is called *ordinarius*.)[37] If a slave wanted to have a *contubernalis* it was clearly much to his, and their, advantage if she was also his *vicaria*. He could achieve this perhaps by buying his existing *contubernalis* from his owner, or by buying a slave from outside (or inside) the household in order to make her his *contubernalis*. Although she, and any children they had, theoretically went to swell the owner's property, in fact they belonged to him at one remove and would be more under the male slave's control. If the man was freed and allowed to take his *peculium* with him (perhaps in return for cash), then he would completely own the woman and would be able to free her. This accounts for the wives who are freedwomen of their husbands who are also of freed status. The advantage of this situation was that the *coniunx et liberta* (woman freed by her husband) owed no services to an outside patron and indeed was not expected to pay a freedwoman's services to her husband[38] (although she might perform the same functions *qua* wife).

If a male slave did not have a *vicaria* for his *contubernalis*, it might still be possible for him to buy out his mate when he was freed or persuade her owner to give or bequeath her to him.[39] It appears to have been uncommon for a woman slave to own her *contubernalis* as her *vicarius*. But, although it was in general improper for a free woman to free a slave in order to marry him, it was perfectly in order if they had been slaves together, she had been freed and he had been given to her specifically so that she might manumit him and marry him.[40]

Outside the civil service, then, most slaves lived in *contubernium* with other slaves, usually in the same household (Tertullian *Ad uxorem* 2.8.1), not with free persons. It might happen that one was freed before the other. As soon as the woman was freed, any subsequent children would be born free; even those born before she was freed might be recovered by their parents.

The flavor of family life created by *contubernium* is reflected by an unusually detailed record by a priest of the cult of the emperor, probably a retired civil servant, at Aquincum on the Danube.

> To the Spirits of the Departed.
>
> T. Flavius Felicio, Augustalis of the colony of Aquincum, set this inscription up during his lifetime to himself and Flavia Secundina formerly his fellow-freedwoman and wife who lived 55 years and to T. Flavius Felicissimus formerly his natural son who lived 23 years, and to T. Flavius Ingenuus his legitimate son, and to T. Flavius Felix his natural son and to Flavia Felicula his natural daughter, and to Flavia Felicissima his granddaughter, all still alive. T. Flavius Felicio saw to (the erection of this monument) for his family and himself. (*AE* 1939 10)

From the above example, we can see that three children were born when the parent's union was *contubernium,* that is, while at least one of the parents was still a slave. Of the two natural sons, Felix was probably the elder, although Felicissimus died first. The chronological sequence of Felix, "Lucky," and Felicissimus, "Very Lucky," is normal. The natural daughter Felicula and eventually the granddaughter were also named after the father. This was a common practice among slaves, partly perhaps for the convenience of slave owners and administrators—as racehorses nowadays are given names derived from sire or dam or both—partly to make clear a family relationship to which the law denied existence. So, although slave children theoretically had no father or mother, we find that the sons of slave men (by slave or freed mothers) may take the father's name direct: Agathonicus after Agathonicus (*CIL* 6. 11234), Antiochus from Antiochus (Ibid. 12082), Blastus son of Blastus the Elder (Ibid. 13608). Daughters take the feminine form: Agathainis daughter of Agathias (Ibid. 11234), Aglaus and Aglais, son and daughter of Aglaus (Ibid. 12037). Or, as here, several children all take names based on that of the father. If the mother was free and the father slave, the middle name would derive from the mother. But we also find the third name being chosen to commemorate the mother. The same patterns occur when the parents are free, but it is when the father is a slave that his relationship with his children particularly needs to be underlined by giving last names derived from his, as we see here.

The mother and Felicissimus are named first (after Felicio himself) because they were already dead when the tomb was dedicated. Then the one legitimate child takes precedence over his brother and sister. The name "Ingenuus" suggests that, besides being the only child born after his parents were living in Roman marriage, he was the only one who was born free, for that is what the name means. In that case, the other three were presumably born slaves and subsequently freed, either by their mother's owner, who is presumably one of the Flavian emperors, or by their parents who had acquired them. But this is not spelled out, much as the freed status of their parents is only alluded to when Felicio calls his wife his fellow-freedwoman. The one legitimate child was of course the youngest of the family.

Thus, slaves emulated the values and often the vocabulary of legal marriage. *Contubernia*, in fact, often survived to become valid marriage. Also, and this is more surprising, slave owners and jurists began, in the second century if not earlier, to respect this family relationship and to see slave families as entities which should be left undisturbed insofar as possible. This can be seen from the passages which show that the nonworking "wives" and children of farm staff were to be regarded as part of the farm staff. If a testator bequeathed the human equipment of a farm, it was clear that they were to be included in the legacy. (It might indeed be difficult to decide where else they could be said to belong.) To these legal and practical reasons, however, Ulpian[41] adds "nor must we believe that he (the testator) enjoined a cruel separation." (". . . *neque enim duram separationem iniunxisse credendus est.*") This is interesting, because it implies that the lawyer will, if possible, protect the reputation of his client by interpreting his will humanely. Public opinion was a safeguard of the slave system. Reports from slaves circulated among the owner's peers could ruin his reputation and have a damaging impact even on his political career.[42] Outsiders had another reason for disapproving of masters who were cruel to their slaves: oppressed slaves might rebel, run away, or murder their owners, so that the whole fabric of society was threatened.[43] So, not only permission to form *contubernia* but also the preservation of existing *contubernia* and, as far as possible, the keeping together of parents and children, become part of rational slave-management.

This does not mean to say, of course, that lawyers always leaned in favor of the slave family. The intention of the testator (explicit or deducible) was crucial: "And the will of the dead man is all-important, for we must examine what he intended." ("*et facit quidem totum voluntas defuncti: nam quid senserit, spectandum est.*")[44] So in one passage Scaevola is asked if, when an agent was bequeathed, his wife and daughter were to be regarded as included in the legacy. The lawyer replied that there was no apparent reason why they should be. Buckland uses this passage to show that "there was nothing to prevent the legacy of a single slave away from his connexions."[45] This is of course true. In legacy of farms and equipment, it can be argued that wives and children of farm workers are part of the equipment: they belong to a category. But a single slave agent was not a category, a family unit. Unless the testator explicitly said, "I bequeath Stichus with his *contubernalis* and children," the lawyer must reply that no reason has been given to show that the family was to go with the father. But what is really interesting is that the question was put to Scaevola (or imagined to be put) at all. Why should upper-class Romans in the second century start thinking that perhaps a slave's family was part of him?[46]

SEXUAL EXPLOITATION

Other intimate relationships involving slave women and freedwomen did not emulate Roman marriage. These included sexual exploitation and *concubinatus* which shall be dealt with here briefly. The casual sexual exploitation of women by the men of the household is an inevitable feature of slave societies.

Various factors might inhibit Roman *domini* from exercising their sexual rights over their slave women—varying attractiveness, the limitations of their physical powers, disapproval on the part of a wife,[47] the jealousies which might be stirred up among male slaves, the possible risk of a hostile reaction by the woman. This last, incidentally, seems unlikely, since slaves were presumably conditioned to think sexual relationships with the owner acceptable, even potentially advantageous, as the elder Seneca says Haterius argued in defending a freedman alleged to have a homosexual relationship with his ex-owner, "Unchastity in a freeborn person is ground for prosecution, in a slave necessity, in a freed person duty."[48] Some protection was offered, if not given, by the law, under a rescript of Antoninus Pius in the mid-second century. Ulpian, in a discussion of masters' cruelty to slaves, explains that if a master forced a slave to "shamelessness and disgraceful violation" he (and this probably includes "she") could flee to a statue of the emperor and appeal to the authorities.[49] Protection was also offered, in special circumstances, against prostitution. If an owner sold a slave with an agreement that she was not to be prostituted, but the buyer, or even a later buyer whose contract had omitted the original clause, made her a prostitute, she was automatically freed or had to be returned to her first owner.[50] The author shares P. A. Brunt's pessimistic view that such covenants cannot have been easy to enforce (*Gnomon* 51, 1979, 445) but they are evidence for a more humane attitude which could exist among slave owners and jurists. In addition, the seduction of other people's slaves was regarded as a breach of good manners and might seriously offend the owner,[51] who might have recourse to one of several types of legal action open to him.[52]

Some masters had children by their slave women. Such children would be born slaves. Martial, quite properly, chose to satirize the insensitivity of a man (doubtless imaginary) who surrounded himself with slave sons fathered on his maids (3.33). It is impossible to be sure if there were many such children, recognized as children but still not freed by their fathers. But the jurists take them into account. They are regarded as standing in a special relationship of affection with their father. If a man was bankrupt and his property was forfeited to his creditors, certain slaves were not to be taken from him: those who were essential to him (*necessarii*) and those with whom he had a tie of sentiment. The latter class included his concubine, natural children and *alumni* (children, often abandoned infants or orphans, whom he was bringing up) (20.1.6:8, Ulpian; 42.5.38, Paul, cf. 17.1.54 pr. Papinian).

No moralizing on the existence of such children appears here, or in a lively inscription put up, no doubt at the father's expense and probably his own composition, to a slave son who remained unmanumitted at 16:

Vitalis, slave of Gaius Lavius Faustus and also his son, a *verna* born in his house, is buried here. He lived 16 years, a hawker at the

Aprian shops, well liked by the people, but he was taken away by the gods. I ask you, passers-by, if I ever gave short measure, to help my father, that you forgive me. I ask you by the gods above and the gods below, to look after my father and mother, Farewell. (*ILS* 7479, from Philippi)

Perhaps the difference between slave and free status did not seem important in the shopkeeping class. That is, however, precisely the class in which slave women could hope to attract the master or his son and be freed in order to marry him. "Freedwoman and wife" and "patron and husband" are fairly common descriptions in funerary inscriptions. When Augustus tried to check the rate of manumissions and established minimum ages of thirty for the slave and twenty for the owner, one of the exceptions was if the owner wished to free a slave to marry her. Marrying a freedwoman was not socially acceptable for the upper classes, but in the lower class intermarriage with ex-slaves seems to have been common. So, in the Republic, a slave girl called Horaea had been so obedient to her aged owners, a husband and wife who had themselves been freed from slavery, and so devoted to one of their freeborn sons that they freed her from slavery and the son honored her with the gown of a Roman matron.[53] Examples could be multiplied, but are rarely as informative as this one.

CONCUBINATUS

In between casual sexual relations with slave women and honorable marriage was *concubinatus*.[54] This, like *contubernium*, was an extralegal institution (though the contrary has been argued, for the period after the Augustan marriage legislation). Unlike *contubernium* it was not intended as a quasi-marital relationship. The concubine might be a freeborn woman[55] as well as a slave or freedwoman. However, the man (at least in our period) is socially superior to the woman and the relationship is not reciprocal. This second point is immediately obvious from the vocabulary: whereas a husband or wife is each *coniunx* to the other, and slave partners each *contubernalis*, in concubinage the woman is *concubina*—and there is no name for the man.

The woman's function and position were to some extent defined as the word implies: she was someone to lie with, her prime function was sexual, and the epitaphs suggest that her virtues were affection and fidelity. The man was expected to keep her, as we see from the early evidence of Roman comedy, but was under no obligation to go on keeping her. "I keep her, but she doesn't keep me," as Aristippus said, a philosophical remark which pleased Cicero.[56] The social superiority of the man is also brought out clearly in Plautus and Terence. The courtesan is either a slave whom the young middle-class citizen wants to buy as his concubine, or a free foreigner, whom he will hire. Since what made a marriage was *affectio maritalis* (the intention to be married), what distinguished concubinage from marriage was the absence of the intention, particularly on the part of the man. Outsiders would judge that a relationship was only *concubinatus* by observing the lack of normal concomitants of marriage such as dowry and a wedding party and by considering the way of life of the couple and their relative social standing.[57] One of the most obvious social gulfs would appear when the man was of high rank and the woman a freedwoman. A relationship between a senator or close male descendant of a senator and a freedwoman would normally be assumed to be concubinage, since marriage was forbidden between them (24.1.3.1, Ulpian).

There is a title in the *Digest* on concubines, but it is extremely brief (25.7). Several jurists there specify the type of woman whom it was permissible to keep as a concubine. They include, apart from women of free status with whom marriage was, for various reasons, impermissible, a man's own freedwoman (*h.t.* 1 pr., 3, Ulpian) or someone else's (*h.t.* 3, Marcianus). Elsewhere in the *Digest* it emerges that a man may have his own slave as concubine (20.1.8, Ulpian; 42.5.38, Paul) but it seems to have been expected that he would free her.[58] Slaves who originally belonged to outsiders would probably need to be bought *in concubinatum* before they counted as official *concubinae*.[59]

A concubine's position was recognized by society. We have seen that she had some protection from the law even if she was a slave, in circumstances when her owner's creditors would otherwise have been in a position to seize her in payment of his debt. She would expect to be supported in a style befitting her lover's station. For the society depicted by the jurists this could mean not only proper maintenance, such as a wardrobe (32.29 pr., Labeo, 32.49.4, Ulpian) but large presents such as slaves and estates (24.1.58 pr.-1,

Scaevola, 39.5.31 pr., Papinian) and rations for her slaves (Scaevola 1.c.). The professional courtesan would no doubt demand her market price, as we see in comedy, but the *concubinae* of the lawyers and the inscriptions are not professionals. They seem rather to be women who would have become wives if they had been social equals of their lovers, or perhaps if they had had a dowry.[60] Quite often they later did marry the same men: we cannot say if the social obstacles had disappeared or if the birth of children and the success of the relationship had triumphed over prudence. This could happen even in the propertied class, unless the lawyers are merely setting themselves puzzles (24.1.58 pr.-1, Scaevola, 39.5.31 pr. Papinian). It is significant that the major difference which Ulpian saw, when considering how a man provides a wardrobe for wife or concubine, was in the regard in which the woman was held: "Clearly there is no difference between them, except in dignity" (32.49.4). But the most famous passage about the social status of a concubine—the social status which results from being a wife or concubine, and the social status which dictates which of the two a woman should be—has particular reference to freedwomen:

> Can a woman who lives in concubinage with her patron, leave him against his will and give herself to another man in marriage or concubinage? For my part I approve of the view that the capacity for marriage *(conubium)* should be taken away from a concubine if she deserts her patron against his will, since it is more honorable *(honestius)* for a patron to have his freedwoman as his concubine than as his wife *(materfamilias)*. (25.7.1 pr., Ulpian)

The elliptical last clause means that a man's own freedwoman who was his concubine *(liberta concubina)* was bound by double ties; she was regarded as having the same obligations as a wife but he was not expected to marry her because of the social disparity between them, created by the fact that he had manumitted her. (Even if he were a freedman himself, he would still have technical seniority and she would still be his dependent.) If the argument sounds imperfect, it is. Two other passages round it out:

> And if a woman gives herself into concubinage to a man other than her patron, I say that she did not have the honor due to a married woman *(matris familias honestatem)*. (23.2.41.1, Marcellus)
> If a woman involved in adultery was not a wife, but was a concubine, the man cannot accuse her *qua* husband, because she was

not a wife, but he will not be prevented from prosecuting her as an outsider (*extraneus*), if only she is the sort of woman who in giving herself into concubinage does not lose the title of married woman (*matrona*), for example a woman who was the concubine of her patron. (48.5.14 pr., Ulpian)

This negative formulation implies that a freedwoman who was concubine to her own patron did not have the honor due to a matron. So the jurists' view can be reconstructed as follows: "It is more honorable for a patron to have his freedwoman as a concubine than as a wife, but it is as honorable for a freedwoman to be the concubine of her patron as the wife of anyone else and more honorable than for her to be the concubine of any other man." The logical consequence of this view was the controversial view that the *liberta concubina* should be assimilated to the *liberta et coniunx*, who was penalized if she unilaterally divorced her patron. Ulpian also argued that a *liberta concubina* could be charged with adultery (48.5.14 pr.).

We cannot say if these severe opinions carried the day: it is probable that other lawyers took a different line, which failed to be made canonical by the early Christian compilers of the *Digest*. We can, however, argue from this evidence that the *liberta concubina* was held in higher regard than other freed *concubinae*.

It is clear from inscriptions that *concubinatus* was an avowable relationship. A man who donates a tomb to his colleagues in a trade guild will say that their wives and concubines are also to be admitted to it (*CIL* 11.6136). So will an individual who dedicates his own tomb and perhaps does not know whether he will have a wife or a concubine or both during his lifetime (*CIL* 9.5256, 11.6257). On the tombs which name individual women, some men have had both wives and concubines, but not, I think, concurrently (e.g., *CIL* 6 1906). Among individual *concubinae* known to us, from Rome, there are no certain freeborn women, freedwomen predominate and some *concubinae* are slaves. Interestingly enough, of the attested freedwomen, few are the jurists' ideal *libertae concubinae*. Most of them lived with men who, as far as we know, had no connection with their earlier life as slaves. It is also striking that many of the men who lived in *concubinatus* were themselves freedmen.[61] Why then, did they not marry their concubines? The reason must be that there was some discernible social gap between the partners. But it is impossible for us to be sure about a gap between Decimus Occius Eros, a freedman, and his concubine Roscia Strategis, freedwoman of a woman, especially when Occius married Roscia Pupa, also freedwoman of a woman (*CIL* 6. 23210). (One could conjecture that perhaps Pupa freed Strategis, which would put her one step below Pupa's husband.) On the other hand, in the Italian towns it is striking that many of the men with concubines are rising freedmen, who could probably look higher than a freedwoman for a wife.

Relationships of *concubinatus* between ex-slaves are not as common as Roman marriage, whether described as marriage or as the *contubernium* which it had ceased to be. Apart from a social gap, apart from the possibility that lack of a dowry debarred some of these women from marriage, their ambiguous sexual history as slaves perhaps formed a barrier. *"Mogli e buoi dei paesi tuoi."* A man would know about a woman who had been a slave in the same household as himself; he might have doubts about a freedwoman whose background he did not know. Such was the life of slave women and freedwomen in the early Roman empire.[62]

Abbreviations

AE = *L'année épigraphique*
CIL = *Corpus inscriptionum latinarum*
ILLRP = A. Degrassi, ed., *Inscriptiones latinae liberae rei publicae* (Florence, 1963)
Digest references are given unprefixed, thus: 39.5.31 pr.

NOTES

1. M.K. Hopkins, "On the Probable Age Structure of the Roman Population," *Population Studies* 20 (1966): 245–264, esp. 260–263.

2. Thus, Julianus, in his book on ambiguities, mentioned a man who left a bequest of two *muli*, but died possessed only of two *mulae*. Servius replied that the bequest held, because female mules were covered by the masculine, *mulorum appellatione etiam mulae continentur, quemadmodum appellatione servorum etiam servae plerumque continentur. Id autem eo veniet, quod semper sexus masculinus etiam femiminum sexum continet.* (32. 62). Cf. 32. 81 pr.: *Servis legatis etiam ancillas quidam deberi recte putant, quasi commune nomen utrumque sexum contineat. . . .* The jurists use both *servae* and *ancillae*.

Also, Ulpian, on the *actio de peculio* (15. 1. 1. 3), says that the person *in potestate* who is covered by the edict may be a woman, though the masculine is used: *de eo loquitur, non de ea: sed tamen et ob eam quae est feminini sexus dabitur ex hoc edicto actio.* The edict covered *filiifamilias* and *filiaefamilias* and slaves of either sex. In some documents, however, the drafter is careful to mention both sexes explicitly: for instance, the edict *de servo corrupto: Ait praetor, "Qui servum servam alienum alienam. . . ."* (11. 3. 1 pr.). In other instances, the masculine might be used and only denote males. The jurists reject indignantly any suggestion that the feminine might ever include the masculine: *exemplo enim pessimum est feminino vocabulo etiam masculos contineri.* (31. 45. pr).

3. See J.P.V.D. Balsdon, *Roman Women: Their History and Habits* (London, 1962) index s.vv., except for Epicharis, on whom see Tacitus, *Annals* 15: 51–57.

4. Some, but not all, of this writing is rhetorically slanted (the loose woman, Epicharis, who is morally redeemed by her courage; the slave maid, Phoebe, whose sense of honor is keener than her mistress's). The biographer Suetonius is an honorable exception: he describes the position of Caenis matter-of-factly and (it seems) objectively, see *Vespasian* 3, *Domitian* 12.3.

5. See, for example, W. L. Westermann, *The Slave Systems of Greek and Roman Antiquity* (Philadelphia, 1955), pp. 85–87, with P. A. Brunt's remarks in his review in the *Journal of Roman Studies* 48 (1958): 166; I. Biezunska-Malowist, "Les enfants-esclaves à la lumière des papyrus," *Hommages . . . Renard* 2, Collection Latomus 102, pp. 91–96.

6. W. W. Buckland, *The Roman Law of Slavery: The Condition of the Slave in Private Law from Augustus to Justinian* (Cambridge, 1908), reprinted 1970, henceforth cited as *RLS*, pp. 397–436.

7. e.g., 27. 1. 32, 29. 5. 1. 10; 32. 27. 2; 32. 102. 2.

8. 21. 1. 14 & 15.

9. 21. 1. 14. 3; cf. Gell., 4. 2. 9. 10; *RLS*, p. 55 n. 8.

10. 18. 1. 8 pr. Future offspring might also be legated (30. 24 pr.; 30. 63).

11. M. Kaser, *Das Römische Privatrecht* 1 (Munich, 1971), p. 549 nn. 38 & 42.

12. 5. 3. 27 pr. The context is *bona fide* possession.

13. 22. 1. 28 pr.

14. Cf. *RLS*, p. 21. Alan Watson, *Tulane Law Review* 42 (1968): 291–95; David Daube, A Parel and T. Flanagan, eds., *Theories of Property: Aristotle to the Present*, Waterloo, 1979, pp. 39–41.

15. A free translation. For a closely parallel use of *non temere* cf. Cicero *To Quintus* 1.1.13.

16. 29.5.14; Apuleius, *Metamorphoses* 2.15; cf. Quintilian, *Declamations* 347.8.

17. Weaver, pp. 104, 205. Boulvert (p. 430) gives the reason for this: the slave had no legal personality and could act directly for his owner.

18. Cf. Treggiari 1975 for more detailed exposition. Occupations of domestic staff of both sexes are examined in Boulvert; also Treggiari, "Domestic Staff at Rome in the Julio-Claudian Period," *Social History/Histoire sociale* 6 (1973): 241–55; idem, "Jobs in the Household of Livia," *Papers of the British School at Rome* 43 (1975): 48–77, with earlier bibliography.

19. It appears that the male doctor (whether free or slave) kept a discreet distance from the patient during labor, relying on the midwife to tell him how labor was proceeding (checking dilatation is specifically mentioned by Galen *On the natural faculties* 3.3). Pope Leo (*Novellae* 48), allowing women's evidence on matters where no male witnesses were available, mentions childbirth as an obvious example.

20. *CIL* 1² 1211 = *ILLRP* 973.

21. *CIL* 1² 1570 = *ILLRP* 977. "P.Ɔ.1." means "freedwoman of Publius and of a woman," the reversed "C." being used to mean "of Gaia" and the *praenomen* Gaia standing for any woman.

22. Cicero *To Atticus* 12.28.3; 12.30.1.

23. The apogee of slave owning by slaves seems to be reached by the slave steward from the Gallic treasury at Lyon who in the time of Tiberius traveled to Rome with a (presumably skeleton) staff of sixteen *vicarii*. (*Inscriptiones latinae selectae* 1795 = Ehrenberg and Jones 158.)

24. Weaver, p. 70.

25. Weaver, p. 102.

26. *De re rustica* 1.8.19. On breeding from slave women, see the moderns cited in n. 5. The *Digest* shows great interest in the children of slave women (*partus ancillarum*: references collected by E. Jonkers, *Economische en sociale Toestanden in het romeinsche Rijk* (Wageningen, 1933), p. 113).

27. 38.1.48 pr.-2, Hermogenianus

> A patron's son or grandson or great-grandson loses the right to the services of the freedwoman, just as a patron does, if he consents to her marriage, for if she has obtained consent to marry she ought to owe duty to her husband [be *in officio mariti*]. But if the marriage to which the patron consents is invalid he is not forbidden to exact services. The exaction of services is not denied to a *patrona*, or to the daughter, granddaughter or great-granddaughter of a patron, if she consents to the marriage, since there is no impropriety in their being paid to them even by a married woman.

This passage must not be pushed too far and its emphasis is on the clash of male spheres of influence—the *officium* (duty) owed to a husband and to a patron. But sexual propriety is involved, or else the clash between duty to a husband and that to a *patrona* would be equally worrisome.

28. [Paul] *Sententiae* 2.19.6, cf. *Tituli Ulpiani* 5.5, 5.9. The formulation is late, so the invalidity of such unions was presumably so obvious that it was hardly worth stating.

29. The most useful modern work is that of Weaver and Rawson; see also Gérard Boulvert, *Domestique et fonctionnaire sous le haut-empire romain. La condition de l'affranchi et de l'esclave du prince*, Paris, 1974; and Andres E.

De Mañaricua y Nuera, *El matrimonio de los esclavos: estudio historico juridico hasta la fijacion de la disciplina en el derecho canonico* (Rome, 1940). Only a fraction of the city population could put up a funerary inscription, which was fairly expensive. R. Duncan-Jones, *The Economy of the Roman Empire: Quantitative Studies* (Cambridge, 1974), index s.v. tombs. Perhaps some were keener to commemorate themselves than others. Of the inscriptions which were set up, only a fraction survive. So we have, as Mommsen said, the remains of remains. For the people who commemorated themselves, the most important thing to mention was their names: other information, which would be useful to us, such as their relationship to each other, their jobs, their legal status (freeborn Romans, enfranchised aliens or freed slaves) is often not explicitly stated. So the comparative rarity of the word *contubernalis* among the roughly 40,000 inscriptions does not mean that only that number of *contubernales* are represented. It is well known, for instance, that many of the couples who call themselves husbands and wives are in fact *contubernales* (Weaver, p. 171).

But those who call themselves *contubernales* are calling attention to the fact that at one stage in the relationship, if not at the time of death, at least one of the partners had been of slave status. This is particularly useful to us because slaves are apparently badly underrepresented in the inscriptions. The overrepresented class is that of freedmen—who seem to have been more anxious to commemorate themselves, because they had one major achievement at least to their credit, that of having obtained freedom, than native Romans were to boast of their free birth. (But during the period the custom of specifying freed origin in the nomenclature gradually dies out, except for prestigious imperial freedmen.)

30. "*Contubernales* in *CIL* 6," *Phoenix* 35 (1981): 42–69.

31. The following inscription is fairly typical:

Felix, slave of Marcus Satellius Tychius, lived 19 years. Hygia slave of Flavia Antiochis dedicated this niche *(columba rium)* with the urns and inscription to him her well-deserving *contubernalis*, and . . . to her daughter Primigenia, who lived 3 years. Aulene Nebris dedicated this niche to Hygia. (*CIL* 6.8022)

Here both "husband" and daughter died young, and Hygia, who is honored with an inscription from a woman friend, probably did not long survive them. This example shows the full nomenclature for slaves. They have one name or, rarely, two. The names are frequently Greek, because Latin did not have a rich stock of suitable names: these names reflect the taste of slave owners or dealers, or the slave parents, rather than the racial origin of the slave, as used to be supposed. Slave status can also be attested more briefly in inscriptions by the slave's name followed by the owner's in the possessive case, e.g., Felix Satelli. Often there is no explicit mention of the owner and slave status is deduced, with varying degrees of certainty, from the single name. By this criterion, the child Primigenia would be identified as a slave. Since her mother was still a slave when she commemorated the child and since children born to slave women were slaves at birth, the criterion can be seen to be valid in this case.

Here is a more doubtful example:

> To the spirits of the departed. To Trophime, homeborn slave of our master Augustus; lived 21 years, 2 months, 28 days. The three Martiales, her father, *contubernalis* and son dedicated this in gratitude. (*CIL.* 6. 27674)

The woman is definitely a slave, belonging to the emperor. If she was a slave, her son must have been born a slave too.

The legal status of the three Martiales is undefined, naturally enough since the monument is dedicated not to them but to Trophime. They play instead on the amusing coincidence that she had found a husband with the same name as her father and on the fact that her child had been named after them, whether by their decision or by that of the managers of the household.

When a man has the three names, first name (*praenomen*), gentile name (*nomen gentilicium*) and surname (*cognomen*), a prerogative of citizenship, or a woman has two (gentile name and surname), free status is clear.

32. My material includes only seven couples where the "husband" is certainly or probably a slave and the "wife" a freedwoman, and six couples where the "husband" is a freedman and the "wife" probably a slave, with no examples where the "wife" is certainly a slave.

33. Weaver, p. 114.

34. This can be seen more clearly when the slave "husband" has achieved freed status and a *nomen*. In my collection there is for example a Julia married to a Ti. Claudius Augusti libertus, where, if the husband was freed by Nero rather than Claudius (in or later than 54 rather than 41–54) the wife is unlikely to be a freedwoman of any of the three Julian emperors (freed in 41 at the latest) (*CIL* 6. 20389). Still less can a Julia married to a freedman of a freedman of Domitian, who was emperior from 81 to 96, be supposed to have been freed before 41: she is surely a granddaughter of an imperial freedman of the Julian period, *vel. sim.* (*CIL* 6. 8768).

35. Weaver (pp. 162–169) gives the most convincing account to date.

36. With certain exceptions, conveniently assembled by *RLS* pp. 399–401.

37. On *peculium* see in general *RLS* pp. 187–238; on *vicarii*, pp. 239–249.

38. 38. 1. 46, Valens.

39. Thus, for example,

> "Let Stichus, the grandson of my nurse, be free: I will ten gold pieces a year to be given to him." Then (after putting in other names) he legated to Stichus his *contubernalis* and children and bequeathed to them the same allowances which he had paid during his lifetime. . . (34.1.20 pr., Scaevola [quoting from a will])

Or, more generously still,

> . . ."but to all my *liberti* (freedmen and possibly freedwomen, the masculine including the feminine) whom I have manumitted in my lifetime or in these codicils or whom I shall have manumitted subsequently, I bequeath their *contubernales* and also their sons and daughters, apart from any whom I

have in my will desired to belong to my wife or have bequeathed or shall have bequeathed to her by name." He later asked his heirs to restore to his wife their coheir a region in Umbria, Tuscany and Picenum with all the slaves who were there, whether they belonged to the town or country staff, and the agents, except for those who were freed. The question was whether the slaves Eros and Stichus, who administered the agency in Umbria and Picenum up to the day of the testator's death, but were the natural children of Dama, whom the testator had freed during his lifetime, should be turned over to Dama by the heirs under the terms of the codicil, or really belonged to his wife according to the words of the letter . . . (32.1.41.2, Scaevola)

At this point the text becomes suspect, but it still seems that the sons were given to their father, who no doubt freed them. Cf. 32. 37.7, Scaevola for legacy of children.

40. 40.2.14.1, Marcianus: "Sunt qui putant etiam feminas posse matrimoni causa manumittere, sed ita, si forte conservus suus in hoc ei legatus est." In general, according to Ulpian, such marriages might be tolerated if the patrona were lower-class, 23.2.13: "If the patroness is so ignoble that even marriage with her freedman is not dishonorable for her. . . ." ("Si patrona tam ignobilis sit, ut ei honestae sint vel saltem liberti sui nuptiae. . . .") But a man also should not marry his freedwoman unless he were of the proper station (40.2.20.2, Ulpian). It is difficult to believe that late-classical attempts to penalize marriages between patrona and libertus were aimed at the lower classes. Severus and Caracalla in 196 encouraged prosecution of a freedman who dared to marry his patroness, her daughter or her granddaughter, and encouraged judges to sentence "in accord with the morals of my times" because such unions were "rightly considered odious" (Code Just. 5.4.3). The Sententiae Pauli (2.19.9) mention the patron's daughter or wife as well as the patroness (but not the latter's descendants) and the penalty (penal servitude in the mines or "public service," depending on the social status [dignitas] of the man). Cf. J. Gaudemet, RIDA 2 (1949): 355.

41. If the text is sound (33.7.12.7). I see no reason to suppose that the words are interpolated, as S. Solazzi, for instance, does. SDHI 15 (1949): 190.

42. Quintus Cicero Commentariolum Petitionis 17; Tacitus Annals 3.36; Martial 7.62.3–4; Lucian The ignorant book-collector 23.

43. Cf. the reasons given by Antoninus Pius for a rescript checking cruelty to slaves, claiming that he was not interfering with the rights of owners but acting in their interests: 1.6.2, Ulpian = Collatio 3.3.1–4, cf. ibid. 5–6, Gaius 1.53. Other sources and discussion in Wynne Williams, Journal of Roman Studies 66 (1976): 76–77.

44. 28.5.35.3, Ulpian; cf. 33.7.18.3, Paul, citing Pedius.

45. RLS p. 77.

46. The same tendency is documented in 33.7.27.1, Scaevola, where a mistress takes some of her farm staff to Rome and dies there. The existence of contubernales, children and parents of these slaves back on the farm is part of the evidence which justifies counting them in the legacy of the farm. There is also what one might perhaps on the model of favor nup-

tiarum call *favor contubernii* in 32.41.5, Scaevola, where legacy of a bailiff with his *contubernalis* and *filii* (sons and perhaps daughters) is held to include grandchildren as well. Cf. also the intended simultaneous freeing of *contubernales* in 35.1.81 pr., Paul., 40.7.31.1, Gaius (two opinions about what happened when the manumission was conditional on the auditing of the man's accounts). Eventually Constantine was to order that when imperial property in Sardinia was divided, "husband" and "wife," parents and children and brother and sister were not to be separated (*Code Theod.* 2.25.1) a ruling apparently given wider application (*Code Just.* 3.38.11).

47. Quintilian *Institutes* 5.11.34 is suggestive. The rhetorical hypothesis "if an affair with a slave is shameful for a mistress, an affair with a slave girl is shameful for a master" is rebutted by the proposition "it is not the same for a master to have sex with a slave girl as for a mistress to have sex with a male slave." Both concentrate on the honor of the free partner. But a man's lapse is likely to be seen as trivial. Some wives might condone (e.g., Val. Max. 6.7.1); others, presumably, would object, as Ovid's mistress objected to his part-time dalliance with her maid (Ovid *Amores* 2.7–8, a fictitious example). Wives, particularly if they had large dowries or influential families, were by no means helpless.

48. *Controversiae* 4 pr. 10. Cf. Trimalchio's remark about his homosexual relationship with his owner, "What a master orders is not shameful." (Petronius *Satyricon* 75.11).

49. Sources cited in n. 43.

50. See *RLS* pp. 70, 550, 603 for sources and discussion.

51. Horace *Epistles* 1.18.72–73; Seneca *de ira* 2.28.7. It was also bad for a man's reputation (*Code Just.* 9.9.24).

52. *Actio de iniuriis* (47.10.9.4, 25; 48.5.6 pr.); *de servo corrupto* (48.5.6 pr., Paul *Sententiae* 2.26.16); under the Aquilian law (47.10.25, 48.5.6. pr.).

53. *CIL* 1² 1570 = *ILLRP* 977.

54. The monographs are Paul Meyer, *Der römische Konkubinat* (Leipzig, 1895); Jean Plassard, *Le concubinat romain sous le haut empire* (Paris, 1921); Carlo Castello, *In tema di matrimonio e concubinato nel mondo romano* (Milan, 1940). All are unsatisfactory, especially in their handling of the epigraphic material. Castello, the best of the three, is also the least accessible. For the epigraphic evidence in particular see Rawson.

55. This is controversial. I rely chiefly on 25.7.3. pr.-1, Marcianus; 23.2.24, 48.5.35 pr., Modestinus, all of which can be interpreted in the opposite sense.

56. Cicero *Ad familiares* 9.26.2: "*Habeo, . . . non habeor a Laide.*"

57. 39.5.31 pr., Papinian: "It is fitting that gifts bestowed on a concubine cannot be revoked, nor, if marriage is subsequently contracted between the same parties, should a gift which was previously legally valid become invalid. But, I replied, the question must be carefully weighed whether *maritalis honor et affectio* preceded the (sc. apparent) marriage, taking into account the relative standing of the parties (*personis comparatis*) and their union in their way of life. . . ." Cf. 23.2.42. pr., Modestinus: "In

unions one must consider not only what is allowed, but also what is honorable."

58. Ibid.; Plautus *Epidicus* 466; *Code Just.* 7.15.3.1.

59. See especially A. Watson, *The Law of Persons in the Later Roman Republic* (Oxford, 1967) pp. 1–10.

60. See Watson (n. 58), pp. 2–5 on ideas attested in Plautus. I find no direct evidence of a real woman being kept as concubine rather than wife because she lacked a dowry, but it seems probable that this happened in Rome as in other cultures.

61. Rawson, p. 289, finds twenty freedmen out of thirty-seven pairs living in concubinage and attested in the inscriptions of the City of Rome.

62. The author gratefully acknowledges the support of the Social Sciences and Humanities Research Council of Canada.

REFERENCES

Boulvert, Gérard. *Esclaves et affranchis impériaux sous le haut empire romain: rôle politique et administratif.* Naples, 1970.

Rawson, Beryl. "Roman Concubinage and Other *de facto* Marriages." *Transactions of the American Philogical Association* 104 (1974): 279–305.

Treggiari, Susan. "Jobs for Women." *American Journal of Ancient History* 1 (1976): 76–104.

———. "Questions on Women Domestics in the Roman West." *Schiavitù, manomissione e classi dipendenti nel mondo antico.* Rome, 1979, pp. 185–201.

Weaver, P.R.C. *Familia Caesaris: A Social Study of the Emperor's Freedmen and Slaves.* Cambridge, 1972.

WIDOWS' RIGHTS IN ANGLO-SAXON LAW

Theodore John Rivers

Women's legal status in England improved appreciably as the Anglo-Saxon period drew to a close. Although this development was characteristic of all women in early English society, widows attained more independence than any other marital class in Anglo-Saxon England.[1] For this reason, it can be said that the most favored women in England were not wives or unmarried daughters, but widows.[2]

Of all the laws which concern women in Anglo-Saxon legislation, several were concerned with a woman's most basic rights: the right to social and sexual protection. Since all women in medieval society were under the protection (*mundium*) of men, either fathers, husbands, brothers, or other male guardians, women in many cases were not legally responsible for their own affairs, save for adultery, incest, homicide, or sorcery. Moreover, if a woman fell victim to a crime, recompense (usually given in the form of monetary compensation) was paid to her guardian, unless the guardian was her husband. In the latter case, payment for any injustice to her was paid to her kindred, since obligations to the kindred were not broken upon marriage. In the early Anglo-Saxon period, monetary compensation for widows likewise went to their kindred. However, in late Anglo-Saxon times women obtained new guardians—the church and the state and with these new guardians, the legal position of women was transformed.

Male protection, of course, is a relative thing, and there must have been Anglo-Saxon families in which the wife was more assertive than her husband, and therefore, less in need of direct control. Yet, no matter how authoritarian a wife may be, Anglo-Saxon

Reprinted from *American Journal of Legal History*, vol. 19, no. 3 (1975): 208–215.

wives were potentially under the legal jurisdiction of their husbands. Widows, however, gained more rights than married women or women who never married. The reason is that, since wives and maidens were under male protection of husband, father, or other guardian, their tutelage was immediate. Such was not the case for widows; instead, they were placed under the protection of the church and the state, which in most cases, became a far more distant type of protection.[3]

Fundamentally, widows were nonetheless treated like all other women in Anglo-Saxon law; that is, they were protected from exploitation because women were viewed as socially inferior.[4] This view of social inferiority is not surprising, since it is men who make this distinction. Yet the absence of direct male control enabled widows to develop more rights than single women or wives.

The majority of laws which concern widows appear late in Anglo-Saxon law, coming mostly from V–VI Aethelred and I–II Cnut. Besides these late laws, there are only four laws from Aethelberht's code and one each from Hlothhere and Eadric's and Ine's which also concern widows. Surprisingly, widows are not discussed in Alfred's code.[5] Anglo-Saxon laws which concern widows protect them from violation of the *mundium*, defend their inheritance rights, stress their financial obligations to the king, or emphasize their social obligations to the Christian community. A detailed description follows.

Widows' most basic right was the *mundium*. The Anglo-Saxon laws which describe this right were primarily concerned that widows be not sexually assaulted. The *mundium* made its first appearance in Aethelberht 75, which protected widows of the nobility; this protection was also extended to widows of the next three classes.[6] If a widow was not only assaulted but also abducted, double the *mundium* was required.[7] This two-fold payment was probably required in order to compensate the widow's guardian, especially if the abductor wished to keep the woman as a wife. Surprisingly, the law just described (Aethelberht 76) did not require that the woman be returned, only that the crime be paid for monetarily. Although this law may not contain every pertinent detail for this offense in early Anglo-Saxon society, its lack of concern that the woman be returned is a good indication of the pre-Christian (that is, totally Germanic) origins of Aethelberht's code.[8]

The next law regarding widows' *mundium* appeared 400 years later. This law was VI Aethelred 39 (A.D. 1008–11), and it indicated that widows were by then placed under the sponsorship of church and state. Although this law does not specify what the payment was if the *mundium* of widows was violated; nevertheless, II Cnut 52 (A.D. 1027–34) indicates that for this crime the offender must render the wergeld of the violated woman.[9] How this payment was divided between the church and the state was not discussed. The assumption of widows' protection by the state had occurred, however, in the reign of Aethelred, not Cnut,[10] while the guardianship that the church gave to widows first appeared in Edgar's reign (959–975).[11] The acceptance of widows' *mundium* by church and state is described below. Suffice it to say here that widows became increasingly significant in late Anglo-Saxon England due to their economic independence, aided by the absence of direct male control.

A widow received financial assistance upon her husband's demise if children had been born from their marriage. In Aethelberht's code, law 78 indicates that this financial assistance equaled one-half of the late husband's property.[12] In Aethelberht's time, the property conferred was rarely landed estates. Property inherited by widows and children was usually movable, either in the form of money or livestock.[13] That the paternal inheritance could be bestowed gradually over a period of years was described by a later law, Ine 38, which provided that six shillings be given every year for support of the late father's child. The law indicated that these six shillings annually were equal to a cow in summer and an ox in winter. An annual supply of a cow and an ox seems extremely extravagant in the light of England's simple economy. What this law may mean is that a cow was milked and an ox harnessed to furnish the family's subsistence at the yearly value of six shillings.[14] It can hardly be assumed that the widow's child was supplied every year with a cow and an ox, since this would have amounted to a considerable sum of money, particularly when the widow had more than one young child, as would usually have been the case.

In addition to these benefits, Aethelberht 78 also obligated the widow's kindred to maintain the late husband's house for widow and children until each individual child reached maturity, which occurred at age ten. Although the widow's kindred maintained the family's residence, the tutelage of the children fell to the late father's kindred, not to the surviving mother. This important fact is given in Hlothhere and Eadric 6. The benefits supplied by Aethelberht 78 also make their appearance in II Cnut 70,1. Here, too, widows and their children inherited from the husbands' estates, with the remaining portion reverting, as in Aethelberht 78, to the paternal kindred. These laws indicated quite clearly that the paternal inheritance destined for widows was more a provision for the children than for the widows, since widows were not entitled to inherit from their late husbands if they had no children.[15]

The inheritance of the husband's property had no bearing on what personal property the wife (widow) could have in her own right, nor do any of the laws described here pertain to the morning-gift, the property which the newly-married husband gave to his bride the morning after their wedding night.

All remaining Anglo-Saxon laws which concern widows appear either in V-VI Aethelred or I-II Cnut. It is not surprising that the majority of these laws concern widows' obligations; increased rights might be expected to bring increased responsibilities. There are eight laws indicating the state's prohibition of remarriage by widows within one year of their husbands' death, a requirement which made its first appearance in the *Poenitentiale Theodori* (A.D. 668–690), the penitential of Bishop Theodore of Canterbury.[16] A widow who married within this allotted time was to lose her morning-gift and all property which she inherited from her deceased husband,[17] even if she was married against her will.[18] The severity of this violation was extended to the husband the bereaved wife married, since he must forfeit his wergeld to the king.[19] Nor were widows to be consecrated as nuns too hastily after their husbands' deaths.[20] The reason for all this frowning on urgency is a simple one. If widows married or entered the convent within the first year of their husbands' death, the king lost the heriot tax, a principal source of revenue. Even if a widow paid the heriot within the first year of her husband's death, she still could not remarry within the same length of time.[21] After the tax was paid and a year had elapsed since her husband's decease, however, the widow could remarry or become a nun if she chose.[22] The remarriage of a widow removed her from the church-state *mundium,* and placed her once again under the *mundium* of her husband. When this happened, her privileged status of a widow ceased, and her duties as a wife began once again. Widows also had social obligations to the Christian community in which they lived. All widows who did not live adulterously received protection from the church, usually the local bishop, and state.[23] As long as they did this, the financial independence which widows obtained in late Anglo-Saxon times allowed them to sue or be sued in court,[24] to will, sell, or inherit property,[25] and to direct their affairs generally as they saw fit. That widows could will, sell, or inherit landed property in late Anglo-Saxon England is proof of the development of widows' rights, since widows were not allowed to inherit other than movable property in Aethelberht's time. A brief look at Anglo-Saxon charters will substantiate this point. Ecclesiastical and monarchical protection could also apply to the disadvantage of widows, however, since they could be exploited by the king's dues[26] or even lose their protection if they violated the law, as for example if they were found guilty of living in adultery. In addition, widows like everyone else in Anglo-Saxon England, were not permitted to marry within the sixth degree of consanguinity.[27]

Widows and widows' rights were continually significant in Anglo-Saxon society. The earliest Anglo-Saxon laws were concerned with the more rudimentary aspects of widows' rights, that is, protection of the *mundium* and defense of the paternal inheritance. Later laws extended these basic rights to obligations as well. The increasing equality of widows with men in England occurred late in the Anglo-Saxon period, and this is supported by the later laws, particularly Aethelred's and Cnut's, and by charters dating from as early as the tenth century. The principal reason for the improved legal status of widows in Anglo-Saxon society was the absence of direct male control.[28] Widows did not lose all of their favored status with the introduction of Norman feudalism in the mid-eleventh century, yet the true flowering of widows' rights appeared within the context of Anglo-Saxon England.

40   Theodore John Rivers

NOTES

1. There are few introductory studies of women in Anglo-Saxon society. In general, see Doris Mary Stenton, *The English Woman in History* (1957), ch. I: "The Anglo-Saxon Woman," pp. 1–28, and Evelyn Acworth, *The New Matriarchy* (1965), ch. III: "The Anglo-Saxon Period," pp. 49–65. A notable example of the political ability of noble English women is evident in the career of King Alfred's eldest child, his daughter Aethelflaed, who, upon her husband's death, ruled Mercia from 911–918. See F. T. Wainwright, "Aethelflaed Lady of the Mercians," in *The Anglo-Saxons: Studies in some Aspects of their History and Culture presented to Bruce Dickins*, ed. Peter Clemoes (1959), pp. 53–69.

2. There are no studies of widows' rights in Anglo-Saxon law. Occasional legal references to widows can be had in: Florence G. Buckstaff, "Married woman's property in Anglo-Saxon and Anglo-Norman law and origin of the common-law dower," *Annals of the American Academy of Political and Social Science*, v. 4, (1894), 233–264; Ernst Young, "The Anglo-Saxon Family Law," in *Essays in Anglo-Saxon Law*, ed. Henry Adams (Boston, 1876), pp. 121–182; Harold Dexter Hazeltine, *Zur Geschichte der Eheschliessung nach angelsächsische Recht* (Berlin, 1905), which was reprinted from the *Festgabe für Dr. Bernhard Hübner* (Berlin, 1905); and Fritz Roeder, *Die Familie bei den Angelsachsen*, Studien zur englischen Philologie, IV (Halle, 1899). Also see legal references in Lorraine Lancaster, "Kinship in Anglo-Saxon Society," *Brit. J. Sociology*, v. 9, 230–250, 359–377 (1958), reprinted, in part, in *Early Medieval Society*, ed. Sylvia L. Thrupp (1967), pp. 17–41.

3. Protection by church and state should not be thought of as a universal type of tutelage which makes widows continually subject no matter where they travel within Anglo-Saxon England. Rather, the authority of the church and crown is too fragmented to give any real substance to this legislated protection. Wives and unmarried daughters live with their husbands and fathers, but widows often live alone (unless they remarry), being supported by their late husband's morning-gift and inherited property.

4. There is no distinction in Anglo-Saxon law for widowers. Unlike women, men are not classified maritally.

5. The relative dates when these laws were promulgated are:
Aethelberht ante 597
Hlothhere & Eadric 685–6
Ine 688–95
V Aethelred 1008
VI Aethelred 1008–11
I–II Cnut 1027–34
All references to these laws are taken from the best edition of the Anglo-Saxon laws: Felix Liebermann, *Die Gesetze der Angelsachsen*, 3 vols. (Halle, 1903–1916, reprinted, Aalen, 1960). (The only exception here is the date from Aethelberht's code. Although Liebermann gives 601–4, this is much

too late. See n. 8 below.) Citations to individual laws referred to in this study are supplied in the first volume of Liebermann's edition. Volumes II and III contain a glossary and commentary respectively. English translations of Anglo-Saxon laws are supplied in F. L. Attenborough, *The Laws of the Earliest English Kings* (1922), and A. J. Robertson, *The Laws of the Kings of England from Edmund to Henry I* (1925).

6. Aethelberht 75,1. See H. Munro Chadwick, *Studies on Anglo-Saxon Institutions* (Cambridge, 1905), pp. 76–102, for a description of classes in Anglo-Saxon England.

7. Aethelberht 76. Cf. Hazeltine, *Eheschliessung*, pp. 19–20.

8. A great deal has been said about the influence of Christianity on Aethelberht's code. The greatest influence that the Church could bring to England with St. Augustine's arrival in 597 is the "Roman tradition" (the written word), but it does not explain many predominantly pagan institutions preserved in Aethelberht's code. The only part of Aethelberht's code which is Christian is its preface, which is now thought to have been appended considerably later than the time the code itself was written down. See Henry G. Richardson and George O. Sayles, *Law and Legislation from Aethelberht to Magna Carta*, Edinburgh University Publications, History, Philosophy and Economics, XX (1966), pp. 1–9. Also see Hans Würdinger, "Einwirkungen des Christentums auf das angelsächsische Recht," *Zeitschrift der Savigny-Stiftung für Rechtsgeschichte, Germ. Abt.*, v. 55 (1935), 105–130. It is reasonable to assume that the influence of the Church on Kentish law occurred gradually, but this does not explain the unusual compensation bishops received if their property was stolen as expressed by Aethelberht's code, although the latter view is upheld in J. M. Wallace-Hadrill, *Early Germanic Kingship in England and on the Continent* (Oxford, 1971), pp. 39–41. That the preface to Aethelberht's code is, indeed, a later addition is also supported by William A. Chaney, "Aethelberht's Code and the King's Number," *Amer. J. Leg. Hist.*, v. 6, 153, n. 9 (1962).

9. Robertson, *Laws*, p. 203, supplies "his" wergeld rather than "the" wergeld. *His* wergeld would make little sense, since monetary compensation is given according to the class of the victim, not of the criminal. Liebermann, *Gesetze*, I, p. 346, also renders *the* wergeld.

10. Cf. Stuart A. Queen and Robert W. Habenstein, *The Family in Various Cultures*, 3rd ed. (1967), p. 219.

11. See A. J. Robertson, ed. and trans., *Anglo-Saxon Charters*, Cambridge Studies in English Legal History, 2nd ed. (1956), pp. 90–93 (#44). Robertson calls this charter: "History of the Estates of Sunbury and Send." Although Robertson does not attempt to date this document more specifically than late tenth century, it is dated ca. 950–968 in P. H. Sawyer, *Anglo-Saxon Charters: An Annotated List and Bibliography*, Royal Historical Society Guides and Handbooks, v. 8, (1968), p. 406 (#1447). Contrary to Sawyer (ibid), however, the estates of Sunbury and Send were not purchased by Archbishop Dunstan, but only placed under his tutelage for the represented widow and child.

12. The other half of the property reverts to the paternal kindred.

13. Eric John, *Land Tenure in Early England: A Discussion of Some Problems*, Studies in Early English History, v. 1, (1960), p. 59. See *feoh* (movable property) in Liebermann, *Gesetze*, v. 2, p. 69.

14. Attenborough, *Laws*, p. 189, believes a cow is given in summer if the husband dies in that season, and an ox in winter similarly. The six shillings itself is derived from the late husband's estate. See Lancaster, *Brit. J. Sociology*, v. 9, p. 360 (1958), (*Early Medieval Society*, ed. Thrupp, p. 32).

15. In early Anglo-Saxon England, the provision for a married woman is slightly different, since she is entitled to one-third of her husband's estate if she wishes to leave her husband. This is supported by Ine 57 in which a wife may leave her spouse if she is innocent of the latter's crime of theft. See Courtney Stanhope Kenny, *The History of the Law of England as to the Effects of Marriage on Property and on the Wife's Legal Capacity* (1879), p. 24. It appears reasonable to conclude that from Ine's time (late seventh century), the wife's inheritance becomes standardized at one-third.

16. *Poenitentiale Theodori*, book II, ch. 12, §9. Arthur West Hadden and William Stubbs, ed., *Councils and Ecclesiastical Dcouments relating to Great British and Ireland*, 3 vols. in 4 parts (Oxford, 1869–1878, III [1878]), p. 199. Also translated in John T. McNeill and Helena Gamer, *Medieval Handbooks of Penance: A translation of the principal 'libri poenitentiales' and selection from related documents*, Columbia University Records of Civilization, v. 29, (1938), p. 209. Here the translation appears as book II, ch. 12, §10.

17. II Cnut 73a. Cf. V Aethelred 21, 1; VI Aethelred 26, 1; and II Cnut 73.

18. II Cnut 73, 2.

19. II Cnut 73, 1.

20. II Cnut 73, 3.

21. II Cnut 73.

22. II Cnut 73, 4.

23. V Aethelred 21 (identical with VI Aethelred 26).

24. Buckstaff, *Annals of the American Academy of Political and Social Science*, v. 4, p. 250 (1894). Although widows could plead their own cases in court in late Anglo-Saxon times, they still remain under the tutelage of church and state. As described above, it is the distance of this form of *mundium* that enables widows to be more independent.

25. For example, see the will of Aethelstan Mannesune (A.D. 986), given in *Chronicon Abbatiae Rameseiensis*, ed. W. Dunn Macray, Rolls Series, v. 83, (1886), pp. 59–61. This will is summarized in C. R. Hart, *The Early Charters of Eastern England*, Studies in Early English History, v. 5 (Leicester, 1966), p. 29 (#21). Also see the will of Aescwen of Stonea: *Liber Eliensis*, ed. E. O. Blake, Royal Historical Society, Camden Third Series, v. 92 (1962), book II, ch. 18 (pp. 93–94). Widows selling land are also illustrated in *ibid.*, ch. 10 (p. 84) and ch. 20 (pp. 95–96). All of the wills cited here date from the second half of the tenth century; they are the earliest examples I have

found which show widows' independence regarding their own property, particularly in regard to the sale of land. For widows' rights concerning inheriting and selling land from the late ninth to the early eleventh century, see the innumerable charters in H.P.R. Finberg, *The Early Charters of Wessex*, Studies in Early English History, v. 3, (1964), and his *Early Charters of the West Midlands*, 2nd ed., Studies in Early English History, v. 2, (1972). Also see the general comments in Willystine Goodsell, *A History of Marriage and the Family*, rev. ed. (1934), pp. 208–209. (The first edition of this work is entitled: *A History of the Family as a Social and Educational Institution* [1930].)

26. H. R. Loyn, *Anglo-Saxon England and the Norman Conquest* (1962), p. 185.

27. VI Aethelred 12 (identical in principle with I Cnut 7).

28. The marriage of a succeeding king to the late king's widow was practiced in Anglo-Saxon England, although both Bede and Asser are shocked by this custom. The first reference to this practice is the marriage of Eadbald, Aethelberht of Kent's son, to the latter's second wife in 616. It is repeated by Aethelbald of Wessex who married Judith, the widow of his father Aethelwulf in 858, as well as by Cnut who married Aethelred's widow, Emma, in 1016. Modern authorities question whether or not this was acceptable custom. It was acceptable only insofar that it strengthened the already existing bonds of kingship. Outside of its utilitarianism, it was not common practice in England. The latter view is supported by William A. Chaney, *The Cult of Kingship in Anglo-Saxon England: The Transition from Paganism to Christianity* (1970), pp. 26–27, and by F. G. Frazer, *Lectures on the Early History of the [sic] Kingship* (1905), p. 244. Cf. Lancaster, 9 *Brit. J. Sociology*, (1958), 241 (*Early Medieval Society*, ed. Thrupp, p. 25).

MERCHET AND WOMEN'S PROPERTY RIGHTS IN MEDIEVAL ENGLAND

Eleanor Searle

Of all the indignities to which women have been subjected in western societies, none has seemed quite so pointless, so humiliating as the necessity of a medieval girl or her family to pay their manorial lord for his permission before she might marry. In England the payment was called *merchet*. Such a fine seems to imply control over the licit sexual activity of peasant girls, the ultimate in needless control over human freedom. Certainly, by the early modern period, it was taken as just this—it came to epitomize the horrors of medieval tenures. At least as early as the sixteenth century, it was equated with sexual rights enjoyed by the lords of the wicked past over the peasant maidens of their estates: the repellent *droit du seigneur*.[1]

The operation of the custom, and its origins, have been debated among historians trying to make sense of the past rather than merely believing the worst of it, as did the early polemicists against customary law and feudal tenures.[2]

There is no disagreement concerning what *merchet* was. It was the term for the payment given the lord by a dependent peasant for license to give his daughter in marriage. For England none of our evidence of this exaction comes from pre-Norman sources. The phrases that describe it look clear enough, though laconic to say the least: "he shall give a payment *(gersumma)* in order to marry his daughter"; "not to marry his daughter without redemption"; "he may not give his daughter without licence." These are not fees for the registration of marriages, for court rolls do not usually recite the couples' names.

This chapter is a revised version of an article, "Seigneurial Control of Women's Marriage: Antecedents and Function of *Merchet* in England," which originally appeared in *Past and Present*, no. 82 (February 1979): 3–43.

Whatever the fee was for, one possibility can be disposed of at the outset. The statements that describe *merchet* are, almost without exception, of the thirteenth century. By that time no lord could prevent a valid marriage, for the church's jurisdiction over the matter was firm. Canonical thinking on the subject of marriage had changed during the twelfth century, but by the time of the Decretals of Gregory IX (1224–41) the minimum requirement had for some time been settled and was set out in that authoritative collection, where Gratian's thinking on the question had been decisive. The consent of a couple of consenting age was the only positive necessity for a valid marriage.[3] The notion of what a marriage was seems gradually to have widened in canonical thought, from the early *Aliter*'s presumption against any union as marriage save one accompanied by expensive and public ceremony and exchange of property, to its final definition in the epoch of St. Francis, when an elopement or the coupling of the homeless beggar could make a valid marriage.[4] This is not to say that churchmen thought of any but the arranged marriage of all European societies as the norm. The church's teaching on the matter was clear: trothplight should be witnessed if the union was to be a marriage without sin, banns should be published, dower and dowry should be bestowed by parental authority at the church door. But if all this were omitted, if all that happened was that the man and the woman mutually consented, even in private and in secrecy, the marriage was no less a marriage, no less under the protection and jurisdiction of the church. The phrase "he is unable to give his daughter in marriage without the licence of his lord" cannot mean what it literally seems to mean. Whatever rights lords may once have had, in the very heyday of the custom the words that describe the custom have literally no meaning. This is not to say that fathers paid license fees for nothing. It is to say that they were not paying for permission to give daughters in valid marriage. The canons remind us that we must look elsewhere to see what the lord could license.

When a villein heir came into his inheritance, he paid his lord an "entry fine," variable "at the lord's will," but probably within customary limits, if the lord had good sense. The noninheriting brother, if sent off to school, or made a priest, paid a similar, but not unnaturally smaller, fine. This is the "forisfamiliated" brother, given his share, and with no further claim upon the heir. Might it not be that, just as the lord was taxing the entering heir, he was taxing the share of the family resources that "set up" the apprenticed boy? It is more than plausible.

And his sister? For the girl who was not herself an heiress, her share in the family property was given her at the time of her marriage as her dowry. It is a usual form of premortem female inheritance. A medieval girl was endowed with her "inheritance" at the church door, and there she was given her dower rights in the groom's property for her support should she outlive him. This was her wedding, and her dowry represented the most that she could claim against her inheriting brother. Surely the lord who taxed the premortem inheritance of her forisfamiliated brother would tax the girl's dowry. That is what I propose the point of *merchet* to have been.

Merchet, at the same time, shares the quality of another seigneurial tax: the fine at a sale *inter vivos*. Whether her father or brother endowed her with the property to make her marriage possible, or whether a girl herself earned wages for her dowry, her possessions were passing into the hands of another, her husband. All property transactions were of great interest to the lord's steward, and all property was held for the lord's profit. Was it not his own at common law? It must not be wasted, it must be used reasonably— he must control, ultimately, its disposal. Profit and control both must be combined in *merchet*, if I read the evidence aright.

Evidence of peasant dowries is abundant. Girls were given land, chattels or coin at, or before, their marriages as their part of the inheritance. Where peasant charters served the interests of the family itself, the gift of land to the daughter and her new husband is explicitly dowry, the marriage gift. Land may be identified as that which a father "gave his [three] daughters as their *maritagium*."[5] Among villein tenants, as with free tenants, a mother's dowry, or even her dower, might be particularly suited to be used as the daughter's dowry, lying perhaps separate from the paternal holding.[6] Such premortem inheritance of land was of particular interest to the lord, and manorial court rolls recorded the transfer though not necessarily the connection with marriage. Where the dowry-land was small, the lord kept track of its transfer and took a fine for the privilege but did not necessarily keep note of the new man responsible for it. The tiny holding might go to a daughter or to a son but the roll does not tell us whether the transfer is to promote a marriage, and *merchet* may go unmentioned, silently included in the entry fine.[7]

Dowries in chattels were very likely more common than land-dowry for those peasant girls fortunate enough to receive a dowry at all. Bracton records it as the custom of the unfree tenants on the ancient demesne manors of Cockham and Bray that if a peasant had only daughters, and all but one had been married "outside their father's tenement with their father's chattels," the one who remained should receive the tenement. If all have been married "outside their father's tenement, with their father's chattels," the eldest inherited the land alone.[8] The composition of dowries is occasionally listed in manorial rolls when the parties seem to wish a recorded marriage settlement like those of the king's court rolls. Thus a prosperous villein in Berkshire gave with his daughter ten bushels of barley, sixteen bushels of oats, several sheep and a cart without iron, promising that half would be paid in August and the rest by the end of September when, presumably, his harvest would be in.[9] More generally chattel-dowries appear in lawsuits. One unhappy husband lost his wife's dowry and came near to being hanged as a felon because his father-in-law gave him a stolen horse as the girl's portion.[10] Other lists of the bride's contribution to her new household are found when disputes over payment came for settlement before manorial courts.[11] Such courts were also sought by disputants over dowry if the couple parted, and such cases make it clear that her dowry was considered the woman's own property.[12] Lords were willing therefore, for a consideration, to put their courts at the peasants' disposal for the registration and enforcement of dowry agreements, once they had established their right to control and to profit from such agreements.

For *merchet* can be seen to have been about property, not girls, and not primarily marriage. The formulary used as a model for the courts of St. Albans preserves the explicit connection: the steward is to inquire "whether any bondman's daughter has married without leave, . . . and what her father has given with her by way of goods."[13] The two are virtually inseparable. Had she been married with leave, the steward would know what goods had been given with her.

We can see this inseparability recorded in the court rolls. When the family was prosperous such concealment brought a heavy amercement. One John Copin of High Easter, Essex, in 1264/5 "concealed the dowry *(maritagium)* of his daughter and gave his daughter without the lord's permission." *Maritagium* here can not have any other meaning than dowry. Yet so inseparable is dowry from marriage that the roll can remark elsewhere that Copin was amerced "because he married his daughter without the lord's permission."[14] In 1339/40 a Berkshire widow was presented for having arranged her daughter's marriage to a free man outside the lord's jurisdiction. All her goods and chattels were ordered to be taken for the lord's fine. At this the widow came, and promising the lord to marry her daughter without chattels, procured his permission, for a fine of 2s.[15] Another Berkshire family was amerced for having married a daughter outside the liberty without permission. Because the case happens to be unusually fully recorded we are able to see the point of marriage control vividly. An inquest concerning the marriage was ordered by the lord and it was found that the girl's father had "alienated with her nine marks' worth of the lord's chattels."[16] A Durham case is equally explicit: Thomas Parkinson, a fourteenth-century reeve, was ordered to be distrained for payment of *merchet* for his daughter's marriage and "to show the court the charter," possibly the marriage contract. When he offered the required evidence, the court roll noted that *merchet* was to be set at half a mark "because he married her with ten marks."[17]

Merchet, then, served as a dowry fine, and therefore it was not usually a fixed fine, either in custumals or as it is recorded in court rolls: it fluctuated with the value of the dowry. Like the entry fine of the villein heir, it was a variable sum. They were in fact related entry fines, for the sister's dowry necessarily lessened the heir's ability to pay the entry fine when the father died. It is therefore significant that when the girl married off the manor the *merchet* was generally set at a higher rate than if she married within the manor and thus kept her portion of the inheritance where the lord would ultimately, at her husband's or her death, receive his share.[18] A number of calculations (not least the father's age and health) must have gone into the settlement of *merchet*. The father of the bride haggled with the father of the groom and on occasion little love was lost between them.[19] Over his daughter's dowry a peasant father was prepared to haggle as well with his lord's steward concerning the *merchet*. We can see the assumption of bargaining in an early description of *merchet* where the tenant is to "pay a fine . . . according as he is able."[20] The matter will usually leave no more trace than the record of the sum. But something more may surface, as in the case of the widow's daughter mentioned above, whose lord went so far as to forbid that any chattels go with the girl out of his jurisdiction. Occasionally, as we shall see, patronage affected the amount paid, or amicability between the family and the steward can be inferred: license to marry is given, and at the next court payment is to be made "according to what is just."[21] A father might even successfully refuse to pay, pleading that the girl had not been in his custody.[22] It was not blood that mattered.

Where the girl was an heiress to land, or a widow with a full tenement or a half-tenement as her dower, the *merchets* recorded are unusually high and permission to marry is almost invariably accompanied by a statement of the lord's acceptance of the man into the woman's tenement. Such *merchets* range, in the rolls studied, between 5s. and £4. Where land is not mentioned, most *merchets* range from 6d. to 2s.[23] None has been found below the lower figure and relatively few between 2s. and 5s. From that figure upwards to £4 there is an even spread in the amount of *merchet* paid. This surely indicates that at the upper end of the economic range, *merchet* was performing the functions of an inheritance tax and control of land tenure. Lower down (at 2s. and below), where one might infer that chattel-dowries were involved, there is still sufficient range to indicate taxation of dowries of varying value. There is no significant difference I have observed between the mid-thirteenth and mid-fourteenth centuries, but any increasing seigneurial desire for profit may have been thwarted by increasing peasant poverty. One cannot tell. In any case, population increase and the spreading liability to the fine would have increased profits from the source somewhat without raising a customary fee. Between 6d. and 2s. nearly every gradation is found, and this suggests that, in general, peasant chattel-dowries fluctuated within narrow limits rather than that *merchet* was a formal profit of lordship.

The variability of *merchet* and the large amounts often actually levied when the girl married a free man outside the lord's jurisdiction must, to some extent, have had the effect of encouraging endogamy, particularly where the jurisdiction was large enough to make the pattern practicable. But such *merchets* were not set at a level that would imply lords' desire to keep girls within the manor or soke. *Merchets* for marriage outside the jurisdiction are only slightly higher than the norm. The large *merchets* levied on such marriages are correlated rather with the family's ascertainable prosperity, or that prominence within the local community that argues prosperity. Large *merchets* were clearly considered worth the price of certain matches, and certain families were prepared, generation after generation, to pay their lords large amounts so that their girls could marry into a wider sphere than the village, obviously aiming to marry the daughter upwards in the social scale. One such family in Berkshire may serve as an example. In the 1290s Richard Young held in villeinage thirty-eight acres in the common fields, a close of unspecified size, two acres of wood and a virgate of arable in the vill of Brightwalton.[24] A villager of such ample prosperity would normally be active as a pledge and office-holder, and so Richard was. He, his heir after him, and his grandson were affeerors, pledges, tithingmen, harvest-reeves. Richard had four children mentioned in the rolls. His son Walter was heir to his lands; a second son, Stephen, was sent away to school (*posuit se ad litteraturam, qui adhuc in scolis residet*, the presentment ran), for which the father paid a *merchet*-like fine. His daughter Felicia was married out of the lord's jurisdiction with a dowry of nine marks for which her father paid *merchet*. Of Juliana, another daughter, the rolls speak but once, concerning a childish prank. Felicia's marriage, with its generous dowry and high *merchet*, was no doubt considered a family asset. Stephen's schooling proved an asset indeed, for he became a steward of his father's lord, riding to other manors on the lord's business and without doubt exercising patronage on behalf of his family. In the following generation the pattern was repeated. Of Walter Young's two sons, John became heir to the family lands while William was given leave, without payment, to become a priest. Walter's daughter, Matilda, was married, like her aunt, out of the lord's jurisdiction. For this the family was charged the unusual *merchet* of 4s.—very probably a reduction of the usual 5s.-or-above *merchet*, arguably an act of favor like the one that attended her brother's taking orders. Primogeniture and the land shortage of the time were met with the device of education and careful marriages for the noninheriting. Those sons and daughters alike were afforded a relatively costly start in life, but the possibilities of return to the family could be considerable, as Stephen's career implies.

The connection between large *merchet* payments and demonstrably prosperous families is strong evidence that such payments were related to property. But we can go still further. We can conclude that although in the custumals *merchet* was a general villein liability, in practice it was a liability of propertied villeins and propertied free men who held in villein tenure. For the fact is that only a relatively small proportion of peasant marriages were taxed in this way. This is particularly striking where the run of court rolls is long and fairly complete. Generation replaces generation within the manor and yet few of the villagers who appear as mere cottagers are forced to pay *merchet*. Now and then a woman who holds a cottage independently will be charged.[25] But those miserable families who appear before their neighbors only as illegal gleaners, thieves of acorns and of kindling—those misdemeanours of the poor—are neither payers of *merchet* nor are they cited for unlicensed marriage. The family arrangements of the landless were informal arrangements at best, and the fact that lords left them untaxed and uncontrolled emphasizes the fact. It is the prosperous peasant who will pay the lord to give his girl a dowry and who will celebrate her wedding with the exchange of property at the church door. Such a man has an honour acknowledged even by his lord and displayed at his wedding feast.[26] He alone can pay the variable fine, just as he alone can afford to purchase the *maritagium* of an under-age villein "heir" for his daughter.[27] One need only trace in the court rolls the few families that pay *merchet* to find land, financial activity and indications of prominence within the village.[28] Virtually never is it recorded that a bride has been excused *merchet* on account of poverty, and I have found no cases in which there was a problem of collection. It is simply the fact that most peasant girls' marriages went untaxed.

The evidence I have been examining links *merchet* with propertied peasant families, and emphasizes its aspect of taxation of dowries. But as with the sure *inter vivos*, there was at the same time a concern over control of land. Precisely because he could not dissolve a marriage, the lord had need of controlling it before the fact when the bride was an heiress, if she were to be allowed to inherit. The common law, with its concept of absolute proprietorship, loosened the lord's hand upon freeholders, but the villein heiress remained as all heiresses had once been, and as her land was, "in the lord's hands." The lord's control has often left its traces merely in the noting of a *merchet* payment or entry fine. The usual occasion when grooms paid to marry was when they married women who were acknowledged heiresses or already in seisin of land. An example can be cited in which we learn only indirectly that the bride was propertied: "Roger Cook gives the lord a silver mark for permission to marry Juliana of Hull and to have seisin of a certain piece of land opposite Juliana's door."[29] But sufficient direct evidence survives for us to see the real function of *merchet* as an entry fine in the case of peasant heiresses, for often the clerk was conscientious enough to record the fine and the lord's acceptance of the husband as the new tenant. Thus, for proffered fines: "it is allowed to John Jordan that he may marry Juliana atte Crouche and hold Juliana's tenement for life";[30] "Walter, son of Richard, has taken Joan, daughter of Ralph of Leagrave, as wife with a half-virgate of land";[31] "Roger of Wooton has received a half-virgate with Alice his wife."[32] In 1286/7 on the same manor Alice, daughter of Molecous, paid 2s. entry fine to hold for life the messuage of her mother, Molecous, and in 1293 a suitor sought license to marry Alice.[33] A more important heiress nearby was allowed in 1288 to inherit her deceased father's half-virgate, and in 1293 a suitor for her paid for license "to have her with a half-virgate" identified as her father's.[34] An adult heiress might be shown, on occasion, unusual favor or confidence. Juliana Godfrend, a Berkshire villein, settled the whole matter at once, paying both for her entry fine, and "that she might marry whom she would."[35] These women were probably adult, but the claims of even small girls were not overlooked. Robert Golion, an active pledge and inquest juror at Chalgrave, died *circa* 1287, evidently leaving a very young heiress, for nothing is heard of her for about fifteen years. For a time her father's land was taken into the lord's hand as unclaimed and without the services performed. Then in 1300 another villager was commanded, and at length forced by distraint, to enter the tenement. There is no mention of formal admission nor is there any entry fine: he did not become the accepted holder but was meant to keep the place up and to perform its services. The land was evidently being detached from demesne management and reverting to tenancy, meanwhile being cared for by an unwilling neighbour. That it was being prepared for the entrance of its "rightful heiress" can be inferred, for two years later Lucy Golion married and she and her husband received her father's land.[36]

It would seem then that in the few cases in which an adult heiress was allowed to purchase prior agreement to whomsoever she would bring as husband on to her land, she paid for the right when she paid her entry fine. More usually the villein heiress without a father appears in the court rolls as inheriting only at the time of her marriage, and in such cases it is her husband who is the central figure. He acts as the payer of the *merchet* and the entry fine for the girl and her land; he is accepted as the tenant responsible to the lord.[37] It is so in the examples we have seen, and clearly so in 1293 when at Romsley, one of the Hales group of properties, a certain Clement offered the lord "half a mark for licence to marry Emma, the heiress *(heres)* of Matilda de Fulfen, and to hold her tenement on the same terms by which the other customary tenants hold."[38] The girl had not yet inherited when her suitor was accepted as tenant.

If the couple were young the father of the bride or groom might be willing to pay a high price to the lord for the marriage of a villein heir or heiress. One villager offered £10 for the marriage of an under-age heiress, to be married to his son, and for permission to have custody of her land on his son's behalf. The marginal note records the offer as "merchet," and here again is evidence that *merchet* is indistinguishable from the purchase of a propertied marriage in any class. A fact of villein life rarely noticed is that whatever the arrangements made for the care of the under-age villein heir and lands, he or she is the ward of the manorial lord in the sense that the lord will control and profit from the marriage. As once had been true of all tenures, the incidents of lordship were not incidental in unfree tenures; they represented the lord's access to what was his own when no accepted tenant was there to perform the services. In the case of this marriage, the steward did not feel able to take full responsibility himself and noted that the arrangement was to stand "if the lord . . . accepts it."[39]

The lord's acceptance of the marriage of the heiress to villein lands was particularly important when she married a man not of the manor, for her lands might all too easily slip into free tenure or under the control of another lord. This can be seen in the corollary, the incentive offered to the male tenant who married in the lord's interest, bringing his wife's land under his own lord's hand.[40] Marriage to another lord's villein was a cause for forfeiture if presented. Thus "they say that Sarah Monk holds a cottage of the abbot of Ramsey and took it to a husband from the homage of the lord Reginald de Grey, wherefore the said cottage was seized . . ."[41] Lords were, after all, accepting men who would do, and ultimately could be made to do, service when they accepted the marriage of a villein heiress. Only if the man were willing to come and accept the full implications of his wife's land tenure were he and his wife allowed to retain her lands; "Elias . . . becomes the earl's villein and gives 2s. to marry Maude, daughter of Henry of Wodethorpe, and to take all her land" heritably.[42] "Richard Scirlet gives the lord 6d. because he married Margery of Coventry without license. And he does fealty to the lord for Margery's tenement, and acknowledges its service . . ."[43] The "outsider *(extraneus)*" Roger of Kinlow was permitted to marry Katherine, the daughter of the reeve of King's Ripton and to take with her a "quarter of land," but on condition that at her death, the "nearest heir of the blood of Katherine" would enter the land—neither lord nor court would accept the land going to Roger or his "outsider" relatives. Another case of marriage between an unfree and a free tenant clearly connects the payment of *merchet* with land tenure. A clerk of Earl Warenne, one Richard del Rode, a villein, married a wife with free land. When the couple's daughter came to be married, Richard gave her a dowry of land from his wife's free tenement, and although called upon to pay *merchet*, he was not finally made to do so.[44]

The control exercised through marriage fines is, then, most importantly, power over the dispersal of chattels and over villein land tenure in the interest of the lord. Since that is so, it follows that this control is associated with a latitude enjoyed by the peasant tenant to leave his property according to his will rather than in accordance with rigid inheritance custom, as long as he secured his lord's permission to do so. The cases above, of the reeve of King's Ripton and the clerk of Wakefield, surely show acts of patronage by lords to valued local villein officials. In particular the reeve's son-in-law had been secured for life even against the customary rights of his wife's "nearer heir." In most of the land held in free tenure, primogeniture had defeated the claims of female and male siblings alike by the thirteenth century, and devise had been severely limited. Whatever the desire of the father, even backed by his lord, to endow children as he liked out of the patrimony, a lawsuit after his death might defeat his act.

Perhaps by analogy with the legal actions for free tenure, villeins have been considered as bound by immutable custom. The point is not unimportant, for research on inheritance, family structure, population growth and economic development will be seriously misdirected if it is assumed that peasant inheritance customs had the same binding power as actions at common law. We should not think of custom as restricting the will of lords, for the very essence of unfree tenure was that it was held at the lord's will. The manorial court was not an impartial tribunal. It was simply not available to rival claimants once a tenant was accepted by the lord. As long as that tenant did the service, and sometimes even longer, the lord's court protected the lord's tenant in possession. His court was the instrument of his will, and no lord was the creature of peasant inheritance custom. He was guided by the findings of his inquest jurors, and influenced, no doubt, by the communal acceptance of his decisions, but his concern was with paid-up rents, labourers, profitably occupied tenements. His goodwill could be secured by petition, and the occasional notes in manorial court rolls to the effect that certain marriages must await his or his steward's decision attest to the fact. This should be enough to remind us that a lord when he held a manorial court was doing far more than providing a service. His court was there to further his interests, and in so far as they were served by acquiescing to the desires of his tenants, he would do so. No doubt often his patronage could simply be purchased. Always it left the traces of its activity in the court rolls in company with the payment of a fine.

In this tenurial world the ability of a villein father to make an heir was as vital as it had once been in the world of knight and baron. In the manorial world bastardy seems rarely to have mattered. "Next kin," *cunder* or "nearest heir" are the phrases used. Juries recognize the rights of sons, but legitimacy is mentioned only in exceedingly rare instances.[45] The legal bastardy of the common law, and even the "plain bastardy" with which the barons contrasted it, seem to have been quite unnecessary classifications within a village. Acceptance by the parental family, acceptability to neighbours and lord were the criteria for inheritance. Though the next of kin be both bastard and a girl, a father could endow her with his holding.[46] Even adoption was possible: Isabel, daughter of William le Blac, gave 1s. to the lord "that she might be the heir of Walter the cowherd," and it was accepted.[47] When a villein father bought the marriage of a villein boy or girl said to be the "nearest *cunder*" of a dead tenant, he was buying several intermingled things: the community's acceptance of himself as custodian of the child's holding and of the child; not least he was buying the lord's agreement that he would accept the child as the next holder of the tenement.[48] It has been seen that fathers transferred their holdings wholly or in part to daughters upon the occasion of their marriage, thereby designating an heir and securing a son-in-law as successor—quite possibly one more to the father's, the lord's and the court's liking than his sons. On manors where youngest sons inherited by custom, a father could bring a boy into court to be recognized as his heir on the occasion of his own remarriage, clearly to deflect the working of custom. Where the custom is primogeniture, the eldest son may be provided for by marriage and a younger son keep the father's holding. Where impartible inheritance is the custom, fathers can be found dividing their tenements and thus, potentially, raising their lord's rent-roll.[49] Not infrequently fathers endowed their daughters with bits of land, for marriage no doubt, but without mention of marriage in the transfer.[50] Men could hand over land to a son and themselves leave.[51] Charters, and the court-roll evidence, it has been seen, show the endowment of peasant girls, specifically "inheriting" at marriage,[52] and court rolls show girls designated as heirs without mention of husbands.[53] A widow who had been allowed to hand over her land to her daughter and son-in-law for care in old age was able to satisfy the court that she was not being properly cared for: she was thereupon allowed to oust the couple and to bestow the land elsewhere and outside her own family.[54]

The strength of the principle of female property rights, and the need felt to control such rights, is strikingly illustrated in the matter of the peasant widow's dower. Nothing makes the function of marriage control clearer than the strict supervision exercised by lord and court over the remarriage of widows with land. As with the dowry given the bride by her father, so the dower given her by her husband at the church door was, from the point of view of the royal courts, a hallmark of freedom. And it is so for the same reason: by the time the *Curia Regis Rolls* began, the notion of proprietorship in land had so circumscribed the lord's will that free tenants could, without purchase of the lord's consent, endow their brides with land to be held for life after their deaths, and warranted by their heirs. Thus a jury in 1220 could be of the opinion that "William was not seised in such a way that he could dower" his wife, for he held unfreely.[55] That did not mean that he could not, within his lord's court, purchase his lord's permission to dower her, nor does it tell us anything about that court's customs for providing for widows whose husbands had left the matter to custom. Indeed, it is well known that, unlike free dower, manorial custom might allow a widow to hold half or all of her husband's tenement for life.[56] Thus it is that the marriage fine of widows is generally higher than maidens' *merchet*, and varies within wider limits. Like the maiden's *merchet*, it is sufficiently variable to imply the transfer of land or goods.[57]

Widows indeed were among the most desirable matches, for as well as being in possession of their own dowries and dower, they might have common property rights to everything acquired after marriage as well.[58] It is not always clear just how strong were the rights of children as against widowed mothers and stepfathers. The mid-thirteenth-century cartulary of St. Peter's, Gloucester, for example, notes that heriot is due at the death of a tenant, and thereafter at the death of his widow, and states that in the case of a widow heriot will be due from her second husband when he dies.[59] One may wonder whether on some manors and in particular cases the peasant heir would ever possess his father's tenement or whether, with the lord's permission, it might pass through a succession of widows and widowers.

Medieval peasants did remarry, and quickly, if for no other reason than that their security of tenure depended upon being able to do their full service. A peasant's wife was so valuable to the household economy that married households might be taxed at a marginally higher rate than widowed ones.[60] The peasant wife was assumed to have so equal a place in the family enterprise that she was often specifically exempted from the harvest boon work or, alternatively, could lead the household to the autumn boon in place of the husband.[61] The Ramsey custumals of Upwood and Wistow note that the widow must give the large sum of 5s. as a commutation for being free of her late husband's services for a month after his death, and certain widows were required "on the day after the husband's death to find enough ploughmen to take the dead man's place."[62] Certainly they were expected to fulfill their husband's obligations if they kept his lands.

In the face of village desire that widows be propertied, in the light of the desirability of the widow as a wife and in the light of their own demand for services, lords were at least as careful to control the marriages of widows as those of maidens. Manorial custumals generally do not list this right, but it is clear enough in articles of inquiry: presentments were required "concerning widows and girls *(de viduis et puellis)* married without the lord's permission."[63] Where it is specified that the widow may hold the full tenement after her husband's death it is also specified "nor shall she take a husband without the lord's permission."[64] The free widow's remarriage was controlled in the interest of the heir, and Magna Carta, cap. 8, controlled the remarriage of widows in the lord's interest—and the control was real enough, especially where the status of land tenure was in danger.[65] Similarly the villein widow lost her dower if she remarried outside the manor. On the other hand, so strong were women's property rights in the manorial world that lords were slow to use their disciplinary powers to oust the incapable widow. The solution of remarriage is one familiar enough to the student of manorial court rolls. A man must be allowed or compelled to marry a widow and keep up her land; the widow must be compelled to take a husband and pay the lord for the marriage. Courts issue the command that widows must provide themselves with husbands; courts distrain men to receive certain widows. This, of course, as the case of the Wakefield rolls shows, must not be taken literally. Often it must have been a means of getting a fine out of a capable and reluctant widow or prospective groom. Immorality, the amercement for which is com mon in medieval court rolls, is particularly the misdemeanour of widows—no doubt more because the freedom of their associations, and their reluctance to marry upon command were sources of profit to lords than because widows were peculiarly lascivious. Certainly capable widows were allowed to hold their tenements without hindrance if they could afford to be taxed at a slightly higher rate than men, the higher rate being the fine to remain single. But what should be made of the many cases in manorial court rolls that record provisional transfer to the next generation with careful stipulations as to the care of an aged parent? They are often assumed to be strictly intrafamilial arrangements, and their specificity is taken as evidence of the distrust between generations. Yet the interests of the lord and of the community should not be overlooked. Such transfers must not infrequently have been forced transfers out of the hands of the incapable, made by (certainly before) the lord's steward and the community, who thereupon assumed a public overseeing of the aged, and who could, as has been seen, be called upon to undo a custody arrangement in the interests of the incapable tenant.

It is this element of public control by the lord, advised by the peasant community, that stands out when one assembles the widespread evidence of *merchet* and the other seigneurial rights concerning women's marriage. At important stages of a peasant woman's life—at marriage, upon widowhood, at remarriage, in incapable old age—she appears under the control of these external agencies rather more than that of her immediate family. Yet it was not her marriages that were at stake. It was her right to inherit and to hold property. A foolish girl, or a poor one, might marry as she liked. But the alliances of medieval peasant girls who had claims to property were, by the logic of peasant society and the claims of lordship, matters of public import as well as of personal and family interest. The control that seems to have been exerted over the marriage was in fact directed at inheritance, and such control was exerted by the lord over male and female alike. The question, then, of whether peasant women in medieval England had more freedom than women of the upper classes is perhaps best approached as a question of property rights. Whether high or low in the social scale, medieval women were protected in their rights to property by their families, their communities—and in the case of peasant women, by courts before which they themselves could and did plead. The right to hold property, and the right to argue like any other member of the community before the courts of that community are aspects of the lives of ordinary medieval women that must have gone a long way towards shaping the expectations of the women who followed them.

NOTES

1. Shakespeare puts the thought in Jack Cade's rantings: "The proudest peer in the realm shall not wear a head on his shoulders, unless he pay me tribute; there shall not a maid be married, but she shall pay to me her maidenhead ere they have it: men shall hold of me in capite . . ." *2 Henry VI*, act 4, sc. 7.

2. For a summary of views in the English historical literature, see Eleanor Searle, "Seigneurial Control of Women's Marriage: the Origin and Function of Merchet in Medieval England," *Past and Present*, no. 82 (1979), pp. 4–5.

3. The age of consent was twelve for a girl and fourteen for a boy. Book four of the Decretals is entirely on marriage: *Corpus juris canonici*, ed. E. Friedberg, 2 vols. (Leipzig, 1879–81), ii, pp. 660–731; see esp. tit. I, cap. ix. The difficulties of establishing free consent without the impediments of pre-contract, consanguinity and affinity were always formidable, much more so than establishing the freedom of the consent, which is not of course to be taken as synonymous with choice. See R. H. Helmholz, *Marriage Litigation in Medieval England* (Cambridge, 1974), esp. chaps. 2–3; the literature on the canons is summarized on pp. 1–5.

4. For *Aliter*, one of the forged decretals of Pseudo-Isadore, see Gratian, *Concordia discordantium canonum*, in *Corpus juris canonici*, ed. Friedberg, i, pt. 2, cause 30, q. 5. The canonical teaching on clandestine marriage is briefly and clearly set out in H. A. Kelly, *Love and Marriage in the Age of Chaucer* (Ithaca, N. Y., 1975), pp. 163–168. For the common occurrence of such marriages and for examples of the many marital problems of villagers, see Helmholz, *Marriage Litigation*, passim; and *Registrum Hamonis Hethe*, ed. Charles Johnson, 2 vols. (Canterbury and York Soc., xlviii, xlix, London, 1948), ii, pp. 911–1043.

5. *Carte Nativorum*, Northern Rec. Soc. XX, Oxford, 1960, ed. Brooke and Postan, no. 300.

6. Ibid, nos. 303, 304, 327. These are charters endowing a single girl, and the lands she is given abut on the land of her future husband and, probably, those of his father. That no. 303 is the donation of the mother's dowry can be inferred from the fact that the charter is the mother's own. No. 327 is again the mother's own, giving other lands, referred to as her

dower *(dote sua)*. No. 304 is that of the bride's brother and includes the lands in no. 303. Some such arrangements naturally enough would be leases for the life of the bride's mother, for her heir or dower-warrantor would be her son: ibid, nos. 382, 385. For such land, used in peasant family settlements, see Edmund King, *Peterborough Abbey, 1086–1310: A Study in the Land Market* (Cambridge, 1973), pp. 62–66.

7. Examples are common in manorial court rolls: P.R.O., D.L. 30/62/752; P.R.O., D.L. 30/63/791, m. 4; P.R.O., D.L. 30/85/1161.mm. 4, 11. In P.R.O., D.L. 30/63/790, m. 15 (1327/8), a father purchases two acres and then transfers them to his under-age daughter, who receives them to hold at the lord's will with her father in immediate possession: fine 18d.

8. *Bracton's Note Book*, ed. Maitland, nos. 951, 988; *Curia Regis Rolls*, xi, no. 1460. A Berkshire family of the early fourteenth century confirms the practice. Ellen Woodward had two daughters, Alice for whom her mother paid 3s. *merchet* that she might marry off the manor, and Matilda, who was accepted as the heir to her mother's holding. P.R.O., S.C. 2/68/153, m. 4.

9. P.R.O., S.C. 2/67/153, m. 6.

10. *Curia Regis Rolls*, viii, pp. 271–272, 277–278.

11. For example, *Court Rolls of the Manor of Wakefield, 1274–1331*, ed. W. P. Baildon, J. Lister and J. W. Walker, 5 vols. (Yorks. Archaeol. Soc. Rec. Ser., xxix, xxxvi, lvii, lxxviii, cix, Huddersfield, 1901–45), iv, ed. Lister, p. 149: a brother is found guilty of detaining the dowry promised his sister, 6s. 8d. and a cow worth 8s.; *Select Pleas in Manorial Courts*, ed. Maitland, p. 46–47: goods worth 35s. 11d.; the defendant claims he owes only 5s. for a mantle (Weedon Bec, Northants.); *Halmota Prioratus Dunelmensis*, ed. W. H. Longstaffe and J. Booth, i (Surtees Soc., lxxxii, Durham, 1889), p. 91: 15(?s.), a brass pot, a feather bed, a chest and various kerchiefs, said to have been left the girl by her mother and detained by her stepmother; P.R.O., D.L.30/85/1160, m.3: the husband sues the wife's brother for a mark "which he agreed to give him in aid for marrying his sister *(in auxilium maritandi sororem suam)*." The brother acknowledged the debt.

12. P.R.O., D.L. 30/85/1161, m.2ᵛ (1313/14): Lucy, whose father Adam Smith had given Richard three roods and twenty perches of land, asks for an inquisition as to whether or not her father had done so "in order that he should marry Lucy *(ea de causa quod eandem Luciam desponsaret)*." The inquest replies that the land was given Richard so that he would marry her. The court therefore adjudges the land to Lucy and amerces Richard.

13. *The Court Baron*, ed. F. W. Maitland and W. P. Baildon (Selden Soc., iv, London, 1891), p. 102.

14. P.R.O., D.L. 30/62/751, m. 1.

15. P.R.O., S.C. 2/69/153, m. 10. The presentment in the case of the widow was that "Cristine Sket est in conventione maritanda Aliciam filiam suam cuidam libero extra liberatem." It was not a marriage, but the terms of a marriage contract before the marriage had taken place, that concerned the lord.

16. P.R.O., S.C. 2/67/153, m. 12: "alienavit cum eadem ad valanciam ix marcarum de catallis domini." The father paid half a mark to the lord (1294–5).

17. *Halmota prioratus Dunelmensis*, ed. Longstaffe and Booth, pp. 51, 59.

18. Even when in custumals it seems to be fixed, it was not in practice. It is commonly stated in custumals that *merchet* would be higher if the girl were married off the manor or outside the soke. A survey of court rolls indicates that stewards carefully questioned whether the girl were to be married to a free man (from whom heriot would, of course, not be due to the lord) or outside the manor, where the husband's heriot, augmented by her contribution, would go to another lord. In both circumstances the *merchet* is consistently higher than average, whether or not the right is a recorded custom.

19. *Curia Regis Rolls*, ix, p. 60. At the church door the fathers argued hotly over the girl's dowry (an ox) and her father evidently became so rattled that he neglected to force a specific statement of dower from the groom's father, although he began with the intention of doing do. The groom died soon after and the girl was turned out by her father-in-law.

20. *Ibid.*, xi, no. 2626: "finem faciet . . . secundum quod potuerit."

21. P.R.O., D.L. 30/488/43. Gloucester Abbey's well-known "Scriptum Quoddam" insists that every reeve has the power to license the marriage of any unfree girl, even if she is marrying outside the lord's land, if he has received safe pledges for the making of her marriage fine at the next court, for fear that she might not marry if the bailiff (who should be the authorizing official) should be long absent. *Historia et cartularium monasterii sancti Petri Gloucestriae*, ed. W.H. Hart, 3 vols. (Rolls ser., xxxiii, London, 1863–7), iii, p. 219. See also *Court Rolls of the Manor of Hales, 1270–1307*, ed. J. Amphlett, S. G. Hamilton and R. A. Wilson, 3 vols. (Worcs. Hist. Soc., Worcester, 1910–33), iii, pp. 183, 188, where the amount of *merchet* is respited "until, he has discussed it with the abbot *(quousque colloquium cum Abbate habuit).*"

22. P.R.O., D.L. 30/62/756, m. 1 (1279–80). The girl was presented as married without license and her father was ordered attached. "He . . . came, saying that she was not in his custody, nor did he know anything . . ." The girl eventually paid her own *merchet.*

23. The counties best represented are Durham, Yorkshire, Lincolnshire, Essex, Worcestershire, Bedfordshire, Berkshire and Sussex. As early as the Shrewsbury privileges recorded in Domesday Book, the widow was more valuable than the maiden, paying twice the amount for her remarriage. *Domesday Book*, i, p. 252.

24. The family is found in the rolls of Brightwalton manorial court: P.R.O., S.C. 2/67/153. The rental is on m. 15. The virgate is entered and crossed out, whether because it was later sold or because it was a scribal error is not evident.

25. For example, at Gidding, Hants., in 1290, Sarra le Monck was presented for having married a man of the homage of Lord Reginald de Grey.

Her cottage was seized by the reeve, who put a lock on the door. Sarra came and broke the lock with a stone, falling into mercy for housebreaking. She was ordered to satisfy the lord for having married without license, her messuage for the time remaining in the lord's hand. Her amercement was 6d.: *Select Pleas in Manorial Courts*, ed. Maitland, p. 98.

26. *Cartularium monasterii de Rameseia*, ed. W. Hart and P.A. Lyons, 3 vols. (Rolls ser., lxxix, London, 1884–93), i, p. 338; on virgaters at Broughton in 1252: "But on the day of his wedding he will reward *(respiciet)* the servants of the *curia* with bread, ale [and] meat as becomes his honour *(secundum quod suum honorem deceat)* and is suitable to his means *(et suae competat facultati)*." On virgaters at Upwood in 1252: "On the very day on which he takes a wife, he will according to his means *(secundum facultatem suam)* honourably reward *(honorifice respiciet)* the servants of the abbot's *curia* with bread, ale [and] meat or fish": ibid., p. 347. These virgaters owed *merchet* as well: ibid., pp. 335, 344.

27. For example, P.R.O., S.C. 2/67/153, m. 15. in 1296/7 a customary tenant at Brightwalton offered ten marks "to have the *maritagium* of Adam de la Grene . . . for benefit of Matilda his daughter," promising to pay in several installments. Adam's father had held 25½ acres and one virgate in the common fields, plus two acres of wood, and had been the lord's forester. In another similar case at Waltham and High Easter in 1326/7, a customary tenant paid 100s. for the custody and *maritagium* of an underage heir: P.R.O., D.L. 30/63/791, m. 4.

28. A few references must serve to underscore a general observation: *Court Roll of Chalgrave Manor, 1278–1313*, ed. M. K. Dale (Beds. Hist. Rec. Soc., xxviii, Streatley, 1950), under Wootton, Lane, Hockliffe, Ingeleys, Algor, Bacun; *Court Rolls of the Manor of Hales*, ii, ed. Amphlett and Hamilton, under Galfridi (Lucy, William), Marmiun, Hem, Teyng (or Teining), Schirlet. A clear example is found in *Court Rolls of the Manor of Wakefield*, iii, ed. Lister, in the Sunderland family, esp. pp. 15, 18, 19, 76, 77, 110, 111; see also Sonderland, William.

29. *Court Rolls of the Manor of Hales*, ii, ed. Amphlett and Hamilton, p. 161. For another similar case, see ibid., p. 146: Robert Bunch gave 20d. because he married Edith, daughter of Roger Marmion, without license. "Et dictus Robertus fecit feoditatem"—clearly for her land. *Merchet* is occasionally paid for sons, presumably when they were allowed by the lord and court to receive land on the occasion of their marriages. Some courts even adopted as customary the payment of *merchet* by men: Levett, *Studies in Manorial History*, p. 237.

30. P.R.O., S.C. 2/69/153, m. 25: fine, 6s. 8d.

31. *Court Roll of Chalgrave Manor*, ed. Dale, p. 24: fine, 2s.

32. Ibid.: fine, 16s. A third case at the same court probably concerns the marriage of an heiress, but the formula is less clear: "Simon le Swon . . . has taken Amabel le Chapman as wife by the lord's permission, and the lord has granted them land and tenement according to the custom . . . fine, 3s."

33. Ibid., pp. 17, 25. The suitor had found a pledge, but the fine was not yet settled. At Chalgrave there were evidently minor "drives" on villein women's marriages, probably when a responsible official arrived. Thus in 1306 "all those who have married bondwomen shall remain in their former condition until they have given satisfaction . . .": ibid., p. 55.

34. Ibid., pp. 22, 25. The girl paid an entry fine of 10s., the man one of 6s. 8d. The girl seems to have run the holding herself until her marriage; she was at any rate amerced in 1290 for avoiding suit at the lord's mill: ibid., p. 24.

35. P.R.O., S.C. 2/67/153, m. 10ᵛ. Another abnormal case is in *Court Rolls of the Manor of Hales*, ii, ed. Amphlett and Hamilton, p. 183: "By special grace Christina O the Green has permission to marry and for this grace she gives 12d. to the lord for the renunciation of custom *(dat domino xiid renunciando consuetudine)* . . .".

36. *Court Roll of Chalgrave Manor*, ed. Dale, pp. 4, 10, 18, 42, 44, 46. Lucy's marriage was unlicensed (the lord had ordered her to marry the tenant who was farming her land), but the couple was not amerced. They paid an entry fine for her land.

37. As in the examples above. See *Court Rolls of the Manor of Hales*, i, ed. Amphlett and Hamilton, p. 108, where a suitor pays half a mark and receives Edith de Kakemore's land, conditionally upon holy church permitting the marriage. The fine was not invariably paid by the suitor, as for example, in *Court Rolls of the Manor of Wakefield*, ii, ed. Baildon, pp. 172–173: Maude, daughter of William de Horbiry, gave 2s. to enter her deceased father's bovate. At the same time she paid 1s. for license to marry. She thereupon surrendered the land and received it back in joint tenancy with Ralph Wolf, her new husband. They paid a further 2s. fine. See also *Chertsey Abbey Court Rolls Abstract* (Surrey Rec. Soc., xxxviii, [London], 1937), ed. F. Toms, introduction, pp. xxxvii–xxxix. In other cases a man is found paying for marriage without the scribe bothering even to mention the woman: *Court Roll of Chalgrave Manor*, ed. Dale, p. 56.

38. *Court Rolls of the Manor of Hales*, ii, ed. Amphlett and Hamilton, p. 170.

39. P.R.O., D.L. 30/85/1161, m. 12ᵛ. "Si dominus Michael de Melden acceptaverit." In a similar case the custody of a virgate, along with the marriage of its four-year-old heir or, if he were to die, the marriage of his sister, were given for a fine and a yearly rent. The children's paternal uncle had asked for custody of them and their land, but the court denied his request on the usual grounds that he was their heir: P.R.O., D.L. 30/63/791, m. 4. In another case in a different part of the country, one Ely gave the lord ten marks "to have the marriage of Adam de la Grene, son and heir of John de la Grene for the benefit of his [Ely's] daughter Matilda." John had held twenty-five and a half acres, plus a virgate and a small wood: P.R.O., S.C. 2/67/153, mm. 14, 15.

40. *Historia et cartulariam . . . Gloucestriae*, ed. Hart, iii, p. 141: Richard does lighter service than the others, "because a certain woman of Wick,

from whom the abbot and convent had a certain salt-pan (*salinam*) there, had married on to the said land (*maritata fuit ad dictam terram*), on account of which one day of boon-reaping was remitted." Clearly the convent felt more secure in its acquisition of her salt-pan once the woman had married a villein.

41. *Select Pleas in Manorial Courts*, ed. Maitland, p. 98. She had, needless to say, married without permission.

42. *Court Rolls of the Manor of Wakefield*, i, ed. Baildon, p. 224.

43. *Court Rolls of the Manor of Hales*, ii, ed. Amphlett and Hamilton, p. 153.

44. For King's Ripton, see *Select Pleas in Manorial Courts*, ed. Maitland, pp. 121, 126; for a discussion of a similar case from King's Ripton, see Homans, *English Villagers*, p. 122. For the villein clerk, see *Court Rolls of the Manor of Wakefield*, i, ed. Baildon, pp. 120, 125.

45. *Carte Nativorum*, ed. Brooke and Postan, no. 390, records a virtually unique case of a disputed claim to inherit. The successful claimant rested her case on the fact that the other had been born before the parents' marriage. However, the lord's interest in the outcome lay with the successful claimant, who was willing to quitclaim the land to the lord and receive it back at an increased rent. When it is also realized that the land had originally been acquired from another lord, the court that agreed to the dubious action is shown clearly enough to be acting for the lord, and not disinterestedly. Any excuse might have served. For the frequent use of *cunder*, see P.R.O., S.C. 2/69/153.

46. P.R.O., D.L. 30/63/790, P.R.O., D.L. 30/63/792: a half-messuage, thirty-eight acres of land, six acres and one rood of pasture, and a little over an acre of meadow. The land escheated after her death and her bastardy was then mentioned.

47. P.R.O., D.L. 30/62/752: "ut posset esse heres Walteri le Couherd."

48. For example, n. 39 above, and P.R.O., S.C. 2/69/153, m. 12. The eleven-year-old child of a virgater is allowed to pay 60s. to hold his father's land, but in full court the boy agrees to lease it for ten years to John le Wynd who, during that time, will find him decent food and clothing. This is done with the lord's consent and with the advice of the boy's uncle. The boy further accepts John le Wynd's daughter as his wife with the lord's permission, paying 60s. John is conceded permission to give his daughter.

49. For example, *Court Roll of Chalgrave Manor*, ed. Dale, p. 32. The fine for dividing the tenement was 6s. 8d.; this is true devise, for the separation was not to take place until after the father's death. For the custom, here, of primogeniture, see ibid., p. 10. Similar cases of devise are to be found in *Court Rolls of the Manor of Wakefield*, i, ed. Baildon, pp. 108, 183, 279, 286.

50. P.R.O., D.L. 30/85/1161, mm. 4, 11, 12: membranes that record almost nothing but *merchets* and resignations of land to children.

51. *Halmota prioratus Dunelmensis*, ed. Longstaffe and Booth, i, p. 57: Fayr-Jon is ordered to return and to dwell with his household. He had made an agreement with his son whereby the son would have the preced-

ing year's crops for 21s. and would pay the reaper and the lord's farmer for the previous year. Beyond that the son would pay his father 21s. annually. The son had died, but his wife (with her child) was able to renegotiate the agreement.

52. For example, the endowment of Agnes Gere by her parents at her marriage to Simon in le Wro consisted of an acre lying next to her father's arable, another acre in the furlong called the Appletree, abutting on her father's arable, an acre in Edgerley, an acre at Faleholm to be held of her father and his heirs, and a further "Appletree" acre, plus a half-acre of meadow lying between her father's meadows. All the lands were to be held jointly. It is arguable that Agnes was receiving a premortem inheritance split off from her father's holding at the expense of other heirs. *Carte Nativorum,* ed. Brooke and Postan, nos. 119–22. For these two prosperous villein families, Gere and le Wro, see King, *Peterborough Abbey,* pp. 110–11. King points out that the land with which Agnes was endowed was free land, acquired by her father, who also acquired other lands for the endowment of two sons. The acquisitions amounted to fifteen acres, of which Agnes received five and a half.

53. *Select Pleas in Manorial Courts,* ed. Maitland, p. 40: William the clerk surrenders into the lord's hands, for the use of his daughter, a half-virgate. Afterwards, at her desire, the father is put in seisin for life "with the object that on his death [she] will be his next heir." That he had other heirs is evident from the entry.

54. P.R.O., D.L. 30/63/790, mm. 14, 15ᵛ. The widow was the accepted tenant and therefore the court acted for her, not for the son-in-law, who had not yet paid an entry fine.

55. Curia Regis Rolls. vol. viii, p. 343.

56. The free tenant dower was one-third of the husband's tenement. For peasant dower, or "free bench," see Homans, *English Villagers,* ch. 13, and Hilton, *The English Peasantry in the Later Middle Ages,* pp. 99–100. At Chalgrave and on the manors of Durham Priory, the widow kept the entire holding. The Chalgrave custom is stated almost stridently: "But the custom of the manor, however, is that no man bound by custom *(nullus custumarius)* may enter such land after the death of his father while his mother is still alive unless with her agreement *(nisi matri placuerit),* and that the mother will hold her land for her whole lifetime if she so wishes." *Court Roll of Chalgrave Manor,* ed. Dale, p. 10. The same court awarded a third of her husband's tenement to a peasant widow; she may have been a free tenant holding in fact from her lord's court: ibid., p. 16.

57. I have found variations, from a fine excused "quia pauper est" to a five-mark entry fine, plus a £4 marriage fine for a widow with six acres. So few regularities are there, that 2s. and 20s. happen to be the most common sums in the evidence I have gathered.

58. *Select Pleas in Manorial Courts,* ed. Maitland, pp. 44–45.

59. *Historia et cartularium . . . Gloucestriae,* ed. Hart, iii, pp. 56, 88, 117. Since heriot included the transfer of the best beast to the lord and the

second-best to the vicar, with a high death rate and remarriage rate peasant families must often have seen their herds swiftly melting away. The claim of a lord to separate death duties from husband and wife, even when a wife predeceases her husband, is striking in the Ramsey Abbey cartulary. In the lands of the rectories of Wistow and Warboys the vicar was to receive, at the death of the husband, the best beast except for horses; at the death of a wife whose husband is still living, the vicar was to receive the family's second-best beast, while the husband received the best beast (thus, it would seem, defeating a child's immediate inheritance from its mother); at the death of a widow, the vicar was to receive the same as that of a husband. *Cartularium . . . Rameseia*, ed. Hart and Lyons, i, pp. 306, 353.

60. Ibid., i, p. 331; *Curia Regis Rolls*, xi, no. 830; *Select Documents of the English Lands of the Abbey of Bec*, ed. M. Chibnall (Camden Soc., 3rd ser., lxxiii, London, 1951), p. 56 (for the wife's work), and passim, for the customary taxes.

61. *Cartularium . . . Rameseia*, ed. Hart and Lyons, i, p. 347: "He himself or his wife will come with his entire working household *(cum tota familia operante) . . ." Curia Regis Rolls*, xi, no. 830 (Surrey): the virgater comes to the "great boons" and to the "alebedripe" boons with all his household save his wife and his shepherd. H. H. E. Craster, *The Parish of Tynemouth* (A History of Northumberland, viii, London, 1907), p. 223, cites the Tynemouth cartulary: "And he shall do the great auth-rep with his whole family of his house except the housewife." The place of such a peasant wife in the household is clear from a reference to peasant dues in 1227, when the wife of a lord's peasant is called the "domina domus": *Curia Regis Rolls*, xiii, no. 25.

62. *Cartularium . . . Rameseia*, ed. Hart and Lyons, i, pp. 347, 350.

63. For example, *Court Rolls of the Manor of Hales*, i, ed. Amphlett and Hamilton, pp. 116–17.

64. *Halmota prioratus Dunelmensis*, ed. Longstaffe and Booth, i, p. 1.

65. *Glanvill*, ed. Hall, vii. 12. *Court Rolls of the Manor of Hales*, i, ed. Amphlett and Hamilton, p. 196, refers specifically to Magna Carta in distraining a second husband. Ibid., pp. 268, 273: an inquest to see whether the stepmother of a free heir should lose her dower since she has married a villein. All the free tenants of the manor were to be there by afforcement. The tenurial problem was settled by the widow making over the land to her stepson in return for a quarter of oats annually. At Hales, as at probably most manorial courts in the thirteenth century, free and villein tenants attended together and held their land from the court.

THE MARRIED WOMEN'S PROPERTY ACTS, 1839–1865: REFORM, REACTION, OR REVOLUTION?

Linda E. Speth

The English common-law fiction of marital unity and its corollary, the loss of the wife's property rights, survived colonization and the American Revolution. Although property rights and inheritance patterns varied from colony to colony and later among territorial and state jurisdictions, the general principle remained constant: once a woman married she became a nonentity as far as the common law was concerned. This essay examines the American woman's legal status and property rights in the first half of the nineteenth century, specifically the origin and impact of the legislation collectively referred to as the "married women's property acts."[1]

Prior to the enactment of the married women's property legislation, marriage for all practical purposes ensured a woman's "civil death." A wife could neither sue nor be sued. She could not execute a will or enter into a contract. The wife's civil disabilities and limitations were mirrored by a loss of economic autonomy. Her personal property became her husband's at the moment of marriage. He owned her jewels, furniture, or goods, whether she brought them with her to the marriage or thereafter acquired them, and he could sell or give away even the clothes on her back. In addition, any wages she received for work performed outside the home belonged to her husband. Though he could not sell her real estate without her permission, he acquired rights to control and manage her land. Any proceeds derived from improving the property, harvesting and selling crops, or leasing her land belonged to the husband alone. The common law also recognized the husband's total authority within the confines of the family. He could legally chastise his wife and had the sole right to appoint guardians of the children even while the mother was alive.

In his *Commentaries on the Laws of England*, a standard legal reference work popular on both sides of the Atlantic, Sir William Blackstone explained the wife's subordinate position at common law as follows:

> By marriage, the husband and wife are one person in law; that is, the very being or legal existence of the woman is suspended during the marriage, or at least is incorporated and consolidated into that of the husband; under whose wing, protection, and cover, she performs every thing. . . . Upon this principle, of an union of person in husband and wife depend almost all the legal rights, duties and disabilities that either one of them acquires by the marriage.[2]

Recently, legal historian Lawrence M. Friedman put the matter more succinctly: "Essentially, husband and wife were one flesh; but the man was the owner of that flesh."[3] Although the rules of equity and the frontier experience ameliorated the traditional disabilities of some married women, the common law doctrine of coverture (marriage) operated to deprive generations of American wives of legal and economic equality.[4]

During the second quarter of the nineteenth century, state legislatures and constitutional conventions began to make inroads on the common-law fiction of marital unity by enacting married women's property acts. Mississippi became the first state to enact such legislation in 1839, followed by Maryland in 1843. Later, states as geographically and economically diverse as Maine, Massachusetts, Iowa, and New York followed suit.[5] By the end of the Civil War, a total of twenty-nine states had passed married women's property acts that seemed, at first glance, to herald a revolution in the legal and economic relationship between husband and wife.[6]

Unlike other aspects of American women's legal history, these legislative reform efforts have received considerable scholarly treatment. Over the past century and a half, lawyers, feminists, historians, judges, and legal historians have analyzed the acts from different philosophical and ideological orientations. General works on American law or women's history have noted the legislation in passing, while scholars Mary Beard, Norma Basch, Joan Hoff Wilson, Peggy A. Rabkin, Kay Ellen Thurman, Elizabeth Bowles Warbasse, and Lawrence Friedman have explored the married women's property acts or related aspects in considerable detail.[7]

Some writers, such as Elizabeth Cady Stanton, a nineteenth-century feminist, as well as some contemporary women's historians have viewed the acts as a response to feminist agitation—a legislative reform effort that had its roots in demands made primarily by women for women's equality, and thus part and parcel of the women's rights movement. On the other hand, scholars such as Rabkin and Thurman downplay or dismiss the impact of the women's rights movement and treat the acts as a small part of the larger nineteenth-century drive for codification—a movement concerned with "rationalizing" American law and stripping it of its English feudal trappings such as coverture and the legal disabilities associated with it. Legal historians, Friedman, for example, do not even mention the women's rights movement in discussing the married women's property acts; instead they develop an external, economic rationale, arguing that the acts flowed from attempts to regulate debtor-creditor relations and thus reflected a desire to make the law better fit the needs of a commercial market economy.[8]

The scholarly debate over the married women's property acts does not revolve solely around the question of their origin; similarly diverse arguments exist concerning their impact. The legislation has been hailed as inaugurating "sweeping changes" in women's legal status. It has also been analyzed as simply extending principles long recognized by equity to wider segments of the population. More recently, it has been viewed by historian Joan Hoff Wilson as part of a complex process that left women in an economic and procedural limbo, making the nineteenth-century woman's overall societal position more restrictive than that enjoyed by her colonial counterpart.[9]

These diverse analyses of the married women's property acts result from contemporary attention to women's legal and domestic status, a growing interest in both legal history and women's history, and increasing scholarly emphasis on interdisciplinary methods. The legislation signifies something different to the bench, the bar, the historian, the feminist, and the legal historian. For a variety of reasons, sophisticated analytical approaches ensure that many recently published works dealing with the legislation are confined to a single jurisdiction. Norma Basch, for example, in her excellent article "Invisible Women," has conducted an intensive study of married women's property rights in New York.[10] This essay will take a somewhat different approach and present a preliminary overview of the earliest women's property acts from a comparative perspective, sketching the diverse origins of the legislation and the overall limiting effect of its impact.[11]

In the turbulent years before the Civil War, America was swept by multiple currents of reform. Although abolitionism received the greatest public attention and precipitated the most vehement debate, other reform movements stirred the American consciousness. During the 1820s and 1830s several individuals petitioned state legislatures and traveled the country arguing for codification, for better and more equitable care for the insane, and for temperance as well as for women's equality.[12] Within this larger reform milieu, a few individuals began to publicly attack the common-law disabilities associated with marriage. In 1832 Mary Jane Robinson and Robert Dale Owen signed a marriage contract in New York in which Owen rejected his legal "rights" as the "barbarous relics of a feudal, despotic system."[13] A few years later Sarah Grimké, a noted Quaker abolitionist, published her *Letters on the Equality of the Sexes* in which she proclaimed that the very word "husband" was synonymous with tyranny for nineteenth-century women.[14]

Despite these early objections to common-law inequities associated with coverture, the first married women's property acts in the nation had little to do with either feminist agitation or concern for female equality. Instead, initial legislative inroads on the common-law fiction of marital unity stemmed from many factors and were often supported by conservative groups.

In the winter of 1839, Mississippi led the way by enacting the nation's first married women's property act.[15] The legislation was limited, however, and referred mainly to the wife's property rights in slaves. In fact, the act was passed not so much to improve women's rights but rather to protect family property, particularly slaves, from attachment by creditors. At common law the husband and wife were one; a woman's property therefore was liable for debts contracted by her spouse. The Mississippi law represented an initial tentative attack on the fiction of marital unity by altering the traditional economic relationship of the marriage unit with third parties (creditors). Four of the act's five sections dealt with the wife's slaves and specified that such "property" was no longer liable for the husband's debts. In addition, the act stipulated that this "economic protection" included slaves owned by the wife at the time of marriage or later acquired by gift or inheritance. This last feature was especially important because wealthy fathers often bequeathed slaves to their married daughters. Such bequests represented an important source of wealth, and the legislators wanted to make sure that such family property would not be seized for the husband's debts.[16]

Paradoxically, this protection of family property worked to the advantage of both husbands and fathers. A father could ensure that his daughter would not be destitute if her husband proved improvident and dissipated the family wealth; the slaves would serve as minimal protection from economic disaster. Husbands also supported the Mississippi legislation. The act was prompted by the Panic of 1837 when planters, faced by hard times, were forced to declare bankruptcy. Warbasse has viewed this legislation as a clearcut attempt to save planter families from ruin by placing the wife's slaves beyond the reach of her husband's creditors. The husband engaged in the hazards of speculation and faced with mounting indebtedness could be secure in the knowledge that his wife's slaves would not be seized for debts. If he could retain some slaves, he could still have the plantation worked, or he could sell slaves to raise needed capital. Although the Mississippi act altered the traditional common-law relationship between husband and wife by creating a wife's separate estate, it accomplished little else. The husband still retained the sole right to manage and control the slaves and to enjoy any profits from their labor.[17]

On March 10, 1843, another southern state whose planters were burdened by debts and economic difficulties passed a married women's property act. Maryland's legislation was similar to that of Mississippi in dealing primarily with the wife's property in slaves, and appears to have been passed for much the same reason. Overall, both the Mississippi and the Maryland acts, and later the Arkansas act of 1846, were limited in scope and represented a conservative effort to safeguard family property rather than an attempt to expand women's rights.[18]

These legislative reform efforts were based on principles that had evolved under equity jurisprudence. In England, courts of chancery furnished equitable remedies when no redress was available at common law. Traditionally, equity courts had recognized the existence of the wife's separate estate through the devices of trusts or antenuptial contracts. A woman's property thereby escaped merging with her husband's. These devices were often used by fathers to protect their daughters' properties from improvident spouses or by shrewd widows entering a second marriage. In many ways what the southern legislatures of the 1830s and 1840s were doing was making the wife's separate estate available to planters who held slaves without the necessity of creating trusts that had to be administered by equity courts. The legislation, of course, did not reproduce the equity device of the wife's separate estate *en toto;* it merely protected her property from being seized by her husband's creditors, and not one of the southern states gave the wife any control over that property. Despite the piecemeal and fragmentary nature of the acts, these statutory reforms had extended principles long available at equity and made them more accessible to certain groups.[19]

The conservative efforts to protect family property and safeguard the wife's original economic assets from the husband's creditors were apparent in other jurisdictions as well. In 1844 Michigan passed an act stipulating that any personal or real property a woman received either before or after her marriage remained her separate estate. Within the next two years, Ohio, Indiana, and Iowa passed more limited legislation declaring that a wife's real estate could not be seized for her husband's debts.[20]

By leaving the husband with the common-law right of management and control of his wife's property, yet preventing that property from being seized for his debts, the early married women's property acts left the husband in a better position to withstand the hazards of the nineteenth-century economy. The risks of speculation and investment were reduced and the danger of economic ruin and bankruptcy, if not eliminated, was at least minimized by placing the wife's property beyond the reach of her husband's creditors.[21]

States along the eastern seaboard began altering the common-law fiction of marital unity during the same period. New England legislatures moved hesitantly to give law courts the power to enforce equity principles. As in the South, much of this legislation attempted to mitigate indebtedness, but the need may have been even stronger in New England. Unlike other American jurisdictions, New England states did not have a strong tradition or familiarity with equity principles. This antipathy to special equity courts had developed during the colonial era and was reinforced during the Revolution and national period when New Englanders rejected the idea of special courts and judicial discretion as symptomatic of tyranny. As the economic need arose during the nineteenth century, and after other states had transferred principles of equity into law, New England began to embrace the notion of the wife's separate estate to resolve indebtedness problems.[22]

In the North, however, other factors along with creditor-debtor relations were at work in securing the passage of the married women's property acts, the codification movement and growing demands for female equality chief among them. In 1847, for example, Clarina I. Howard Nichols attacked the proprietary disabilities of married women in Vermont in a series of editorials in the *Windham County Democrat*. While Nichols's editorials deplored the inequities enshrined by the common law and helped persuade Senator Mead to introduce a married women's property bill, the issue of creditor-debtor relations undoubtedly ensured its passage. Once again the law was limited, and it protected the profits of a wife's real estate from liability for her husband's debts.[23]

The complex interplay of factors which led to the implementation of the nation's first married women's property acts can best be illustrated by examining one jurisdiction in some detail. New York's 1848 legislation sprang from both conservative and liberal impulses, from tangled currents of nineteenth-century reform movements, and was supported by members of ideologically opposed factions.

In New York the codification movement led "inexorably" to the early married women's property act. Following the Revolution, many citizens of the new republic began to object to the legal heritage derived from England. The English common law was regarded as a feudal, anachronistic system that had little applicability to an egalitarian society. Both the common law and, at times, equity were perceived as judge-made rules that subverted the will of the people. It was argued that law should be known and rational, approved by the people via state legislatures and available to all by codification.[24] During the 1820s proponents of codification turned to the works of Jeremy Bentham, the English utilitarian philosopher, who argued that codified law would ensure the greatest good of the greatest number. Besides attacking the common law, other codifiers also objected to trusts and uses as the trappings of and for an aristocratic elite. During the 1820s and 1830s New York began a conscious effort to "defeudalize" its law of real property and weaken equity as a separate system of law, available primarily to the wealthy.[25]

Scholars such as Rabkin, Warbasse, and Friedman have emphasized the impact that the philosophies and works of such men as Bentham, Edward Livingston, William Sampson, and David Dudley Field had on revising American property law in the nineteenth century.[26] The codification movement in New York, like so many other nineteenth-century reform movements, was complex and tortuous in its progress. The myriad events, their chronology, and the several personalities who played important roles have been treated in detail by many scholars, but especially important for our purposes is an understanding of how the codification movement led to the married women's property acts. The first significant efforts to codify New York's substantive law of property created gaps in legal procedures by eliminating certain traditional devices. The Revised Statutes of 1828, for example, abolished nominal trusts and subsequent laws weakened equity as a separate system of law.[27]

These first efforts to codify the law were not motivated by a concern for women's rights, although many codifiers attacked the common-law fiction of marital unity and its associated disabilities.[28] Ironically, in their efforts to simplify the law, the codifiers created more confusion, and New York families who had made use of trusts to protect family property were left with reduced options.

While the larger codification movement was not concerned with women's rights, and at first left women in a more limited and restricted legal position, the resulting effort that culminated in the 1848 Married Women's Property Act did have feminist supporters. The mixture of codification and feminism (two philosophies not always related and at times antithetical) can be seen in the person of Judge Herttell and his efforts during the 1830s to urge legislative reform of the law.

In 1836 Judge Herttell, concerned that preliminary efforts toward codification left married women in a worse position by emasculating equity without giving them any legislative protection, and opposed to feudal common-law principles, introduced a resolution in the New York Assembly. Herttell attacked the 1828 Revised Statutes because they did not go far enough in stripping the law of its feudal taint. In objecting to the revisions, Herttell gained the support of many fathers whose wealth was not in land but in bonds and cash. The Revised Statutes permitted the creation of trusts in real estate only, and a father who wished to transfer other types of wealth (personal property) to his married daughter and protect it from her husband could not do so. The limited nature of the early attempts to codify the law simply reinforced and generated growing objections that the system of British property law was out of date for a commercial economy and that more legislative reforms were needed. Herttell, however, was not merely concerned about making the law a viable instrument for a market economy. Much of his argument was phrased in Enlightenment rhetoric of equality, and his philosophy has been characterized by Rabkin as having feminist shadings.[29]

While Herttell rejected the common law as feudal, and thus demonstrated a close affinity with the codifiers, the feminist strand of his argument captured the attention of a wholehearted advocate of women's rights. Ernestine Rose arrived in New York the same year that Judge Herttell introduced his resolution in the New York Assembly, and she immediately entered the debate about reforming existing laws.

Ernestine Rose, a twenty-six-year-old Polish immigrant who had been involved in at least two legal cases in Europe that centered on a woman's property rights, believed that the economic dominance afforded the husband by law was nothing short of criminal.[30] In 1836 she began a long battle to educate the public and convince the New York State Legislature to remedy the proprietary disabilities of the married woman. She lectured and traveled throughout the state in an effort to stir public consciousness but was able to obtain only six women's signatures (including her own) for a petition she drafted demanding equal property rights for wives. Initially, Rose's effort met with indifference or ridicule from both men and women, but she stubbornly persisted in attacking the legal disabilities of wives. By 1840 she was joined by other feminists such as Paulina Wright Davis and Elizabeth Cady Stanton. At this time, however, Rose's work probably constituted the most important feminist agitation for the legislation. Between 1837 and 1848 when New York passed its married women's property act, Rose drafted several more petitions and helped keep the issue of equal property rights before the politicians.[31]

On January 8, 1848, Judge Fine of St. Lawrence introduced a bill in the New York Senate that became the basis for the New York married women's property act. Fine, a conservative judge, who wanted to safeguard his wife's property from his creditors, also received overwhelming support from wealthy Dutch landowners who wanted to protect their married daughters' property from wasteful and improvident husbands. In addition, the bill was supported as a first step toward equal property laws by advocates of women's rights as well as by those who felt that the legislature rather than the courts constituted the appropriate lawmakers.[32]

Although the 1848 New York law was broader than the southern legislation and recognized the wife's title to both her real and personal property, it too was limited and failed to remove any other common-law disabilities. Poorly drafted and fragmentary, the act precipitated litigation over whether the wife had the right to mortgage her own property. In addition, another limitation or perhaps oversight in the 1848 law generated increased confusion. New York families faced the somewhat anomalous legal difficulty that although wives now had the legal title to their own property, they still retained most of their civil disabilities, and under the new law neither husband nor wife could convey her property.[33]

In fact, the 1848 legislation offered the wife less economic and legal autonomy than an antenuptial contract could. Many of these contracts, traditionally enforced by equity courts, had recognized the wife's right and ability to convey her property or to enter into contracts. The 1848 legislation, following two decades of legal simplification and attacks on equity, left the New York wife in a "procedural limbo" and is, in part, responsible for the assertion that nineteenth-century women had fewer legal rights and options than their colonial counterparts.[34]

As the courts moved to resolve the uncertainties inherent in the married women's property acts, neither the bench nor the bar seemed interested in improving women's legal status. As in other jurisdictions such as Maine, most of the cases in New York courts revolved around debtor-creditor relations and had little to do with the domestic or legal relationship between husband and wife. In addition, judges reared on common-law doctrines expounded by Blackstone construed the laws narrowly, and the earliest legislation both in intent and impact was not revolutionary as far as women were concerned.[35]

Despite the intent or impact of the legislation, women did have some effect. Liberal feminist reform impulses became increasingly important in the twelve years before the Civil War. The limitations in the early legislation as well as the overall disabilities suffered by married women in other jurisdictions came under increasing attack by the fledgling women's rights movement. Three months after the property act became law in New York, a group of three hundred middle-class women and sympathetic men met at Seneca Falls, New York, to discuss the social, political, economic, and legal inequities that plagued American women. Historians date this meeting as the official birth of the women's rights movement, and the Declaration of Sentiments issued by the convention, couched in Enlightenment rhetoric and modeled on the Declaration of Independence, has become a landmark document in the history of American feminism.[36] The Declaration demanded the right to vote, equal pay for equal work, the full participation of women in American society, and an end to the legal subjugation of women. In detailing "man's tyranny to woman," the document condemned the common law as the historic tool of man's economic and domestic exploitation of woman.

He has made her, if married, in the eye of the law, civilly dead.

He has taken from her all right in property, even to the wages she earns.

He has made her, morally, an irresponsible being, as she can commit many crimes with impunity, provided they be done in the presence of her husband. In the covenant of marriage, she is compelled to promise obedience to her husband, he becoming, to all intents and purposes, her master—the law, giving him power to deprive her of liberty, and to administer chastisement.

He has so framed the laws of divorce, as to what shall be the proper causes, and in case of separation, to whom the guardianship of the children shall be given, as to be wholly regardless of the happiness of women—the law, in all cases, going upon the false supposition of the supremacy of man, and giving all power into his hands.[37]

As historian Mary Beard has pointed out, such vehement rhetoric ignored the historically ameliorating effects of equity jurisprudence for some married women.[38] Nineteenth-century feminists, however, were on firmer ground when they attacked the piecemeal nature of the earliest acts. In many ways, while feminists were not solely responsible for the first legislation, they played instrumental roles in pinpointing and publicizing its weaknesses.

In 1851, for example, Ernestine Rose, whose speaking ability earned her the title "Queen of the Platform," focused on the most glaring flaws in the New York married women's property legislation. In a speech before a national women's rights convention, she condemned the efforts of the New York State Legislature:

According to a late act, the wife has a right to the property she brings at marriage, or receives in any way after marriage. Here is some provision for the favored few; but for the laboring many, there is none. The mass of the people commence life with no other capital than the union of heads, hearts, and hands. To the benefit of this best capital, the wife has no right. If they are unsuccessful in married life, who suffers more the bitter consequences of poverty than the wife? But if successful, she can not call a dollar her own. The husband may will away every dollar of the personal property, and leave her destitute and penniless and she has no redress by law. And even where real estate is left she receives a life-interest in a third part of it, and at her death, she can not leave it to any one belonging to her; it falls back even to the remotest of his relatives. This is law, but where is the justice of it? Well might we say that laws were made to prevent, not to promote, the ends of justice. . . .[39]

During the 1850s New York feminists mounted intensive lobbying and organizational drives to obtain a wife's rights to her own wages, a right that Rose had indicted the American legal system for systematically denying her. Two other women played critical roles as well in achieving some redress for married women in New York—Susan B. Anthony and Elizabeth Cady Stanton.

Anthony, whose flair for organization was to serve the women's rights movement for decades, provided a sound base for the effort to give New York wives the right to control and manage their own wages. In 1854 she initiated an intensive lobbying effort to convince the New York State Legislature that their constituents believed that wives had the moral right to wages earned by their labor and that such monies should not legally be under the management of their spouses. Without the right to vote, Anthony believed that women could bring political pressure to bear only through their right to petition, and in 1854 she appointed women to spearhead a petition campaign in every district of the state. In less than three months, Anthony's group had trudged throughout New York State in midwinter "knocking at every door" until they had obtained six thousand signatures supporting better property rights for married women. In an effort to focus the legislators' attention on the reform, Anthony also organized a women's rights convention in Albany while the legislature was in session. The petitions were used to persuade the assembly to hold a hearing on women's issues.[40]

With the careful organizational groundwork that Anthony had established, the next move was to present the case before the politicians. Elizabeth Stanton, the articulate theorist of the early women's rights movement, spoke before the Joint Judiciary Committee, the first woman to publicly address both houses in the state. Despite Stanton's eloquence, careful arguments, and legal documentation, the bill was defeated.

Advocates of women's rights continued their efforts, however, and in 1855 Anthony undertook a joint petition-gathering and lecture tour throughout the state. This time, she gathered 13,000 signatures and once again delivered them to the New York politicians. Although some were beginning to support the ideal of equal property rights, the concept of women's rights generated hostility and ridicule, and it would be years before it was taken seriously. When the Joint Judiciary Committee issued its report about wives' property rights, it ignored the petitions and statistics that the women had assembled. The committee overlooked the common law disabilities that women such as Anthony, Rose, and others were attacking in conventions, public meetings, and speaking tours. The report issued by the committee argued (tongue in cheek) that men, not women, suffered the most in American society.[41]

> . . . the ladies always have the best place and choicest titbit at the table. They always have the best seat in the cars, carriage and sleighs; the warmest place in the winter and the coolest place in the summer. . . .
>
> . . . if there is any inequity or oppression in the case, the gentlemen are the sufferers. They, however, have presented no petitions for redress; having doubtless, made up their minds to yield to an inevitable destiny. On the whole, the Committee have concluded to recommend no measure, except as they have observed several instances in which husband and wife have signed the same petition. In such case, they would recommend the parties to apply for a law authorizing them to change dresses, that the husband may wear petticoats and the wife the breeches, and thus indicate to their neighbors and the public the true relation in which they stand to each other.[42]

Although such a facetious response was discouraging, Anthony persevered. In 1848 with funds made available by sympathetic supporters, she gave lectures in the major New York cities and towns, calling for both a wife's right to her wages and an equal role in appointing guardians for her children. By 1860, the groundwork laid by Anthony, Rose, and Stanton began to show results. During the winter of 1860, Anthony visited the legislators in Albany and urged them to support several amendments to the original 1848 measure. When some of the amendments were passed by the Senate, she called on Stanton's eloquence to present the case once again before the public and the politicians. In March 1860 Stanton addressed a joint session of the legislature, and the following day the Married Women's Earning Act became law. In addition, New York wives gained greater rights and received equal power and authority with their husbands in guardianship matters.[43]

Limitations in the first married women's property acts spurred feminists to action in other states as well. Mary Upton Ferrin of Salem, Massachusetts, for example, dissatisfied with the early legislation in the 1840s, spent years persuading men and women to

sign petitions for property rights for wives. Her work reached frui-
tion in 1854 when Massachusetts passed a married women's property act that gave wives title to their property and allowed them to
enter into contracts and make valid wills. In their later *History of
Woman Suffrage*, Stanton, Anthony, and Matilda Gage praised Ferrin's contribution:

> . . . for six years, after her own quaint method [she] poured the hot
> shot of her earnest conviction of woman's wrong into the Legisla-
> ture. In circulating petitions, she traveled six hundred miles, two-
> thirds of the distance on foot. Much money was expended, besides
> her time, and her name should be remembered as that of one of the
> brave pioneers in this work.[44]

Similarly, Ohio feminists who felt that the act of 1845 was too
limited agitated for more extensive property rights. As early as
1848 a women's rights convention in the state sent a memorial
written by Mary A. Johnson to the Ohio State Constitutional Convention. The memorial asked: "We earnestly suggest that in the
new constitution you are about to form for the state of Ohio,
women shall be secured, not only the right of suffrage but all the
political and legal rights which are guaranteed to men." Feminist
lobbying efforts continued in Ohio and eventually culminated in a
broader married women's property act in 1861.[45]

By the outbreak of the Civil War, the American woman's legal
status and her corresponding proprietary disabilities differed in
each jurisdiction. While generalizations need to be tested by systematic studies of each state, overall, northern wives had obtained
more redress in their traditional legal disabilities than had southern
wives.[46] This rough geographical breakdown reinforces the supposition that the early women's rights movement had some connection with the most liberal legislation. At this time, the women's
rights movement was primarily a northern phenomenon. Certainly
feminist efforts were important in changing the original and tentative acts in the North.

Of course, feminist concern for equality intersected with both
liberal and conservative recognition that the first laws were at
times confusing and vague and that they created more problems
than they resolved. It is doubtful that the women's rights movement alone could have forced legislative changes in the legal status

of women. Some support was grudgingly won, as well as a few sincere converts, but the acts were enacted because so many groups supported them for a variety of reasons.

The origins of the married women's property acts should not be viewed either as the vanguard of a feminist revolution nor as single-minded conservative effort to protect family property from the hazards of the marketplace. Either explanation, while in part true, does not satisfactorily capture the complexities of the nineteenth-century political process. Those who emphasize that the acts were reactionary efforts designed solely to facilitate property flow in the economy tend to ignore or downplay the real work such women as Ferrin, Rose, Stanton, and Anthony undertook to better women's economic and legal status.

After the Civil War, feminists continued to fight for additional legislation for equality, although as in the earlier period, legislation was not passed solely in response to feminism. Isabella Beecher Hooker, a prominent New England advocate of women's rights, daughter of Lyman Beecher and half-sister of Harriet Beecher Stowe, led a vigorous campaign during the 1860s and 1870s in Connecticut that culminated in the 1877 Married Women's Property Act. As in other jurisdictions, this act amended an earlier one and established broader principles of female property rights; the Connecticut wife's earnings were placed under her sole control, and her property was not liable for the debts contracted by her husband.[47] Similarly, during the 1870s, Myra Bradwell, an Illinois teacher who founded and edited the *Chicago Legal News* (the first legal journal in the West) wrote and then lobbied for the law that gave married women in that state the right to their own wages.[48]

Despite such efforts, the battle for female legal and economic equality was far from won and seemed in abeyance, especially after the 1870s as the women's rights movement increasingly emphasized suffrage as the panacea for sex-based inequality. Ironically, the married women's property acts helped fuel and intensify the drive for the vote, often at the cost of obtaining other reforms for women. Rabkin and others argue that the acts stimulated feminist agitation for suffrage, and Rabkin concludes her perceptive study of New York's 1848 act with Elizabeth Cady Stanton's analysis:

What is property without the right to protect that property by law? It is mockery to say a certain estate is mine, if, without my consent, you have the right to tax me when and how you please, while I have no voice in making the tax gatherer, the legislator or the law. The right to property will, of necessity, compel us in due time to the exercise of our right to the elective franchise, and then naturally follows the right to hold office.[49]

Although feminists such as Stanton, Susan B. Anthony, and Ernestine Rose had some input into the earlier married women's property acts, the initial nineteenth-century inroads on the doctrine of marital unity sprang from diverse origins and reflected a wide sweep of regional variety. The drive for codification, conservative efforts to protect family property, the American experience with equity jurisprudence, as well as the embryonic women's movement, all coalesced to produce a climate receptive to the passage of these acts. While diverse groups and individuals supported the legislation, they did so for very different reasons and motives. The married women's property acts were not the result of a coherent national movement for female rights, but rather flowed from the demands of very different and at times contending factions.

In conclusion, although the acts sprang from diverse origins, their total impact was remarkably similar. Poorly drafted, piecemeal, and narrowly construed, the legislation did not inaugurate any sweeping changes in the American woman's legal status in the antebellum years. Heralding a possible revolution in women's legal and economic status, they, in effect, ratified the status quo by codifying principles of equity and as such stirred little real debate. Despite these caveats, the married women's property acts cannot be dismissed as ephemeral occurrences. The legislation made inroads into the century-old common-law doctrine of coverture, established a framework for future efforts, and marked a beginning in the battle for women's rights. Full legal equality for women, however, in property and guardianship matters as well as in political participation, remained for future generations to achieve. The legal fiction of marital unity, while battered in the first half of the nineteenth century, proved resilient and has endured in some forms to influence domestic law and public perceptions to the present day.[50]

NOTES

1. The focus of this essay is on the American woman's legal status and property rights at common law. Woman's legal position in community property states such as Texas, California, and Louisiana, has not been considered.

2. Analyses of the legal status of the *feme covert* (wife) usually begin with Sir William Blackstone, *Commentaries on the Laws of England in Four Books*, ed. George Sharswood (Philadelphia: J. B. Lippincott Co., 1904, originally published in 1765–69), 1:432–46. See also James Kent, *Commentaries on American Law*, 4 vols., 11th ed., ed. George F. Comstock (Boston: Charles C. Little and James Brown, 1867, originally published in 1826–30); Tapping Reeve, *The Law of Baron and Femme*, 3d ed. (Albany, N. Y.: William Gould, 1862, originally published in 1816).

3. Lawrence M. Friedman, *A History of American Law* (New York: Simon and Schuster, 1971), p. 184; also see Justice Black's dissenting opinion in United States v. Yazell, 382 U.S. 341, 86 S. Ct. 500, 15 L. Ed. 2d 404 (1966).

4. Several scholars have suggested that some of the common-law disabilities associated with coverture were not enforced in frontier communities both because women were in short supply and hence more valued, and because some common-law technicalities were simply unknown. In addition, equitable principles, originally developed in England and transplanted to some American jurisdictions, incorporated ways to avoid the contractual disabilities of the *feme covert*. See Richard B. Morris, *Studies in the History of American Law*, 2d ed. (New York: Octagon Books, 1963, originally published in 1938), Chaps. I and III; Julia Cherry Spruill, *Women's Life and Work in the Southern Colonies*, with an introduction by Anne Firor Scott (New York: Norton, 1972, originally published in 1938), pp. 3–19, 340–66; Roger Thompson, *Women in Stuart England and America: A Comparative Study* (London: Routledge & Kegan Paul, 1974); Mary R. Beard, *Women as Force In History: A Study in Traditions and Realities* (New York: Macmillan, 1946), pp. 82–95, 109, 111, 113–14, 123–28, 131–44, 158–59, 196–203, 205; Joseph Story, *Commentaries on Equity Jurisprudence as Administered in England and America*, 2 vols. (Boston: Charles C. Little and James Brown, 1839, originally published in 1836).

Despite the possible ameliorating effects of either equity or the American colonization experience, the common-law fiction of marital unity endured in American society. See, for example, Norma Basch, "Invisible Women: The Legal Fiction of Marital Unity in Nineteenth Century America," *Feminist Studies* 5 (1979): 346–66; Marylynn Salmon, "Equality or Submersion? Feme Covert Status in Early Pennsylvania," in *Women of America: A History*, ed. Carol Ruth Berkin and Mary Beth Norton (Boston: Houghton Mifflin, 1979), pp. 92–111; Linda E. Speth, "Woman's Sphere: Role and Status of White Women in 18th Century Virginia" (M.A. thesis, Utah State University, 1980), pp. 8–12; Joan Hoff Wilson, "The Illusion of

Change: Women and the American Revolution," in *The American Revolution: Explorations in the History of American Radicalism*, ed. Alfred F. Young (Dekalb, Ill.: Northern Illinois University Press, 1976), pp. 383–445.
    5. See Laws Miss. 1839, ch. 46; Laws Md. 1843, p. 293; Laws Me. 1844, p. 104; Mass. Rev. Stats. 1844, ch. 74; Laws Mass. 1845, p. 531; Laws Ia. 1845, ch. 5; Law N.Y. 1848, ch. 200.
    6. Basch, "Invisible Women," p. 362, note 14.
    7. See notes 8 and 9 below.
    8. Beard, *Women as Force in History*, pp. 158–69; Basch, "Invisible Women," pp. 346–66. The author would like to thank Dr. Joan Hoff Wilson for sending the galley proofs of "Hidden Riches: Legal Records and Women, 1750–1825." The article has since appeared in Mary Kelley, ed., *Woman's Being, Woman's Place: Female Identity and Vocation in American History* (Boston: G. K. Hall, 1979).
    The legal status of American women in the nineteenth century has been explored in several dissertations. Particularly important are Kay Ellen Thurman, "The Married Women's Property Acts" (LL.M. dissertation, University of Wisconsin Law School, 1966); Elizabeth Bowles Warbasse, "The Changing Legal Rights of Married Women, 1800–1861" (Ph.D. dissertation, Radcliffe College, 1960); Peggy A. Rabkin, "The Silent Feminist Revolution: Women and the Law in New York State from Blackstone to the Beginnings of the American Women's Rights Movement" (Ph.D. dissertation, State University of New York, Buffalo, 1975). Also see Rabkin, "The Origins of Law Reform: The Social Significance of the Nineteenth-Century Codification Movement and its Contribution to the Passage of the Early Married Women's Property Acts," *Buffalo Law Review* 24 (1974–75): 683–760.
    Essentially, Friedman agrees with Thurman in arguing that the acts were motivated by economic reasons. See Friedman, *History of American Law*, pp. 184–86. Important analyses of nineteenth-century legal development also include Roscoe Pound, *The Formative Era of American Law* (New York: Peter Smith, 1950); and Morton J. Horwitz, *The Transformation of American Law, 1780–1860* (Cambridge, Mass.: Harvard University Press, 1977).
    Elizabeth Cady Stanton stresses feminist impact, although she notes the legislation was supported by the Dutch aristocracy who wanted to protect their married daughters' properties. See *Eighty Years & More: Reminiscences, 1815–1897*, with a new introduction by Gail Parker (1881; reprint ed., New York: Schocken, 1971), pp. 150–51. For recent works which emphasize that feminists supported the legislation, see Eleanor Flexner, *Century of Struggle: The Woman's Rights Movement in the United States* (1959; reprint ed., Cambridge, Mass.: Harvard University Press, 1975), pp. 62–64; Gerda Lerner, *The Woman in American History* (Menlo Park, Calif.: Addison-Wesley Publishing Co., 1971), pp. 80–81; Leo Kanowitz, *Woman and the Law: The Unfinished Revolution*, 2d ed. (Albuquerque: University of New Mexico Press, 1975), pp. 40–41, p. 263, notes 45–46.

9. Initially, some nineteenth-century advocates of women's rights underestimated the enduring nature of the common-law fiction of marital unity. See Elizabeth Cady Stanton, Susan B. Anthony, and Matilda Joslyn Gage, eds. *History of Woman Suffrage*, vol. I (Rochester, N. Y.: Charles Mann, 1881), p. 64 (hereafter cited as Stanton et al., *HWS*). Scholars who argue that the acts attempted to codify rules of equity include Basch, "Invisible Women," p. 356; and Rabkin, "Origins of Law Reform," p. 692. Basch, however, goes on to suggest that in interpreting the acts, the courts subverted the legislature's reform impulses. In this respect her analysis is similar to Wilson's in "Hidden Riches."

10. Basch, "Invisible Women."

11. Rabkin shares Basch's legal historical approach and also confines her in-depth analysis to the jurisdiction of New York. See "Origins of Law Reform."

12. For a discussion of nineteenth-century reform movements, see Alice Felt Tyler, *Freedom's Ferment: Phases of American Social History from the Colonial Period to the Outbreak of the Civil War* (New York: Harper and Row, 1962, originally published in 1944).

13. The marriage contract is reproduced in Stanton et al., *HWS*, I:294–95.

14. Sarah M. Grimké, *Letters on the Equality of the Sexes and the Condition of Woman* (New York: Lennox Hill, originally published in 1838), p. 85. Also see pp. 74–83 for Grimké's attack on the common-law disabilities associated with marriage.

15. Laws Miss. 1839, ch. 46.

16. Ibid.; also see Friedman, *History of American Law*, pp. 185–86.

17. Warbasse, "Changing Legal Rights," pp. 137–60.

18. Ibid.; and *Acts, Memorials and Resolutions of the State of Arkansas*, 1845, pp. 38–39.

19. Warbasse, "Changing Legal Rights," pp. 164–81. Several legal treatises discuss principles of equity. In addition to the work of Story cited above, see generally Frederick William Maitland, *Equity* (Cambridge, 1926).

20. Thurman, "Married Women's Property Acts," pp. 3–4; Warbasse, "Changing Legal Rights," pp. 204–05; see also Mich. Acts 1842, no. 66; Laws Ohio 1845, p. 75; Laws Ind. 1847, ch. 6; Laws Ia. 1845, ch. 5.

21. Thurman, "Married Women's Property Acts," pp. 25–26.

22. Warbasse, "Changing Legal Rights," pp. 182–91. For a discussion of American attitudes toward English legal traditions and special courts, see generally George Athan Billias, ed., *Law and Authority in Colonial America* (Barre, Mass.: Barre Publishers, 1965); David H. Flaherty, ed., *Essays in the History of Early American Law* (Chapel Hill, N. C.: University of North Carolina Press, 1969); and George Lee Haskins, *Law and Authority in Early Massachusetts: A Study in Tradition and Design* (New York: Macmillan Co., 1960).

23. Stanton et al., *HWS*, I:171–72. The act also allowed Vermont wives

the right to make a will, see Warbasse, "Changing Legal Rights," p. 192.
    24. For a discussion of codification, see Charles Malcolm Cook, "The American Codification Movement: A Study of Antebellum Legal Reform" (Ph.D. dissertation, University of Maryland, 1974).
    25. Rabkin, "Origins of Law Reform," pp. 687–716.
    26. Ibid., pp. 694–715; Warbasse, "Changing Legal Rights," pp. 57–87, 216–26; and Friedman, History of American Law, pp. 153–55, 250, 340–47, 351–53, 470, 557. Also see Horowitz, Transformation of American Law, pp. 17–18, 257–58, 265–66.
    27. The Revised Statutes of 1836 abolished trusts and required that previously equitable estates were now legal. Because a married woman's legal estate still belonged to her husband, the statutes worked to a woman's disadvantage. They denied her an equitable estate without enabling her to hold a legal estate, and this incomplete reform generated increased confusion.
    Attacks on equity as a separate system continued. In 1846 the New York Constitution abolished Chancery. For background on this development and its relationship to women's legal rights, see Rabkin, "Origins of Law Reform," pp. 716–25.
    28. During the 1820s and 1830s a vigorous debate took place in several magazines and scholarly journals about the pros and cons of codification and the common-law doctrine of coverture. Caleb Cushing, a lawyer, was hostile to Blackstone's emphasis on the wife's common-law disabilities, but he was not motivated by feminist ideology. He believed that women were inferior to men and was opposed to granting them suffrage. See "Legal Conditions of Women," North American Review 26 (April 1828): 316–356.
    29. Rabkin, "Origins of Law Reform," pp. 762 832; see also Thomas Hertell, Argument in the House of Assembly of the State of New York in the Session of 1837 in Support of the Bill to Restore to Married Women "The Right of Property" as Guaranteed by the Constitution of This State (New York: Henry Durell, 1839).
    30. For further information about Rose, see Yuri Suhl, Ernestine L. Rose and the Battle for Human Rights (New York: Reynal and Company, 1959).
    31. Rabkin, "Origins of Law Reform," pp. 749 50; and Stanton et al., HWS, I:99. Paulina Wright Davis also worked for the cause of women's rights in subsequent years. Her feminist newspaper, The Una, helped publicize the movement.
    32. Andrew Sinclair, The Better Half: The Emancipation of the American Woman (New York: Harper and Row, 1965), p. 87; Stanton, Eighty Years, pp. 150–51; and Warbasse, "Changing Legal Rights," pp. 226–27.
    33. Thurman, "Married Women's Property Acts," pp. 38–40.
    34. Basch, "Invisible Women," p. 356; and Wilson, "Hidden Riches."
    35. Thurman, "Married Women's Property Acts," pp. 28–29.
    36. "Declaration of Rights and Sentiments, 1848," in Stanton et al., HWS, I: 70–73.

37. Ibid. Scholars who argue that the married women's property acts launched the women's rights movement emphasize that the Seneca Falls Convention was held three months after the 1848 New York act became law. While historians tend to refer to the convention as the official beginning of the women's rights movement, no philosophy or reform springs into existence full blown at a given instant. Feminist ideology which provided the wellsprings of the movement was evident prior to 1848. On this point see Flexner, *Century of Struggle,* pp. 3–77; and Carol V. R. George, ed., *"Remember the Ladies": New Perspectives on Women in American History* (Syracuse, N. Y.: Syracuse University Press, 1920), pp. 59–65.

38. Beard, *Woman as Force in History,* pp. 113–21.

39. Rose's speech is contained in Stanton et al., *HWS,* I: 237–41.

40. Flexner, *Century of Struggle,* pp. 86–87; and Stanton, *Eighty Years,* pp. 191–92.

41. Ernestine Rose, "Petitions Were Circulated," in *Feminism: The Essential Historical Writings,* ed. and with an introduction and commentaries by Miriam Schneir (New York: Random House, 1972), pp. 125–27; Flexner, *Century of Struggle,* pp. 86–87; and Alma Lutz, *Susan B. Anthony: Rebel, Crusader, Humanist* (Boston: Beacon Press, 1959), pp. 39–41.

42. The report is contained in Stanton et al. *HWS,* I: 629–30.

43. Lutz, *Susan B. Anthony,* pp. 76–78; and Flexner, *Century of Struggle,* pp. 88–89. During the Civil War, the liberal 1860 act was amended. The wife no longer had equal guardianship rights with her husband, although she had to give her written consent before her husband could apprentice their child or appoint a guardian in his will.

44. Although Beard believes the women's rights movement overstated the legal subjugation of American women, she recognizes its role in effecting some changes and believes the tribute paid to Ferrin in *History of Woman Suffrage* was justified. See Beard, *Woman as Force in History,* p. 162.

45. Paulina W. Davis, comp. *A History of the National Woman's Rights Movement* (New York: Source Book Press, 1970, originally published in 1871), pp. 8–9.

46. Systematic studies need to be done of the court records of each state to determine the overall legal status of women from 1800 to 1860. As previously noted, Basch has done so for New York, but additional studies for other jurisdictions are needed in order to facilitate our understanding of the nineteenth-century woman's changing legal position.

47. Hooker's diaries, correspondence, and related materials have been filmed by The Stowe-Day Foundation. A clothbound edition of the Guide/Index is available. See *The Isabella Beecher Hooker Project,* ed. and with an introductory essay by Anne Throne Margolis (Hartford, Conn.: The Stowe-Day Foundation, 1979).

48. On Myra Bradwell's contribution to women's rights, see Karen DeCrow, *Sexist Justice* (New York: Random House, 1974), pp. 30–31.

49. Quoted in Rabkin, "Origins of Law Reform," p. 760.

50. Two works by Leo Kanowitz refer to the lingering impact of the

concept of coverture on women's legal status. See Kanowitz, *Women and the Law*, pp. 35–99, and Kanowitz, *Sex Roles in Law and Society* (Albuquerque, N.M.: University of New Mexico Press, 1973), pp. 42–74, 183–244. See also Barbara Allen Babcock et al., *Sex Discrimination and the Law: Causes and Remedies*, Law School Casebook Series (Boston: Little, Brown and Co., 1975, originally published in 1973), esp. pp. 561–818.

Suggested Readings for Part III

Norma Basch, "Invisible Women: The Legal Fiction of Marital Unity in Nineteenth Century America," 5 Feminist Stud. 346 (1979).

Gail M. Beckman, "Estate Planning: A Woman's Perspective," 114 Tr. & Es. 136 (1975).

Grace Blumberg, "Sexism in the Code: A Comparative Study of Income Taxation of Working Wives and Mothers," 21 Buffalo L. Rev. 49 (1971).

Carol S. Bruch, "Property Rights of De Facto Spouses Including Thoughts on the Value of Homemakers' Services," 10 Fam. L. Q. 101 (1976).

Jane R. Chapman and Margaret Gates, eds., *Women into Wives: The Legal and Economic Impact of Marriage* (Beverly Hills, Calif.: Sage Publications, 1977).

Linda G. De Paul, "Women and the Law: The Colonial Period," 6 Hum. Rts. 107 (1977).

Mary Ann Glendon, "Modern Marriage Law and its Underlying Assumption: The New Marriage and the New Property," 13 Fam. L. Q. 441 (1980).

Joan R. Gundersen and Gwen Victor Gampel, "Married Women's Legal Status in Eighteenth Century New York and Virginia," 39 Wm. & Mary Q. 114 (1982).

John D. Johnston, Jr., "Sex and Property: The Common Law Tradition, the Law School Curriculum and Developments toward Equality," 57 N.Y.U. L. Rev. 1033 (1972).

Herma Hill Kay and Carol Amyx, "*Marvin v. Marvin:* Preserving the Options," 65 Calif. L. Rev. 937 (1977).

Linda K. Kerber, "From the Declaration of Independence to the Declaration of Sentiments: The Legal Status of Women in the Early Republic, 1776–1848," 6 Hum. Rts. 115 (1977).

Barbara A. Kulzer, "Law and the Housewife: Property, Divorce and Death," 28 U. Fla. L. Rev. 1 (1975).

Richard Morris, *Studies in the History of American Law* (New York: Columbia University Press, 1930), especially chapter 3, "Women's Rights in Early American Law," pp. 136–173, on the married woman's proprietary capacity.

Sarah B. Pomeroy, *Goddesses, Whores, Wives, and Slaves: Women in Classical Antiquity* (New York: Schocken Books, 1975).

Peggy A. Rabkin, "The Origins of Law Reform: The Social Significance of the Nineteenth Century Codification Movement and its Contribution to the Passage of the Early Married Women's Property Acts," 24 Buffalo L. Rev. 683 (1974–75).

Marjorie D. Rombauer, "Marital Status and Eligibility for Federal Statutory Income Benefits: A Historical Survey," 52 Wash. L. Rev. 227 (1977).

Mary M. Wenig, "Sex, Property and Probate," 9 Real Prop. Prob. Tr. J. 642 (1974).

Joan Hoff Wilson, "Hidden Riches: Legal Records and Women, 1750–1825," in *Woman's Being, Woman's Place, Female Identity and Vocation in American History,* ed. Mary Kelley (Boston: G. K. Hall, 1979).

Judith T. Younger, "Community Property, Women and the Law School Curriculum," 48 N.Y.U. L. Rev. 211 (1973).

PART IV

Protecting Women's Interests: Family and Sex Roles

The effect of the changing status of women on the field of family law occupies an important place in legal textbooks.[1] Several essays in Part IV of this collection explore traditional family law topics, such as marriage and divorce. The historical influence of the changing nature of sex roles on many areas of law has not been as well documented. The remaining essays in this section discuss the impact of changing sex roles on several other areas of law, including criminal law, labor law, and social welfare legislation. Stereotypical views of women's nature and gender roles have influenced the *formulation* of law in these areas. That is, these stereotypical views have contributed not only to the development of marriage and divorce policy, but also to the emergence of thirteenth-century criminal procedure, twentieth-century protective labor legislation, and social insurance for wives and mothers.

The double-edged sword of protective laws based on women's innate characteristics and gender roles has resulted in special policies for women-only in a number of areas of law. Protective legal policy originates primarily from judicial and legislative solicitude for women as childbearers and childrearers.

However, preferential treatment has its drawbacks. Gender-based classifications stemming from protective motives have resulted historically in women being denied admission to the legal profession, the right to vote and to hold public office, and to serve on juries, among other disabilities.[2] Although the purported rationale of this legal policy is protection, such benign discrimination often embodies and reinforces traditional stereotypes and gender role identification. Moreover, as some commentators have suggested, such preferential treatment for women also works to the disadvantage of men.[3]

95

Essays in this section focus on different aspects of the double-edged sword of protection by exploring women's interests in a variety of contexts. Ruth Kittel explores a woman's right to seek redress for injury to her body. Because rape was one of only two crimes for which women could play an active part in initiating the legal process, this offense occupies a unique position in thirteenth-century English criminal procedure.

In early Norman times, the traditional way of initiating a legal action against another party was trial by battle. Women, however, were exempt from this procedure. Since a woman never had to risk her life to seek redress for a wrong, a societal concern arose that women would undertake legal actions fraudulently.[4] This concern resulted in limitations on women's rights to initiate suits: Women could initiate suits only in cases of rape and the death of a husband.

Kittel also examines the procedure, sanctions, and outcomes of 142 rape cases during this period. Her objective is to compare legal theory with the actual practice of the local and royal courts. She finds that although treatises and statutes proclaimed harsh punishment as the sanction for rape, legal reality differed. The odds favored the offender's acquittal. Even if convicted, the rapist suffered at most a fine or imprisonment; capital punishment never resulted.

D. Kelly Weisberg's essay examines the formulation of divorce law in Puritan Massachusetts from 1639 to 1692. When the colonists arrived in the Massachusetts Bay Colony in 1630, the marital bond could not be severed. English law did not permit divorce, but only granted separation in limited cases. In contrast, divorce law in the Bay Colony reveals several differences. Not only was divorce available, but also, divorce was more frequently granted to women than to men.

Weisberg explores the procedure, grounds and outcomes of seventeenth-century divorce petitions, as well as the social conditions which contributed to the emergence of this liberal divorce policy. These social conditions include: 1) Puritan dependence on the family as a primary agent of social control; 2) Puritan concern with sin and with the temptation facing married women separated from their husbands; 3) the community concern with dependent women draining public coffers; and 4) the overall scarcity and value of women. Legal policy was thus based on an ambivalence toward women. Women were perceived as evil beings to be prevented from tempting others' husbands. In addition, women were also seen as dependent and in need of protection from cruel, bigamous and deserting husbands. These social conditions and predominant attitudes resulted in colonial women acquiring a legal privilege which their English counterparts would not gain for two hundred years.

The essay by Michael Hindus and Lynne Withey, "The Law of Husband and Wife in Nineteenth-Century America: Changing Views of Divorce," examines changes in divorce law in three states, from the Revolution to the Civil War. The states include: Massachusetts, Virginia, and South Carolina.

State statutes vary considerably concerning the specific grounds and procedures for divorce. In this period, both Massachusetts and Virginia had statutory grounds and procedures for divorce; however, South Carolina granted only separate maintenance. Despite this difference, similarities existed in the common grounds upon which marriages could be severed. These grounds included: adultery, desertion, cruelty and the criminal conviction of a spouse.

Another major difference concerned divorce procedure. Judicial decrees were awarded in Massachusetts, whereas the legislature played a more active role in Virginia. In addition, differences existed in the factors influencing the judiciary and legislature. Divorce policy in Massachusetts and Virginia was influenced by the contractual basis of marriage. On the other hand, in South Carolina, marriage and separation were regarded primarily as a property-based rather than a contractual relationship.

Hindus and Withey emphasize that nineteenth-century divorce law evolved from a concern for the protection of women. This concern mirrored nineteenth-century beliefs about the fragility of women. Much of the foundation of nineteenth-century divorce law, then, involved attempts by courts and legislatures to offer protection for the injured and dependent wife.

Nancy Erickson's essay explores the historical background of a landmark United States Supreme Court decision. Erickson examines the public and feminist response to the case of *Muller* v. *Oregon*.[5] This early twentieth-century decision had an important impact on women's legal status in regard to employment. In *Muller*, the Court upheld restrictions on the number of hours that women were permitted to work—restrictions that did not apply to men.

Prevailing ideas about woman's role as wife and mother constitute the judicial rationale for the decision. The Court reasoned that preferential treatment was permissible because women need protection due to their physical characteristics and childbearing function.

Erickson's essay reminds us that reaction to developments in the law may play a role in the emergence of new legal rules. Specifically, reaction and opposition to the *Muller* decision by a small group of outspoken feminists foreshadowed the contemporary feminist challenge to protective but unequal treatment for women.

Grace Blumberg's essay, "Adult Derivative Benefits in Social Security: A Women's Issue," explores the Social Security Act, originally enacted in 1939 to provide economic benefits to large classes of individuals. Women constitute a significant percentage of the beneficiaries of this social welfare legislation—either as derivative beneficiaries (collecting on the accounts of their retired, disabled, or deceased husbands) or as beneficiaries themselves.

Blumberg explores the history of the legislation, its underlying assumptions and its capacity to adapt to social, economic, and legal change. Her central argument is that the derivative benefits scheme contains many inconsistencies. In part, she attributes this to Congress's piecemeal approach to both the enactment and revision of the legislation. However, many of the problems inherent in the legislation stem from protective motives and stereotypical views about dependent women. These fundamental assumptions work to the detriment of the system's beneficiaries.

NOTES

1. See Barbara Allen Babcock et al., *Sex Discrimination and the Law: Causes and Remedies* (Boston: Little, Brown & Co., 1975), chapter 3, pp. 561–

818; Herma Hill Kay, *Text, Cases and Materials on Sex-Based Discrimination,* 2d ed. (St. Paul, Minn.: West Publishing Co., 1981), chapter 2, pp. 163–482; Leo Kanowitz, *Sex Roles in Law and Society* (Albuquerque: University of New Mexico Press, 1973), pp. 183–298; and Judith Areen, *Cases and Materials on Family Law* (Mineola, N.Y.: Foundation Press, 1978), chapter 2, pp. 93–143.

2. In Bradwell v. Illinois, 83 U.S. 130 (1873), the United States Supreme Court denied a woman's application for a license to practice law because she was a female; in Minor v. Happersett, 88 U.S. 162 (1874), the Court ruled that the states could limit the right to vote to men alone; and in Hoyt v. Florida, 368 U.S. 57 (1961) the Court upheld statutory limitations on a woman's ability to serve on juries.

3. See the discussion in Kay, "Men as Victims?" pp. 12–26; and Leo Kanowitz, *Equal Rights: The Male Stake* (Albuquerque: University of New Mexico Press, 1981).

4. The belief that women falsely accuse men of sexual attacks is one of the rationales given for corroboration requirements. See generally, Babcock, pp. 843–863. This concern was voiced by Matthew Hale in his *Pleas of the Crown* 635 (1778): rape "is an accusation easily to be made and hard to be proved, and harder to be defended by the party accused though never so innocent." This statement has often been reiterated in court decisions. See, for example, People v. Scott, 407 Ill. 301, 95 N.E.2d 315 (1950).

5. 208 U.S. 412 (1908).

RAPE IN THIRTEENTH-CENTURY ENGLAND: A STUDY OF THE COMMON-LAW COURTS

Ruth Kittel

The thirteenth century is the earliest period in English history for which records of the common-law courts exist. The plea rolls with their laconic entries of court action are imperfect, but they offer sufficient information to make possible a comparison between the theoretical statements of the law and the practice of the courts. In particular, the plea rolls provide the basis, however rudimentary it may be, for the study of women as plaintiffs in the royal courts and their attempts to achieve redress for specific complaints.

Legal theory in the thirteenth century allowed a woman relatively few rights in bringing criminal charges before the common-law courts. A man could bring charges for any one of a large group of crimes: homicide, mayhem, wounding, false imprisonment, arson, robbery, burglary, and larceny. A woman, on the other hand, was restricted to two areas: the unnatural death of her husband and injury to her body, which was often narrowly interpreted to mean rape.[1]

This limitation on a woman's right as plaintiff may have stemmed from the procedural advantages she enjoyed in prosecuting her case.[2] Since Norman times, the usual method of initiating court action for serious crimes was the appeal of felony.[3] Traditionally, trial had been by judicial battle and whoever was victorious in combat won the case. Women, the clergy, and aged or crippled men were exempted from this procedure, and, instead, underwent trial by ordeal.[4] When the Fourth Lateran Council in 1215 abolished the ordeal, defendants charged by women were convicted or acquitted by a jury. A woman, unlike a man, never had to risk her life in prosecuting a complaint of felony. Because it was relatively easy for a woman to bring charges, there may have been a societal concern that a woman would undertake an appeal

101

falsely, and consequently, a strong social pressure to limit a woman's right to the crimes "which most injured her and where it was most essential that she should herself make suit."[5] This attempt at the limitation of a woman's right to appeal was understandable in Norman times when a male plaintiff offered battle by his own body. However, by the middle of the thirteenth century, trial by battle had ceased to be the ordinary means of adjudication. Although men continued to talk of fighting, the battle rarely materialized.[6] Both men and women had recourse to the same method of settling disputes: trial by jury. The rationale for limiting the rights of women had disappeared, but throughout the century, the major legists, although they might express doubts about trial by battle, generally accounted it the normal mode of proof, and in turn, declared a woman's rights of appeal to be those involving death of a husband and rape.[7]

Many women brought cases outside of these two areas, but to do so, meant to run the risk of a challenge being raised in court.[8] An analysis of rape cases, therefore, has a particular significance in the legal study of thirteenth-century English women. Rape was one of two complaints where a woman's right to bring charges was not questioned. It was also the complaint which intimately concerned her own well-being. Other relatives could and did appeal the death of a woman's husband. However, only rarely did a husband or parent bring charges of rape on behalf of a woman.[9] It is noteworthy that the injured woman herself initiated all but a few of the rape cases entered on the plea rolls. Unlike other cases, the appeal of rape was clearly and uniquely a woman's right and responsibility.

Despite this official sanction, the relatively small number of cases in the records suggests that many women did not bring charges in the royal courts.[10] Many women may have been too ashamed or intimidated to initiate the royal judicial process. Some may have preferred to seek redress within the local courts. Those who were poor and humble—for example, field-laborers, thresher-women, and gleaners—had virtually no way of appealing rape.

A few women, however, did proclaim their wrongs publicly in the common-law courts. This essay is concerned with the outcome of these women's efforts to secure justice.

Legal treatises and statutes provide general knowledge of the legal framework within which the royal courts operated and specific information concerning the prescribed penalties for rape and the accepted grounds for acquittal. In our attempt to understand the attitudes of thirteenth-century society towards rape, it is useful to examine both the theoretical operation and the actual practice of the law courts.

Women who brought appeals could hope—at least in theory—to secure harsh punishments for a convicted rapist. Bracton, a legal writer of the mid-thirteenth century, commented that in the past, rape had been a capital crime subject to the death penalty.[11] Concerning his own time, he wrote that in some cases the appropriate punishment should be castration and blinding in order that the "defiler be punished in the parts in which he offended."[12] "The offender should lose his eyes which gave him sight of the maiden's beauty for which he coveted her . . . and the testicles which excited his hot lust."[13] One case suggests that the injured woman herself, by the judgment of the court, should be the one to tear out the eyes and cut off the testicles.[14] The anonymous author of another legal tract, Placita Corone, written in 1274–75, echoes Bracton. This author states that the judges in cases of rape might decree blinding or castration or both, according to their discretion. However, he notes one special provision. If the wrongdoer were a married man, his wife could come before the rendering of judgment and "could claim her husband's testicles as her own property." "Thereupon, according to strict law, he would be merely blinded for the trespass."[15]

Castration and mutilation were reserved for the most outrageous cases. According to Bracton, the degree of punishment depended on the status of the woman: whether she be a virgin, nun, widow, matron, concubine, or prostitute.[16] Bracton sang the praises of purity and the horror of its loss: "Virgins and widows as well as nuns are dedicated to God and their defilement is committed not only to the hurt of mankind, but indeed, in scorn of Almighty God Himself."[17] Nevertheless, virgins, widows, and nuns were not the only ones to be protected. Bracton emphasized that the king "for the preservation of his peace" must guard all women, and that whatever the woman's status, the penalty was to be severe.[18] Unfortunately, Bracton does not elaborate further. Presumably, the specific degree of punishment would be decided in individual cases according to the discretion of the judges.

If a woman desired to prosecute fully her charges of felony, punishment was harsh. But—and this is important—if a woman initiated a suit and failed to complete it, the situation changed. At this point, the king could choose to let the case drop or he could take up the prosecution in her place. If the case was taken over by the king and the man convicted, punishment was less severe. Rape—like mayhem, wounding and false imprisonment—was, in Henry III's time, a crime whose penalties depended on the method of prosecution.[19] When the king charged an offender with the violation of a woman, the defendant was subject only to fine and imprisonment. The First Statute of Westminster in 1275 fixed two years of prison and a fine at the king's pleasure as the punishment.[20] This distinction between punishment for rape based on the appeal of a woman and that based on the indictment by the king lasted only until 1285. In that year, a statute provided the death penalty for all cases of rape—for a "married woman, a maiden, or other woman"—even when the rapist was convicted at the king's suit.[21] All women were now equally protected, and the method of prosecution no longer made a difference. In the course of the century, the judgment of society, as reflected in its statutes, proclaimed rape to be an increasingly serious infraction of the king's peace.

Among all the harsh penalties, there are several notes in the legal treatises concerning grounds for acquittal. Several of these are specific to charges of rape. For example, if the accused declared that he had not defiled the woman and that she was still a virgin, four law-abiding women were to examine her body. If they said that she was still a virgin, the accused would depart free.[22] This primitive method of proof depended on the woman's virginal status being apparent to observers.

Another evidence of innocence depended, surprisingly enough, on a woman's pregnancy. Britton and other legal writers declared that if the woman at the time of the alleged rape had conceived, then the man was innocent "because no woman can conceive if she does not consent."[23] This legal ruling that pregnancy is evidence of consent was based on the state of medieval science. Although the major thinking about conception, as represented by Aristotle in the works of Aquinas, declared that only the male seed was necessary,[24] thinkers such as William of Conches insisted that the woman produced a seed towards the conception of a child just as the man did. When the woman consented, the seed was emitted. Therefore, in cases of alleged rape, pregnancy proved consent. In these instances, although the woman may have been unwilling at first, her desires of the flesh prevailed, and hence the seed was released.[25] Both the man and woman freely and actively contributed towards conception.

For the single man, there remained one additional means of avoiding punishment: marriage to his victim. When the girl was willing to marry her alleged rapist, that agreement brought the case to a close. The background to this provision stretches to the distant Germanic past. Roman law did not allow the injured woman to marry her attacker.[26] Germanic custom, however, at least in the Ripuarian and Visigothic laws did permit such a marriage. Ripuarian law emphasized the importance of the girl's free choice, while Visigothic law stressed the wishes of both the girl and her relatives.[27] Not until 1140 did canon law support the Germanic practices.[28] Gratian permitted such marriages provided the alleged rapist had done penance, and both victim and parents consented.[29] These teachings of Gratian were repeated in the thirteenth-century English penitential of Thomas of Chobham.[30]

By the mid-twelfth century, canon law teachings permitted the marriage between the alleged rapist and his victim. So did the customary law of France. Certain areas of France were acquainted with a practice called "grace by marriage," which applied to men accused of a wide variety of crimes.[31] At the moment just before hanging, if a woman stepped forward from the crowd and proclaimed she wished to marry the condemned, the judge could grant a pardon. In northern France not only were rapists pardoned through marriage, but also murderers and thieves. The practice of grace through marriage was more sweeping in France than it was in England—where it was limited to rape. But the writer of an addition to Bracton's treatise may be close to the truth when he attributes the origins of the rapist's pardon through marriage to both contemporary Church law and French practice.[32]

English custom, however, differed in one important aspect from that in France. On the continent, a woman could wait until *after* judgment with her offer of marriage; in England, the commitment of the two parties to marry had to be made *before* judgment. This English variation brought with it certain problems. The danger, as Glanvill noted, was that a woman might be tempted to force a man into marriage by alleging an attack of rape.[33] The accused, unless convinced that the court would acquit him, would be under considerable pressure to consent to marriage. There was no way to stop fraudulent appeals, although Glanvill protested that a lower-class woman should not be allowed to use an accusation as a means of forcing a noble man into a disparaging union. He stated that the two parties to the suit might be reconciled to each other by marriage only "if they have license from the King or his justices and the consent of their families."[34] However, in the middle of the thirteenth century, Bracton altered Glanvill's teaching. Bracton stated that a serf or a common woman might claim a nobleman as her husband, "for this lies wholly in her discretion."[35] Marriage, regardless of the social status of the parties, would end in the dismissal of all charges.

In general, to secure acquittal, the accused had to prove either that intercourse had never occurred or that the woman had consented to the act. Pregnancy, according to the accepted science of the time, was the clearest evidence of consent; a history of previous sexual relations with the accused or other men might serve the same purpose. Finally, if the parties married, all charges were dropped—regardless of the guilt or innocence of the defendant.

What happened to appeals in actual legal practice? How often were men punished by castration? How often were they acquitted? What could a woman who brought a suit reasonably expect?

To answer these questions, the author analyzed 142 rape cases contained in twenty rolls of pleas heard before itinerant justices.[36] The rolls come from different parts of England with their varying social structures: from Oxford and Bedford with their open-field social system; Kent, Norfolk, and the Chiltern Hills where personal freedom and partible inheritance were usual; the frontier areas of the Kentish Weald and the Warwickshire Forest of Arden; and the growing urban areas of London and Bristol.[37] This analysis attempts to reflect a representative sample of thirteenth-century society. The dates of the rolls range from 1202 to 1276. They cover the period where prosecution by a woman could result in castration, and prosecution by the king in a fine. They do not cover the period after 1285 when prosecution by any means could result in death. That must remain a subject for another study. The rape cases, for purposes of analysis, can be divided into two broad categories. In the first group are those cases in which women brought the initial charges and then subsequently dropped their pleas. The second group comprises those cases which women fully prosecuted.

In the majority of cases concerning rape (56 percent), the woman for one reason or another did not continue the prosecution of her appeal.[38] In each of these cases where the woman failed to follow through her appeal, she would either be amerced or committed to jail for her fault. Only in cases of extreme poverty or youth would the penalty be remitted. With this punishment the likely outcome, why then did women choose to abandon such a large number of cases? Unfortunately, the court rolls do not comment directly on the problem, but they do suggest some possibilities.

In a few instances, an appeal of rape was the prelude to a marriage. The percentage of such cases is not high. Only two trials out of 142 ended in the union of the alleged rapist and his victim.[39] Rarely can we determine the circumstances behind these decisions to marry. In one case in the early thirteenth century, Lucy accused Stephen Hoket of taking her into a booth, keeping her there all night, and raping her. When she cried out, his relatives came and put a lock on the door, so she could not escape. Stephen came into court and gave evidence which would tend to imply her consent; he said she had been his mistress for the past year. The serjeant of the hundred, however, bore witness that Lucy "was seen bleeding"; Stephen then gave five marks to the king for license to marry.[40] In this instance, there had been a long-term relationship between the two parties, but the charge of rape seems to have been substantiated. Since Stephen's family had helped him in this attack, perhaps they had an interest in a possible marriage. Could Lucy have been an heiress and the rape a means of pressuring her into marriage? It is tempting to make such a guess, but unfortunately, the records do not provide a clear answer.

Marriage was possible only when the parties were single and willing to make a lifelong commitment. An easier and less demanding means of settlement was a concord or agreement. In such a concord, the alleged rapist would typically give the woman a sum of money in compensation for the injury. In return, she would then cease to prosecute the case. There are eighteen concords in this sample. It is necessary, however, to point out that the money which the injured woman received from such concords could be quite small. In a case from 1202, the woman received half a mark.[41] On the other end of the scale, in 1242, Matilda was to receive from Adam, the defendant, four marks for her injury.[42] Unfortunately, the records do not reveal the terms of most agreements, so there is no way of determining the average amount of payment, or how often the agreements involved land instead of, or in addition to, money.[43] What is apparent is that a woman, hoping for some compensation, might bring an appeal of rape, but in only a minority of these cases would she achieve her aim.

Marriage or other agreements account for only a small number of the appeals which a woman dropped. What about the results of all other cases which she failed to prosecute? If a woman did not appear in court, then the king, for the preservation of the peace, might prosecute in her place. The king, however, did not prosecute every abandoned suit. In this sample, there are at least four cases in which the king did not act. In these last instances, the accused escaped with impunity.

In the majority of trials, however, the king *did* prosecute. The judges would order: "Let the truth of the matter be inquired into by the country."[44] A jury would then assemble and render its verdict. Of thirty-two accusations settled in this manner, twenty-seven men (84 percent) were acquitted. Only five (16 percent) were found guilty. In this sample, the penalties for those convicted ranged generally from four to ten marks. In an exceptional case in the King's Bench where the accused had raped a woman and kept her imprisoned for two years, he paid ten pounds to the king.[45] Ten pounds appears a large sum of money, but as a punishment it is negligible compared to blinding and castration. As the trials show, the accused had little to fear. The chances overwhelmingly favored acquittal, and even if convicted, he would suffer at most imprisonment or amercement. From the large number of cases in which a woman failed to appear in court, and from the consequences which that entailed, the evidence suggests that the man and his kin may often have exerted considerable pressure on the woman to withdraw from her suit. It is even possible that the community itself discouraged the woman from seeking full vengeance. A large minority of women (44 percent) did attempt to prosecute fully their cases. For whatever the reasons, they were motivated enough to pursue their appeals. In those situations in which the accused had reason to believe that a woman would continue her suit and that a court would find him guilty, he fled. If he did not appear at four successive courts and the jurors testified to his guilt, he was declared an outlaw.[46] As a result, he was deprived of every proprietary, possessory, and contractual right.[47] It was the duty of every man to pursue an outlaw and capture him as though he were a wild beast.[48] If an outlaw were seized, the justices would send him to the gallows as soon as the mere fact of his outlawry was proved.

In the cases involving rape, proceedings for outlawry were initiated against thirty-two men. The disabilities incurred by these men were heavy, but rarely were outlaws captured and hanged. Most seem to have departed from the area and succeeded in evading further punishment; very few appear in later plea roll entries.[49]

There was one other alternative for the man who did not wish to stand trial. The accused rapist could seek as sanctuary a consecrated monastery, church, or chapel with a graveyard. The neighborhood then surrounded the holy place and sent for the coroner. The coroner, in turn, offered the refugee the choice of trial or abjuration of the realm. If the refugee chose abjuration, he swore on the gospels to leave the realm of England and never to return except with the express permission of the king or his heirs.[50] Possibly few abjurors left the kingdom. It has been surmised that many abjurors sooner or later left the highway on their trip to the coast and simply took up residence unmolested elsewhere.[51] For the abjuror who was caught, however, punishment was harsh. His fate was that of the captured outlaw. If his abjuration could be proved, he was promptly hanged. A minority of malefactors, two from this sample, chose the option of abjuration.[52]

Some men, however, did not flee, but chose instead to stand trial. Probably they believed that they would be acquitted. Of twenty-three cases brought before the court, twenty men were acquitted and three found guilty. And for various reasons, none of the three convicted men faced castration. Two were clergymen and due to the privilege of their order, were handed to the ecclesiastical courts for punishment.[53] The canon law courts did not dispense either mutilation or execution as punishments. The third case was actually prosecuted by the king. In this instance, the woman had not dropped suit, but her appeal had been quashed due to deficiencies in the pleading; the king had continued her plea. As a result, the convicted rapist was simply fined two marks.[54]

The leniency of the juries is startlingly apparent. Acquittal is the order of the day. No woman succeeds through prosecution in securing a harsh punishment for a rapist. There are no instances of castration or mutilation.

The pattern of court action in cases of rape bears a certain resemblance to judicial decisions regarding homicide. The rate of conviction in both instances is low: 8 percent in homicide, 6 percent in rape.[55] However, there is an important difference. The full punishment, execution, is carried out in 7 percent of homicide cases.[56] The extreme penalty for rape, on the other hand, is never put into effect.

In summary, thirteenth-century legal writers and statutes proclaimed strong sanctions against the sexual violation of women; rapists were to be severely punished. In reality, however, if this sample is representative, these sanctions remained a dead letter. They may have had some deterrent effect, but if men had any awareness of the probability of a woman dropping her suit and the unwillingness of juries to convict, even that effect may have been minimal. It is true that some men accused of rape fled. Forced to find new homes elsewhere in England, these men probably suffered most for their deeds. Those who remained to stand trial were generally acquitted.

By the fourteenth century, cases of rape would no longer occupy the unique legal position which they hold for a study of women in the thirteenth century. The limitations on the right of a woman to appeal only rape and the death of her husband were becoming less important. Procedure by way of appeal was giving way to the process of indictment on the one side and to the action of trespass on the other.[57] In both developments, trial by battle, which had formed the basis for the restrictions on female plaintiffs, was eliminated. As a result of these changes, a woman's legal position dramatically improved; she was now able, with the full sanction of the law, to gain redress more easily for a wide variety of complaints.

Beyond the scope of this essay, however, is the separate, more complex issue of whether women in the fourteenth century experienced any improvement in securing convictions for charges of rape.

NOTES

1. Bracton, *De Legibus et Consuetudinibus Angliae*, ed. G. E. Woodbine (New Haven, 1942). Bracton, *On the Laws and Customs of England*, trans. S. E. Thorne (Cambridge, Mass., 1968), f. 148b (hereafter cited as Bracton). See also Britton, trans. F. M. Nichols (Washington, D.C., 1901), p. 96 (hereafter cited as Britton). For a fuller discussion, see M. R. Kittel, "Married Women in Thirteenth-Century England: A Study in Common Law" (unpublished Ph.D. dissertation, University of California, Berkeley, 1973), pp. 171–73.

2. J. M. Kaye believes that for a man not to be able to offer battle was a disadvantage in the early days when inquests were looked upon with suspicion. J. M. Kaye, ed., *Placita Corone* or *La Corone Pledee devant Justices*, Selden Society Supplementary Series, vol. 4 (London, 1966), p. xxxi. A lawyer in 1313–14 voices the same complaint, see F. W. Maitland, L. Harcourt, and W. C. Bolland, eds., *Year Book of the Eyre of Kent, 6 and 7 Edward II, 1313–14*, Selden Society, vol. 24 (London, 1909), p. 114.

3. The word "appeal" as used in this chapter does not have a contemporary equivalent. Above all, it should not be confused with the current American usage of the word "appeal" in reference to a court of second instance. Whereas today the state and the state's representative (the district attorney) bring criminal charges (e.g., People v. John Doe), in the thirteenth century an individual could bring charges against another. In this context, the appeal was "an accusation made in a set form and according to customary procedure by a plaintiff, known as the appellor *(appelator)* against one or more defendants, known as the apellees *(appelati)*." C. A. F. Meekings, *Crown Pleas of the Wiltshire Eyre, 1249*, Wiltshire Record Society, vol. 16 (1961), p. 69. For a discussion of appeals, see Bracton, ff. 137–146b.

4. Sometimes women were sent to the ordeal of iron and men to that of water. See F.W. Maitland, ed., *Select Pleas of the Crown (1200–1225)*, Selden Society, vol. 1 (London, 1887) no. 12 (1201), and D. M. Stenton, ed., *Pleas Before the King or His Justices, 1198–1202, II*, Selden Society, vol. 68 (London, 1952), no. 359 (1201). Other times both men and women performed the same ordeal. See Stenton, ibid., no. 732 (1201).

5. Meekings, *Crown Pleas*, p. 88.

6. Kaye, *Placita Corone*, p. xvi.

7. Britton in the 1290s describes trial by battle as the expected outcome

of an appeal of felony (Britton, pp. 83, 88). However, he seems to prefer the jury as a method of proof. He counsels that it is better to proceed by writs of trespass than by appeal in order to avoid the "perilous risk of battle" (ibid., p. 103). And Fleta, although he says that "resort may not be lightly had to battle," sees trial by battle as a real possibility. He goes to great lengths to give the correct form of the words of affirmation and denial to be said before battle. H. G. Richardson and G. O. Sayles, eds., *Fleta*, vol. 2, Selden Society, vol. 72 (London, 1955), p. 84 (hereafter cited as *Fleta*).

8. For cases which illustrate challenges in court, see Maitland, *Select Pleas*, vol. 1, no. 32 and no. 117. For another case, see R. E. Latham and C.A.F. Meekings, eds., "The Veredictum of Chippendum Hundred, 1281," *Collectanea*, Wiltshire Archeological and Natural History Society, Records Branch, vol. 12 (1956), p. 128 (1267–68).

9. For a plea brought by parents, see F. W. Maitland, ed., *Pleas of the Crown for the County of Gloucester, 1221*, Selden Society (London, 1884), no. 483. For pleas brought by husbands, see G. O. Sayles, ed., *Select Cases in the Court of King's Bench Under Edward I*, Selden Society, vol. 57 (London, 1936), no. 8; H. G. Richardson and G. O. Sayles, eds., *Select Cases of Procedure Without Writ Under Henry III*, Selden Society, vol. 60 (London, 1941), no. 132.

10. In twenty eyre rolls from five counties, 3,492 people were accused of homicide, compared to only 142 accused of rape. For a study of homicide see J. B. Given, *Society and Homicide in Thirteenth-Century England* (Stanford, 1977).

11. Bracton, f. 147.

12. Ibid.

13. Ibid. See also W. J. Whittaker, ed., *The Mirror of Justices*, Selden Society, vol. 7 (London, 1895). "This crime was punished by tearing out of eyes and loss of testicles, because of the appetite which entered through the eyes and the heat of fornication which came into the reins of lechers." Ibid., p. 141.

14. Maitland, Harcourt, and Bolland, *Eyre of Kent*, p. 134.

15. Kaye, *Placita Corone*, p. 9.

16. Bracton, f. 147.

17. Ibid.

18. Ibid.

19. F. Pollock and F. W. Maitland, *History of English Law* (Cambridge, England, 1898), 2d ed., vol. 2, p. 491.

20. First Statute of Westminster, c. 13, *Statutes of the Realm*, vol. 1 (London, 1810), p. 87.

21. Second Statute of Westminster, c. 34, *Statutes of the Realm*, vol. 1 (London, 1810), p. 29.

22. Bracton, f. 148.

23. Britton, p. 96. See also *Fleta*, bk. 1, c. 33; and Whittaker, *Mirror of Justices*, p. 103. For a case, see *Year Book 30–31 Edward I*, Rolls Series, p. 520.

24. Thomas Aquinas, *Summa Theologiciae*, Ia, 92, 1.

25. Guillaume de Conches, *De Philosophia Mundi*, vol. 4, p. xii, in PL 172 (erroneously ascribed to Honorius); also in *Dialogus de Sustantiis Physicis* (Strassburg, 1567, rpt. Frankfurt, 1967), vol. 6, pp. 241–42.

26. *Code of Justinian*, IX, 13, 1, 2.

27. P. Lemercier, "Une curiosite judiciare au moyen age: la grace par mariage subsequent," *Revue historique de droit francais et etranger*, 4th ser., 33 (Paris, 1955), p. 471.

28. A. Esmein, *Le mariage en droit canonique*, vol. 1 (Paris, 1891), pp. 391–93.

29. C 36 q.2 d.p.c. 6, c.9, 10, d.p.c. 11. See J. Brundage, "Rape and Seduction in the Medieval Canon Law," unpublished paper, 1976.

30. Thomas de Chobham, *Summa Confessorum*, ed. F. Broomfield, *Analecta Medievalia Namurencensia*, vol. 25 (1968), p. 354.

31. Lemercier, "Une curiosite judiciare," p. 470.

32. Bracton, f. 147b.

33. G.D.G. Hall, ed., *Tractatus de Legibus et Consuetudinibus Regni Anglie Qui Glanvilla Vocatur* [The treatise on the laws and customs of the realm of England commonly called Glanvill] (London, 1965), pp. xiv, 6.

34. Ibid.

35. Bracton, f. 148.

36. The author owes this sample to the kindness of Dr. James Given. These are the same twenty rolls he used in his study of homicide; therefore, the comparison between conviction and acquittal rates of rape and homicide are based on records from the identical area.

37. The counties are Bedford (eyres of 1202, 1227, 1247, 1276), Gloucester—only Bristol (1221, 1248), Kent (1227, 1241, 1255), Norfolk (1250, 1257, 1268–69), Oxford (1241, 1247, 1261), Warwick (1221–22, 1232, 1247) and London (1244, 1276). For the methodological difficulties posed by this sample, see Given, *Society and Homicide*, chapter 1.

38. There was also a high rate for dropped charges in other crimes. J. B. Given found 48.3 percent of appeals dropped in homicide cases. Given, *Society and Homicide*, p. 98.

39. Kent, J. I. 1/358, 27 (1227) and G. H. Fowler, ed., *Calendar of the Roll of Justices on Eyre, 1247*, Bedfordshire Historical Society, vol. 21 (1939), p. 177, no. 740. The last case appears unusual, because despite the marriage, the jurors convicted the accused and ordered him to be guarded.

40. Stenton, *Pleas Before the King*, vol. 68, p. 395.

41. D. M. Stenton, ed., *The Earliest Lincolnshire Assize Rolls, 1202–1209*, Lincoln Record Society, vol. 22 (London, 1934), no. 916.

42. K. E. Bayley, ed., "Two Thirteenth-Century Assize Rolls for the County of Durham," *Miscellanea*, II, Surtees Society, vol. 127, no. 335. See also C. T. Clay, ed., *Three Yorkshire Assize Rolls for the Reigns of King John and King Henry III*, Yorkshire Archeological Society, vol. 44, p. 40; also printed in Stenton, *Pleas Before the King, 1202*, IV, vol. 84, no. 3491, where the plaintiff received twenty shillings.

43. For a curious case involving land, see Kent J. I. 1/359, 35d.

44. Meekings, *Crown Pleas*, p. 70.

45. Sayles, *Select Cases*, vol. 55, no. 75.

46. E. H. Chadwych-Healey, ed., *Somersetshire Pleas (Civil and Criminal) from the Rolls of the Itinerant Justices, Close of Twelfth Century—41 Henry III,* Somerset Record Society, vol. 11 (1897), no. 794; D. M. Stenton, ed., *Rolls of the Justices in Eyre for Gloucestershire, Warwickshire, and Shropshire (1221–2),* Selden Society 59 (London, 1940), no. 858; Maitland, *County of Gloucester, 1221,* no. 313.

47. Pollock and Maitland, *History of English Law,* vol. 1, p. 477.

48. The words with which the courts decreed outlawry were, "Let him bear the wolf's head" *(Caput gerat lupinum);* Pollock and Maitland, *History of English Law,* p. 467; Bracton, f. 125b; F. W. Maitland, ed., *Select Pleas of the Crown,* Selden Society, vol. 1 (London, 1888), no. 47; *Year Book 20–21 Edward I,* Rolls Series, p. 237.

49. Because outlaws do not generally appear on later rolls, it is extremely difficult to determine where they settled—whether they took up residence in towns or small villages in England or whether they left the country.

50. For forms of the oath, see Bracton, f. 136; Britton, p. 54; *Fleta,* bk. 1, c. 29; Whittaker, *Mirror of Justices,* p. 34; *Abjuratio et Juramentum Latronum* in *Statutes of the Realm,* vol. 1 (London, 1810), p. 250. For a summary see R. F. Hunnisett, *The Medieval Coroner* (Cambridge, England, 1961), p. 45.

51. Hunnisett, *The Medieval Coroner,* p. 49. See also A. Reville, "L'Abjuratio Regni," *Revue Historique,* L (1892), pp. 26–27.

52. Norfolk J.I. 1/569a, 4 (1268–69). Two men fled to sanctuary. Jurors say that one raped the woman and the other helped.

53. Norfolk J.I. 1/565, 28d (1250) and D. M. Stenton, ed., *Rolls of the Justices in Eyre, Being the Rolls of Pleas and Assizes for Gloucestershire, Warwickshire, and Staffordshire, 1221–2,* Selden Society, vol. 59 (London, 1940), no. 858, p. 776.

54. Norfolk J.I. 1/565, 13d.

55. See Given, *Society and Homicide,* p. 92. The exact figure is 8.2 percent.

56. Ibid. Of 3,492 accused, 247 (7.1 percent) were found guilty and executed; 38 (1.1 percent) clerics were found guilty also and released to the ordinary.

57. With the process of indictment, communal accusation has been added to private accusation. The jury of presentment had Anglo-Saxon origins, but its use as a routine process began with the Assize of Clarendon in 1166. From that point, it slowly grew in popularity. See N. D. Hurnard, "The Jury of Presentment and the Assize of Clarendon," *English Historical Review,* vol. 56 (1941), pp. 347–410; A. Harding, *The Law Courts of Medieval England* (London, 1973), p. 40, and T. F. T. Plucknett, *A Concise History of the Common Law* (London, 1948), p. 404.
Actions of trespass also increased during the thirteenth century. Inci-

dents which in the 1240s served as grounds for appeals of felony had by the later part of the century come to serve more and more as cause for actions of trespass. Meekings, *Crown Pleas*, p. 83. The popularity of actions of trespass is reflected in the growing percentage of cases brought before the King's bench. In Michaelmas of 1273, 58 percent of the cases were those of trespass; in Trinity of 1290, 67 percent; and in Trinity of 1307, 77 percent. Sayles, *Select Cases*, vol. 57, pp. cxii–cxiii.

UNDER GREAT TEMPTATIONS HERE: WOMEN AND DIVORCE LAW IN PURITAN MASSACHUSETTS

D. Kelly Weisberg

One of the most rapidly developing areas of women's studies is the subject of women and the law. This area of study first began to attract considerable attention in the mid-1960s. Following the passage of Title VII of the Civil Rights Act of 1964,[1] the critical topic of discussion was discrimination in employment.[2] Kanowitz later broadened the focus of attention to include discrimination against the single and married woman in such areas as property rights, family law and criminal law.[3] The past several years have witnessed the publication of three major texts on women and the law.[4] Much of the prior research has been written by members of the legal profession. Comparatively little research has been contributed to the field by either historians or sociologists.[5] Perhaps this fact explains the absence of research that examines specific legal problems concerning women in their historical context or that inquires into the social conditions influencing the formulation or evolution of a particular body of law affecting women.[6]

This paper represents an exploratory study of the social conditions affecting women in Puritan Massachusetts from the years 1639 to 1692 and the influence of these social conditions on the formulation of American divorce law. Although the subject matter on divorce law in America is voluminous, locating the problem

Reprinted from *Feminist Studies*, vol. 2, no. 2/3 (1975): 183–194, with minor revisions, by permission of the publisher, *Feminist Studies*, Inc., c/o Women's Studies Program, University of Maryland, College Park, Md. Copyright © 1975 by *Feminist Studies*, Inc.

within this specific historical context proves difficult. Original material concerning divorce in Massachusetts during the period of the first charter may be found in the records of the Court of Assistants—the only primary sources available pertaining to this period. Grounds for divorce and the types of dissolutions are not defined by statutes, but rather must be sought in the cases themselves. However, the records of these early courts are sketchy, ambiguous, inconsistent and contain large gaps. Adding to the difficulties of the search is the fact that there is no title or index listing of "Divorce" in the early editions of these records (a fact which shows that divorce policy was indeed in its incipient stages of formulation).[7]

Regrettably, there is a lack of secondary sources that deal in depth with divorce records in this period of Massachusetts history. Howard's compilation is perhaps the most comprehensive.[8] Howard searched the original material and compiled a list of divorce petitions for the years 1639–1692, revealing the date, facts, grounds, court, and decree of each divorce action. From this compendium emerged the fact that divorce was available to women in Massachusetts in this early period.

Puritan Massachusetts provides an ideal laboratory for the study of the relationship between social conditions and the formulation of divorce law. In fact, the roots of American divorce law are to be found in the colonial period in New England. At the time of the colonists' arrival in the Massachusetts Bay Colony in 1630 there existed in England virtually no way to sever the marital tie.[9] Marriage was held to be indissoluble; that is, marriage was a sacrament and what God had joined, no man could cast asunder.

In contrast, early English law had granted women some rights in this regard. Before the Norman Conquest English law specified that "if she [the wife] wish to go away with her child, let her have half the property. If the husband wish to have them, (let her portion be) as one child. . . ."[10] However, with the establishment of feudalism, women were deprived of this and other legal rights. "Loss of legal status, disability and incapacity as to legal rights, subjugation to marriage rights of the lord, theological questioning as to whether or not she could have a soul, these were the afflictions visited upon wives and women by feudalism and the church."[11] Absolute divorce (*a vinculo matrimonii*, from the bonds of marriage), which released the parties from their matrimonial obligations and permitted remarriage, was not readily available to women or men in England until the Matrimonial Causes Act was passed in 1857, providing for the introduction of judicial divorce on the ground of adultery.[12] Prior to that time marriage could be terminated only by death, annulment, or by act of Parliament. Annulments, declaring in effect that a marriage never existed, could be obtained in ecclesiastical courts on the ground of impediments existing at the time of marriage. Such impediments consisted of precontract (prior espousal to another before marriage) or prohibited degrees of consanguinity and affinity. Such annulments, however, were primarily available to members of the upper classes and to "disgruntled husbands."[13]

Divorce by act of Parliament provided another means of dissolving a marriage. Henry VIII furnishes the most noteworthy example of parliamentary divorce. During the reign of Elizabeth, however, remarriage after parliamentary divorce was forbidden. It was not until 1688 that remarriage was permitted following a parliamentary divorce. Other problems, in addition to the issue of remarriage, were inherent in the process of obtaining this type of divorce. First, parliamentary divorces were granted only rarely. Secondly, because of the tremendous costs involved, ranging from £600 to £1000, such divorces were available only to the upper classes. (As Mueller notes, the average income in England in 1688 was £2,800 for lords, while that of shopkeepers and tradesmen was £45 and that of laborers £15.) Finally, not only were parliamentary divorces rarely granted and costly, but they were generally granted only to men. In the entire history of parliamentary divorce in England before 1857, only four parliamentary divorces were granted to female petitioners.[14]

Another possible legal means for releasing parties from marital bonds in England was divorce *a mensa et thoro* (from bed and board). Such a divorce, also granted by ecclesiastical courts in instances of gross misconduct of a spouse such as adultery and cruelty, suspended the requirement of cohabitation and separated the parties; it did not permit remarriage. Such separations were also difficult to obtain[15] and the costs, although more in reach of the middle classes,[16] were similarly prohibitive. Although these separations were theoretically available to both women and men, it appears that more men than women may have availed themselves of this legal remedy.[17] Thus, at the time the first colonists crossed the Atlantic Ocean, divorce in the mother country was a rarely granted privilege accorded primarily to the upper classes and generally only to men.

The situation in the Massachusetts Bay Colony, however, reveals some startling departures from English divorce policy. When Massachusetts adopted many features of the common law of England, it did not adopt ecclesiastical law pertaining to marriage and divorce. The concept of marriage in the colony owed much to the Reformation view of marriage as a civil contract based on the mutual consent of both parties, as opposed to the prevailing doctrine of the Anglican church that marriage was a sacrament lying within the jurisdiction of ecclesiastical courts.[18] Marriage and divorce became civil matters. Within two decades after the colonists' arrival at Massachusetts Bay, the colonial Court of Assistants was officially empowered to hear and determine all causes of divorce.[19]

Between the years 1639 and 1692, Massachusetts colonial courts issued only absolute *a vinculo* decrees in the forty actions for divorce which have been discovered.[20] As Howard notes: "It is significant that during the seventeenth century not a single clear case of divorce from bed and board (*a mensa et thoro*) has been discovered in any of the Massachusetts records."[21]

Third and most significant, divorces were more frequently granted to women than to men in this period. The records for this period reveal that the number of women who brought actions for divorce ("petitions") was almost four times greater than the number of men and the women were successful in the majority of their petitions.[22]

Thus, while the doctrine of marital indissolubility was operative in the mother country, it was no longer adhered to in Massachusetts Bay Colony. Not only were marital bonds dissoluble, but women were granted such marital dissolutions more frequently than men.

In order to understand the nature of the social conditions which contributed to the emergence of a new divorce policy in the New World, it is helpful to examine the social organization of colonial society. The migration to New England, unlike that to Virginia and the southern colonies, was one of families. Haskins maintains that the majority of the emigrants bound for the Massachusetts Bay Colony were members of large family groups, which encompassed servants and apprentices as well as parents, children and close relatives.[23]

In the Puritan view, the family was at the foundation of both religion and government. That is, the assumption under which such Puritan leaders as John Winthrop acted was that the state resulted from "many familyes subjecting themselves to rulers and law."[24] The family was the basic social unit of the Massachusetts Bay Colony. It was also the primary unit of social control. The family was responsible for holding a "watchfulle eye" over the conduct of every individual and for enforcing the laws of God. The Puritans believed that religion, morality, obedience to the laws, deference to authority, and good conduct originated in the home. The chief problem for the state, according to Morgan, was to see that family governors did their duty.[25] So important was the family as a source of social control that the earliest laws enacted in the colony (in the first year of settlement) attempted to organize all individuals under family government and ordered the servants of the Massachusetts Bay Company into artificial families (with the stipulation that the "cheife in the familie bee grounded in religion").[26] Later stipulations prescribed strict punishment for any threat to familial authority—prescribing the death penalty for disobedient children and servants.

In addition, legislation in 1679 provided for the establishment of public officers (tithingmen) to root out disorders in families under their charge and to report on negligent heads of families. The state, as a general principle, took action against family governors who were deemed unfit, in some cases taking children and servants away to place them with a family head who was more worthy.

It goes almost without saying that when the Puritans spoke of these "cheifes of familyes," they were referring to men. The social order was based on the Biblical order—the world was created for man, man was created for God. Such writers of the period as John Eliot described how "the Child is implicitely comprehended in the Fathers Covenant, the Wife is explicitely comprehended in her Husbands."[27]

In Puritan ideology, woman was clearly subordinate to man. The proper conduct of a wife consisted of submission to her husband's instructions and commands. He was the head of the family and she owed him obedience. Woman was the weaker vessel in both body and mind. Intellectual pursuits were not deemed appropriate for members of the female sex. When the wife of the governor of a neighboring state went insane, Governor Winthrop attributed the reason to the time she spent in reading and writing: "For if she had attended her household affairs, and such things as belong to women, and not gone out of her way and calling to meddle in such things as are proper for men, whose minds are stronger, etc., she had kept her wits and might have improved them usefully and honorably in the place God had set her."[28] Considering that Puritan ideology conferred such an inferior status upon women, it is all the more remarkable that divorce law in the new country was so favorable to women. Such a development was possible because of a peculiar set of conditions—one of which was Puritan dependence on the family as an agency of social control.

In most divorce petitions brought by women, the cause of the petition was some breach of their husband's familial duties. The cause most frequently cited by women in divorce petitions was desertion. Bigamy, adultery and failure to provide were the next most frequently cited grounds. Adultery *alone* was not sufficient ground for a woman to be granted a divorce, although it was sufficient for a man to secure a divorce. In order for women to be successful in adultery petitions, the act had to be compounded by desertion, cruelty, or failure to provide. Divorce cases successfully brought by women all reveal the husband to have had an unfit character for family government. Undoubtedly, the court responded favorably to women's petitions, influenced by the Puritan concern with maintaining the family as an agent of social control. By granting a woman a divorce and thereby permitting her to remarry a more fit family head, she would become a member of a better family government. And, since the "guilty" party of the divorce was not permitted to remarry, the negligent male was out of circulation (stigmatized and often sent out of the colony) and hence no longer a threat to the community's basis of social control.

A factor which indirectly contributed to easier access to divorce for women was the Puritan attitude toward deviance. Erikson notes that few deviants could slip through the Puritan network without attracting public attention.[29] Colonial courts dealt not only with what we term "crimes," but with many kinds of deviant behavior—persons who drank too much, were without the use of their reason, lived a scandalous life, dressed in inappropriate clothes, or let their hair grow too long, who swore, bragged, or talked too much, disobeyed their parents or engaged in frivolous games. Thus, individual dereliction of family duties was automatically considered deviant behavior and received due attention by colonial courts.[30]

The Puritan attitude toward single women and men undoubtedly also affected the granting of divorce. The Puritans held that single persons (whether unmarried, or married and temporarily living apart from their spouse) were subject to sin and iniquity— "the companions and consequences of a solitary life."[31] Legislation of the New England colonies was replete with regulations governing the conduct of single persons. Unmarried men were not permitted to dine and lodge alone, and instead were ordered to live with other families. In some cases, they were taxed for their solitary living. Single women too, or wives whose husbands were away were similarly subject to legislation. They were prohibited from entertaining lodgers or overnight guests lest they give "the appearance of sin."[32]

Occasionally, married couples were temporarily separated, as when the husband preceded the wife to the new continent with the intention of sending for her after he was well established. In other cases, wives returned to England, discouraged by the hardships they suffered in New England. Occasionally too, husbands returned to England on mercantile ventures. The Puritans believed that these individuals too were shadowed by sin and iniquity. An act of the Massachusetts general court is illustrative of the Puritan concern with such situations and the sanctions subsequently imposed:

> Whereas divers persons both men and woemen living within this Jurisdiction whose Wives, and Husbands are in England, or elsewhere, by means wherof they live under greet temptations heer, and some of them committing lewdnes and filthines heer among us, others make love to woemen, and attempt Marriage, and some have attained it; and some of them live under suspicion of uncleannes, and all to the great dishonour of God, reproach of Religion, Commonwealth and Churches, it is therfore ordered by this Court and Authoritie therof (for the prevention of all such future evils)

That all such married persons as aforesaid shall repair to their said relations by the first opportunitie of shipping upon the pain, or penaltie of twenty pounds. . . .[33]

The Puritan concern with the temptations afflicting single people may be seen as well underlying the courts' decisions to grant women divorce in cases of desertion. It is likely that more husbands than wives were guilty of desertion, as it was easier for men to travel, having greater access to funds (married women were subject to male management of their property) and greater freedom of movement. In Puritan eyes, a husband's desertion resulted in the woman's being subject to considerable temptation. In accordance with Biblical antecedents of Puritan ideology, woman was the weaker vessel in both body and mind. It was thought that woman was less able to resist temptation (although men were certainly no paragons of virtue in Puritan eyes). Very likely, the courts were predisposed to grant divorces in order to remove women from the path of temptation and free them to remarry. Such women would no longer pose a threat to the stability of other households.

Bigamy presented another troublesome problem for the colonists. In the course of one divorce action in Plymouth colony, it was discovered that the husband had three other wives—one in Boston, one in Barbados, and one in England.[34] Calhoun maintained that it was an exceedingly common offense for an immigrant who had left a spouse in England to attempt a new alliance in the colonies.[35] As mentioned above, husbands occasionally traveled to the New World alone with the intention of sending later for their wives in England. However, the trip across the Atlantic was costly and it took time for a man to get settled (to build a house, clear land, and plant crops) and provide for the necessary funds. Consequently, men often courted women in the new continent and in order to do so without public censure, masqueraded as single. Some married men may never have intended to send for their wives. Men who could not divorce their wives in England may have deserted them with plans of subsequent remarriage in the colonies.[36] Given the state of colonial society (a wilderness where it took time for news to travel) and the vast distances between England and the colonies, bigamy was easily concealed. When it was discovered, however, it provided immediate grounds for terminating a marriage. Divorce in cases of bigamy may be seen as once again serving to strengthen the family as an agent of social control. The husband was publicly recognized as an unfit family governor and was put out of circulation—often ordered to leave the colony. (Apparently, it mattered little that the man may have continued in his career of bigamy, as long as it was not within the colony's boundaries.) An unfit family head thus removed from his position of responsibility no longer posed a potential threat to the community, and the wife was free to join a better family government through remarriage.

Still another factor which may have influenced the granting of divorce to women was the concern with public burdens draining the state coffers. Puritan ideology held that it was the state's duty to provide assistance to those who could not help themselves. Women whose husbands had deserted them fell in this category. Without the benefit of a husband to support them and their children, women were at the mercy of the community.[37] The concern with this issue of public welfare was reflected in various court decisions of the time, such as the following: "William Flint beeing a married man haveing gotten a slutt with child is fined 20 lb whereof 10 lb is left to the Toune of Salem to bring up the child with, and the other ten pound to the Publique, and to lye in Prison till hae pay it, or give security."[38] The Puritans took various measures to prevent this potential burden to the state in cases of desertion. Legislation was passed which required deserting husbands to return to their wives and to support them, and to put up sureties lest their families become public charges. In addition, by the end of the 1600s in Massachusetts, laws were passed which enabled spouses to remarry after a three-year absence of their mates who had gone aboard ship and were never heard from again.[39]

Probably the most influential factor in the formation of liberal divorce policy was the combined scarcity and value of women in Puritan Massachusetts. Most of the women who comprised part of the first migrations to the new continent were already situated in families with husbands and children. The number of women in the New World was further reduced by illness. Women, like men, suffered from the multitude of diseases and starvation afflicting the colonists. They were also subject to another danger—childbirth—which further decimated their numbers. Demos suggests that the seven-year shorter life expectancy of colonial women reflected the hazards of childbirth and adds that twenty percent of the deaths of adult women resulted from causes connected to childbirth.[40] A similar scarcity of women was also the plight of the southern settlements. These settlements resolved the dilemma by importing and selling women from England. As Miller describes:

> A group of stockholders of the Virginia Company formed a subsidiary company whose purpose was to supply the planters with wives. In 1620, ninety young women, certified as "pure and spotless," were put up at auction for 120 pounds of tobacco a head. . . . In 1621, when 38 additional women arrived, the price was raised to 150 pounds of tobacco per head. All told, 140 marriageable women were sent to Virginia and none lacked for husbands. Supplying women to the colonists was the only financially rewarding enterprise undertaken during the existence of the Virginia Company.[41]

Why Massachusetts did not choose this solution to the problem is open to speculation. It may be hypothesized that the majority of the Massachusetts settlers constituted members of a higher social class (Virginia had been settled primarily by individual adventurers, convicts and slaves) and hence were reluctant to acquire wives in this manner. Whatever the reason, the fact remained that women were not in plentiful supply in the Massachusetts Bay Colony in these early decades.[42] Although the supply of marriageable women was low, the demand remained quite high. Women were valuable partners in the New World. The New England home was a nearly self-sufficient unit. A wife was a necessity in the management of household tasks. Moreover, women were valuable in their role as childbearers.

The importance of children in colonial America cannot be overestimated. Calhoun notes that families of ten and twelve children were common and families of twenty or twenty-five children were "not rare enough to call forth expression of wonder."[43] As Miller further explains: "In colonial America, large families were the rule not because there was no effective method of birth control, but because the abundance of land and the scarcity of labor made children a valuable asset. Not only did Americans feel they could afford to have numerous children: they felt that they could *not* afford not to have them."[44] In addition, since the infant mortality rate was high, women were essential in order constantly to renew the labor supply.

Women were so scarce and such a valuable asset that they were usually married before getting far into their twenties, some as early as sixteen. Widows were courted practically at their husband's funeral. As Howard describes: "Thus Judge Sewall went home with Widow Denison from her husband's funeral and 'prayed God to keep house' with her."[45] It is extremely likely that this shortage of women influenced the granting of divorce to women. In freeing women from marriages that were undesirable to them, divorce would result in increasing the number of available marriageable women in the colony. Divorce thus may have served as a practical solution to a simple problem of supply and demand.

I do not intend to convey the impression that colonial courts willingly and frequently granted divorce in Puritan New England. In fact, colonial courts took considerable pains to deal with domestic tensions before they reached the divorce stage. Courts interfered in several cases to order separated couples to "repair" to their spouses. Husbands and wives were often reproved for "living in contention one with the other and admonished to live otherwise."[46] Occasionally too, spouses were whipped and fined for acts contributing to marital discord. The court's chief aim in domestic affairs was to restore the family to an acceptable state of tranquility. Yet, significantly, when this objective was not possible, the courts of the Massachusetts Bay Colony did not hesitate to grant divorces.

It is without question that the legal code which governed colonial Massachusetts was heavily indebted to the legal tradition of the mother country. However, at a time when English women were locked into their marital vows for life, women in the Massachusetts Bay Colony enjoyed an enviable legal advantage. Within only a few decades after their arrival, the women of the Bay Colony had access to divorce—a legal status which their English contemporaries would not obtain for another two hundred years. This development can only be attributed to the peculiar social conditions which characterized this colonial settlement—the Puritan dependence on the family as a primary agent of social control, the Puritan concern with sin and the temptation of married women separated from their husbands, the community concern with draining the public coffers, and the overall scarcity and importance of women in the Massachusetts Bay Colony.

NOTES

1. 42 U.S.C. §2000e to e-15 (1970), *as amended* by Equal Employment Opportunity Act of 1972, Pub. L. No. 92–261, §2, 86 Stat. 103, codified at 42 U.S.C. §§2000e to e–17 (Supp. IV 1980).

2. See, for example, Pauli Murray and Mary Eastwood, "Jane Crow and the Law: Sex Discrimination and Title VII," 34 *George Washington Law Review* 232 (1965); Robert S. Miller, "Sex Discrimination and Title VII of the Civil Rights Act of 1964," 51 *Minnesota Law Review* 877 (1967); Note, "Classification on the Basis of Sex and the 1964 Civil Rights Act," 50 *Iowa Law Review* 778 (1965); James Oldham, "Sex Discrimination and State Protective Laws, 44 *Denver Law Review* 344 (1967).

3. Leo Kanowitz, *Women and the Law: The Unfinished Revolution* (Albuquerque: University of New Mexico Press, 1969).

4. Herma H. Kay, *Sex-Based Discrimination: Text, Cases and Materials* (St. Paul: West Publishing Co., 2nd ed. 1981); Leo Kanowitz, *Sex Roles in Law and Society: Cases and Materials* (Albuquerque: University of New Mexico Press, 1973); Barbara Babcock, Ann Freedman, Eleanor H. Norton and Susan D. Ross, *Sex Discrimination and the Law: Causes and Remedies* (Boston: Little, Brown & Co., 1975).

5. The only exception is research on women and crime. For an annotated bibliography of this literature, see David M. Horton and Marjorie Kravitz, *The Female Offender: A Selected Bibliography* (Washington, D.C., U.S. Department of Justice, 1979).

6. This void in the literature may not be at all surprising considering that few studies in the related field of sociology of law have dealt at any length with the relationship between particular laws and the social setting in which those laws emerge. But see Jerome Hall, *Theft, Law and Society* (Indianapolis: Bobbs-Merrill, 1939), and William J. Chambliss, "A Sociological Analysis of the Law of Vagrancy," 12 *Social Problems* 67 (Summer 1964). It must be acknowledged that English historiography is far more advanced in this regard. For a brief discussion of the reasons contributing to this state of American legal history, see Lawrence M. Friedman, *A History of American Law* (New York: Simon and Schuster, 1973), pp. 9–10.

7. For the early records of the Court of Assistants for the years 1641–1644, see William H. Whitmore, ed., *A Biographical Sketch of the Laws of the Massachusetts Colony from 1630 to 1686 in which are Included the Body of Liberties of 1641 and the Records of the Court of Assistants 1641–44* (Boston: Rockwell & Churchill, City Printers, 1890).

8. George E. Howard, *A History of Matrimonial Institutions* (Chicago: University of Chicago Press, 1904), II, 333. Further examination of the early colonial records might reveal additional cases. Such a search would be valuable especially in terms of shedding light on pleading procedure, rules of evidence, questions of jurisdiction and appellate procedures of early divorce cases.

9. English annulments declared that a marriage never existed and divorce *a mensa et thoro* merely constituted a separation. Neither fit the concept of divorce in its legal sense as we know it today, as a termination of marriage. Only the rarely granted parliamentary divorces accomplished this.

10. Cited in Henry H. Foster, Jr., "Common Law Divorce," 46 *Minnesota Law Review* 50 (1961).

11. Ibid.

12. Joseph W. Madden, *Handbook of the Law of Persons and Domestic Relations* (St. Paul: West Publishing Co., 1931), p. 256.

13. Foster, "Common Law Divorce," p. 51.

14. Gerhard O. W. Mueller, "Inquiry Into the State of a Divorceless Society: Domestic Relations Law and Morals in England From 1660 to 1857," 18 *University of Pittsburgh Law Review* 545, 551 (1975).

15. Madden, *Handbook,* p. 157. "It was necessary to establish by the strictest proof that not only the offense complained of had been committed, but that the parties were not colluding to escape their marital obligations, that the complaining party was free from guilt, and that the offense had not been condoned. Hence a divorce *a mensa et thoro* could not be had solely upon the confessions of the parties themselves, nor if collusion, connivance, condonation, or recrimination could be proved." Ibid.

16. Mueller, "State of Divorceless Society," p. 553.

17. Foster notes the frequency with which noblemen sought divorces *a mensa et thoro* and also the frequency with which they violated the prohibition against remarriage, "Common Law Divorce," p. 52.

18. Richard B. Morris, *Studies in the History of American Law* (New York: Columbia University Press, 1930), p. 126.

19. See Whitmore, *Laws of the Massachusetts Colony,* p. 14.

20. As recorded by Howard, *Matrimonial Institutions,* p. 333.

21. Ibid., p. 339.

22. Based on the author's analysis of Howard's data. See Howard, *Matrimonial Institutions,* especially pp. 330–40.

23. George L. Haskins, *Law and Authority in Early Massachusetts: A Study of Tradition and Design* (New York: Macmillan Co., 1960), p. 79.

24. Edmund S. Morgan, *The Puritan Family: Religion and Domestic Relations in Seventeenth Century New England* (New York: Harper & Row, 1971), p. 144.

25. Ibid., p. 143.

26. Ibid., p. 144.

27. As quoted in Morgan, ibid.

28. As quoted in Morgan, p. 44. Erikson suggests that the reason the colony elders were so irritated with Anne Hutchinson was because she was a woman and because she possessed keen intelligence. Similarly deviating from the norm, the girls who were first accused of witchcraft in Massachusetts attracted public attention because they "began to live in a state of high tension and shared secrets with one another which were hardly becoming to quiet Puritan maidens." Kai T. Erikson, *Wayward Puritans: A Study in the Sociology of Deviance* (New York: John Wiley & Sons, 1965), p. 441.

29. Erikson, *Wayward Puritans,* p. 170.

30. Powers notes another factor, finding that New Englanders were a litigious people, attributable to "the readiness with which one could file a suit without incurring lawyers' fees or appeal a case without elaborate briefs." Edwin Powers, *Crime and Punishment in Early Massachusetts, 1620–1692: A Documentary History* (Boston: Beacon Press, 1966), p. 437.

31. Morgan, *Puritan Family,* p. 145.

32. John C. Miller, *The First Frontier: Life in Colonial America* (New York: Dell Publishing Co., 1966), p. 59.

33. Cited in Whitmore, *Laws of the Massachusetts Colony,* p. 37.

34. John Demos, *A Little Commonwealth: Family Life in Plymouth Colony* (New York: Oxford University Press, 1970), p. 93.

35. Arthur W. Calhoun, *A Social History of the American Family: Colonial Period,* vol. 1 (New York: Barnes & Noble Publishers, University Paperbacks, 1945), p. 141.

36. See the discussion on "self-divorce" in Mueller, "State of Divorceless Society," pp. 563–73.

37. See Demos, *A Little Commonwealth,* on the function of the Puritan family as a welfare institution, especially p. 184. Mueller notes that England was also concerned with acts of desertion for the reason of the burden imposed on the community's poor relief funds. "To state the whole in a simpler manner: society was bothered about spousal walk outs only when it was hurt financially," Mueller, "State of Divorceless Society," p. 572.

38. Cited in Whitmore, *Laws of the Massachusetts Colony,* p. 285.

39. Howard, *Matrimonial Institutions,* p. 340.

40. Demos, *A Little Commonwealth,* p. 66. Concerning the surplus of young single men, Flaherty notes that the Pilgrims in 1620 ordered "all single men that had no wives to join with some family as they thought fit, that so we might build fewer houses." David Flaherty, *Privacy in Colonial New England* (Charlottesville: University Press of Virginia, 1972), p. 176.

41. Miller, *First Frontier,* p. 28.

42. The scarcity may have lessened in later decades if Massachusetts Bay's demographic trends followed those of Plymouth Colony. Demos notes for Plymouth Colony at the end of the century spinsters became somewhat more common as demographic trends worked to create a surplus of females in some of the older towns. Demos, *A Little Commonwealth,* p. 77.

43. Calhoun, *A Social History,* p. 87.
44. Miller, *First Frontier,* p. 209.
45. Howard, *Matrimonial Institutions,* p. 157. Widows were especially valued because of their dower rights.
46. Cited in Demos, *A Little Commonwealth,* p. 93.

THE LAW OF HUSBAND AND WIFE IN NINETEENTH-CENTURY AMERICA: CHANGING VIEWS OF DIVORCE

Michael S. Hindus and Lynne E. Withey

The increasing divorce rates of the late nineteenth and early twentieth centuries, and the debate which raged over the meaning of that increase, are well known to historians.[1] However, this increase occurred independently of any significant change in divorce law. The legal changes, which made it easier to obtain a divorce and provided the necessary basis for a rising divorce rate, occurred decades earlier between the end of the Revolution and the 1850s. These changes, which liberalized both the grounds for divorce and divorce procedures, were not prompted by a major change in attitudes about marriage and divorce. Nor were they intended to encourage the dissolution of marriage. On the contrary, the inviolability of the marriage bond and the need to discourage easy divorce continued to be major concerns of the courts. Liberalization of divorce laws seems to have been prompted by a gradual change in the definition of conditions which made marriage intolerable, and by increased efforts to insure justice for mistreated husbands and wives. Although there is little evidence to suggest that legal changes were accompanied by an increasing incidence of divorce during the antebellum period, the level had undoubtedly risen compared with the colonial years. However, towards the end of the nineteenth century, when attitudes about marriage changed and more people sought divorces, the liberalized laws of the early nineteenth century were put to uses that had not been envisioned by the lawmakers responsible for them.

A fundamental belief in the sanctity of marriage and family bul-

Based on a paper presented at the Annual Meeting of the American Society for Legal History, Chicago, Illinois, October 1978.

warked the divorce laws of the early nineteenth century. This was tempered only by the realization that there were some evils even greater than divorce—notably adultery and exceptionally cruel treatment of either spouse. A related belief, almost as powerful, was the view of women as fragile and helpless, requiring the protection of husbands. If a husband withdrew his protection by desertion or cruel treatment, it was the court's role to interfere and insure protection for the injured wife. Much of the change in divorce law involved facilitating divorce for cruelty and desertion, and reflected a growing concern about the protection of women. Such concern was hardly restricted to law; the antebellum years saw the general development of attitudes about women as delicate and helpless, which hardened into a nearly unshakeable ideology by the Civil War. In theory, husbands as well as wives could obtain divorce for cruelty and desertion, but most cases were initiated by women. The motives behind the laws seem to be the protection of women.

In Virginia, for example, almost all the men who petitioned the legislature for divorce before 1847 named adultery or previous sexual incontinence as grounds, while women invariably sued for cruelty or desertion—never for adultery.[2] In South Carolina, which did not allow divorce at all but did grant separate maintenance, these motives were clear—separate maintenance was a remedy for women only, and was justified with much rhetoric about female helplessness. The remedy prescribed, however, did not always work.

One South Carolina woman endured life with a cruel husband until his death and then tried to collect alimony from his estate. Her request was denied with the explanation that she should have sued during his lifetime. She had not done so because she feared violence from her husband against her male relatives and friends; when she had once attempted such a suit, he challenged her attorney to a duel.[3]

Marriage was sacred not only for moral reasons, but also because it was a contract, equally sacred to the nineteenth-century legal mind. To a certain extent, marriage could be dissolved for the same reasons that contracts could be broken—fraud and insanity, for example. However, the moral and legal views of marriage sometimes conflicted, and marriage came to be viewed as a special kind of contract, one which could not be broken as easily as others. This view underscored the belief that marriages should be dissolved only in extraordinary circumstances. This paper is a preliminary inquiry into changes in divorce law before 1870. It considers these changes within the context of three states: (1) Massachusetts as a legally innovative northern state, (2) Virginia as a representative southern state, and (3) South Carolina as the only state not permitting divorce. Despite their differences, all states except South Carolina had statutorily established grounds for divorce and procedures for obtaining them. And in all these states, the courts interpreted those statutes as narrowly as possible as a matter of policy.[4] In South Carolina, where no divorce statutes existed, the courts held religiously to the viewpoint that the absence of statutes prevented them from dissolving marriages under any circumstances. South Carolina courts, however, did grant separate maintenance, and the statutory silence forced the courts to establish the conditions under which separate maintenance would be permitted. In Massachusetts and Virginia, the courts confined their role to interpreting the meaning of statutory changes. In Massachusetts and South Carolina the analogy between marriage and contract was also a source of some discussion in determining grounds for divorce or alimony.

The state statutes varied considerably on the specific grounds and procedures for divorce. There was general agreement, however, on the exceptional nature of divorce and on the general conditions under which it might be granted. Throughout the nineteenth century, most states granted divorce for adultery, desertion, cruelty, and criminal conviction only. They distinguished between these causes and another set of conditions which were grounds for annulment: impotence, insanity, consanguinity, affinity, and bigamy.[5] Most states also distinguished between divorce from the bonds of matrimony (a vinculo), and divorce from bed and board (a mensa et thoro), which did not allow the parties to remarry. In the early nineteenth century, the former was usually granted only for adultery.

Similarity existed among the states also in their general trend toward liberalizing the grounds for divorce and toward granting more divorces a vinculo. In Massachusetts, for example, divorce from bed and board was eliminated by statute in 1870.[6] In addition, divorces became easier to obtain in a procedural sense. In states such as Virginia, where divorces were granted only by legislative action at the beginning of the century, there was a trend toward shifting more responsibility to the courts. Differences among the states were matters of detail and procedure; the trend toward limited liberalization of divorce—while maintaining the official view of divorce as a social evil which could be justified only in exceptional circumstances—occurred throughout the country.

Both Massachusetts and Virginia liberalized their divorce laws between the 1820s and 1870s. However, the liberalization in Virginia started from a more conservative position and proceeded more slowly. In the eighteenth century, both states granted divorces only by special act of the legislature, but Massachusetts passed a law in 1785 shifting this responsibility to the Supreme Judicial Court. The Court was permitted to grant divorces from the bonds of matrimony for adultery, impotency, and criminal conviction carrying a prison sentence of seven years or more, and from bed and board for cruelty, desertion, and nonsupport of wife. This statute remained substantially unchanged until 1838.[7] Virginia, however, continued the practice of legislative divorce until 1827, when county courts were given limited jurisdiction to grant annulments and divorces from bed and board for adultery and cruelty. Power to grant divorces *a vinculo* remained in the legislature until 1847, when the courts were authorized to grant such divorces for adultery only. In 1853, the grounds for court-determined divorces *a vinculo* were expanded to include desertion for five years or more and criminal conviction or prostitution prior to the marriage.[8] This was the limit of divorce in Virginia in the period up to 1870; complete divorces remained extremely restricted, and the limited divorce from bed and board was the preferred procedure. Legislative divorces were substantially reduced, but not completely eliminated.

Until 1838, the major difference between divorce in Massachusetts and in Virginia was procedural. Massachusetts residents could obtain divorce by the Supreme Judicial Court, but the grounds for and the distinction between the two types of divorce were similar. In 1838, however, desertion for a period of five years or more was made a cause for divorce *a vinculo*. This was the first time that such a decree could be obtained for action which did not carry a criminal sanction.[9] This statute opened the way for further liberalization of the grounds for divorce. In the 1850s some minor additions were made. The next important change occurred in 1857 when a statute was passed allowing any divorce from bed and board to become a complete divorce after five years. The logical culmination of this trend was the elimination of divorce from bed and board in 1870.[10] Virginia did not take comparable action until the twentieth century.

In Virginia, divorce was so infrequent, and the use of the legislature as a final court of appeal on divorce matters so persistent, that the courts played virtually no role in interpreting divorce law. In Massachusetts, however, as the grounds for divorce were liberalized, the courts found it necessary to rule on the precise meanings of the new statutes. Adultery, always the most compelling cause for divorce, never raised serious problems of interpretation. The courts confined their concern with adultery to insuring that husbands and wives did not collude (by refusing to accept confession as the sole evidence of adultery)[11] and to establishing that an act of adultery once forgiven could not later become grounds for divorce.[12]

Cruelty and desertion, however, posed more difficult problems, especially after they became grounds for divorce *a vinculo.* Early in the nineteenth century, the Massachusetts courts established a narrow definition of cruelty, stating that mere threats of violence, without actual physical cruelty, were insufficient to permit divorce.[13] The courts also distinguished between cruelty and adultery cases on the issue of condonation. A wife who continued to live with her husband despite his cruelty was not considered to have condoned his action and could therefore still sue for divorce; however, a partner who continued to live with his or her spouse after an act of adultery was not so entitled. This distinction was justified by the argument that an abused wife might continue to live with her husband in the hope that his conduct would improve.[14]

Arguments concerning the definition of cruelty were rare after the first decade of the century. The more serious issue was the definition of desertion, which became increasingly broad. Eventually desertion encompassed cruelty, a point which helps to account for the decline in decisions citing cruelty as the primary cause for divorce. *Pidge* v. *Pidge*,[15] in 1841, was the first discussion of the statutory change of 1838 which permitted divorce *a vinculo* after a desertion lasting five years. This case established the narrowest possible definition of desertion under the change in statute. In *Pidge*, the libellant, who had left her husband more than five years earlier because of his extreme cruelty, argued that she had been forced from her home by his actions and that this, therefore, constituted desertion. In rejecting her claim, the court stated that cruelty, desertion, and nonsupport were all grounds for divorce from bed and board; that the new statute had specifically added desertion to the grounds for divorce *a vinculo;* and that therefore it could be assumed that cruelty and nonsupport were intended to remain grounds for divorce from bed and board only.[16] "To hold otherwise," the opinion stated, "would be adding to the provisions of this statute, and opening a door for the greatest latitude in granting divorces."[17] This case provides one of the clearest examples of the courts' extreme reluctance to do anything which indicated judicial creation of law in the area of divorce, and of their continuing commitment to the narrowest possible interpretation of divorce statutes. The dissent in *Pidge* maintained that the wife was just as effectively abandoned in this situation as if her husband had actually left the town.[18] It was too narrow an interpretation of the statute, the dissent argued, to define desertion as a complete removal of one party from the other.[19]

Eventually the dissenting justice's opinion in *Pidge* became law in Massachusetts. The 1857 divorce statute broadened the definition of desertion to allow suits to be filed by an individual forced to leave her/his spouse because of cruelty or nonsupport. This change meant, in effect, that a divorce *a vinculo* could be obtained for cruelty or nonsupport after the parties had been separated for five years. Cruelty and desertion involving separations of less than five years remained grounds for divorce from bed and board, but the same statute also provided that such divorces could be decreed *a vinculo* after five years, so the result ultimately was the same.

Two cases in the 1860s tested the limits of the definition of desertion under the 1857 statute. The court in *McGrath* v. *McGrath*[20] granted a divorce where a wife claimed desertion, even though her husband continued to provide her some financial support. The husband contributed to his wife's support at the instigation of the overseers of the poor, while refusing to resume living with her. The court ruled that this refusal constituted desertion, stating that "There is no more important right of the wife, than that which secures to her in the marriage relation the companionship of her husband and the protection of his home."[21] A husband has a legal obligation to support his wife, the court argued, but provision of such support did not absolve him from other marital obligations.[22] The court in Lea v. Lea [23] decided that a divorce for desertion was improper where it was clear that the separation of husband and wife was voluntary. In Lea, a woman left her husband with his consent. After the statutory five years, he filed for divorce. The husband's attorney argued that desertion did not necessarily imply nonconsent on the part of the abandoned party.[24] Capitalizing on the courts' history of interpreting divorce statutes narrowly, the attorney pointed out that the 1857 statute omitted a clause from earlier laws stating that desertion must be without the consent of the person deserted in order for a divorce to be granted. This omission, he claimed, in effect allowed divorce in cases of desertion by mutual consent.[25] Entering into this battle of semantics, Chief Justice Bigelow stated that the clause had been removed from the later statute because of the provision that a divorce could sometimes be granted to the deserting party, if such desertion had been caused by the cruelty or neglect of the other. In such instances, the desertion was "voluntary," and the wording of the statute had to be changed. The change was not intended, however, to countenance divorces where both parties agreed to the separation.[26]

These two cases continued the longstanding practice of narrowly interpreting the divorce statutes. Despite the general broadening of grounds for divorce, the courts were not prepared to sanction what appeared to be a voluntary agreement to separate. The inclusion of desertion as a cause for divorce a vinculo and the broadened definition of desertion made this narrow interpretation particularly important because it was now easier for a husband and wife to collude to get a divorce. Consequently, the court maintained an anticollusion vigil on desertion just as they had on adultery.

By 1870 it was much easier to obtain a divorce in both Massachusetts and Virginia than it had been fifty years earlier, although Massachusetts had moved much farther in that direction. The basic attitudes underlying divorce law, however, had not changed significantly in either state, and the similarities between the states were more important than the differences.

Divorce continued to be a necessary evil, used only when essential to protect an individual from extreme moral or physical harm. At the beginning of the nineteenth century, divorce from bed and board was the widely accepted compromise measure between upholding the sanctity of marriage and insuring justice for wronged wives and husbands. In an intellectual sense, the limited divorce did not quite break the marriage bond; in a practical sense, it denied remarriage and was therefore a remedy which would be sought only as a last resort. Over the next several decades, legal attitudes gradually moved toward more sympathetic definitions of cruelty and desertion and greater willingness to grant complete divorces. By 1864, Joel Bishop, in his treatise on marriage and divorce law, wrote that divorce from bed and board was dying out in America, and characterized it as an obsolete and unnatural institution.[27] Such changes in attitudes were possible without questioning fundamental beliefs in the sanctity of marriage and the evil of divorce.

South Carolina policy illustrates many widely held views on marriage and divorce carried to their logical conclusion. Despite its prohibition of divorce, South Carolina did recognize some of the same problems that led other states to grant divorces, and made allowances by granting alimony, or separate maintenance. Because of the absence of statutory provisions, the conditions under which alimony was granted were worked out in the equity court. In South Carolina, antebellum attitudes about marriage and divorce are seen in sharp relief, coupled with some interesting exceptions to the prevailing beliefs in other parts of the country. Alimony was granted for cruelty and desertion. In practical terms, there was relatively little difference between South Carolina's provision for alimony and other states' provisions for divorce from bed and board. The only significant difference between the states was that under the South Carolina system, women who received alimony did not regain the contract and property rights of single women.

Virginia courts also occasionally permitted alimony without divorce. As in South Carolina, such cases were determined by equity courts.[28] It was apparently not widely used as a substitute for divorce in Virginia, however. In Massachusetts the issue did not arise until 1868, when a woman petitioned for alimony without divorce because of religious scruples against divorce.[29] The court, after duly noting the South Carolina and Virginia examples, denied her petition on the grounds that she had a legal remedy, and her disinclination to use it did not justify creating a new remedy for her. She might appeal to the legislature for such a remedy, but the court did not have the power to create new law.[30]

The similarity between cases of divorce from bed and board and cases of alimony suggests that even intransigent South Carolina shared the fundamental views of other states concerning the nature of marriage and the circumstances under which it might be dissolved. One might argue, in fact, that the differences between South Carolina and other states were semantic rather than real. In two critical areas, however, South Carolina differed from other states. No distinction was recognized there between divorce and annulment; no court had the power to declare a marriage void, for any reason whatsoever. Additionally, in South Carolina, adultery was not recognized as a cause for alimony, whereas other states treated it as the most compelling reason for divorce.

South Carolina's absolute prohibition on dissolution of marriage was based on a rather contorted reading of its English legal heritage. More than any other state, South Carolina adopted the English legal system without modification. In England, divorce and annulment were the province of ecclesiastical courts. Since such courts did not exist in the United States, and since the state legislature had not expressly granted these powers to any court, South Carolina jurists concluded that they had no power to dissolve marriages. Nevertheless, as early as 1784, the courts recognized the need for protecting wives' physical safety and financial security in unusual situations. An 1801 case in the equity court of appeals established the principle of alimony without divorce on the grounds that women were entitled to protection from abusive husbands, that they clearly had no remedy at law, and that therefore the equity courts must have jurisdiction.[31] The defendant in this case argued that English courts did not have the power to grant alimony without divorce, and that therefore South Carolina courts were also prohibited from doing so.[32] The court acknowledged its lack of power to grant divorce, but refused to carry the logic of English precedent so far as to prevent it from assuming the power to grant alimony.[33]

A series of cases in the early nineteenth century reiterated these principles, and clearly established alimony without divorce as the remedy for abused wives. In all these cases, cruelty was the ground for alimony.[34] In 1826, in *Rhame* v. *Rhame*,[35] the court not only reiterated its jurisdiction in alimony cases, but for the first time made an explicit statement of the grounds for which alimony might be granted.[36] This case differed from earlier ones, because the wife had left voluntarily as a result of alleged mistreatment, although no instance of actual physical cruelty was proved. In addition, the husband attempted to impeach his wife's character, accusing her of having venereal disease at the time of their marriage. These accusations were not clearly proved, but were sufficiently convincing that the court took them into account. The court concluded that there was insufficient justification for alimony, but that, since the husband refused to take his wife back, she was entitled to support.[37] The decision then looked to English precedent to define the specific grounds for alimony.[38] Because alimony was granted in England only in connection with divorce from bed and board, the court argued that they should grant alimony for the same causes for which divorce would be granted in England. In fact, however, the only point on which the court followed English practice was in granting alimony for cruelty; here they specified that actual physical danger or threat of same must be proved in order to sustain a petition for alimony.

On other points South Carolina courts diverged from English practice, despite their stated intentions. In *Rhame* v. *Rhame*[39] the court for the first time explicitly stated that desertion might be a cause for alimony, although this was not permitted in English courts.[40] The remedy for desertion in England was a suit for restitution of conjugal rights, a procedure which had never been used in the United States. In the absence of such a remedy, the South Carolina court concluded that alimony was an appropriate substitute. More significantly, South Carolina courts did not allow adultery as a ground for alimony. In 1858, in *Hair* v. *Hair*,[41] the court asserted that a suit based on adultery could not be sustained. In

Hair the court again defined the specific grounds for alimony as cruelty, desertion, and "obscene and revolting indecencies practiced in the family circle."[42]

South Carolina practice further diverged from that of England and the other states in the denial of any distinction between divorce and annulment. In *Mattison* v. *Mattison*,[43] a case for annulment because of insanity, the court denied the appeal on the grounds that their powers were limited to granting alimony, and that no distinction might be made between the power to grant divorce and the power to grant annulment.[44]

An apparent contradiction is presented in South Carolina's alimony decisions. Although alimony was granted for cruelty and desertion, the grounds which were considered most compelling in dissolving marriages in other states (adultery, impotence, insanity, and close relationship by blood or marriage) were denied in South Carolina as causes for alimony. The explanation for this pattern may be found in the fact that alimony was perceived as a remedy for women only. It was justified by the argument that innocent and helpless women must be protected from abusive husbands or husbands who refused to support them. As one lower court judge explained, "God knows, the condition of all women, but especially of married women, is bad enough by the common law of England, and advancing civilization loudly demands its amelioration. But that law, which almost enslaves the wife, makes the husband liable for her support."[45] The notion of helpless women requiring protection and relief was consistent with antebellum ideas about women. Under the same set of attitudes, male adultery was not perceived as a serious offense. As long as a woman was being supported and protected, she had no cause for complaint if her husband was not always faithful. If a wife committed adultery, however, and her husband turned her out of his house as a result, the court would not sustain her claim for alimony.[46]

South Carolina's attitude on adultery is also apparent from the fact that it was one of the few states that did not prosecute adultery as a criminal offense. Relying upon English precedent as justification for this practice, South Carolina courts determined, in an 1831 case, that adultery was not indictable at common law because in England adultery was tried in ecclesiastical courts rather than law courts.[47] A husband's remedy for adultery was instead a civil suit against his wife's lover. Nothing was said of a wife's remedy; it was, presumably, nonexistent.

The second major concern expressed in South Carolina alimony cases, in addition to an abstract and idealistic commitment to the protection of women, was a commitment to the protection of property. Alimony was designed not only to allow victims of cruel husbands to live separately, but also to insure the financial security of women, particularly propertied women. On this point, moral issues such as adultery had no place, except insofar as they were taken into consideration in determining the amount of alimony.

One line of South Carolina cases reflects the importance of property. In *Prather* v. *Prather*,[48] the court held that a woman's claim to alimony was strengthened if she had brought considerable property to the marriage, although she was entitled to alimony regardless of her premarital financial status if the circumstances warranted it. In *Rhame* v. *Rhame* and an anonymous case in 1810 where the grounds for alimony were deemed insufficient but the women involved had had substantial property of their own, provision was made for their support from the income of their property.[49] Most alimony cases involved wealthy couples, a point which was emphasized in *Prince* v. *Prince*,[50] where alimony was granted out of the husband's daily income. The husband in *Prince* argued in defense that alimony could only be granted from the proceeds of capital, not from daily income. The court, however, decreed that the husband, although not possessed of extensive property, nevertheless had an income sufficient to support both himself and his wife. The protection of alimony, it declared, was not intended to be limited to the wealthy.

The circumstances, both financial and moral, of individual cases governed the amount of alimony granted. Hence, the man who had no property but a regular income was not expected to provide as handsomely for his wife as a wealthy plantation owner. And the woman who had brought property to her marriage was entitled to a larger income than one who had not. Additionally, a husband's adultery entitled his wife to a larger income.[51] But no circumstances changed a husband's essential property rights. The husband might be forced to pay alimony from the proceeds of property brought to the marriage by his wife, but nothing could take away his right to hold that property and to control the income from it. This principle was stated most specifically in *Converse* v. *Converse*,[52] where the wife deeded by a marriage settlement some of her property to her husband but kept some apart for her separate use. She did not sue for alimony because she had enough property of her own to support herself, but sued instead to have all her property restored to her on the grounds that she acted under duress when she deeded part of it to her husband. The court determined that she had adequate grounds for alimony, if that had been the nature of her suit, but that nothing could interfere with a husband's right to his wife's property—regardless of how reprehensible his conduct might have been.[53] The court found no evidence of duress in her agreement to the marriage settlement, and decreed that the property deeded to her husband should remain in his hands.[54] John Belton O'Neall dissented from the majority opinion, but not because of any liberal notions about women's property rights. He argued that it was to be assumed that a woman grants property to her husband only under his orders, and that therefore she might be said to have acted under duress.[55] A similar case occurred in Virginia, when a woman sued to be permitted to keep a slave which had belonged to her before marriage.[56] The court, after reviewing the precedents giving them the authority to grant separate maintenance and determining that the woman was indeed entitled to such maintenance, dismissed her suit on the grounds that she had no claim on any specific part of her husband's property.

Alimony without divorce provided South Carolina courts with a way of striking a balance between the sanctity of marriage and what was perceived as the demands of justice for innocent women. In particular, it was seen as a way of providing justice for the wealthy woman who enriched her husband with her property (which became his upon marriage) and was then abused by him. The courts stopped short, however, of simply returning such women's property to them. Just as the marriage bond was so sacred that it could not be challenged under any circumstances, so too property rights were equally sacred. Other states were also reluctant to tamper with the marriage bond, and often compromised by granting divorce from bed and board. But even these limited divorces restored to the women involved all the property they had brought to marriage, and allowed them to resume the property and contract rights of single women.[57] In a Massachusetts case, *Dean* v. *Richmond*,[58] which first established the *feme sole* status of a woman divorced from bed and board, the court drew a clear distinction between alimony or separate maintenance on the one hand, and divorce from bed and board on the other, with regard to women's legal status. Without the right to sue and hold property in her own right, they argued, a woman would have no way of enforcing payment of alimony, or of protecting her property in general. In short, "the law, instead of protecting her from the oppression and abuse of power of the husband, has merely released him from an inconvenient connection, reserving to him the right to deprive her of all comfort and support."[59] The South Carolina solution, however, not only denied couples the right to remarry, but insured that a woman, once married, would never again have the right to contract or hold property in her own name until her husband's death.

Given the context of familial and sexual politics in the nineteenth century, prior to the Progessive Era, and given the traditional hostility to divorce in the legal and social system until very recently, the antidivorce posture of the above discussed case law does not seem startling. The question that arises is how were judicial decisions reached and upon what legal principles were they based.

In today's era of marriage and nonmarital contracts, it should not be a surprise to find contract law lurking at the heart of these issues. Nineteenth-century jurists might well have been appalled by *Marvin* v. *Marvin*,[60] but they certainly would have understood it. The interesting feature about the contractual approach to marriage and divorce in the nineteenth century, however, was its result-orientation. Judges, at least in Massachusetts and South Carolina, saw no inconsistency in invoking the principles of contract law to preserve a marriage, while rejecting traditional contract defense when parties tried to end a marriage.

Thus, for example, contract principles were used to a great extent to defend and justify South Carolina's extreme stance on divorce. The court in *Devall* v. *Devall*[61] saw marriage as a contract based on interest, not love, between two competent parties. Therefore, the parties had to abide by the state-imposed terms of that contract. A South Carolina jurist, discussing this issue in 1830 in the short-lived *Carolina Law Journal*, described marriage in similar terms:[62]

> With us, the contract [of marriage], on whose unchangeable and continued existence during the lives of the parties, so much of the happiness, the peace, order, and morality of society depends, is regarded as so sacred, that when once formed, the act of God can dissolve it.

Thus, in declaring a marriage between an uncle and his niece valid for inheritance purposes, the South Carolina court based its decision on the primacy of a civil contract, unaffected by canonical notions of consanguinity.[63]

Contract principles were applied in defense of marital stability, but contract defenses were not admitted to dissolve marriages. This doctrinal double standard was enunciated in *Mattison v. Mattison*.[64] In *Mattison*, in spite of the alleged insanity of one party to the marriage, the court found the marriage nevertheless inviolate. Although normally insanity would invalidate a contract, it did not entitle a party to an annulment. The opinion in *Mattison* expressed the general attitude of South Carolina officials: "Cases of individual hardship have occurred, and will occur; but the observation of a different policy in other States, as well as the experience of our own, has served only to confirm the conviction that it is better to tolerate occasional suffering than to jeopardize the peace of society, and open a wide door to fraud, imposition and other immorality."[65]

While Massachusetts and South Carolina adopted widely divergent policies on divorce, both states supported the sanctity of marriage on contract principles and departed from those principles when the effect would apparently invalidate a marriage. In Massachusetts this policy is evident in two lines of cases involving the validity of marriage. The first situation involved marriages contracted in foreign jurisdictions which would not have been valid in Massachusetts; the second concerns the validity of marriages in which the wife was pregnant at the time of marriage by a man other than her husband. In *The Inhabitants of Medway* v. *The Inhabitants of Needham*,[66] the validity of a marriage between a white woman and a mulatto man was at issue. Since at the time of the marriage (prior to 1770) such a marriage was illegal in Massachusetts, the couple went to Rhode Island, which had no such ban, in order to marry. This case provided the first test in Massachusetts of two apparently conflicting principles: first, that a marriage which is valid according to the laws of the jurisdiction in which it was solemnized is valid in any other jurisdiction; and second, that a contract which is repugnant to the laws of the domicile is not valid in that domicile.

Chief Justice Parker, however, specifically exempted marriage from the latter general principle of contract law, "on principles of policy."[67] Chief Justice Parker offered no cases in support of his policy principle, although English cases were routinely cited to uphold the recognition of marriages valid in a foreign jurisdiction. As a matter of policy rather than law, this principle was not unlimited; a state was not obliged to recognize incestuous marriages which might be valid in the state where contracted. Parker reiterated this point ten years later in *Putnam* v. *Putnam*.[68] Marriage was a special form of contract law. A state would not enforce usurious or gaming contracts even if valid in the state in which they were consummated. However, Parker was not entirely happy with this position and called upon the legislature to reconcile this discrepancy.[69]

The strong social policy supporting marital stability was expressed most vividly in *Hervey* v. *Moseley*.[70] In *Hervey*, a mother sued for recovery of the services of her daughter who was enticed into marriage at the age of thirteen in violation of the minimum age for marriage in Massachusetts. The court held that although ordinary contracts in violation of penal statutes are void, "in the case of marriage this principle has been, for sound and obvious reasons, disregarded."[71] Thus, the court found the marriage was valid and the mother was not entitled to recover.

A second line of cases which discussed the contractual nature of marriage conformed to common-law principles, but the common-law notions were statutorily supported. In these cases the wife was pregnant at marriage by another man. Under contract doctrine, the wife's pregnancy might constitute fraud. However, under the characteristic divorce pattern in Massachusetts, this type of fraud could not invalidate a marriage until expressly permitted by statute, a change made in 1855.[72]

Although the 1855 statute permitted divorce for fraud, the courts were not required to apply common-law principles to determine the elements of fraud. In *Reynolds* v. *Reynolds*,[73] Chief Justice Bigelow noted that even though marriage is a civil contract which may be set aside on grounds of fraud, "it is not to be supposed that every error or mistake . . . concerning the character or qualities of a wife or husband . . . will afford sufficient reason for annulling an executed contract of marriage."[74] Anticipating the modern spirit of full disclosure, Bigelow suggested that the parties take it upon themselves to inquire into the character and chastity of their spouses. In short, despite the statutory change, the principles of contract law alone would leave little room to challenge a marriage. As Bigelow noted, however, "The only doubt which has arisen as to the wisdom or expediency of this doctrine has been occasioned by cases of ante-nuptial incontinence and want of chastity in females."[75] While this is apparently a clear statement of a sexual double standard, it is consistent with Bigelow's subsequent and explicit conception of marriage as the basis for legitimizing offspring. Thus, a double standard in this area was biologically determined, rather than a reflection of an inconsistency in morality.

Since principles of contract law governed even this fraud exception, a due diligence standard had to be met before a case for fraud could be asserted. In *Reynolds*, the divorce for fraud was granted only because the husband met such a test and, upon discovery of the fraud, took immediate steps to annul the marriage.[76] Within the next four years, the diligence issue came up two more times. In *Donovan* v. *Donovan*,[77] Bigelow perceived the issue in terms of a material misrepresentation of fact which induced the other party to enter into a contract which he would not otherwise have entered into. "This is the general rule applicable to all contracts," Bigelow stated, "and we are unable to see any reason for excepting . . . the contract of marriage."[78] Two years later, however, Bigelow applied a "reasonable man" test to the prenuptial inquiry and refused to grant a divorce or annulment because the petitioner failed to prove deception and false and fraudulent representation.[79]

Since women are traditionally the parties seeking the majority of divorces, liberalized divorce laws have usually been seen as an index to improving the status of women. This preliminary examination of divorce doctrine from the Revolution through the Civil War indicates that the law evolved from a concern for a woman's need to be protected, not her need to be free from the proverbial bonds of matrimony. At a time when courts refused to scrutinize the adequacy of consideration in contract cases, courts granted equitable relief to individual spouses whose marriage contracts had proved to be a "bad deal." Ever sensitive to a divorced woman's (and especially a divorced mother's) value in the demographic marketplace of the nineteenth century, courts granted divorce to victims of cruelty and desertion, extracting alimony and child support in the process.

For propertied women, where the paternal interests of the state were not as crucial, the marriage contract was simply rescinded and the property returned to the woman. Only South Carolina took the extreme position that marriage was based on property, not on contract, and refused to permit divorce where the logical accompaniment would have been to return a married woman's previously separate property. The feudal barons of this most aristocratic state had erected a sexual and racial double standard in which the planter's wife retained her security in return for overlooking her husband's liaisons with slaves. But the minority of women who were unconvinced that this system allegedly was in their own best interests paid a high price for a little freedom. These women could never remarry and their property was confiscated in return for alimony which might be unequal to its annual yield.

The South Carolina example, while extreme on its facts, cannot be dismissed. For despite the contractually based ideology in Massachusetts,[80] some of the South Carolina attitude existed. Marriage in Massachusetts was a contract, but it was a special contract, interpreted according to the strict moral standards of the men who wrote the opinions. The law of divorce developed in a context of religious disapproval and societal concern for spousal and child support (lest divorce increase the number of public charges). Only after these concerns were addressed could the happiness of the individuals be considered. As a contract, marriage was indeed a hard bargain for all too many nineteenth-century women.

NOTES

1. William L. O'Neill, *Divorce in the Progressive Era* (New Haven, 1967).

2. Of sixteen male petitions for divorce, ten were for adultery, two for previous sexual incontinence, three for desertion, and one resulted from a wife's attempt to murder her husband. Of twenty female petitions, eleven were for cruelty, seven for desertion, one for a husband's criminal sentence, and one for impotence. Two of the desertion cases also involved bigamy, and two of the cruelty cases also involved adultery; but here cruelty was cited as the primary cause for divorce. Legislative petitions, Virginia State Library, Richmond.

3. Anon., 2 S.C. Eq. (2 Des.) 198 (1803).

4. Joel Prentiss Bishop, *Commentary on the Law of Marriage and Divorce and Matrimonial Suits* (Boston, 1864), pp. 32, 89.

5. Bishop discusses the distinctions between divorce and annulment, and between void and voidable marriages; he also discusses the justifications for and history of the various grounds for divorce. Ibid., pp. 105–06, 704–833.

6. Mass. Acts, 1870, Ch. 404, Sec. 1. See also ibid., pp. 28–30.

7. Rev. St., 1835, Ch. 76. On Massachusetts divorce in the colonial period, see Nancy F. Cott, "Divorce and the Changing Status of Women in Eighteenth-Century Massachusetts," *William and Mary Quarterly* 33 (1976): 586–614, and "Eighteenth-Century Family and Social Life Revealed in Massachusetts Divorce Records," *Journal of Social History* (Fall 1976): 20–43.

8. 1833 Supp. to Rev. Code, Ch. 115; Va. Acts 1847–48, Ch. 122; Code of Va., 1849, Ch. 109; Va. Acts 1852–53, Ch. 28.

9. See Pidge v. Pidge, 44 Mass. (3 Met.), 257, 260 (1841).

10. General Statutes, 1860, Ch. 106.

11. See Pierce v. Pierce, 20 Mass. (3 Pick.) 299 (1825); Holland v. Holland, 2 Mass. 154 (1806); Baxter v. Baxter, 1 Mass. 345 (1805).

12. See Anon., 6 Mass. 146 (1809); North v. North, 5 Mass 320 (1809).

13. French v. French, 4 Mass. 586 (1808) and Hill v. Hill, 2 Mass. 150 (1806) established that a single action of violence was sufficient to permit divorce. Warren v. Warren, 3 Mass. 320 (1807) rejected a husband's refusal to support his wife as a sufficient definition of cruelty.

14. Gardner v. Gardner, 68 Mass (2 Gray) 434 (1854).

15. 44 Mass. (3 Met.) 257.

16. Ibid. at 260.

17. Ibid.

18. Ibid. at 265.

19. Ibid.

20. 103 Mass. 577 (1870).

21. Ibid. at 579.

22. Ibid.

23. 90 Mass. 418 (1864).

24. Ibid.
25. Ibid.
26. Ibid. at 419.
27. Bishop, pp. 28–30.
28. Purcell v. Purcell, 14 Va. (3 Hen. & M.) 507 (1809) established that equity courts could grant alimony. *Purcell* was decided in 1809 before courts had power to grant divorces. Almond v. Almond, 25 Va. (4 Rand.) 662 (1826) noted that equity courts had assumed the power to grant separate maintenance, but that no rules had been established to regulate the procedure.
29. 100 Mass. 365 (1868).
30. Ibid.
31. Jelineau v. Jelineau, 2 S.C. Eq. (2 Des.) 45 (1801). For earlier cases see Anon., 1 S.C. Eq. (1 Des.) 112 (1784); Greenland v. Brown, 1 S.C. Eq. (1 Des.) 196 (1789).
32. 2 S.C. Eq. (2 Des.) 45.
33. Ibid.
34. Boyd v. Boyd, 5 S.C. Eq. (Harp. Eq.) 118 (1824); Williams v. Williams, 4 S.C. Eq. (4 Des.) 183 (1811); Taylor v. Taylor, 4 S.C. Eq. (4 Des.) 165 (1811); Anon., 4 S.C. Eq. (4 Des.) 93 (1810); Devall v. Devall, 4 S.C. Eq. (4 Des.) 79 (1809); Prather v. Prather, 4 S.C. Eq. (4 Des.) 32 (1809).
35. 6 S.C. Eq. (1 McCord Eq.) 197 (1826).
36. Ibid. at 206.
37. Ibid. at 209.
38. Ibid. at 204–05.
39. 6 S.C. Eq. (1 McCord Eq.) 197.
40. Ibid. at 207.
41. 28 S.C. Eq. (10 Rich. Eq.) 163 (1858).
42. Ibid. at 174.
43. 20 S.C. Eq. (1 Strob. Eq.) 387 (1847).
44. Ibid. at 392–93.
45. Prince v. Prince. 1 Richardson Eq. 282 (1845).
46. Boyd v. Boyd, 5 S.C. Eq. (Harp. Eq.) 118 (1824) stated that a wife cannot support a claim for alimony if her conduct was such that her husband was provoked to retaliate. Slight misconduct, however, did not invalidate her claim. Devall v. Devall, 4 S.C. Eq. (4 Des.) 79 (1809).
47. State v. Brunson and Miller, 8 S.C. Eq. (Bail. Eq.) 149 (1831).
48. 4 S.C. Eq. (4 Des.) 33 (1809).
49. In the first case, the husband refused to take his wife back into his household; in the second, the husband was given a choice between taking her back and providing for her support. Anon., 4 S.C. Eq. (4 Des.) 93 (1810); Rhame v. Rhame, 6 S.C. Eq. (1 McCord Eq.) 114 (1826).
50. 18 S.C. Eq. (1 Rich. Eq.) 282 (1845).
51. Thompson v. Thompson, 31 S.C. Eq. (10 Rich. Eq.) 416 (1859).
52. 30 S.C. Eq. (9 Rich. Eq.) 535 (1856).
53. Ibid. at 563.

54. Ibid. at 566–67.
55. Ibid. at 567–68.
56. Almond v. Almond, 25 Va. (4 Rand.) 662 (1826).
57. The Massachusetts statute of 1785 allowed wives to regain posses-sion of their real estate in every case except where they had committed adultery. An additional act passed in 1806 allowed the court to grant wives all or part of their personal property in divorces *a vinculo*. An 1828 statute extended this provision to divorces from bed and board. Rev. St. 1835, Ch. 27 and 28; West v. West, 2 Mass. 223 (1806). See also Babcock v. Smith, 39 Mass. 61 (1840); Page v. Estes, 36 Mass. 269 (1837); Dean v. Richmond, 22 Mass. 461 (1827). A Virginia statute passed in 1827 decreed that all prop-erty brought to marriage by the injured party be restored, in both types of divorces. Code of Virginia, 1849, Ch. 165, Sec. 3.
58. 22 Mass. 461 (1827).
59. Ibid. at 465.
60. 18 Cal. 3d 660, 557 P.2d 106, 134 Cal. Rptr. 815 (1976).
61. 4 S.C. Eq. (4 Des.) 79 (1809).
62. "The Effect of Foreign Divorces on South Carolina Marriages," *Carolina Law Journal* 1 (1830): 378.
63. Bowers v. Bowers, 31 S.C. Eq. (10 Rich. Eq.) 551 (1859).
64. 20 S.C. Eq. (1 Strob. Eq.) 387 (1847).
65. Ibid. at 393.
66. 16 Mass. 157 (1819).
67. Ibid. at 160.
68. 25 Mass. 433 (1829).
69. The difference between Medway v. Needham and Putnam v. Put-nam was that in the latter case, the marriage was contracted by a divorced party who was unable to remarry under Massachusetts law. This deliber-ate evasion so criticized by Parker was rectified by Ch. 76, Sec. 39 of the Revised Statutes. Litigation on this point includes Commonwealth v. Bet-sey Hunt, 58 Mass. 49 (1849) and Lyon v. Lyon, 68 Mass. 367 (1854).
70. 73 Mass. 479 (1856).
71. Ibid. at 483.
72. Mass. Acts, 1855, Ch. 27.
73. 85 Mass. 605 (1862).
74. Ibid. at 607.
75. Ibid. at 608.
76. Ibid. at 611.
77. 91 Mass. 140 (1864).
78. Ibid. at 141.
79. Foss v. Foss, 94 Mass. 26 (1866).
80. We found no similar contract cases in Virginia.

HISTORICAL BACKGROUND OF "PROTECTIVE" LABOR LEGISLATION: *MULLER V. OREGON*

Nancy S. Erickson

In the 1908 case of *Muller* v. *Oregon*,[1] the United States Supreme Court held that women's working hours, unlike men's, could be restricted by law even in employment that was not generally considered especially hazardous to health. *Muller* could have opened the door to labor legislation for men too, but labor turned toward unions rather than legislatures for protection, so *Muller* is now a mere footnote in labor history. *Muller* is still important in legal education, primarily cited as an early example of "legal realism" and as the origin of what has come to be called the "Brandeis brief"—a brief which includes not only legal arguments, but scientific, psychological, and sociological data as well.

Not enough attention has been paid to *Muller's* significance for women's history. The *Muller* holding is based on two distinct but connected premises, both of which reflect traditional views of woman's "sphere." The first premise is that women are less able to protect themselves than are men; the second, that the state has a right to protect women, all viewed as potential child-bearers, in order to protect "the race." Both premises were challenged by feminists a decade later at the height of the women's rights movement and thereafter.[2] Immediate opposition to *Muller* by feminists in 1908, however, has not been researched until now. This paper will explore both the general reactions and the feminist responses of the time to the *Muller* decision.

INTRODUCTION

From the mid-nineteenth century to the early twentieth, many state legislatures passed laws restricting the number of hours that workers were permitted to toil for hire. Some of these laws applied to all workers; others applied only to women or children. Women's

work was also regulated in other respects: employers were prohibited from employing women workers for certain hours during
the night and in occupations deemed dangerous to their physical
or moral well-being.[3]

Employers mounted legal challenges to maximum-hours laws on
the theory that they impaired the workers' constitutional right to
freedom of contract.[4] State courts ruled both ways on the issue,[5]
but in 1905, in Lochner v. New York, the Supreme Court of the
United States held that a maximum-hours law for workers in
bakeries was unconstitutional as an unreasonable interference with
their liberty to contract in relation to their labor.[6] Lochner was a
harsh blow to Progressive reformers who were attempting to improve labor conditions by legislation.

Most bakery workers were male, and the Supreme Court in Lochner seemed to assume they all were,[7] but in fact the New York law
covered both male and female workers. Therefore, when three
years later the Court addressed the issue of "protective"[8] legislation for women only (specifically, maximum hours for women in
laundries),[9] those who sought to uphold the law had to convince
the Court that there was a difference between working in a bakery
and working in a laundry,[10] or that there were unique and overriding reasons for regulating the hours of women workers. The second approach was chosen, and it succeeded. In Muller v. Oregon
the Court held that the state had significant interests justifying
"protection" of women workers—interests that did not exist with
regard to male workers. First, women are inherently more in need
of protection from overwork because of their physical structure,
especially when performing their "maternal functions," and are
inherently incapable of asserting fully their own rights as well as
men.[11] Secondly, women are the bearers of the race; therefore, the
well-being of society depends on their well-being, and their freedom can be restricted for the sake of the unborn child and society.[12]

At the time, Muller was seen as a victory for the friends of labor,
because it eroded the Lochner rule that the legislature was not empowered to protect the health of the worker by maximum-hours
laws. Muller is viewed in a somewhat different light today. From a
modern feminist standpoint, the first justification for the holding
in Muller is unacceptably paternalistic: it "protects" women, who

are adult human beings equally capable of making their own decisions and looking out for their own interests as men are, even when women may prefer to risk a certain degree of harm in their pursuit of a desired goal.[13] Additionally, even if the law truly helped all women workers and harmed none,

> legislative classifications which distribute benefits and burdens on the basis of gender carry the inherent risk of reinforcing the stereotypes about the "proper place" for women and their need for special protection.[14]

The second justification is even more objectionable because it treats women as objects: as means rather than ends. That is, for the sake of "the race"—not even for the sake of a particular fetus that is already in existence—women's rights may be curtailed.[15]

We know that the paternalistic bases of *Muller* were strongly opposed, only a decade thereafter, by women workers in the printing industry and by women transit workers.[16] The Woman's Party, formed in 1913,[17] also rejected them unequivocally. The Equal Rights Amendment, which they drafted and for which they lobbied for over fifty years, leaves no room for such principles, and protectionism in employment was finally laid to rest by the Civil Rights Act of 1964.[18] Yet historians have uncovered no feminist opposition to *Muller* in 1908. "Progressive" social reformers, both men and women, supported paternalistic legislation of the type upheld in *Muller* and wrote the famous "Brandeis brief" in that case.[19] It is not difficult to understand why they, and others disappointed by the decision in *Lochner*, supported *Muller*. Half a loaf often seems better than none, especially if one is convinced that obtaining the half loaf will present no barrier to obtaining the entire loaf eventually.[20] It is difficult to understand, however, why history appears to be totally devoid of feminist[21] opposition to Progressive paternalism at the time of *Muller*. One cannot merely assume that the drive for suffrage consumed American feminists so fully that the question of "protective" labor laws was entirely ignored.

The answer is that history is not devoid of such opposition; it is only that historians have not yet discovered it. In fact, *Muller* immediately generated what appears to have been a bitter controversy among women in the suffrage movement. Some of that

controversy will be documented in this paper; we must then put
our historical tools to work to uncover the rest.[22]

I. THE *MULLER* CASE

The *Muller* case arose out of a 1903 Oregon law prohibiting the
employment of any female in "any mechanical establishment, or
factory, or laundry in this State more than ten hours during any
one day."[23] Violation of the statute was a crime, subject to a fine. In
1905, Curt Muller, the owner of a Portland laundry, was convicted
and fined for requiring a certain Mrs. Gotcher to work more than
ten hours in his laundry. He appealed to the Supreme Court of
Oregon, arguing that the law under which he was convicted was
unconstitutional in that it violated women's rights to contract to
work for as many hours as they wished. The Oregon court upheld
the statute and his conviction.[24] Muller appealed again—this time
to the Supreme Court of the United States.

The National Consumers League then got wind of the appeal.
The NCL, founded in 1899, was devoted to improving wages and
working conditions, especially for women. One of the Consumers
League projects was to encourage consumers to buy only those
products manufactured by "good" companies, but the League and
its affiliates also lobbied for legislation to protect workers against
poor working conditions.[25] When the Consumers League of Oregon heard that Muller was going to take his case to the United
States Supreme Court, they notified the NCL, and that organization's board decided to ask an eminent New York lawyer, Joseph
H. Choate, to represent the NCL in a brief to the Court. Choate is
reported to have said that he could see no reason why "a big husky
Irishwoman should not work more than ten hours a day in a laundry if she and her employer so desired."[26] Choate undoubtedly
objected to all labor legislation for workers, including "protective"
legislation for women, but at least he sensed that not all women fit
the stereotype of the small, frail, and weak female.

Florence Kelley, who was then general secretary of the NCL,
was not disappointed by Choate's attitude toward the case.[27] On
the contrary, it gave her an excuse to take the case to another
lawyer whom she considered more sympathetic to labor and to the
objectives of the NCL—Louis D. Brandeis, a Boston attorney and
brother-in-law of her colleague in the NCL, Josephine Goldmark.

Brandeis agreed to write a brief in favor of the Oregon law. He also agreed to argue the case before the United States Supreme Court if the Oregon attorney general would invite him to do so as an official representative of the State of Oregon. This was arranged. Then work began on what has come to be known as the "Brandeis brief" (although Josephine Goldmark and other women of the NCL deserve equal credit for it). To the modern lawyer, "Brandeis brief" has become a generic term for a brillant combination of social, economic, or scientific knowledge that tends to persuade the court of the soundness of the legal arguments.

Very few modern lawyers have ever read the original "Brandeis brief"; if they did, most would be shocked.[28] Its legal argument is almost nonexistent,[29] and the social and scientific data appear very unscientific to the modern eye.[30] Especially questionable are the attempts to justify the law's coverage of women only. It is not difficult to show that overwork is damaging to any worker, and the brief contains many "authorities" on that general point.[31] Additionally, it could be argued convincingly that there is a significant difference between factory or workshop labor and work performed elsewhere, in terms of pace, variety, and opportunity for rest; this argument was also made in the Brandeis brief.[32] However, the strategy that Brandeis chose was not simply to show that the type of work regulated by the law was especially taxing.[33] He also tried to prove that the type of worker "protected"—the woman worker—was in special need of protection. He based his argument on four "matters of general knowledge":[34] first, women are physically weaker than and otherwise physically different from men;[35] second, damage to a woman's health might affect her future reproductive capacity;[36] third, the health of a child may be damaged by overworking its mother[37] (for example, by affecting the quality or quantity of milk she produces); and fourth, excess hours of labor deprive the family of her services in the home. It should be noted that three of the four rationales for this "protective" labor legislation concerned not the woman herself, but rather her actual or potential family.[38] Additionally, one of these rationales involved not physical differences between the sexes but social sex roles with regard to childcare and housework.

Finally, Brandeis argued that the law would not harm women workers in their competition with men workers because women workers do not compete with men. There are "women's jobs" and "men's jobs," he argued, and substitution of men for women as a result of the limits on women's hours would be quite unlikely. Although it is true that the job market was (and is) sex segregated, Brandeis assumed that it was so by nature. He also assumed that the only issue was whether the Oregon law and others like it would "result in contracting the sphere of [women's] work."[39] The issue of whether the law would prevent women from expanding the "sphere" of their work was ignored, on the apparent assumption that women had already expanded their "sphere" as far as it could or should be expanded. Laws that totally prohibited the employment of women in certain jobs were assumed to be valid.[40] Thus, Brandeis's argument of lack of harm to women may be criticized on the ground that he cited already existing discrimination against women as a reason for further discrimination.[41]

Two other briefs were presented to the Court: a separate brief for the state of Oregon and the brief for Muller. There were no *amicus* briefs from women's organizations or any other groups or individuals on either side of the issue.[42] If there were groups or individuals opposed to "protective" labor legislation on feminist grounds, they may have assumed that the Court would, as one state supreme court did,[43] overturn such a law on the freedom of contract grounds used in *Lochner*.

The brief for the state of Oregon was oriented more toward legal precedent than toward the social or scientific "data" cited by Brandeis, but the legal precedent was based on most of the same assumptions about women as the Brandeis "data." The state argued that every state has the inherent power (known as the "police power") to make all laws "necessary and proper to preserve the public security, order, health, morality and justice."[44] The state recognized that maximum hours laws might "work a hardship" on women, but concluded that "the welfare of the individual will not be considered when it is placed in the balance against the welfare of the state at large."[45] This statement is significant because it indicates that "protection" of the individual against her will might not be valid without a showing of possible harm to the *public* welfare. In fact, later in the brief the state indicated its doubt on this point:

We are free to admit that if the evil results of long-continued hours of work by women in such employments were confined to the individual, there might be a question, if this were not an unreasonable and illegal use of the police power of the state . . .[46]

What harm to the *public* good would occur if women worked long hours? The state's answer was the same as Brandeis's, but without the "scientific" data: overworking women would harm their reproductive capacities so as to damage future generations[47] and would "render them incapable of bearing their share of the burdens of the family and the home."[48] "Burdens" apparently refers not only to childbearing but also to housework.[49] The state also made reference to the possibility that women might not be "as fully able to assert [their] rights and care for [themselves] as [are men]."[50] All these arguments had been accepted by the Oregon Supreme Court,[51] and the state merely reiterated them to the United States Supreme Court.

Clearly, the state's primary concern, like Brandeis's, was the effect on "the race" of overworking women. Brandeis and the state of Oregon were merely expressing a concern about race degeneracy that was part of the prevailing culture of their time. Darwinism was a reigning philosophy, and Darwinism taught that race degeneracy could be avoided only by valuing the race above the individual. In practical terms, this meant that women's lives, and especially women's employment, would have to be regulated for the sake of the children they were expected to bear.[52]

Muller's brief, on the other hand, relied on the argument of equality between the sexes that had been successful in persuading one state supreme court to overturn its women-only hours legislation.[53] The argument sounds a bit strained, coming as it did from the employer, not the woman.[54] Yet there is a decidedly modern feminist ring to Muller's insistence that women have the same rights as men and do not need the "protecting arm of the legislature"[55] any more than do men. Furthermore, the brief recognizes that some women may not want the "protection" of the law because to them it may be a restriction rather than a real protection: "The woman employed by [Muller] . . . may have been a widow, and had the care of a family of dependent children; she may have been and no doubt was perfectly willing to contract with [Muller] for the services forbidden."[56]

Even more remarkable is the brief's insight that what we today would call "sexual stereotyping"[57] may underlie the law:

> For reasons of chivalry, we may regret that all women may not be sheltered in happy homes, free from the exacting demands upon them in pursuit of a living, but their right to pursue any honorable vocation, any business not forbidden as immoral, or contrary to public policy, is just as sacred and just as inviolate as the same right enjoyed by men.[58]

We also tend to think that analogizing sex discrimination to race discrimination is a modern phenomenon, but Muller's brief uses this approach with no indication that such an analogy is new:

> But if the statute had forbidden employment for more than ten hours, of all persons of white color, the statute would have had application to all of that class, and yet no one would contend that the classification was reasonable or one that could be sustained.[59]

Muller denied that protection of a woman's own health was a sufficient reason for the law: "It is difficult to imagine any employment that may be dangerous to women employees that would not be equally dangerous to men."[60] Further, although he recognized that some constitutional authorities accepted the power of the state to restrict the employment of women who were actually pregnant,[61] Muller flatly disputed the argument that women could be "protected" for the sake of "possible children":

> Suppose that the woman employed was an adult, single woman, and that the work in the laundry was peculiarly suitable to her sex. Can the Court say that her contract to work ten and a half hours in that service tends to impair the public health, and that in the distant and remote future the possible children which she may bear will need the protection of this statute?[62]

Finally, Muller concluded his brief by pointing out that the statute might not have been passed to help women, or, even if passed for that purpose, might not serve that purpose:

> Women, in increasing numbers, are compelled to earn their living. They enter the various lines of employment hampered and handicapped by centuries of tutelage and the limitation and restriction of freedom of contract. Social customs narrow the field of her en-

deavor. Shall her hands be further tied by statutes ostensibly framed in her interests, but intended perhaps to limit and restrict her employment, and whether intended so or not, enlarging the field and opportunity of her competitor among men?[63]

On February 8, 1908, after oral argument and submission of the briefs, Justice Brewer handed down his opinion for a unanimous Court. The Court rejected Muller's brief almost in its entirety and picked portions of the other two briefs to support its opinion, adding a few of its own thoughts here and there, including a few references to the history of male domination and to possible psychological differences between men and women.[64]

Justice Brewer's summation is a sufficient indication of the influence on the *Muller* opinion of the two briefs for the state:

> The two sexes differ in structure of body, in the functions to be performed by each, in the amount of physical strength, in the capacity for long-continued labor, particularly when done standing, the influence of vigorous health upon the future well-being of the race, the self-reliance which enables one to assert full rights, and in the capacity to maintain the struggle for subsistence. This difference justifies a difference in legislation and upholds that which is designed to compensate for some of the burdens which rest upon her.[65]

The Court acknowledged its debt to Brandeis by quoting extensively from his brief in a footnote.[66] Thousands of law students have thereby been led to believe that the Brandeis brief was responsible for the Court's validation of the Oregon law. *Muller* is supposed to represent the Court's first acceptance of social, scientific, and economic facts as a basis for its opinions.[67] Looking at the opinion more closely, however, one perceives that the "women need protection" argument and the "bearer of the race" argument are at its center. Those arguments were not created by Brandeis and were urged in the state's brief as well as in Brandeis's. It is likely that the Court would have accepted these arguments even without Brandeis's "authorities." The Brandeis brief may be significant for later legal developments, but the *Muller* holding probably would have been the same even without that brief. Paternalistic protectionism toward women was a feature of American law long before the Brandeis brief.

II. THE PRESS RESPONDS TO *MULLER*

Although *Muller* is now recognized as a landmark case, the institutional press did not consider *Muller* the most important news item of the day on February 25, 1908. The *New York Times* omitted to mention the case at all; the top news of the day was that, as part of the entertainment at Mrs. Waldorf Astor's charity ball, Mrs. James B. Eustis draped a live boa constrictor over her shoulders.[68]

The case was considered only page two news in the *Chicago Daily Tribune*; the front page headline story concerned a congressional bill to award medals to people who had saved the lives of victims of a shipwreck in 1860.[69] The Supreme Court did make page one, however, with its opinion in the Great Northern Railway's fight to avoid fines under the Elkins Act.[70] The news article on *Muller,* entitled "High Court Aids Women Workers," was a mere two-paragraph introduction to two paragraphs of the opinion, the latter being divided by a subheading "Sex Justifies Separate Law."[71]

The *Los Angeles Times* considered the opinion significant enough to be page one news, but it was still overshadowed by an article speculating on the future of Portugal after the assassination of the King and Crown Prince on February 1.[72] The *Muller* story was again a mere two-paragraph paraphrase of parts of the opinion, headed by "Decision Favors Women," and "Justice Brewer Holds that Welfare of Race Demands Consideration of Her Frailty."[73]

The "Oregon Case" was awarded the greatest prominence by the *Washington Post,* which gave it four headlines: "Has Right of Her Own," "Supreme Court Holds Woman Above Man in Law," "Decision in Oregon Case," and "Law Limiting Hours of Labor for Laundress Declared Valid for Reasons of Sex—Woman Regarded in Class by Herself, to Be Protected by Legislation. Opinion by Mr. Justice Brewer."[74] Six paragraphs of quotes and paraphrases of the opinion are introduced by two paragraphs of commentary, the second of which explains how the Court differentiated the Oregon statute from the "New York Bakery Law" at issue in *Lochner* three years before. The first paragraph is the clearest indication of the relative significance of *Muller:* "Labor had an inning yesterday in the United States Supreme Court's decision that the Oregon law limiting to ten the hours of labor for women in laundries in that State was valid."[75] *Muller* was seen as a small victory for labor on a day when the biggest news was of a Supreme Court decision believed to be a significant defeat for labor—the "Danbury Hatters" case, in which the Court held that labor boycotts by the Hatters union and the American Federation of Labor were in violation of the Sherman antitrust law.[76] That opinion had been handed down three weeks before, but an article by Samuel Gompers, President of the A.F.L., attacking the opinion, made front-page news on February 25, overshadowing *Muller*. One wonders, in fact, whether the news of *Muller* might not have been relegated to the back pages of the paper, had Gompers published his attack on the Court a day later.

In succeeding days, several papers published editorials and other news items related to *Muller*. The *Chicago Daily Tribune* carried a story on February 26 about a speech by Florence Kelley, urging the state of Illinois to pass a law limiting women's hours of work, since the Supreme Court had now made it clear that such laws were constitutional.[77] *Muller* was a great victory for Kelley, not only because of her involvement in *Muller* itself, but also because it effectively overruled the 1895 Illinois Supreme Court opinion declaring unconstitutional the Illinois eight-hour law for women that she had worked so hard to enact and to enforce.[78]

The *Los Angeles Daily Times* editorial of February 27, entitled "Woman's Work," is notable for its naiveté juxtaposed with an attempt to paint a brutally severe picture of the depths to which American womanhood would have fallen without the protection of state legislatures and the United States Supreme Court. After praising the *Muller* opinion as "wonderfully clear and profound," and highlighting the law's purpose—"to protect women . . . that as mothers of the race they may bear children capable of development into full manhood and womanhood"—the editorial made a statement that would have infuriated Florence Kelley: "We do not suffer much yet in this country from the overworking of women in factories, therefore the results are not concrete facts before our eyes."[79] Had no one read or even heard of Kelley's detailed reports on the horrendous conditions under which women labored in the factories of Illinois?[80] But the editorial concluded with a passage that could have been written by Kelley herself:

> The laboring classes of older races, where factory work has gone on for centuries and where women have worked side by side with their brothers in mills generation after generation manifest the degener-

acy contemplated as possible by the decision here referred to. No doubt the employment of the men during excessively long days, the putting of children to work too early and the permitting them to work too long, have aggravated this evil. But leaving all this out of the question, no one can look clearly at the meager frames, bent shoulders and hollow chests of factory women of Europe and fail to conclude that these can never be the mothers of a robust race.[81]

Thus far we have seen unanimous agreement with the Court's opinion, with nary a hint that a discordant position could be imagined. Such hints were dropped, however, in an editorial in the *New York Times* and an article in the *Washington Post*.

Having failed to report the case at all on February 25th,[82] the *Times* more than made up for that omission the next day with a lengthy editorial entitled "The Position of Woman," commencing with the following pronouncement on the proper place of women in society:

> That woman is a ward of the State, that she is set apart in a class by herself, and placed under the fostering care and special protection of the law, not because of consideration for her individual comfort and interests, but in the interest of the human race and of posterity, is a principle that has just been affirmed by the Supreme Court of the United States. It is held, even, that she may be constitutionally deprived of certain rights in the exercise of which she might incur risk, rights with which, in the case of the male sex, the State would not upon any similar ground interfere.[83]

The tone of the editorial and its choice of words leaves no doubt but that the writer agreed with the Court. In fact, the *Times* went farther than the Court in indicating woman's distinct status— Justice Brewer did not use the words "ward of the State."[84] The editorial continued with the facts of *Muller* and a lengthy excerpt from the opinion, followed by a list of states with similar laws and a criticism of the 1907 New York Court of Appeals decision in the *Williams* case holding unconstitutional that state's prohibition on night work for women.[85] The writer recognized that the Court's broad interpretation of the police power might

> work a hardship to her individually, since her freedom of contract is interfered with and her power to earn a subsistence may be diminished." But, says the court, the policy embodied in the statute has in view "not merely her own health, but the well-being of the race."

This repeats with great exactness the principle of Nature as expressed by TENNYSON:

So careful of the type she seems
so careless of the single life.[86]

The Darwinian philosophy of the time was thus clearly expressed.[87] The writer then opined that the same "principle of Nature" embodied in *Muller* could be used to sustain other laws that treat men and women differently:

[The principle of protecting women in order to secure the well-being of the race] accords, also, with the policy of exemptions in favor of woman that prevails in all civilized countries, and largely, even, among primitive savages, exemptions, that is, from jury duty and military and constabulary service. It is in harmony, likewise with the laws that compel support of the wife by the husband, and provide for alimony when divorces are granted. It will be observed that these laws, and the opinion of the court sustaining their constitutionality, do not spring from sentiment. They rest rather upon a maxim of highest social policy. To the end that the race may be preserved, that the health, vigor, and soundness of posterity may be assured, that class of society charged with the chief functions of race preservation must be surrounded with peculiar safeguards, and securely sheltered against risks and perils that the law permits men freely to incur in their daily affairs.[88]

The broader principle from which this principle concerning women was supposed to be derived—namely, that "private interest [is] subservient to the general interests of the community"[89] had been denied the very day before in the editorial pages of the *Times*, when the "private interest" was a utility company's interest in its rates rather than a woman's interest in her job.[90] Additionally, the *Times* generally opposed labor legislation on freedom of contract grounds.[91] Its approval of *Muller* should be seen as consistent with, rather than opposed to, its generally conservative views on public issues.

Finally, the writer of "The Position of Woman" took a poke at suffragists, who were not generally well treated on the editorial pages of the *Times*: "We leave to the advocates of woman suffrage to say whether this decision makes for, or against, the success of their cause."[92] Clearly the message intended was that woman's position as a "ward of the State" is incompatible with her exercise of the franchise. Suffragists were challenged to show why that should not be so.

The favorable press reports of *Muller* indicate that it was not seen as a serious threat to "freedom of contract" or to business interests generally and that it did not challenge prevalent attitudes concerning the place of women in society. Next we must investigate the views of women toward *Muller* to see whether the conservative underpinnings of the case spurred opposition from suffragists.

III. THE FEMINIST DEBATE OVER *MULLER*

"Justice Brewer's decision has no bearing directly upon the suffrage issue," declared Rev. Anna H. Shaw, M.D., President of the National American Woman Suffrage Association (NAWSA) in an interview reported in the *Washington Post* on March 1st.[93] "Not granting women the power to protect themselves," she stated, "the state recognized that it owes them protection, but if they had the ballot they could back their demands for shorter hours with it."[94] In regard to the issue of whether women need special "protection," her reply (or the report of her reply) was a trifle unclear, but she seemed to concede the need for "protective" labor laws, whether passed by a legislature elected by men or a legislature elected by both men and women: "I agree with Justice Brewer that women need special protection. They are physically weaker in a sense, but when it comes to endurance, I believe they are as strong as men, after all."[95] On its face, such a concession would seem to contradict the NAWSA "Declaration of Principles" of 1904, which demanded that "all constitutional and legal barriers shall be removed which deny to women any individual right or personal freedom which is granted to man."[96] To examine other women's views, we must turn to the suffrage newspapers of 1908 to see whether there was general agreement on the need for "protection" for women workers, and, if so, how this protectionism was harmonized with the demand for equal rights and freedoms.

In 1860 the suffrage movement split into two separate organizations.[97] The more radical group, led by Elizabeth Cady Stanton and Susan B. Anthony, formed the National Woman Suffrage Association, and its official organ was the *Revolution*, published in New York by Stanton. The more conservative faction, led by Lucy

Stone, her husband Henry B. Blackwell, and others, formed the American Woman Suffrage Association and published their newspaper, *The Woman's Journal*, in Boston. By 1908, however, the two organizations had merged into one (NAWSA) and only *The Woman's Journal* remained; it was published weekly by Alice Stone Blackwell, the daughter of Stone and Blackwell.[98]

The *Muller* decision was announced in the February 29 issue of *The Woman's Journal* under the headline "An Important Decision."[99] It is strictly a matter of reporting, without commentary, concluding with three paragraphs from the opinion. Only from the title and from the lack of criticism can one surmise that the author, presumably Alice Stone Blackwell, must have been favorably disposed toward the decision.

In the next issue, however, it became apparent that trouble was brewing. The following editorial appeared:

Justice Brewer's Opinion

It is natural that there should be some difference of opinion among suffragists, as well as among anti-suffragists, in regard to the important decision of the U.S. Supreme Court upholding the constitutionality of the Oregon law limiting the number of hours per day that women may be required to work in factories, laundries, etc. Those who wish to see the arguments in favor of such limitation clearly set forth with the history of the legislation in this line in the different States should read the third and fourth chapters of Mrs. Florence Kelley's book, "Some Ethical Gains through Legislation," published by MacMillan.

Some benighted opponents of equal suffrage are boasting over the decision as though there were something in it incompatible with political rights for women. Justice Brewer evidently does not think so, for he is an advocate of woman suffrage. And, in fact, where is the inconsistency in a man's believing that women should be protected against excessive and inhuman overwork, and at the same time believing that they should be protected against taxation without representation?

A.S.B.[100]

Alice Stone Blackwell recognized that the *Muller* opinion had dangerous potential; Justice Brewer's words were inconsistent with some of the main suffragist arguments. Her task then was either to deny the inconsistency or to show *Muller's* consistency with other suffragist arguments.

Woman suffrage arguments gradually shifted from the early

days of the woman's rights movement to the victory in 1920.[101] In the early period, suffragists emphasized the equality of all people and their natural right to the ballot. To support this argument, they cited the principles of the American Revolution, as embodied in the Declaration of Independence, especially the themes of consent of the governed and no taxation without representation.[102]

In later years, when American men of older stock were questioning the equality of the new immigrants and of the native inhabitants of the new American colonies, the argument based on equality lost some of its power.[103] "[N]ew arguments for suffrage evolved, emphasizing the ways in which women differed from men. If the justice of the claim to political equality could no longer suffice, then the women's task was to show that expediency required it."[104] The expediency argument took three main forms: the vote would make her a better mother, wife, and citizen; women could protect themselves with the franchise by passing laws that women needed, such as "protective" labor laws; and women would vote for the social reform measures that the Progressive desired.[105] It should be noted that each of these is based on an assumption that women are different from men; thus, the expediency arguments tend to contradict the equality arguments. Additionally, the assumptions of sex differences underlying the three expediency arguments are themselves dissimilar and perhaps even incompatible. The argument that the franchise would improve women assumed that they were prevented from developing to their full potential by the lack of it.[106] On the other hand, there was the assumption that because women are somehow ethically better than men, they would vote for all societal reforms.[107] The protection argument, of course, assumes either that women need more protection than men against third parties who are trying to oppress them both[108] or that women need protection against men.[109]

For those people who were, or who tended toward being, "true feminists,"[110] mouthing the expediency arguments must have been painful. Elizabeth Cady Stanton would seem to belong to this group.[111] For those people who wanted women to vote primarily in order to accomplish social reform objectives, the equality argument would have been irrelevant. Florence Kelley[112] and Jane Addams[113] probably fall into this category. For those in the middle, who believed that women should by right have the vote, and who were convinced that to get it women would have to stage a single-issue campaign, setting aside any other feminist goals, the expediency arguments were simply expedient.[114] Alice Stone Blackwell may have been one of those.[115]

Blackwell's first reaction to the "difference of opinion" in regard to *Muller* was to devise her clever but inaccurate and convoluted analogy between "believing that women should be protected against . . . overwork, and . . . believing that they should be protected against taxation without representation."[116] She knew that the Court had said that *only* women could be protected against overwork, because of "the inherent difference between the two sexes, and . . . the different functions in life which they perform."[117] If women could be treated differently from men in this instance, perhaps they had no substantial claim of a right to the ballot. Yet, it is interesting that Alice Blackwell's response contained a slogan from the natural equality arguments for suffrage, rather than the expediency arguments. Those were to come later. In the meantime, however, she could not resist publishing a few words of praise for the decision and for Brandeis in the "Notes and News" column of the same issue of the *Journal.*[118]

Two weeks later what seems to be a radical feminist protest against *Muller* appeared on the pages of *The Woman's Journal:*

Against Justice Brewer's Decision

At a recent meeting of the Woman's Henry George League in New York, the following resolution was unanimously passed:

Whereas, Woman is a human being just as much as man is, and therefore possesses an inalienable right to life, liberty and the pursuit of happiness; and

Whereas, Woman in a primitive state, unhampered by natural restrictions, not only fulfilled all of woman's special functions, but also performed the heaviest labors of the tribe; and

Whereas, For the successful propagation of the human species, fatherhood is as important as motherhood; and

Whereas, No woman who is not free physically, mentally, morally and economically, is fit for motherhood; and

Whereas, The so-called protection afforded her by man-made laws has so far secured her nothing better than subjection; robbed her of the fruits of her labor, and even denied her the right to her own children; and

> Whereas, The recent decision of Justice Brewer is not in accordance with facts or with equity; therefore be it
>
> Resolved, That the Woman's Henry George League of Manhattan protests against the said decision of Justice Brewer of the Supreme Court, as unjust and humiliating to women; as tending to sex slavery; as opposed to economic freedom, and as inimical to the best interests of present and future generations; and be it further
>
> Resolved, That a copy of these resolutions be sent to the newspapers.[119]

Undoubtedly, Alice Stone Blackwell was not happy about publishing this resolution, but perhaps she feared that if she refused, the Henry George League itself, with chapters all over the world,[120] would retaliate, to the detriment of the woman suffrage movement. Additionally, the resolution was clearly feminist. An antisuffrage attack on *Muller* could have been referred to the *Remonstrance,* the main antisuffrage journal of the time,[121] but an attack on feminist grounds would seem to belong in *The Woman's Journal,* whatever Blackwell might have thought of it personally.

Although Alice Stone Blackwell's first editorial on *Muller* implied that many suffragists were concerned about the decision, the Woman's Henry George League resolution condemning the *Muller* decision is the only item critical of that decision published in *The Woman's Journal.* The views of other individuals and women's organizations are difficult to locate.[122]

We do not know who authored the Woman's Henry George League resolution or whether it is representative of the views of the organization.[123] There is no readily apparent connection between Henry George's philosophy and the feminism of the resolution on *Muller. Progress and Poverty,* George's widely read and highly influential work,[124] is neither profeminist nor antifeminist. Undoubtedly various passages could be cited to support either side of the controversy.[125] When George ran for the mayor of New York on the ticket of the newly formed labor party, "equal pay for equal work without distinction of sex" on public works was a plank in his platform.[126] Other than this, there is little evidence that George was strongly in favor of women's rights.

Woman's Henry George Leagues existed in several cities in the United States by 1908,[127] but it is not clear whether all of them were as feminist as the resolution against *Muller* appeared to be. In fact, there is some evidence that they were not. At the fourth annual banquet of the Woman's Henry George League of New York, on February 12, 1908, Mrs. Christine Ross Barker, "the able advocate of 'equal pay for equal work,' " spoke on the subject of "Wages for Women."[128] She began her talk by chastising some Single Taxers for their sexist attitudes—"heresies," she called them—and emphasizing that the Single Tax philosophy is "built upon the rock of equal rights for *all* including women and special privileges for *none*—not even women."[129] She continued with a passage that echoes the "sex slavery" theme of the resolution against *Muller:*

> So long as women are dependent upon men for a livelihood there can be no normal human relation between them—no real comradeship—no real love. It is a commonplace of our philosophy that the man who is dependent upon another man for a living is that other's slave. Why are we not frank enough to make it an equal part of our propaganda that the woman who is dependent upon a man for a living is that man's slave?[130]

After describing various forms of sex discrimination in the marketplace and advocating wages for housework,[131] she concluded that women must "take [their] work out of the home and into the open labor market" and ended with a statement of the connection between the Single Tax and economic independence for women:

> The chief beauty of the Single Tax to me is that it will give woman her place in the economic world, and so shall we stand as simple separate persons with our feet planted on the earth, self supporting, self respecting human units, owing no man anything. The Single Tax will not solve all problems, but it will solve absolutely and forever the problems of unearned riches and undersired [sic] poverty, and will clear the air of all the rottenness that flows from these two sources and so establish a healthy human fellowship among men and women.[132]

Perhaps the resolution against *Muller* was a result of the inspiration of Mrs. Barker's speech rather than settled principles of the Woman's Henry George League, or perhaps it is evidence of a large group of feminist precursors to the Woman's Party members of the 'twenties.[133] Whichever is the case, Alice Stone Blackwell was not going to allow these women to get the last word. Into the same issue of *The Woman's Journal* she slipped a paragraph about *Muller* in a column headed "Concerning Women":

Miss Josephine Goldmark did much of the research work for the brief on which Justice Brewer's opinion as to the constitutionality of limiting women's hours of labor was based. In an article in "Charities," she points out that men's labor in mines is limited by law to eight hours a day in eight States of the Union, and that the men's value and dignity as citizens is not thought to be lessened thereby; nor is their right to vote impaired. Miss Goldmark is a suffragist.[134]

Finally, a whole month later, she published an article by Florence Kelley entitled "Justice Brewer's Decision"[135] that was the coup de grace to the Woman's Henry George Leaguers. Kelley explained her delay by stating that she had "waited for the published text" of *Muller* before writing about it. Then the famous lawyer, orator, and social reformer explained to her suffragist audience why *Muller* was a victory for those who supported protective labor legislation for all workers, men and women alike:

> The ground taken by the Court is clear. It must be shown that a law restricting freedom to contract really protects the health of the person thus restricted. Henceforth both men and women need only show a clear relation between their working hours and their good or bad health in order to have statutory restrictions upon their working day sustained by the Supreme Court of the United States.
> As women attain more power, they will undoubtedly follow the example of the voting working-men, and establish leisure for themselves in many more industries and in a much larger measure.[136]

She was correct in her prediction that the Court would ultimately uphold protective labor laws for men as well as women.[137] However, by that time men had long since abandoned the effort.[138] More importantly in terms of feminism, Kelley did not see anything in *Muller* dangerous to the women's movement:

> The only unsatisfactory thing about this decision is that women had no voice in enacting the statute of Oregon, or in electing the men who did enact it; no voice in electing the judges who sustained it in Oregon, and will, except in four free States, have no share in enacting the beneficent legislation which will naturally follow upon this decision.[139]

Kelley ignored the fact that *Muller* undermined the natural rights argument for woman suffrage,[140] and she proceeded to state what may have appeared to be a straightforward expediency argument for the vote. In fact, it was a straightforward argument for "protective" labor legislation, which she believed would come sooner and be more comprehensive if enacted by the representatives of women voters. That she was not really arguing for the franchise probably did not worry Alice Stone Blackwell and her readers. It was close enough; if it helped in the campaign for woman suffrage, that was sufficient.

CONCLUSION

In 1908 *Muller v. Oregon* was generally viewed, by women as well as men, as a victory for modern Progressive reform—as a recognition by the Court of the harsh conditions under which women workers toiled and their special need for protection by the state. In fact, the *Muller* holding that the state may take a paternalistic "protectionist" stance toward women, even against their will, is not modern but is based on traditional views of women and their "proper" roles. It has taken over seventy more years for the Court to overcome the protectionist stance and to assume an egalitarian stance toward women, and the transition is not yet complete. Viewed as a chapter in women's history, therefore, *Muller* was not "progressive."

This paper has raised the issue of whether feminists in 1908 recognized the conservative—even reactionary—nature of the case with respect to women's rights. At first the historian, seeing no obvious opposition to *Muller*, is tempted to say "Well, we can't expect that their consciousness will be raised to the same degree as ours!" Alternatively, one could conclude that feminists were simply engrossed with the "single issue" of the day—the vote—and did not have the time or energy to scrutinize Supreme Court opinions. In fact, at least one small group of feminists opposed the "protective" labor legislation upheld in *Muller* on the ground that it violated their ultimate principle of equality between the sexes, and they expressed their view in *The Woman's Journal*, the main suffrage newspaper of the time. The editor of the newspaper also recognized the antifeminist bases of *Muller*, but did not criticize the case and the social reformer suffragists, such as Florence Kelley, who had participated in it. After the feminist attack on *Muller* in *The Woman's Journal*, the social reformers counterattacked in the same newspaper, and the controversy within the women's movement was stilled until after the vote was gained. It is not that women were too busy with the vote to notice *Muller;* those who placed "Progressive reform" above the vote or who favored the vote at any price simply outnumbered the true feminists.

NOTES

1. 208 U.S. 412 (1908).
2. See notes 16–18 *infra* and accompanying text.
3. For the history of these laws, see J. Baer, *The Chains of Protection: The Judicial Response to Women's Labor Legislation,* 3–41 (1978)(hereinafter cited as *Chains*).
4. Freedom of contract was thought to be a liberty guaranteed by the fourteenth amendment's due process clause: "nor shall any state deprive any person of life, liberty, or property, without due process of law." See L. Tribe, *American Constitutional Law* § 8–1 (1978).
5. *Compare* Ritchie v. People, 155 Ill. 98 (1895) *with* Commonwealth v. Hamilton Manufacturing Co., 120 Mass. 383 (1876); Wenham v. State, 65 Neb. 394 (1902); and State v. Buchanan, 29 Wash. 602 (1902).
6. 198 U.S. 45 (1905).
7. Ibid. at 56 ("Is this . . . an . . . interference with the right of the individual to . . . enter into these contracts . . . which may seem to him appropriate or necessary for the support of *himself and his family?"*), 57 ("There is no contention that bakers as a class are not equal in intelligence and capacity to *men* in other trades . . . or that they are not able to assert their rights and care for themselves without the protecting arm of the State. . . ."), and 64 ("[T]he real object and purpose were simply to regulate the hours of labor between the master and his employees *(all being men, sui juris)* in a private business not dangerous . . . to the health of the employees") (emphasis added).
8. This article follows the practice in B. Babcock et al., *Sex Discrimination and the Law: Causes and Remedies* (1975) (hereinafter cited as Babcock) of putting the term "protective" in quotation marks "whenever it refers to laws for women only to emphasize that such laws are often in fact not protective but discriminatory." Ibid. at 19 n. 1.
9. Muller v. Oregon, 208 U.S. 412 (1908).
10. The Supreme Court had held ten years earlier that the working hours of miners could be restricted to eight hours per day. Holden v. Hardy, 169 U.S. 366 (1898). Of course, even if the Court had held that the hours of work in laundries could be restricted, it could still have held the Oregon law in *Muller* unconstitutional in that it covered only women. However, the state legislature would not have been foreclosed from passing a law covering all laundry workers.
11. Muller v. Oregon, 208 U.S. at 421 and 422.

12. Ibid.

13. Cf. Weeks v. Southern Bell Tel. & Tel. Co., 408 F.2d 228 (5th Cir. 1969):

> Men have always had the right to determine whether the incremental increase in remuneration for strenuous, dangerous, obnoxious, boring or unromantic tasks is worth the candle. The promise of Title VII is that women are now to be on equal footing.

14. Orr v. Orr, 440 U.S. 268, 283 (1979). This is not to say that paternalism is dead. See Erickson, "Equality Between the Sexes in the 1980's," 28 *Cleveland State L. Rev.* 591, 598–603 (1979).

15. In the 1973 abortion cases, the Supreme Court held that, subsequent to "viability" of the fetus, the state may prohibit all abortions except those necessary to preserve the woman's life or health. Roe v. Wade, 410 U.S. 113, 163–65 (1973). The state's interest was stated in terms of "protecting potential life," which seems to refer to the life of the particular fetus. See Erickson, " Women and the Supreme Court: Anatomy is Destiny," 41 *Brooklyn Law Review* 209, 238–55 (1974). On the other hand, in Maher v. Roe, 432 U.S. 464 (1977), the Court indicated that the interest in the life of the particular fetus is not the only valid state interest:

> In addition to the direct interest in protecting the fetus, a State may have legitimate demographic concerns about its rate of population growth. Such concerns are basic to the future of the State and in some circumstances could constitute a substantial reason for departure from a position of neutrality between abortion and childbirth.

Ibid. at 478 n. 11. The Court did not delineate the circumstances under which the state could "depart . . . from a position of neutrality between abortion and childbirth," that is, whether a state could prohibit abortion if the state's population began to drop slightly or only if most of the population were destroyed by a nuclear holocaust. However the state's interest is defined, it looks uncomfortably similar to the *Muller* bearer-of-the-race theory.

16. The Women's League for Equal Opportunity and the Equal Rights Association were formed in 1915 and 1917 in response to the displacement of women printers in New York City because of the 54-hours law and the prohibition of night work in 1912 and 1913. E. Baker, *Protective Labor Legislation*, 189–90 (1925) (hereinafter cited as Baker). The New York legislation affecting women transit workers was enacted in 1919 and repealed in 1920. *See* M. Winslow, *The Effects of Labor Legislation on the Employment Opportunities of Women*, 268–86 (1928).

17. I. Harper, *The History of Woman Suffrage* 381, 675–78 (1922) (hereinafter cited as 5 H.W.S.); I. Irwin; *History of the Woman's Party*, (1921).

18. *See* 5 H.W.S. at 678 for one of the first references to the E.R.A. The controversy between E.R.A. supporters and those who opposed it on the ground that it would nullify "protective" labor laws is described in Babcock, *supra* note 8, at 247–87 (1975). For later criticism of *Muller, see also*

Crozier, "Constitutional Law—Regulation of Conditions of Employment of Women. A Critique of Muller v. Oregon," 13 *Boston U. L. Rev.* 276 (1933).

Title VII of the Civil Rights Act of 1964 prohibits sex discrimination in employment. 42 U.S.C. §2000-e *et seq.* See *Chains, supra* note 3, at 149–74.

19. The National Consumers' League (NCL) was in the forefront of the movement for "protective" labor legislation. *See* Baker, *supra* note 16, at 157–62; M. Nathan, *Story of an Epoch-Making Movement* (1926). *See* the description of the compilation of materials for the brief by Josephine and Pauline Goldmark, Florence Kelley and others of the NCL in J. Goldmark, *Impatient Crusader: Florence Kelley's Life Story,* 143–59 (1953) (hereinafter cited as *Crusader*).

20. Hill, "Protection of Women Workers and the Courts: A Legal Case History," 5 *Feminist Studies* 247, 252 (No. 2, 1979). *See* notes 135–40 and accompanying text.

21. Feminism is a philosophy, not an organization or a "movement," although there have been two "waves" of feminist activity in America and many feminist organizations have attempted and are attempting to change society by bringing it into line with feminist philosophy. Webster defines "feminism" as "the theory of the political, economic, and social equality of the sexes." (*Third New International Dictionary* 837, 3d ed., 1964.) The author prefers to define it as the belief that women and men are inherently equal in intelligence, talents and abilities, and that sex-stereotyped societal roles should be discarded in favor of freedom of the individual to choose what role(s) s/he wishes to play in society. Unlike O'Neill, who calls them "social feminists," (W. O'Neill, *Everyone Was Brave* x, 1969) (hereinafter cited as O'Neill, *Brave*), this author does not term the social reformers feminists at all. Some were, but most were not.

22. This article is part of a more extended research project by this author to uncover evidence of the *Muller* controversy that exists in public and private sources, especially suffrage publications and letters of women who were active in women's issues at the time.

It would be surprising to discover a lack of feminist opposition to "protective" labor legislation in the United States before *Muller.* In England in the late nineteenth century there was strong opposition in the form of the Women's Rights Opposition Movement, which began in the 1850s. One historian of women's labor history states: "The Movement opposed statutory protection largely on the ground that it was an interference with the freedom of the individual to work for as many hours and on whatever terms she chose. Such interference was regarded as even more objectionable because it emanated from an all-male Parliament." W. Creighton, *Working Women and the Law* (1979).

23. Statute quoted in Muller v. Oregon, 208 U.S. at 416–17.

24. State v. Muller, 48 Ore. 252, 85 Pac. 855 (1906). The briefs of the Supreme Court of Oregon were never recorded or bound in the Oregon Supreme Court library, although such was the usual practice; this omis-

sion is unexplained. Letter to the author from R. Andrus, Librarian, Supreme Court of Oregon, undated (approx. January 8, 1979).
25. See sources cited in note 19 *supra*.
26. A. Mason, *Brandeis: A Free Man's Life* 248 (1946).
27. This episode is taken from *Crusader, supra* note 19, at 143–55.
28. The brief was published, together with the United States Supreme Court opinion, in L. Brandeis & J. Goldmark, *Women in Industry* (1908).
29. The legal argument comprises two pages.
30. For a criticism of this data, *see* Baer, *supra* note 3, at 59–61.
31. *See*, for example, Brief for Defendant in Error at 28–36, Muller v. Oregon, 208 U.S. 412 (1908) (hereinafter cited as Brandeis Brief).
32. *See*, for example, ibid. at 24–27.
33. A small portion of the brief was, however, devoted to such "evidence." *See* ibid. at 104–09.
34. Muller v. Oregon, 208 U.S. at 421.
35. Brandeis Brief at 18–23.
36. Ibid. at 22, 33, 35, 36–42, 49–55, 61.
37. Ibid. at 33, 35, 38, 42, 49, 59.
38. Ibid. at 20, 33, 42, 48–51, 93, 97.
39. Ibid. at 82–84.
40. *See*, for example, Bradwell v. Illinois, 16 Wall. 130 (1872). As late as 1948, the Supreme Court upheld a law prohibiting women (except wives and daughters of bar owners) from tending bar. Goesart v. Cleary, 335 U.S. 464 (1948). Such laws have now been outlawed by Title VII of the Civil Rights Act of 1964. *See* Baer, *supra* note 3, at 194–67.
41. The author has argued elsewhere that the Supreme Court is still allowing discrimination to justify further discrimination. *See* Erickson, "Equality Between the Sexes in the 1980's," 28 *Cleveland State L. Rev.* 591, 596–97 (1979).
42. An *amicus curiae* (friend of the court) brief is one submitted by an individual or organization not a party to the action who has an interest in the outcome and presumably can aid the court in its deliberations.
The New York Women's Trade Union League (NYWTUL) petitioned the American Federation of Labor to argue in favor of the Oregon law. President's Report for November, 1907, NYWTUL, Minutes of Executive Board Meeting Held Tuesday, November 26, 1907, p. 1. The A.F.L. did not do so, however. For the relationship between the National Women's Trade Union League and the A.F.L., *see* O'Neill, *Brave* 98–102.
Nancy Schrom Dye reports that the National Women's Trade Union League was divided over the issue in the period after *Muller*, but did decide to support such legislation. Dye, "Creating a Feminist Alliance: Sisterhood and Class Conflict in the New York Women's Trade Union League, 1903–1914," in J. Friedman & W. Shade, eds., *Our American Sisters* 284–86, 293–94 (2d ed. 1976). Dye states, however, and this author's research confirms, that there is no evidence of such a dispute in the NYW-TUL at the time of *Muller*. In fact, it appears that "protective" labor

legislation was unquestioningly accepted. N. Dye, *The Women's Trade Union League of New York 1903–1920* 400 (Ph.D. Thesis, University of Wisconsin, 1974). In May, 1907, the NYWTUL Secretary's Report notes: "I have twice met with the Committee of the Women's National W.U.L. of the National Child Labor Committee to consider recommendations to the U.S. Bureau of Labor on the conditions of women [sic] and childrens [sic] work." NYWTUL Secretary's Report, Month Ending May 22, 1907, p. 5. The following month, she reported on People v. Williams, 189 N.Y. 131 (1907), *aff'g* 100 N.Y.S. 337 (Sp. Sess. 1st Div. N.Y.C. 1906):

> I have to report that the law limiting women's work to the hours between six a.m. to 9 p.m. has been declared unconstitutional on the grounds of the state having no right to interefere [sic] with the freedom of contract of women, that it was sentimental to claim that she was not as capable as the man to do a full days work.

NYWTUL Secretary's Report to the Executive Board, Month Ending June 27, 1907, p. 8. *Williams* was again referred to in the Annual Report 1907–1908 of NYWTUL (March 27, 1908), which noted at p. 7 the following resolution of the national convention of women unionists called by the NYWTUL for July 14, 1907: "(4) Endorsing woman suffrage, particularly on the ground of the recent decision in New York declaring limitation of night work for women, illegal."

There is no doubt that the national organization, as opposed to the New York branch, approved of *Muller*. One of their general goals was the eight-hour day, but, more specifically, their 1909 Convention Handbook referred to *Muller* and to "Mr. Brandeis' brief" to support their argument that ten hours of work per day was excessive and damaging to the health of waitresses. *See* NYWTUL 1909 Convention Handbook 25, the NYWTUL archives.

The NYWTUL archives are located in the New York State Labor Library, Two World Trade Center, Room 26, 68th floor, New York City. The author gratefully acknowledges Zofia Doliwa, librarian and Magister Juris, for assistance in the search through these records.

43. Ritchie v. People, 155 Ill. 98 (1895).

44. Brief for the State of Oregon at 8, Muller v. Oregon, 208 U.S. 412 (1908), (hereinafter cited as State's Brief) quoted from *Black's Constitutional Law*, a leading treatise of the time.

45. Ibid. at 9.

46. Ibid. at 11.

47. Ibid. at 10, 12, 19.

48. Ibid. at 14, citing Wenham v. State, 65 Neb. 400, 405, (1902).

49. *See* Crozier, *supra* note 18 at 289.

50. State's Brief at 19.

51. State v. Muller, 48 Ore. 252 (1906).

52. *See*, for example, E. Clarke, *Sex in Education* (1873) (argument against higher education for women on the ground that it destroys their reproductive capacity and general health).

53. Ritchie v. People, 155 Ill. 98 (1895).

54. Employers often opposed hours laws because they feared that employers in states without such laws would have a competitive advantage. *See,* for example, S. Kingsbury, *Labor Laws and Their Enforcement with Special Reference to Massachusetts* 49 (1911).

55. Brief for Plaintiff in Error at 16, Muller v. Oregon, 208 U.S. 412 (1908) (hereinafter cited as Muller's Brief).

56. Ibid. at 19.

57. Orr v. Orr, 440 U.S. 268 (1979).

58. Muller's Brief at 24.

59. The race-sex analogy had, in fact, been used by Mathew Carpenter in his argument that the state could not deny to women on the basis of sex the right to be admitted to the practice of law. Bradwell v. Illinois, 83 U.S. 130, 134 (1872).

60. Ibid.

61. Ibid. at 23, citing R. Tiedeman, *Limitations of the Police Power* § 86 (1886).

62. Ibid. at 19–20. *See also* ibid. at 26.

63. Ibid. at 31.

64. Muller v. Oregon, 208 U.S. 413, 421–23 (1908). *See* Baer's analysis of *Muller* in *Chains, supra* note 3, at 61–67.

65. Muller v. Oregon, 208 U.S. at 422–23.

66. Ibid. at 419 n. 1.

67. See, for example, J. Appleman, *Persuasion in Brief Writing* 7 (1968); Biklé, "Judicial Determination of Questions of Fact Affecting the Constitutional Validity of Legislative Action," 38 *Harv. L. Rev.* 6, 12–14 (1924).

68. *New York Times,* February 25, 1908, p. 1, col. 7. *Muller* was not even mentioned under "Supreme Court Decisions" of February 24, 1908, on page 8 of the *Times* of the 25th, col. 1.

69. *Chicago Daily Tribune,* February 25, 1908, p. 1, col. 7.

70. Ibid. at col. 1. *See* Great Northern Railway Co. v. United States, 208 U.S. 452 (1908).

71. *Chicago Daily Tribune,* February 25, 1908, p. 2, col. 5.

72. "Struggle for Life—Monarchy in Danger of Extinction," *Los Angeles Times,* February 26, 1908, p. 1, col. 7.

73. Ibid. at col. 5.

74. *Washington Post,* February 25, 1908, p. 1, col. 5.

75. Ibid.

76. Loewe v. Lawlor, 208 U.S. 274 (1908). Ironically, *Loewe* proved to be much less significant for labor than *Muller* was for women. The Clayton Act was passed only six years later, and Section 20 of that Act exempted labor organizations from the operation of the antitrust laws, although it was not interpreted in accord with Congressional intent until 1940. *See* R. Gorman, *Labor Law* 621–27 (1976).

77. *Chicago Daily Tribune,* February 26, 1908, p. 8, col. 7.

78. Ritchie v. The People, 155 Illinois 98 (1895). Kelley was appointed Chief Inspector for Factories for Illinois in 1893, after having written several reports and studies relied on by the state legislature in passing the first

182   Nancy S. Erickson

factory law for Illinois. She also led the campaign for its passage. *See Crusader*, supra note 19, at 33–47, and F. Kelley, *Some Ethical Gains Through Legislation* 139–45 (1905). A ten-hour law was passed in 1909 and sustained in 1910. Ritchie & Co. v. Wayman, 244 Ill. 509 (1910).

79. *Los Angeles Daily Times*, February 27, 1908, p. 4, col. 4.
80. *See* note 78 *supra*.
81. *Los Angeles Daily Times*, February 27, 1908, p. 4.
82. *See* text accompanying note 68 *supra*.
83. *New York Times*, February 26, 1908, p. 6, col. 1.
84. The Court's words were: "As minors, though not to the same extent, she has been looked upon in the courts as needing especial care that her rights may be preserved." 208 U.S. at 421.
85. People v. Williams, 189 N.Y. 131 (1907), *aff'g* 100 N.Y.S. 337 (Sp. Sess. 1st Div. N.Y.C. 1906). Florence Kelley is reported to have been more concerned about this decision than about *Lochner*, since men could secure shorter hours for themselves through union activities and, in hazardous occupations, through the power of the vote. Women had neither. *See Crusader, supra* note 19, at 147–49.
86. *New York Times*, February 26, 1908, p. 6, col. 2, quoting from Section 55 of Tennyson's poem "In Memoriam" (1850).
87. Tennyson's suggestion of the principle of natural selection nine years before Darwin's *Origin of the Species* (1859) is not as surprising as might seem at first glance. Tennyson was familiar with the works of the pre-Darwinian scientists, Lyell, Herschel, and Chambers. E. Mattes, "Further Reassurances in Herschel's Natural Philosophy and Chambers's Vestiges of Creation," in R. Ross, *In Memoriam: An Authoritative Text, Backgrounds and Sources, Criticism* (1973). In fact, the two lines quoted by the *New York Times* could be a poetic translation of the following passage from Chambers:

[T]he individual, as far as the present sphere of Being is concerned, is to the Author of Nature a consideration of inferior moment. Everywhere we see the arrangements for the species perfect; the individual is left, as it were, to take his chance amid the mêlée of the various laws affecting him.

R. Chambers, *Vestiges of the Natural History of Creation* 25 (1844; 1945 ed.)
But the species was not necessarily safe from extinction, according to Tennyson. Nature "seems" to be "careful" of the species and "careless" of the individual life, but this is just an illusion. Section 56 of "In Memoriam" continued:

"So careful of the type?" but no.
From scarped cliff and quarried stone
She cries, "A thousand types are gone:
I care for nothing, all shall go."

This conclusion is probably based on Lyell's *Principles of Geology* (1830–1833): "The inhabitants of the globe, like all the other parts of it, are subject to change. It is not only the individual that perishes, but whole species." C. Lyell, 2 *Principles of Geology* title page (1830–1833). *See* Mattes, "The

Challenge of Geology to Belief in Immortality and a God of Love," in Ross,
supra, at 122.
   88. *New York Times*, February 26, 1908, p. 6, col. 2. For the current
constitutional status of laws exempting women from jury duty *see* Taylor
v. Louisiana, 419 U.S. 522 (1975), disapproving Hoyt v. Florida, 368 U.S.
57 (1961). Women-only alimony laws have been held unconstitutional. Orr
v. Orr, 440 U.S. 268 (1979). Title VII now prohibits exclusion of women
from the police force. 42 U.S.C. § 2000e *et seq.* (1972). It appears, however,
that differential treatment of women in the military may be condoned by
the Court on the authority of *Muller!* See Kahn v. Shevin, 416 U.S. at 356
n. 10:

> Gender has never been rejected as an impermissible classification in all
> instances. Congress has not so far drafted women into the Armed
> Services, . . . The famous Brandeis Brief in *Muller v. Oregon.* . . on which the
> court specifically relied . . . that the special physical structure of women has a
> bearing on the "conditions under which she should be permitted to toil."

Many would argue, however, that under the Supreme Court's later opinions (for example, Craig v. Boren, 429 U.S. 190 [1976]), sex discrimination
in the military would be outlawed. *See* Goodman, "Women, War, and
Equality: An Examination of Sex Discrimination in the Military," 5
Women's Rts L. Rptr. 243 (1979). In Rostker v. Goldberg, 101 S. Ct. 2646
(1981), the Court held the male-only draft registration law constitutional
because the purpose of registration is a ready supply of combat-eligible
inductees, and women, by federal law, are not combat-eligible. The law
making women non-combat-eligible was not challenged, however, and
the Court did not rule on its constitutionality.
   89. "The Position of Woman," *New York Times*, February 26, 1908, p. 6,
col. 2 (paraphrasing *Muller*).
   90. "Property and the Constitution," *New York Times*, February 25,
1908, p. 6, col. 1, commenting on Trustees of the Village of Saratoga
Springs v. Saratoga Gas, Electric Light, and Power Co., 191 N.Y. 123
(1908).
   91. "Property and the Constitution," *New York Times*, February 25,
1908, p. 6, col. 1, commenting on Adair v. United States, 208 U.S. 161
(1908).
   92. *New York Times*, February 26, 1908, p. 6, col. 2. For antisuffrage
editorials, *see*, for example, editorials of December 6, 1908, p. 12, col. 1;
December 20, pt. 2, p. 10, col. 1; December 25, p. 6, col. 2.
   93. "Brewer Equal Suffragist," *Washington Post*, March 1, 1908, p. 1,
col. 7.
   94. Ibid. Dr. Shaw then described Justice Brewer as being a more radical feminist than the suffragists: "[H]e is the most radical suffragist I know.
He went so far as to say in a speech that he hoped the time would come
when a woman would be president of the United States. No woman hopes
that." The *Post* picked this up in its headlines: "President of Association
Does Not Agree With His Wish to See a Woman President." Dr. Shaw's
position on woman suffrage, however, was firm. "As for the idea that

184 Nancy S. Erickson

voting is one of the things that will impair the functions of race preservation, I don't see why it should. . . . "(Ibid.) The antisuffragists disagreed,
of course. They considered "woman's physical constitution as too delicate
to withstand the turbulance of political life." A. Kraditor, *The Ideas of the
Woman Suffrage Movement 1890–1920*, 15 (1971) (hereinafter cited as
Kraditor, *Ideas*).

95. "Brewer Equal Suffragist," *Washington Post*, March 1, 1908, p. 1,
col. 7.

96. 5 H.W.S., *supra* note 17, at 742, reprinted in W. O'Neill, *The Woman
Movement: Feminism in the United States and England*, 133–35 (1969)
(hereinafter cited as O'Neill, *Woman Movement*).

97. The split is described in O'Neill, *Brave, supra* note 21 at 14–30.

98. The *Revolution* ceased publication in 1870. E. Flexner, *Century of
Struggle* 153 (1968 ed.) (hereinafter cited as Flexner). The reunion of National and American took place in 1890. Ibid.

99. 39 *The Woman's Journal*, February 29, 1908, no. 9, p. 33, col. 2.
(hereinafter cited as *W.J.*).

100. 39 *W.J.* no. 10, March 7, 1908, p. 38, col. 1.

101. Kraditor, *Ideas, supra* note 94, at 38–63.

102. Ibid. at 38–42. The "Declaration of Sentiments" adopted by the
Seneca Falls Convention of 1848 is modeled on the Declaration of Independence. This document is reproduced in E. Stanton, S. Anthony, and
M. Gage, 1 *History of Woman Suffrage* 70–71 (1881) (hereinafter cited as 1
H.W.S.); A. Kraditor, ed., *Up From the Pedestal: Selected Writings in the
History of American Feminism* 184–88 (1968); O'Neill, *Woman Movement,
supra* note 94, at 108–10. *See also* Kraditor, *Ideas* at 58 n.5 for other instances in which suffragists cited the principles of the Declaration of Independence; and the records of the woman's right convention of 1870 (called
by the Stanton-Anthony faction) in P. Davis, *History of the National Rights
Movement* (1871, reprinted 1971) *(passim)*.

103. The influx of "new" immigrants was disturbing to the older inhabitants in many ways. *See* R. Wiebe, *The Search For Order 1877–1920* 54,
62, 210 (1967). Some newly arrived groups from particularly unfamiliar
cultures were especially threatening. The Chinese laborers, for example,
were at one time totally ineligible for citizenship, and therefore, the vote.
See United States v. Wong Kim Ark, 169 U.S. 649, 702 (1898). The Supreme
Court had to determine whether the natives of the American colonies were
entitled to certain rights previously considered basic and afforded even to
women. *See* Dorr v. United States, 195 U.S. 138 (1904) (trial by jury). For
the effect of the "new" immigration on the suffrage movement, *see*
Kraditor, *Ideas* at 105–37.

104. Kraditor, *Ideas* at 39. Expediency arguments were not unknown in
the early period. *See*, for example, speech at an equal rights convention in
1848 (after the Seneca Falls Convention) reported in 1 H.W.S. 77, reproduced in O'Neill, *Brave, supra* note 22, at 49–50.

105. Kraditor, *Ideas* at 39.

106. Ibid. at 45.

107. Ibid at 90–91.

108. This was the argument in *Muller*, of course.

109. Examples of statutes of which reformers might have approved that women could enact to protect themselves against men would be laws raising the age of consent for statutory rape and making drunkenness a ground for divorce.

110. See note 21 *supra*.

111. *See* Kraditor's discussion of Stanton in *Ideas* at 39–42.

112. *See* note 19 and text accompanying notes 27 and 79–81 *supra* and notes 135–40 *infra*.

113. *See*, for example, her essays "Why Women Should Vote" and "The Larger Aspects of the Women's Movement" in C. Lasch, ed., *The Social Thought of Jane Addams* (1965).

114. Kraditor, *Ideas* at 39.

115. Alice Stone Blackwell once stated: "The God I would like to believe in wouldn't squash individuals for the good of the whole if it wasn't for their own good as well." Such a statement could be seen as consistent with "protective" labor legislation if such laws were believed to help women themselves, as well as the race. Blackwell also joined the Women's Trade Union League, which supported "protective" labor legislation. "Alice Stone Blackwell," in I. E. James, J. James, and P. Boyer, *Notable American Women* 157 (1971). For the position of the Women's Trade Union League, *see* note 42 *supra*.

116. 39 *W.J.* no. 10, March 7, 1908, p. 38, col. 1, quoted in text accompanying note 100 *supra*.

117. Muller v. Oregon, 208 U.S. at 423.

118. 39 *W.J.* no. 10, March 7, 1908, p. 40, col. 5:

Louis D. Brandeis of Boston deserves gratitude from all those who rejoice in the decision of the U.S. Supreme Court upholding the constitutionality of the Oregon law that forbids employers to require women to work more than 10 hours a day in factories, laundries, etc. The decision is said to be due to the exhaustive brief prepared by Mr. Brandeis. He devoted a great deal of time and labor to the case, and has refused to take any pay.

119. 39 *W.J.* no. 12, March 21, 1908, p. 48, col. 1. The statement that manmade laws have "robbed her of the fruits of her labor" refers to the fact that, before the Married Women's Property Acts, a married woman's wages belonged not to the woman herself, but to her husband, who could demand them from her employer and then spend them as he wished. L. Kanowitz, *Women and the Law* 35–41 (1969). The reference to a denial of "the right to her own children" is an allusion to the common-law rule that, upon divorce, custody of children was awarded to the father. *See* Zainaldin, "The Emergence of a Modern American Family Law: Child Custody, Adoption, and the Courts, 1796–1851," 73 *N.W.U. L. Rev.* 1038 (1979). The "tender years" doctrine preferring the mother was a mid-nineteenth century development. Ibid at 1072–73.

120. 1908 issues of the *Single Tax Review*, the journal of the Henry George League (or Single Tax League, as it was also called), report on activities of the League in Australia, England, and New Zealand, among others. The journal was later entitled *Land and Freedom*.

121. *The Remonstrance* was published in Boston from 1890–1919. *See* Flexner, *supra* note 98, at 295.

122. *See* note 22 *supra.*

123. The Robert Schalkenbach Foundation in New York City was set up to further the educational work of Henry George. Ms. Frances Soriero of that organization, Mr. Philip Finkelstein, Director of the Henry George School, and Dr. Robert Clancey, formerly director of the school, have no knowledge of the existence of WHGL of N.Y., although one still exists in Chicago. Telephone conversations with the author, January 26, 1979. The papers of Henry George are in the New York Public Library but no reference to the WHGL of New York is evident in the index to the papers.

124. H. George, *Progress and Poverty* 406 (13th Printing 1940).

125. For example, contrast his judgment that political and legal equality has "reached its full expression in the American Republic" (ibid. at 529) with his view that "[w]e cannot go on educating boys and girls in our public schools and then refusing them the right to earn an honest living" (552).

126. J. Commons, 2 *History of Labor in the United States* 449 (1918).

127. J. Miller, *The Single Tax Yearbook* 444–45 (1917). *See also* ibid. at 25, for mention of the fact that single tax women of the United States held their own conventions at times.

128. 7 *Single Tax Review* no. 4 (March–April 1908) 41.

129. Ibid at 42 (emphasis in original).

130. Ibid.

131. Ibid. at 42–43.

Political economists must take their share of the blame for woman's status in the home, inasmuch as they have ignored her work as part of the production of wealth. The shopkeeper, it is explained, is as much a producer as the manufacturer. But it is where the shopkeeper stops that production begins for the homemaker. The goods delivered at the housekeeper's door are to her raw material and tools of production and still to be modified by human exertion and adapted by human labor to gratify human desire. This producer also is worthy of her product, this laborer worthy of her wages—and no more. Anything more is charity; anything less is slavery. It is precisely in order that we may keep the best things of life out of the domain of barter that we must take our stand squarely on the ground of working for wages.

132. Ibid. at 43.

133. *See* note 17 *supra* and "Declaration of Principles of Woman's Party" in J. Johnson, *Special Legislation of Women* 99–101 (1926).

134. 39 *W.J.* no. 17, March 21, 1908, p. 45, col. 5.

135. 39 *W.J.* no. 17, April 25, 1908, p. 68, col. 1.

136. Ibid. at col. 2.

137. Bunting v. Oregon, 243 U.S. 426 (1917).

138. The AFL in 1914 reversed its earlier support of maximum hours laws. Babcock, *supra* note 8, at 247.

139. 39 *W.J.* no. 17, April 25, 1908, p. 68, col. 1.

140. *See* text accompanying note 102 *supra.*

ADULT DERIVATIVE BENEFITS IN SOCIAL SECURITY: A WOMEN'S ISSUE

Grace Ganz Blumberg

Millions of Americans, most of them women, are derivative beneficiaries of workers covered by Old Age, Disability, and Survivors Insurance.[1] The Social Security Act Amendments of 1939[2] introduced derivative benefits four years after passage of the original Social Security Act of 1935.[3] Developments since 1939 have increasingly called into question the desirability of continuing to treat large classes of adults as derivative beneficiaries.[4] Such developments include a dramatic rise in female labor-force participation, an equally dramatic increase in the divorce rate, and basic changes in state marital property law. Congressional attempts to reflect these developments in the scheme of derivative benefits have produced anomalous results.[5]

This article explores the current derivative benefits system: its history, its underlying assumptions, and its capacity to adapt to social, economic, and legal change. The article then briefly examines alternative proposals for achieving the goals of the present system, as well as other goals arguably appropriate to it.

More than 95 percent of the aged derivative social security beneficiaries are women who collect benefits on the accounts of their retired, disabled or deceased husbands. Of the 26 million aged social security beneficiaries, about 15.8 million are women. Fifty-nine percent of those women (about 9.3 million) receive benefits as wives or widows of retired or disabled workers. In contrast, virtually all of the 10.2 million aged male social security beneficiaries collect benefits on their own accounts. Less than 1 percent of all aged male beneficiaries (54,258) receive benefits as the husbands or widowers of female workers.[6]

This is an abbreviated version of an article "Adult Derivative Benefits in Social Security," that originally appeared at 32 Stanford Law Review 233–292 (1980).

For the reader unfamiliar with Old Age, Disability, and Survivors Insurance[7] [OASDI], a brief description follows. The system provides monthly benefits to workers and, in certain instances, their dependents, in a manner designed to partially replace income lost on account of death, severe disability or retirement. Payments are made from current contributions paid by both employee and employer.[8]

In general, to achieve minimum eligibility for himself and his dependents, a worker now must have engaged in covered employment one quarter of the time from each year after 1950 or age twenty-one, whichever is later, until he dies, is disabled, or reaches retirement age.[9] In addition, to be eligible for disability benefits, a worker must have engaged in covered employment during half the quarters in the ten-year period immediately preceding disability.[10] Once basic eligibility is established, the level of payments is computed by averaging monthly earnings in covered employment since 1950, after excluding the lowest five years.[11] The formula for calculating benefits favors low-income workers because the insured receives a markedly higher percentage of his first portion of average monthly earnings than he does of the rest. The amount payable to an insured worker at retirement age is called the Primary Insurance Amount[12] [PIA]. All benefits payable to the insured's dependents are computed as a percentage of the insured's PIA. For example, a dependent spouse's benefit is 50 percent of the insured's PIA,[13] a surviving spouse's benefit is 100 percent of the insured's PIA;[14] a surviving dependent child's benefit is 75 percent of his deceased parent's PIA.[15]

For convenient reference, adult derivative benefits[16] are schematized on the next page.

I. HISTORY OF THE SOCIAL SECURITY ACT AND OF DEPENDENTS' BENEFITS

A. Development of the Act and Derivative Benefits

The original social security scheme[17] adopted in 1935 represented one-half of a federal program designed to assure old-age income security. The plan, to be financed in the early stages by equal contributions from selected groups[18] of employers and employees,

TABLE 1

Adult Dependents' Benefits—Calculated as a Percentage of
Worker's PIA and Subject To Earnings Test

Intact Marriage	*In Divorce*
WIFE'S ALLOWANCE—50% H's PIA	DIVORCED WIFE'S ALLOWANCE— 50% H's PIA
granted when H is retired or disabled *and* W is over 65 (62)* or has in her care a qualifying child.	granted when H is retired or disabled if ex-W is over 65 (62)* and H-W marriage lasted at least 10 years.
(for men? By statute only if H is over 65 [62]* and is economically dependent on W. The support requirement was declared unconstitutional in *Califano* v. *Goldfarb*, 430 U.S. 199 [1977].)	(for men? Not by statute but see note 58 *infra*.)
SURVIVING MOTHER'S ALLOWANCE—75% H's PIA	SURVIVING DIVORCED MOTHER'S ALLOWANCE—75% H's PIA
granted when H is dead and there is a qualifying child.	granted when H is dead and there is a qualifying child.
(Each child gets 75% PIA as well—up to a family maximum of 150–180% PIA.)	(Each child gets 75% PIA as well—up to a family maximum of 150–180% PIA.)
(for men? Not by statute but benefits were constitutionally extended to men in *Weinberger* v. *Wiesenfeld*, 420 U.S. 636 [1977].)	(for men? Not by statute but see note 58 *infra*.)
WIDOW'S ALLOWANCE—100% PIA	SURVIVING DIVORCED WIFE'S ALLOWANCE—100% PIA
At age 65, 100% of H's PIA. An actuarially reduced benefit can be claimed at age 60 or, if W is totally disabled, at age 50, also actuarially reduced (by 50%).	same as widow's allowance if H-W marriage lasted at least 10 years.
(for men? Same as Wife's Allowance above.)	(for men? Not by statute but see note 58 *infra*.)

THE EFFECT OF REMARRIAGE

Generally, remarriage terminates derivative beneficiary status. There is an exception for widows and widowers who remarry after age 60. They may elect treatment as the beneficiary of the current or deceased spouse (at 50%, however, not 100%). As of January 1, 1979, widows and widowers over 60 may remarry without any alteration of their derivative surviving spouses' benefits.

*If claimed between age 62 and 65, the benefit is actuarially reduced.

was to be supplemented by another catchall scheme: federal funding of state old age assistance under the categorical Old Age Assistance [OAA][19] welfare program. It was expected that private savings and private pensions would establish a third tier of old-age income replacement.[20]

Social Security is a system in which today's workers pay taxes on earnings that are distributed to aged retired workers in some rela tion to the taxes paid by the retired workers to support the preceding generation of retirees.[21] The two original drawing cards of an employer-employee financed retirement income scheme were its promise not to drain the federal budget[22] and its capacity to encourage retirement of workers in order to free jobs for younger workers.[23] The second reason, as forcefully argued by one historian,[24] is the primary explanation for the system's reliance upon the mechanism of labor-force participation. The Civil Service Retirement Act of 1920 and the Railroad Retirement Acts of 1934 and 1935, models for the social security scheme, were largely conceived as a means for retiring older workers.[25] The legislative history of the social security program also indicates that the retirement of older workers was a significant factor in its adoption.[26]

Concern centered on whether the level of benefits would be high enough to ensure this goal.[27] The earnings test[28] and extremely unfavorable social security tax treatment of workers over age 65[29] are explained in part by the legislative goal of retiring superannuated workers. The 1935 scheme relied entirely upon labor-force participation as the basis for eligibility. To the extent that we have since repudiated the goal of retiring aged workers,[30] it seems useful to bear in mind the origin of social security's worker-related focus. The tie-in between labor-force participation and old-age income security is neither inevitable nor universal.[31]

The survival and growth of social security did not rest, however, on its potential or actual capacity to retire superannuated workers. The system's continuing vitality is due to its ability to accommodate both a concern for social adequacy and a concern for individual equity. Individual equity is what one expects from an annuity: the purchaser receives payments directly related to the amount of his contributions and actuarial expectations. Social adequacy or welfare requires that benefits provide basic comfort for all recipients.[32]

Congress's mixing of equity and adequacy in the original design of the social security system has been important to its continuing strength. The assurance of adequacy within a system nominally based on principles of equity explains much of the system's appeal. Social security survived and grew because of the appeal of the illusion it created. Taxes are "contributions"; recipients were, at first, "annuitants" and, later, "beneficiaries." Retirement benefits are "earned" and come "as of right."[33] While the packaging of the system provides the iconoclast[34] with an irresistible target, the illusion maintains its vitality for the working and retired public.

Congress has varied the balance between equity and adequacy during the history of social security. The original act of 1935 emphasized individual equity.[35] The scheme it proposed was based on the principle of contribution and included few welfare elements. The proposed system relied entirely on labor-force participation as the basis for eligibility and created a benefit structure not unlike that of many private annuities.[36] Benefits, scheduled to begin in 1942, were to be based on a worker's lifetime earnings record.[37] The worker was to receive payments determined by his contributions and those of his employer prior to his reaching age 65.[38] Two provisions, however, were designed for social adequacy. Benefits were to be progressive: the lower the worker's lifetime earnings, the greater would be the percentage of earnings replaced. Additionally, the act placed a ceiling on monthly benefits.[39] Even so, the concern for equity mainly characterized the system and no provision was made for direct benefits to retired workers' dependents.

A provision amended to the 1935 scheme before it went into effect provided derivative benefits for dependents, thus introducing significant adequacy elements into the system. The Senate Finance Committee charged the first Advisory Council on Social Security, appointed in May 1937, with considering the advisability of extending benefits to "survivors of individuals entitled to such benefits."[40] Exceeding the scope of its charge, the council recommended benefits not only for widows and children of deceased retired workers but also benefits for survivors of workers who died before retirement age.[41] Even more surprisingly, the council recommended that wives of living retired workers receive 50 percent of the husband's benefit.[42]

B. The Wife's Benefit

The wife's benefit introduced a pure adequacy measure to a system originally based strictly on earnings of individuals. Spouses of retired married workers would receive an additional supplement—50 percent of the retired worker's benefit—despite the fact married earners contributed no more in taxes than single workers. The council recommended this because benefits payable during the early years of the social security program would generally be inadequate to support single recipients, much less recipients who shared their benefits with family members.[43] Noting that in 1930, 64 percent of men aged sixty-five and over were married, the council saw the wife's allowance as a means of adequately supporting a greater number of needy people in a less expensive way than a general increase in the level of benefits.[44]

The council recommended the allowance as an alternative to the wife's claim on her own earnings account. She could collect one or the other, but not both.[45] Moreover, the recommendation conditioned eligibility for a wife's allowance on the husband's retirement and the wife's reaching retirement age, then sixty-five. While it recognized that many wives were younger than their husbands, the council thought the second requirement was necessary for internal consistency: Since the single woman could not claim benefits until age sixty-five, the retired worker's wife should not be able to do so either.[46]

C. The Widow's Benefit

The 1939 amendments also provided for widows. Under the amendments, a widow is not eligible for any benefits—unless she has in her care a child entitled to the child's benefit[47]—until she reaches retirement age. At that time, she can claim a widow's benefit on her deceased husband's account[48] or she can claim a retirement benefit on her own earnings account—but not both.[49] No mechanism exists for building the widow's contribution record on top of her deceased husband's.

D. The 1950 Amendments: Husbands' and Widowers' Benefits, Divorced Wives' and Widows' Benefits

Congress has made no subsequent changes of the magnitude of

the 1939 amendments. The 1950 amendments created husband's and widower's benefits, eligibility for which, unlike wife's and widow's benefits, required proof that the husband was economically dependent upon his wife.[50] Congress also extended to the divorced mother caring for a child of her deceased former husband the "mother's benefit" payable to widows in similar circumstances.[51] Like the widowed mother's benefit, the divorced mother's benefit terminated when the youngest child reached eighteen. Unlike the widow's benefit, however, it did not resume when the divorced mother reached retirement age. However, in 1965 Congress introduced the equivalent of the wife's benefit for the divorced woman who reached retirement age and satisfied three conditions: that she have been married for at least twenty years to the retired man on whose account she claims; that she not be presently married to another; and that she either receive actual support from her former husband or have a legal claim to such support.[52] In 1972, Congress eliminated the support requirement,[53] and the 1977 amendments reduced the required duration of marriage from twenty years to ten.[54] But a major difference in treatment between a divorced woman and a wife still exists: Unlike a current wife of a retired or disabled worker, who may collect a wife's benefit either when she reaches retirement age *or* when she has a qualifying child in her care, [55] the divorced spouse of a retired or disabled worker is eligible for a wife's benefit only when she reaches retirement age.[56] The payment of derivative benefits to a divorced wife or surviving divorced wife does not reduce the maximum family benefit otherwise payable on the insured worker's account.[57] Congress has not legislated any benefits for divorced men.[58]

II. A CRITIQUE OF THE ASSUMPTIONS UNDERLYING THE CURRENT SOCIAL SECURITY SYSTEM

The derivative benefits scheme, viewed as a whole, contains many inconsistencies and seemingly irrational distinctions. Some of this confusion is attributable to Congress's piecemeal approach to social security reform. But much of the problem stems from two assumptions made by Congress about the nature of family life and the role of women in society: the core notion of dependency and norms of labor-force participation.

A. The Core Notion of Dependency

The 1939 amendments, which introduced the notion of dependents' benefits, reflected a complex of generalizations, many of them gender-based, about labor-force participation and family life. The family is composed of one wage earner and one housewife. The wage earner provides all the family's dollar income. If a woman, generally assumed to be single, works, her income is used solely for her own support. Other family members are not economically dependent upon a woman's earnings. Marriage is terminated only by death.

Although these generalizations qua generalizations were valid in 1939, the frequency of individual exceptions occasioned ameliorative amendments in subsequent years. The 1939 amendments did not provide husband's or widower's benefits on the basis of a wife's covered employment. In 1950, Congress added such benefits subject to an actual dependency test.[59] Similarly, a child could receive a child's benefit on his mother's account only if he was not living with his father and was supported solely by his mother.[60] It was not until the Supreme Court's 1975 decision in Weinberger v. Wiesenfeld[61] that children of women workers received benefits under the same conditions as children of male workers. The increasing frequency of divorce prompted a series of amendments designed to ameliorate, albeit imperfectly, extreme instances of hardship; however, Social Security still ignores most marriages that terminate in divorce.

More resistant to change, however, is the core notion of dependency, that is, that each family includes one wage earner and one homemaker and that if that second adult is gainfully employed at all, her earnings contribute to her support only.[62] The primary legislative expression of this generalization is the choice of individual rather than family earnings as the computation base for retirement benefits. The basis for such a choice in a system designed to replace family income lost by retirement is the assumption that individual and family earnings are generally synonymous. The core notion of dependency also undergirds the requirement that the surviving spouse elect between benefits based on her account and benefits based on the account of her deceased spouse rather than allowing the survivor benefits based on some function of the two accounts.[63] Similarly, application of the earnings test to the benefits of surviving spouses and surviving parents with children-in-care is, to some extent, based on the assumption that the intact family had one wage earner and one housewife.[64] While the use of gender stereotypes informs the content of such a view of the economy of the family, and the author has chosen her pronouns accordingly, gender neutrality does not cure the problems generated by the core notion of dependency.

B. The Use of Male Work Norms

Women have two roles: that of homemaker[65] and that of gainful earner. The social security system fails to take into account the effect of women's dual roles on their participation in the labor force. The three salient aspects of female labor-force participation ignored by the social security system are length of projected worklife, predictable interruptions in worklife, and low earnings compared to those of men. The failure to consider these characteristics of female labor-force participation results in low benefit levels for retired women workers[66] and often results in no benefits at all for disabled female workers.[67]

In 1991, retirement benefits will be based upon a forty-year worklife,[68] which is, not coincidentally, the worklife expectancy[69] of men born between 1940 and 1970.[70] The average monthly wage, upon which benefits are based, is computed by dropping out the lowest five years of earnings and averaging the rest.[71] The omission of the five-year period prevents temporary periods of illness, continuing education, and involuntary unemployment and underemployment from diminishing the retired worker's benefits.[72]

But this method of computing benefits hurts women workers who do not work during their childbearing and childrearing years, and who have, therefore, a far lower worklife expectancy.[73] By using a forty-year worklife, the system forces women workers to include zero or low-earning childrearing years in determining their benefits.[74] Moreover, the effect of using the male norm in calculating benefits is compounded by the disparity between female and male earnings.[75]

Predictable temporary labor-force absence in the female working population age twenty to thirty-four has serious consequences for the disability coverage of working women. Many working women who are otherwise "fully insured" do not meet the "recency-of-work" requirement for disability benefits: that the worker has been employed for twenty of the forty quarters immediately preceding the onset of disability. While elimination of this test would extend coverage to more currently employed women, it would not fully address the special characteristics of female labor-force participation. To the extent that most persons who are currently homemakers are future labor-force participants, eligibility for disability benefits turns on the fortuity of timing. A woman disabled during her homemaking phase generates no benefits, but a woman disabled after her return to work does. Current female worklife projections[77] and labor-force participation rates[78] make it plausible to regard all homemakers as future labor-force participants. In such case, the disability of a homemaker represents the loss of anticipated future income in the same way that the disability of a gainful earner portends such loss.

This discussion suggests two conclusions: that it is inappropriate, in a system designed to replace income lost by retirement, to establish a norm of work longevity that 41 percent of the working population[79] will probably never attain, and that predictable labor-force absence experienced by female workers should excuse zero-contribution years in the same manner that the five-year dropout provision excuses absences for involuntary unemployment and illness. Most of the proposals mentioned in this article directly or indirectly adopt one or both of these conclusions.

III. BENEFIT INEQUALITY IN THE CURRENT SYSTEM

The introduction of the wife's allowance by the 1939 amendments created a number of results unjustified by principles of adequacy or equity. The system created inequality between one- and two-earner couples and between all couples and single persons. Moreover, the system inadequately provided for widows and divorced women.

A. Benefit Inequality Among One- and Two-Earner Couples and Single Persons

The introduction of derivative benefits has led to a system that inequitably favors one-earner couples over two-earner couples and single individuals. Benefit inequality in the system is revealed by comparing: (1) one- and two-earner couples that have received similar earned income streams and have paid equivalent social security taxes; and (2) single persons and husband-wife families that have equivalent standards of living before retirement but receive different social security replacement rates upon retirement.

1. *Benefit inequality between one- and two-earner families.* The following example illustrates the inequality in the system between one- and two-earner families. All spouses in Families A and B reach age sixty-five in 1979. On their sixty-fifth birthdays, the spouses in both families claim old age retirement benefits for the first time. In Family A, the husband alone is eligible for primary benefits. His average monthly wage[80] was $600. In Family B the husband's average monthly wage was $400, and the wife's was $200. Both Family B spouses are eligible for primary benefits, and the wife's primary benefit exceeds the amount—50 percent of husband's primary insurance amount [PIA]—she would receive as her husband's dependent. According to the 1980 schedules, retirement benefits for the two families are: (1) Family A—$735.30 per month; (2) Family B—$613.80 per month.[81] Thus, on the same family earnings and contributions record, Family A receives benefits which are 20 percent higher ($121.50) than those received by Family B.

Benefit inequality, substantial during couple retirement, is sharply accentuated at the death of one spouse. If husband A dies before his wife, she would enjoy a monthly widow's benefit of $490.20,[82] while widow B would receive only $369.30 at her husband's death.[83] Thus the 20 percent gap in retirement income increases to 33 percent in survivorship.

Such a differential in benefits is unjustifiable in a program designed to replace preretirement income.[84] Most commentators perceive a serious unfairness in the differential in benefits among same-income, same-contribution families.[85] They divide on the issue of how this unfairness should be cured. One unsuccessful legislative measure would have achieved parity for some relatively low-income two-earner couples by allowing them to cumulate their earnings up to the individual maximum taxable base and to receive 150 percent of the PIA so derived.[86] An alternative solution would be to adopt the tax concept of income splitting and treat every retiring couple as though it were composed of two single workers, each of whom had earned one-half of the couple's total income.[87] Assuming that the unsuccessful House bill's costs would have resulted in a diminution of basic benefit levels for all recipients, and that the savings derived from income splitting would be redistributed as increased benefits, either change would affect the relative position of single persons. As the next section will demonstrate in more detail, there is no reason why a two-earner retired couple should receive greater retirement benefits than two single persons with the same total earnings and contribution records. Indeed, the only argument for inequality would favor single earners because they are less likely to be able to enjoy the couple's economies of scale. Moreover, the principle of adequacy upon which the wife's allowance is based should never allow the one-earner couple's benefits to exceed the benefits paid to two single persons, each earning half the couple's taxable earnings and paying, together, the same contributions.[88] To allow otherwise is simply to favor married persons.

In short, the current system creates substantial benefit inequality between couples having the same earnings and the same contribution records. In 1939, Congress may have considered this an unfortunate but tolerable inequity affecting only a minority of households—those in which both spouses were gainfully employed. But the situation has changed. In 1976, there were 42,624,000 American husband-wife families in which at least one person was employed. In 55 percent of these families (23,581,000), the wife was gainfully employed.[89] These figures indicate that the working couple has emerged as the new standard family. In this altered context, the favorable treatment accorded one-earner couples is a serious shortcoming.

2. *Inequality between married couples and single persons.* There is obvious benefit inequality between one-earner couples and single persons. For identical contributions the one-earner couple receives an additional 50 percent of the earner's PIA as the wife's benefit. This level of subsidy cannot be justified on the ground that without it the couple will have inadequate support. Indeed, a number of commentators argue that one-earner couples receive unwarrantedly higher replacement rates than do single persons who had "equivalent" preretirement income.[90] They argue that if the goal of

social security is to replace some uniform percentage of income of persons enjoying the same preretirement standard of living, the same income replacement rate should be applied to X income for a single person as is applied to 130–150 percent of X income for a couple since couples enjoy economies of scale. But this is never done; the replacement rate is much lower for single persons.[91]

This benefit inequality is particularly inappropriate since single persons lack adequate retirement income more often than couples. Families headed by a person sixty-five or older enjoy a median income almost two-and-one-half times greater than that of single individuals[92] and more than two-and-two-thirds times greater than that of aged widows and other elderly women not living with a spouse.[93] Couples receive greater social security benefits not only because of the wife's allowance but also because the median social security income of married men is higher than that of single persons.[94] Elderly couples are also more likely than single persons to enjoy asset[95] and second-pension[96] income. As a result, single persons not only receive lower social security benefits, but rely more heavily on those benefits. Thus, inequity exacerbates a problem of inadequacy.

B. Benefit Inadequacy: Intact Marriage, Survivorship, and Divorce

Ironically, the system fails to provide adequately for the persons that the scheme of derivative benefits was precisely designed to protect—the wife and widow of a one-earner couple.[97] The system also fails to provide for a person it only belatedly attempted to protect—the divorced wife.

1. *Derivative benefits in the intact marriage and survivorship.* The American social security system expresses a striking ambivalence toward the economically dependent wife. Some comparable foreign systems virtually ignore her, except for survivorship purposes;[98] others consistently make special provisions for her.[99] No other system, however, gives her so many conflicting signals as ours. Only after she reaches retirement age do we unequivocally acknowledge her economic dependency and entitle her to replacement of the economic support she has lost by her husband's retirement, death, or disability. Earlier in life, her loss of support due to these events is recognized only if she is caring for a dependent

child.[100] This system creates a benefit hiatus that is particularly severe for the widow in the period between her eligibility for surviving mother's and widow's benefits.[101] But the hiatus is also experienced by the wife of a retired or disabled worker whose qualifying child has attained the age of eighteen.[102] Similarly, the late middle-aged homemaker whose husband retires early or dies before she reaches retirement age may wait several years before she is eligible for benefits.

While some justify the hiatus as necessary to maintain parity with the single working woman, parity is maintained at the cost of thrusting women into a job market for which many are ill-prepared. Because the period is short and often comes when the wife is older, investment in extensive rehabilitation would be of questionable value. Moreover, even when the widow is younger, the system discourages her from entering the labor force. The widow's gap occurs not simply because the surviving mother is offered benefits until her youngest child reaches age eighteen. Congress also conditions the receipt of derivative benefits on abstention from substantial labor-force participation.[103] The mother is given a choice between inadequate social security benefits and inadequate gainful earnings.[104]

In response to this problem, the suggestion has been made that the earnings test be abandoned in the case of the surviving mother.[105] The underlying issue of income replacement, however, is broader and has ramifications for all widows. If the surviving mother or widow was employed before the husband's death, her current earnings do not at all replace family income lost by his death. Hence her derivative benefits arguably ought not be reduced by her earnings. Even if she was a housewife before his death, it is highly unlikely that her gainful earnings will effectively replace his. Her absence from the labor force and the wide gap between median male and female wages[106] make it unlikely that her earnings will equal his. To effectuate the goal of replacing family income lost because of a wage earner's death, it is arguable that a surviving spouse should always be eligible for some amount of social security benefits so long as loss of family income exceeds the savings effected by the death of a family earner. Some countries do, in fact, pay a widow's benefit to the younger widow without regard to her earnings or the presence of dependent children[107] and allow the retired widow to collect both her own primary benefit and some portion of a survivorship benefit based on her husband's account,[108] in order for the widow to maintain some semblance of her former standard of living.

As with surviving mother's benefits, the goal of social adequacy supports a more liberal approach to aged widow's benefits. Widows, as a group, are the poorest of the aged.[109] The death of an aged husband often means more than a loss of from one-third to one-half[110] of the couple's social security benefits. In most instances, the husband's pension, if any, does not provide for survivors' benefits.[111] The husband also may have been earning substantial postretirement income[112] that ceases with his death.

While this discussion has focused on the gender-related needs of widows, income replacement of this sort need not be gender-specific. A strong policy in favor of gender-neutrality[113] has prompted Sweden to consider replacing its widow's pension, its last vestige of gender-specific social security, with a surviving spouse's pension available when income loss substantially exceeds the reduction in family costs.[114]

The problems posed by this section are ones that must be faced by any social insurance system, and, as such, are beyond the particular focus of this paper.[115] They have been briefly delineated, however, to indicate that the American social security system, as it now exists, does not ideally serve even the unit for which it was ostensibly designed, the traditional earner-homemaker couple.

2. *Divorce and eligibility for derivative social security benefits.* This section will survey basic divorce data, will then examine the act for internal consistency and rationality, and, finally, will contrast its treatment of divorce with inconsistent state law treatment of the couple's other property interests, including pensions.

Divorce, while not unknown in 1939, was relatively infrequent. The American divorce rate has increased nearly threefold since then,[116] and is now five per thousand of population, the highest rate in the world.[117] The demographers Glick and Norton project that approximately "40 percent of all current and potential marriages among young women now in their late twenties may eventually end in divorce."[118] Moreover, Glick and Norton also estimate that for women who divorce, the median time between the first marriage and divorce is 7.3 years;[119] for women who re-marry and divorce again, the median time between remarriage and divorce is 5.5 years.[120] The chances of remarriage drop off sharply for persons divorced between ages thirty-five and fifty-four.[121] These data are of particular concern to social security because the amount of time spent in and out of marriage, and the frequency with which divorced persons do not permanently attach them-selves to another mate may determine areas of need that the sys-tem currently neglects.

The current treatment and its development. The 1939 amendments did not include any provision for divorced wives. Not only was marriage to a retired primary beneficiary necessary to establish initial qualification for the derivative wife's benefit, but divorce after retirement terminated the former wife's benefit.[122]

While the absence of any provision for divorced wives is not explained in the legislative history, it may be that Congress was influenced by the relative infrequency of divorce in 1939. Moreover, the wife's benefit itself was designed not so much for the wife as to ensure the adequate support of the retired worker.[123] Thus it is not surprising that Congress initially thought it unneces-sary to make provision for the divorced wife.

Since 1939 Congress has attempted, in a piecemeal fashion, to extend benefits to divorced women. In 1950, Congress extended surviving mother's benefits to the divorced widow with a deceased worker's qualifying child in her care.[124] The articulated purpose was to pay benefits to "individuals who have actually been depen-dent upon a deceased worker."[125] In 1965, Congress provided aged wives' and widows' benefits for divorced women, previously married at least twenty years to the insured worker, but not cur-rently married.[126] The provisions were designed to protect "women who have spent their lives in marriages that are dissolved when they are far along in years."[127]

Finally, in 1972, Congress eliminated the requirement in both the 1950 and 1965 amendments that divorced beneficiaries be actually dependent on their former husbands.[128] By eliminating the depen-dency requirements, Congress recognized that social security should address the hardship a wife suffered after the dissolution of a long marriage without regard to actual dependency. Supporting this recognition is a growing acceptance of the idea that a woman divorced after a long marriage deserves a share of the economic fruits of the marriage.

Despite this congressional response, several difficulties remain in the system's treatment of divorced women. Once she has qualified for social security benefits, the divorced woman is treated, with one notable exception,[129] as though she were still the insured worker's wife. When she reaches retirement age, her entitlement depends on two events: her husband must also have reached retirement age,[130] and, if he is under age seventy-two, he must have in fact retired.[131]

In the intact family, the decision whether to retire is based on the community of economic interest; but after divorce, the husband has little personal or economic incentive to consider his former wife's interests. If he delays retirement she may experience hardship. If he retires but then makes excess earnings, her benefits will be reduced just as his are,[132] even though she does not receive any portion of his excess earnings. Moreover, the wife's benefit is 50 percent of his PIA because it is based on the incremental cost of a second adult in the husband's household. At the husband's death, the widow's benefit is 100 percent of his PIA because it will cost her as much to maintain herself as it would have cost him had he been alone. The divorced wife is treated in precisely the same manner as the current wife even though she is not a second adult in a preexisting household and her husband's death is not a matter of economic significance to her.

While these anomalies occur because the divorced wife is treated as though she were still married to and living with her former husband, in two instances the fiction is unaccountably and seemingly irrationally abandoned to the divorced wife's detriment. Whereas a wife under retirement age is entitled to a derivative benefit when she has a disabled or underage child of a retired, disabled, or deceased worker in her care,[133] a divorced mother in the same circumstances is only eligible when her exhusband dies.[134] While her exhusband is alive, the divorced mother will receive no benefit until she attains retirement age. As with aged divorced wives,[135] serious matters of entitlement turn on an economically inconsequential event for most divorced women: the death of a former husband.

Moreover, where the marriage ends in less than ten years—and most divorces occur within this period[136]—the divorced woman is completely ineligible for any benefits based on the marriage.[137] Her contribution record is likely to reflect the low- or zero-earning years attributable to the marriage. Consequently, her benefits may be inadequate.

State treatment of division of pension rights upon divorce. State law better recognizes the duality of women's lives and the high incidence of divorce than does the social security system. In seven of the eight community property states, there are reported cases dealing with dividing pension rights at divorce.[138] In all seven states, pension rights accrued during marriage are property subject to division.[139] There are thirty-seven equitable division states;[140] a majority of those states treat pension interests as divisible property, but reported cases are infrequent.[141]

Most equitable division cases are of very recent vintage. None date before 1975 and many were decided in the last four years.[142] The issue began to assume prominence in the community property states in the late sixties.[143] The timing coincided with state-law adoption of no-fault divorce and the support principles articulated in the Uniform Marriage and Divorce Act.[144]

Under a no-fault system, divorce is effectively available upon one party's demand; the other party, therefore, may have little or no leverage with respect to the economic incidents of dissolution. Under such circumstances, statutory and case law must guard against economic unfairness. The Uniform Act treats marriage as an economic partnership and recognizes homemaking as a valuable contribution to that partnership.[145] At dissolution, the couple's assets are divided accordingly. Because of the undesirability of continuing economic obligations between the parties, the distribution of property substitutes for alimony whenever possible.[146] No-fault divorce will probably cause continuing development in the division of pension rights, particularly in the equitable division states.

There would seem to be little justification for treating social security any differently from other kinds of pensions. But because of federal preemption of the area,[147] Congress, by explicitly providing for divorced wives, has ruled out state distribution of social security benefits.

Congressional treatment of divorce and social security compares poorly with state law treatment of division of pensions. First, most marriages that end in divorce are not taken into account at all by social security because of its ten-year marriage requirement.[148] While the act's ten-year requirement may comport with the divorce provisions' hardship rationale,[149] it is not consistent with state-law economic partnership theory; in those terms, social security either understates or overstates the spouse's proper share. If the marriage has been a very long one, the divorced wife receives one-quarter to one-third of the total benefits, less than the one-half she might have gotten under a state-law distribution. If the marriage has been shorter, say ten or eleven years, the 50 percent PIA benefit overstates the exwife's interest in the marriage. Finally and most importantly, unlike an interest created by state-law division, the interest created by the act is not one the divorced spouse can build upon to achieve her own complete old-age income security. If, after dissolution, she pursues gainful employment and establishes a substantial earnings record, she is unlikely to receive any divorced wife's benefit.

Any proposal for social security reform should look to state law for a more fair and adequate method of treating benefit eligibility after divorce.

IV. PROPOSALS FOR CHANGE

In recent years there have been a number of proposals for change.[150] All of these proposed changes would have the intended or incidental effect of reducing the role of derivative benefits in the social security system. Some would do little more than eliminate current classes of beneficiaries.[151] Others would reduce or eliminate derivative benefits but would attempt to maintain or improve general benefit levels by other adjustments.[152] Still others would, through homemaking coverage, child care credits, or economic partnership treatment of married couples, transform derivative beneficiaries into primary beneficiaries.[153] In this section I will discuss the last-mentioned possibility, economic partnership treatment of married couples.

Income-splitting plans view marriage as an economic partnership in which each adult has equal rights in the wealth generated by either spouse during the marriage.[154] Such plans allocate contributions made to social security during the marriage equally between the two spouses. These plans contain great promise. They offer to cure nearly every problem identified previously. Under such plans, women would develop continuous contribution records that would be portable in the event of divorce or spousal death. The treatment of spousal contributions is consistent with the most progressive state-law treatment of marital property.[155] The problems generated by low female earnings are mitigated by the matching of most female earners with a male earner.[156] Income splitting can end the benefit inequality between one- and two-earner couples, and, by terminating the wife's benefit, can also eliminate much of the replacement-rate inequality between all couples and single earners. Even in a 50-50 split system, social security would continue to subsidize married couples to some extent because of the progressive benefits scheme.[157] Such a subsidy must, however, be compared to the present subsidy in the form of dependents' and survivors' benefits. An income-splitting system need not prove any more expensive than the current system and might even achieve some savings.

Though each possible change has been proposed separately, some measures could be adopted in combination. No proposal is clearly superior to the others. The author finds the partnership approach most attractive. But this is a value-laden choice. In the final analysis, the proposed measures reflect the values of their proponents. Those who would establish independent social insurance for women who are predominantly or exclusively homemakers place a very high value on homemaking and the preservation of this option for married women. Those who propose child-care credits and who would alter the worklife norms of social security so as to include female as well as male workers are primarily concerned that women not be shortchanged by the system when their domestic roles curtail an otherwise substantial role in gainful employment. Those who propose partnership plans take a relatively neutral view toward female roles but strongly espouse the position that, as an ethical matter, marriage should be treated as a sharing partnership.[158] This position finds growing support in state marital property law. Those who, in contrast, value individual autonomy and the freedom of women not to marry[159] tend to prefer alteration of worklife norms and child-care credits for all mothers, whether married or not.

V. SUMMARY

This article has examined the history and development of adult derivative benefits in social security legislation. Such a benefit structure was originally predicated upon the assumption of a worker-homemaker marriage that endured until the death of one of the spouses. This assumption has increasingly been undermined by a dramatic rise in female labor-force participation and an equally dramatic rise in the divorce rate.

The social security system has failed to adapt itself to the pattern of labor-force participation generally experienced by women, who now constitute 41 percent of the labor force. This failure is reflected in relatively low female benefit levels and frequent lapses in disability coverage. The alternative treatment of married persons as either primary or derivative beneficiaries results in substantial benefit and contribution inequality among one- and two-earner couples with equal incomes. Efforts to accommodate divorce have revealed the inflexibility of the derivative benefits structure. Legislative provision for divorce is clumsy, imprecise, and both overinclusive and underinclusive. Nor can it be said that the system works very well for those relatively few for whom it was originally designed. Dependent wives, widows, and surviving mothers experience substantial benefits gaps. The younger dependent wife who enters the labor force after her husband's death finds it difficult to build adequate social security protection because she must choose between two inadequate earnings records. Totally disabled wives and widows are generally treated as though they were able-bodied.[140]

In response to some or all of these problems, various changes have been suggested. Proposals range from relatively minor tinkering with the derivative benefits system to complete overhaul that would curtail or abolish derivative benefits and, in some cases, insure most persons on their own accounts. There is currently no indication that any of these concepts is economically or administratively infeasible. It is helpful, when comparing these proposals, to bear in mind that social security already subsidizes, albeit in an expensive, crude, and inefficient manner, the old age economic security of the homemaker in the intact one-earner family.

NOTES

1. Social Security Act of 1935, ch. 531, 49 Stat. 622 (current version at 42 U.S.C.A. §§401–432 [West 1974 & Supp. 1979]). In this paper, the term "social security" refers to the American system of old age, survivors, and disability insurance. It does not encompass the broad range of social programs characterized as "social security" in Europe.

2. Ch. 666, 56 Stat. 1362 (1939) (current version at 42 U.S.C.A. §402 [West 1974 & Supp. 1979]).

3. Social Security Act of 1935, ch. 531, 49 Stat. 622 (current version at 42 U.S.C.A. §§401–432 [West 1974 & Supp. 1979]).

4. For statistics comparing the incidence of primary and derivative benefits and reasons for the persistence of derivative claims, see Martin, *Social Security Benefits for Spouses*, 63 Cornell L. Rev. 789, 794–809 (1978).

5. *See* notes 118–37 *infra* and accompanying text. A number of recent Supreme Court decisions have further disrupted the basic scheme by disapproving a variety of gender-based distinctions in the Act. *See* Califano v. Goldfarb, 430 U.S. 199 (1977); Weinberger v. Wiesenfeld, 420 U.S. 636 (1975). *But see* Califano v. Webster, 430 U.S. 313 (1977) (greater women's benefits do not violate fifth amendment equal protection as they are direct compensation for past economic discrimination).

6. Social Security Administration, Social Security and the Changing Roles of Men and Women: Chart Book 14–15 (OHR Pub. No. 329, July 1979).

7. 42 U.S.C.A. §§401–432 (West 1974 & Supp. 1979).

8. The 1980 rate for each is 6.13 percent of annual wages up to $25,900. Social Security Amendments of 1977, Pub. L. No. 95–216, §§101, 103, 91 Stat. 1511, 1513 (codified in scattered sections of 26, 42 U.S.C.A. [West Supp. 1979]).

9. 42 U.S.C. §419 (a) (1974).

10. 42 U.S.C. §423(c)(1)(B)(i) (1974. *But see* 42 U.S.C. §423(c)(1)(B) (ii) (1974).

11. As of January 1979, average monthly earnings are indexed and replacement rates lowered accordingly. A person who reaches age sixty-two, becomes disabled, or dies in 1979 or thereafter, will have his earnings in each year after 1950 increased to reflect the increase in average wages since the year in which he earned them. Social Security Amendments of 1977, 42 U.S.C.A. §415(b) (West Supp. 1979); see H. R. REP. NO. 702(I), 95th Cong., 1st Sess. 24–25 *reprinted in* [1977] U.S. Code Cong. & News 4155, 4180–81 (hereinafter cited as 1977 HOUSE REPORT]. There is, however, a five-year "hold harmless" clause for new beneficiaries who would receive higher benefits under the old system. *See* Social Security Amendments of 1977, Pub. L. No. 95–216, §201(a), 91 Stat. 1514 (amending 42 U.S.C. §415[a] [1976].)

12. 42 U.S.C. §§415, 402(a) (1974).

13. 42 U.S.C. §402(b)(2) and (c)(3) (1974).

14. 42 U.S.C. §402(e)(2) and (f)(3) (1974). The Social Security Amendments of 1939, which introduced derivative benefits, provided a widow's benefit of 75 percent of the insured's PIA, ch. 666, §202(d)(2), 53 Stat. 1365 (1939). In 1961, the widow's benefit, also made available to dependent widowers, was raised to 82–1/2 percent, Pub. L. No. 87–64, §§102(a), 104(d)(1). In 1972, it was raised to 100 percent of the insured's PIA, Pub. L. No. 92–603, §§102(a)(2), 86 Stat. 1335 (1972) (codified at 42 U.S.C.A. §402[e][2][A] [West 1974 & Supp. 1979]).

15. 42 U.S.C. §402(d)(2) (1974).

16. One type of adult derivative benefit has been omitted from the schematization because it is not germane to the issues treated in this article: the benefit payable to the aged parent of a deceased insured son or daughter when the parent was receiving at least one-half his support from the insured deceased child and has not married since the child's death, 42 U.S.C. §402(a) (1974).

17. Social Security Act of 1935, ch. 531, 49 Stat. 623 (current version at 42 U.S.C.A. §§401–433 [West 1974 & Supp. 1979]).

18. Coverage is still not universal but has, however, been considerably expanded since the original 1935 Act. Compare the 1935 Act, ch. 531, §210(b), 49 Stat. 623 with 42 U.S.C. §410 (1974), as amended by Social Security Amendments of 1977, Pub. L. No. 95–216, §§311–321, 91 Stat. 1531–1541 (1977).

19. The Social Security Act of 1935, ch. 531, tit. I, 49 Stat. 620 (1935), codified at 42 U.S.C. §§301–306 (1974), repealed effective January 1, 1974 by Pub. L. No. 92–603, tit. III, §303(a), (b), 86 Stat. 1484 (1972). The role of OAA has been taken over by the federally managed Supplemental Security Income [SSI] program for the aged, blind and disabled, Pub. L. No. 92–603, tit. III, §301, 86 Stat. 1465, codified at 42 U.S.C. §§1381–1383(c) (1974 and 1978 Supp.).

20. J. Brown, An American Philosophy of Social Security and Issues (1972) at 55.

21. See, for example, Final Report, Advisory Council on Social Security, S. Doc. No. 4, 76th Cong., 1st Sess. 6; J. Pechman, H. Aaron and M. Taussig, Social Security Perspectives for Reform, 73–74 (1968); and J. Brittain, The Payroll Tax for Social Security, 253 (1972).

22. Edwin Witte, Executive Director of the instrumental 1934–35 Committee on Economic Security, reports that a rather reluctant President Roosevelt was persuaded to endorse a separate social security program by the argument that it would reduce the costs of the noncontributory old age assistance grants [OAA] and that he "apparently formed the idea that the two programs combined would result in decreasing government costs as the years went on." See E. Witte, The Development of the Social Security Act, at 149 (1963). See also Final Report, supra note 21, at 11.

23. The Economic Security Act: Hearings on S. 1130 before the Senate Comm. on Finance, 74th Cong., 1st Sess. 283 (1935) (statement of J. Douglas Brown), 744–49, 754–55 (statement of Murray Latimer).

24. William Graebner, *Retirement and the Corporate State, 1885–1935: A New Context for Social Security* (1978) (unpublished paper on file with author).

25. Ibid. at 2–6 and sources cited therein.

26. *Supra* note 23.

27. Ibid.

28. The first such provision was draconian: "Whenever the Board finds that any qualified individual has received wages with respect to regular employment after he attained the age of sixty-five, the old age benefit payable to such individual *shall be reduced, for each calendar month in any part of which such regular employment occurred, by an amount equal to one month's benefit*" (emphasis added), Social Security Act of 1935, ch. 531 §202(d), 49 Stat. 623. In 1978, the excess earnings provision, 42 U.S.C. §403, or "retirement test," as it is popularly known (see, for example, *1976 Social Security and Medicare Explained*, CCH) allowed unlimited earnings for workers over age seventy-two. Workers age sixty-five or older could earn up to $4,000 without losing any benefits. Workers under age sixty-five may earn up to $3,240 without losing any benefits. Every dollar earned in excess of these limits diminishes both primary and derivative benefits by fifty cents. *1978 Social Security Benefits* 22, CCH.

The 1977 Social Security Amendments increase the amount of exempt earnings for beneficiaries sixty-five and older to $4,500 in 1979, $5,000 in 1980, $5,500 in 1981 and $6,000 in 1982. They also provide that, starting in 1982, the excess earnings test will no longer apply to workers over age 70, Pub. L. No. 95–216, §§301, 302, 91 Stat. 1530 (1977). The evolution from the harsh 1939 measure to the present liberal measures is motivated by more than a concern for basic adequacy in old-age income. Increasingly, it is thought desirable to encourage old persons to work, *Social Security Amendments of 1977*, H.R. Rep. No. 95–702(I), 95th Cong., 1st Sess. 49 (1977), reprinted in (1977) *U.S. Code Cong. & Ad. News* 6414. Old workers continue to pay social security taxes, enhancing the deteriorating ratio between social security contributors and beneficiaries. (In 1975, there were thirty beneficiaries for every hundred workers; in 2030 there will be forty-five beneficiaries for every hundred workers. *Reports of the Quadrennial Advisory Council on Social Security*, H. Doc. 94–75, 94th Cong., 1st Sess. 49 [1975].) Substantial earnings will also bring into play even the present liberal earnings test, effecting a savings in benefits paid out. Employment of the aged also promises to reduce public welfare expenditure.

29. The worker who has reached retirement age continues to pay social security taxes on earnings at the regular rate but is unlikely to receive any additional benefits attributable to those contributions. Additional earnings years per se are not likely to substantially improve his record unless he has many relatively low or no earning years during his preretirement worklife. Some economists characterize the excess earnings test as a tax upon older people. *See*, for example, Milton Friedman, in W. Cohen and M. Friedman, *Social Security: Universal or Selective?* (1972) at p. 30 and Bell, *Social Security: Unfair to Those Who Receive It*, Challenge 18–22 (July-August, 1973).

30. *Supra* note 28.

31. A number of countries have universal flat-rate pensions. Canada, Denmark, Finland, the Netherlands, Norway and Sweden pay substantial flat-rate pensions to all citizens who reach retirement age. These pensions may be augmented by earned supplements as well as hardship supplements based on need. The combination of a flat-rate system and an earnings-related supplement is commonly characterized as a "two-tier" system. See generally, *Organization for Economic Cooperation and Development, Old Age Pension Schemes*, 185, 79 (1977).

32. See text accompanying notes 35–58 *infra*. *See also* J. Pechman, H. Aaron and M. Taussig, *supra* note 21, at 31–33 (1968).

33. The drafters of the scheme intended that perception. *See* J. Brown, *An American Philosophy of Social Security: Evolution and Issues* 21 (1972).

34. See, e.g., W. Cohen & M. Friedman, *Social Security: Universal or Selective?* (1972).

35. Social Security Act of 1935, ch. 531, 49 Stat. 623 (current version at 42 U.S.C.A. §§401–433 [West 1974 & Supp. 1979]).

36. Private pension plans typically base retirement benefits on salary and years of service. *See* W. Greenough & F. King, *Pension Plans and Public Policy* 118 (1976). The largest benefits are given to employees having the highest salary at retirement and the greatest number of years of employment with the company. Survivors' benefits are usually provided only through a joint and survivor option which reduces the monthly payments to offset the increased likelihood of benefit payments over a greater number of years. *See* ibid. at 119.

The original Social Security Act provided for the payment of benefits to covered individuals over sixty-four. The level of benefits depended on whether the employee earned greater or less than $3,000 in wages since December 31, 1936. Social Security Act of 1935, ch. 531, §202, 49 Stat. 623 (repealed 1939).

37. Social Security Act of 1935, 531, §202, 49 Stat. 623 (repealed 1939). Moreover, if the worker were to die before retirement, his contributions would be returned to his estate. Ibid. §203(a). If the worker were to reach retirement but fail to qualify for social security, his contributions would be returned. Ibid. §204(a).

38. Ibid. §202 (current version at 42 U.S.C.A. §402 [West 1974 & Supp. 1979]).

39. Social Security Act of 1935, ch. 531, §202(b), 49 Stat. 623 (repealed 1939).

40. *Final Report, supra* note 21, at 1 (emphasis added).

41. Ibid. at 5, 16–19.

42. *Final Report, supra* note 21, at 5, 15–16.

43. *Final Report, supra* note 21, at 15.

44. Ibid. The cost of the wife's benefit was consciously allocated to single beneficiaries. *See Final Report, supra* note 21, at 16. The 1939 Advisory Council chose the same approach in financing widows' benefits. Ibid. at 17.

45. *Final Report, supra* note 21, at 5. This has been aptly characterized as an implicit dependency test. V. Reno, *Women and Social Security: Alternatives to Dependency in Family Protection* (Sept. 1977) (unofficial draft report prepared for the Social Security Administration, U.S. Department of Health, Education, and Welfare). If the wife is eligible for greater benefits on her account, she is presumed not to be an economic dependent of her husband; if she is not so eligible, she is presumed an economic dependent and hence receives the wife's allowance. Ibid. To receive greater benefits on her husband's account rather than on her own, a wife's average monthly earnings must be less than one-third of her husband's—less than one-quarter of the couple's total income. For husbands and widowers, the corresponding actual dependency test required a man to show that he received at least one-half his support from his wife. 42 U.S.C. §402(c)(1)(C), (f)(1)(D) (1976) (repealed 1977). The Supreme Court disapproved this gender-based distinction in Califano v. Goldfarb, 430 U.S. 199 (1977).

46. *Final Report, supra* note 21, at 16.

47. The "mother's benefit" is 75 percent of the deceased husband's PIA. 42 U.S.C.A. §402(g)(2) (West Supp. 1979). Initially, the widow's eligibility for the mother's benefit was strictly coextensive with her children's eligibility for children's benefits. Social Security Admendments of 1939, ch. 666, §202(e)(1)(E), 53 Stat. 1365. The Social Security Amendments of 1965 extended children's benefits, previously available only to disabled children and nondisabled children under the age of eighteen, to nondisabled children under the age of twenty-two who are full-time students. 42 U.S.C. §402(d)(1)(B) (1976). Such students between the age of eighteen and twenty-two, while themselves qualified for children's benefits, do not, however, qualify their mothers for mothers' benefits. 42 U.S.C.A. §402(s)(1) (West Supp. 1979).

48. The widow's benefit was set at 100 percent of her husband's PIA in 1972. *See* note 14 *supra.*

49. 42 U.S.C.A. §402(c) (West 1974 & Supp. 1979).

50. Social Security Amendments of 1950, ch. 809, §101(a), 64 Stat. 482 (codified at 42 U.S.C. §402 [c][1][C], [f][1] [D] [1976] [repealed 1977]); *see* note 45 *supra.*

51. Social Security Act Amendments of 1950, ch. 809, §101(a), 64 Stat. 482 (codified at 42 U.S.C. §402[g] [1][1976]); *see* note 47 *supra.*

52. Social Security Amendments of 1965, Pub. L. No. 89–97, §308, 79 Stat. 375 (current version at 42 U.S.C. §402[b][1] [1976]).

53. Social Security Amendments of 1972, Pub. L. No. 95–603, §114, 86 Stat. 1348 (amending 42 U.S.C. §402 [b][1] [1976]).

54. Social Security Amendments of 1977, Pub. L. No. 95–216, §337, 91 Stat. 1548 (codified at 42 U.S.C.A. §§402, 416 [West Supp. 1979]).

The divorced woman who satisfies the requirements for a wife's benefit is further eligible for a surviving widow's benefit if her former husband is dead and she has attained retirement age. 42 U.S.C. §402(e) (1976).

55. 42 U.S.C. §402(b)(1)(B) (1976).

56. Ibid. This provision was unsuccessfully challenged in Mathews v. DeCastro, 429 U.S. 181 (1976). For discussion of the divorced wife's benefits, see Martin, supra note 4, at 819–24.

57. 42 U.S.C.A. §403(a)(3)(C) (West Supp. 1979). This provision effectively socializes the social security cost with respect to divorce. Under the present ten-year provision, it is not inconceivable that a retired or disabled worker might have three present and former spouses claiming full wives' or widows' benefits on his account. Compare France, where the surviving spouse and the eligible divorced ex-wife share one surviving spouse's pension. Cockburn and Hoskins, *Social Security and Divorced Persons*, 29 Int'l Soc. Security Rev. 111, 116 n.2 (1976).

58. Gender-neutral treatment of divorced husbands and surviving divorced husbands is probably constitutionally required by the fifth amendment due process clause, which embodies the equal protection doctrine. *See* Califano v. Oliver, No. C-7623975C (N.D. Cal. June 24, 1977) (extending divorced wives' benefits to divorced husbands).

59. Social Security Amendments of 1950, ch. 809, §101(a), 64 Stat. 482 (codified at 42 U.S.C. §403(c)(f) (1974). The gender-based distinction with respect to the issue of economic dependence was declared unconstitutional in Califano v. Goldfarb, 430 U.S. 199 (1977).

60. Social Security Amendments of 1939, ch. 666, §202(c)(4), 53 Stat. 1364.

61. 420 U.S. 636 (1975).

62. The problem with this formulation is that the couple "depends" on all income the spouses earn. The effect of this approach is to disregard a certain quantum of income in need of replacement: that generated by the so-called "dependent" wife.

63. 42 U.S.C. §402(e)(1)(D) (1974).

64. See discussion in text accompanying notes 98–108 *infra.*

65. It is highly likely that a woman will marry at least once. The percentage of women never married has remained relatively constant in this century between 4 percent and 5 percent. Bureau of the Census, U.S. Dep't of Commerce, *Population Characteristics; Marital Status & Living Arrangements,* March 1976, at 3 (1977). Whether or not a woman ultimately enters an enduring marriage, the belief that she may affects her job opportunities, choice of occupation, investment in training, and opportunities for advancement.

66. The average monthly social security payment for female workers retiring in November 1978 was $215. For men, it was $325. U.S. Dep't of Health, Education, and Welfare, *Social Security and the Changing Roles of Men and Women,* 10 (1979) (hereinafter cited as HEW REPORT).

67. *See* text accompanying notes 71–78 *infra.*

68. *See* text accompanying note 11 *supra.*

69. The term "worklife expectancy" includes periods of participation in market employment and involuntary unemployment. Household work

and other forms of unpaid employment are not included. Fullerton and Byrne, "Length of Working Life for Men and Women," 1970, Monthly Lab. Rev., Feb. 1976, at 31, 34 n.1.

70. Ibid. at 32.

71. *See* text accompanying note 11 *supra*.

72. *See* J. Brown, *supra* note 20, at 176–77.

73. Worklife expectancy reflects the average number of years a woman will work if mortality and labor-force participation rates hold constant throughout her lifetime at the level recorded in the year of her birth. Fullerton and Byrne, *supra* note 69, at 34 n. 3. The worklife expectancy at birth for a woman has risen from twelve years in 1940 to twenty-three years in 1970. Ibid. at 32 (table 1). Under current projections, worklife expectancy in 1990 will be twenty-seven years. (In 1970, 43 percent of all women were in the labor force. The projected rate for 1990 is 51 percent. Bureau of Labor Statistics, U.S. Dep't of Labor, *U.S. Working Women: A Databook* 5, 65 (1977) [hereinafter cited as *Databook*]. Applying the ratio of the 1970 rate to the 1990 rate (43:51) to 1970 worklife expectancy indicates a 1990 worklife expectancy of twenty-seven years: 43/51 = 23/27.)

74. Because of the 1950 "new start" provisions, Social Security Amendments of 1950, §104(a), 42 U.S.C. §409 (1976), women have not yet experienced the full effect of the forty-year worklife standard. *See* Mallan, *Women Born in the Early 1900's: Employment, Earnings, and Benefit Levels*, Soc. Security Bull., Mar. 1974, at 3, 20–21.

75. In the United States, women earn dramatically less than men. In the last two decades, median annual earning figures for year-round full-time workers have shown a slow but steady decline in women's earnings as a percentage of men's from 63 percent in 1955 to 59 percent in 1975. By including all persons who worked at any time during 1975, the figure drops to 41 percent. *Databook, supra* note 73, at 34–35.

Social security's weighted benefit formula does relatively little to redress the inequality of earnings. *See* note 66 *supra*.

76. 42 U.S.C. §423(c)(1)(B)(i) (1976).

77. *Supra* note 73.

78. In 1976, there were 38,414,000 women in the labor force. Women comprised 41 percent of the total labor force. *Databook, supra* note 73, at 5.

79. *Supra* note 78.

80. Because the distinction between "wages" and "earnings" is not significant to this discussion, they are used interchangeably. Prior to the Social Security Amendments of 1977, the statutory term was "average monthly *wage*," 42 U.S.C. §415(b) (1976) (emphasis added). The 1977 amendments introduce the term "average indexed monthly earnings." Social Security Amendments of 1977, Pub. L. No. 95–216, §201(b), 91 Stat. 1517 (codified at 42 U.S.C.A. §415(b) (West Supp. 1979); *see* note 11 *supra*.

81.   TABLE 1

Old-Age Benefits for One-Earner and
Two-Earner Couples

Family	AMW	Old-Age Benefits
A (one-earner)		
Husband	$600	$490.20 (PIA)
Wife	0	245.10 (Wife's allowance)
Total per month		$735.30
B (two-earner)		
Husband	400	369.30 (PIA)
Wife	200	244.50 (PIA)
Total per month		$613.80

82. This figure equals 100 percent of husband *A's* PIA.
83. Widow *B* is entitled to 100 percent of her husband's PIA. 42 U.S.C.A. §402(b) (West 1974 & Supp. 1979).
84. For further discussion, *see* Blumberg, *Adult Derivative Benefits in Social Security,* 32 Stan. L. Rev. 233, 248–49.
85. *See* e.g., *Economic Problems of Women: Hearings Before the Joint Economic Committee,* 93d Cong., 1st Sess., 317 (1973) [hereinafter cited as *Economic Problems of Women*]; *Future Directions in Social Security: Women and Social Security: Hearing Before the Senate Special Comm. on Aging,* 94th Cong., 1st Sess. pt. 18, 1751 (1975) (hereinafter cited as *Future Directions in Social Security*) (statement of Arthur S Flemming, Chairman, U.S. Commission on Civil Rights); ibid. at 1769 (statement of Hon. Robert M. Ball, former Commissioner of Social Security); Citizens' Advisory Council on the Status of Women, *Report of the Task Force on Social Insurance and Taxes* 68–78 (1968); J. Pechman, H. Aaron and M. Taussig, *supra* note 21, at 81–82, 87, 217–19; U.S. Comm'n on Civil Rights, *Toward Elimination of Sex-Based Differentials in the Social Security System* 18021 (Dec. 1974) (unpublished report on file with *Stanford Law Review*).
86. H.R. 1, 92d Cong., 1st Sess. §110 (1971); H.R. Rep. No. 1605, 92d Cong., 2d Sess. 38, *reprinted in* [1972] *U.S. Code Cong. & Ad. News* 5372; *see* H.R. Rep. No. 231, 92d Cong., 2d sess. 10, 48–49, 268–70, reprinted in [1972] *U.S. Code Cong. & Ad. News* 4989, 4997, 5034–35, 5253–56.
87. *See* text accompanying notes 155–58 *infra*.
88. Here I compare a one-earner couple, which can claim 150 percent of the husband's PIA, and two single persons, each earning half as much as the couple. The comparison does not consider two-earner couples or two single persons with unequal earnings whose total earnings equal the earnings of the one-earner couple. However, so long as each individual's primary benefit exceeds his derivative benefit, the benefits of couples or pairs

of single persons do not vary significantly from those of two single persons with equal earnings.

89. *Databook, supra* note 73, at 37. In 1976, the rate of female participation in the labor force was 47.3 percent, 61 percent of the rate for males. Ibid. at 5. In 1976, the male labor-force participation rate was 77.5 percent. Ibid. The rate of female labor-force participation is currently projected to reach 73 percent of the male rate. Board of Trustees of the Federal Old-Age and Survivors Insurance and Disability Insurance Trust Funds, 1975 Annual Report, H.R. Doc. No. 135. 94th Cong., 1st Sess. 48 (1975).

90. J. Pechman, H. Aaron and M. Taussig, *supra* note 21, at 82–89. Equivalent income is the income at which each household has the same standard of living.

91. In contrast to a replacement rate of 97 percent for a single person with AMW of $350, an equivalent, single-earner couple receives from 127 percent to 133 percent replacement, and an equivalent 2-earner couple, each earning half the income, receives 107 percent to 115 percent. (This second comparison was not made by Pechman, Aaron, and Taussig in their study. *See* J. Pechman, H. Aaron and M. Taussig, *supra* note 21. In their analysis, they use the term "married couple" to mean "one-earner couple.") Two-earner couples get a higher replacement rate than single persons because of the progressivity of the benefit schedule and the economies of marriage. One-earner couples claiming the wife's benefit get the highest replacement rate because the benefit schedule is not sufficiently progressive to reflect the economies of marriage.

92. *See* D. Fowles, *Income and Poverty Among the Elderly*, 1975, at 3–6 (HEW Pub. No. (OHD) 77-20286, 1977); D. Fowles, *Elderly Widows*, (HEW Pub. No. (OHD) 77–20015, 1976).

93. *See* D. Fowles, *Elderly Widows,* at 3, 9.

94. U.S. Dep't of Health, Education and Welfare, *Preliminary Findings from the Survey of New Beneficiaries: The Income of Newly Entitled Beneficiaries,* 1970, at 16 (Rep. No. 10, June 1973) (report by A. Fox).

95. Ibid. at 4.

96. Ibid.

97. *See* text accompanying notes 42–46 *supra.*

98. In Germany, for example, there is no wife's allowance. In countries with a two-tier system consisting of universal grants to provide adequate support for the aged and earnings-related supplements, the supplement does not include any notion of a spouse's benefit. Such two-tier systems exist in Canada, Finland, Norway, and Sweden. Organization for Economic Cooperation and Development, *supra* note 31, at 185–87.

99. Australia, Belgium, Ireland, and the Netherlands, for example, have unitary systems which pay derivative benefits to wives of any age. Ibid.

100. 42 U.S.C. §402(b)(1)(B) (1976).

101. This hiatus has come to be known as the "widow's blackout period." It generally occurs when a widow is in her fifties or late forties. The

lack of full protection for middle-aged widows seems to have been recognized in 1939 but was considered unavoidable in view of parity and cost. Neither the Advisory Council nor the Social Security Board seemed to have pinpointed the "gap" difficulty. *Final Report, supra* note 21, at 18–19. Instead, the 1939 Social Security Board contemplated that middle-aged widows might be ineligible because their youngest child had already reached eighteen. But the Board's suggestion that widows might rely on savings accumulated during the marriage apparently overlooked the "gap" experienced by the widow with young children. H.R. Doc. No. 110, 76th Cong., 1st Sess. 8 (1939).

102. 42 U.S.C. §402(b)(1) (1976).

103. Her benefits are subject to the earnings test described in note 28 *supra*.

104. Mallan, *Young Widows and Their Children: A Comparative Report*, Soc. Security Bull., May 1975, at 3.

105. *See* ibid. at 18.

106. *See* note 75 *supra*.

107. *See* D. Hoskins and L. Bixby, Women and Social Security, Law and Policy in Five Countries 25 (1973); Reference Div., British Information Services, Pub. No. R5455/77, *Social Security in Britain* 12–13 (1977).

108. *See* N. Eisen, *The Working Woman in Israel* 78–79 (1975); D. Hoskins and L. Bixby, *supra* note 107, at 27.

109. *See* notes 92–93 *supra*.

110. If the wife receives more as a derivative beneficiary than on her own account, at her husband's death total benefits to the family will be reduced from 150 percent of his PIA to 100 percent of his PIA, the aged surviving spouse's benefit. *See* 42 U.S.C.A. §402(b), (e) (West 1974 & Supp. 1979). If she received more on her own account than she would have as a derivative beneficiary, her husband's death could cause a loss of up to 50 percent of family benefits. Such reduction would occur if they had equal average monthly earnings. In this latter case her choice would be between 100 percent of her PIA and 100 percent of her deceased husband's PIA. *See* ibid. §402(e).

111. *See* Thompson, *Aged Female OASDI Beneficiaries: Income and Characteristics*, 1971, Soc. Security Bull., Apr. 1977, at 32–33.

112. Ibid.

113. Recent Supreme Court decisions would seem to indicate that such provision would have to take a gender-neutral form. *See, e.g.,* Orr v. Orr, 440 U.S. 268 (1979); Califano v. Goldfarb, 430 U.S. 199 (1977); Weinberger v. Wiesenfeld, 420 U.S. 636 (1975). *But see* Califano v. Webster, 430 U.S. 313 (1977).

114. *See* C. Jonung, Women and Social Security: The Case of Sweden, B-53 to -54 (Mar. 1978), *reprinted in* N. Gordon, The Treatment of Women in the Public Pension System of Five Countries (Urban Institute Working Paper No. 5069-01 Mar. 1978)

115. *See* HEW REPORT, *supra* note 66 at 39, 59–62, 85.

116. The divorce rate per 1,000 married women fourteen to forty-four years old was fourteen in 1939–1941 and thirty-eight in 1977. *See* H. Carter and P. Glick, *Marriage and Divorce* 395 (1976) (data through 1974), Glick and Norton, *Marrying, Divorcing and Living Together in the U.S. Today*, Population Bull., Oct. 1977, at 5.

117. Glick and Norton, *supra* note 116, at 4.

118. Ibid. at 18. Using data derived from the Census Bureau's Current Population Survey for June 1975 and assuming that the future divorce experience of young adults "will mirror that of older adults in recent years," Glick and Norton project that "about 38% of women now in their late twenties may end their first marriage in divorce. Of the three-quarters who will later remarry, about 44% may redivorce." Ibid.

119. Ibid. at 7–8.

120. Ibid.

121. Age is an important factor in predicting the likelihood of remarriage after a divorce. The 1975 Population Survey indicates that of women aged fourteen to twenty-nine at divorce, only 24% had not remarried when they were surveyed a median of 3.4 years after divorce, and of women aged forty to seventy-five at divorce, 72% had not remarried when they were surveyed a median of 6.5 years after divorce. Ibid. at 20.

122. Social Security Amendments of 1939, ch. 666, §202(b)(1), 53 Stat. 1364 (current version at 42 U.S.C.A. §402 (West 1974 & Supp. 1979)).

123. *See* Social Security Amendments of 1939, ch. 666, §§202(b)(1)(C), (e)(1)(C), 209(m), 53 Stat. 1365, 1378 (repealed in 1957).

124. Social Security Amendments of 1950, ch. 809, §101(a), 64 Stat. 485 (codified at 42 U.S.C. §402(g) (1976)).

125. S. Rep. No. 1669, 81st Cong., 2d Sess. 55, *reprinted in* [1950] *U.S. Code Cong. & Ad. News* 3287, 3317. To ensure actual dependency, the surviving divorced mother was eligible for the mother's benefit only if she had received one-half her support from her husband pursuant to an agreement or court order. Social Security Amendments of 1950, ch. 809, §101(a), 64 Stat. 486 (current version at 42 U.S.C.A. §402[g] [West 1974 & Supp. 1979]).

126. Social Security Amendments of 1965, Pub. L. No. 89–97, §308, 79 Stat. 375 (current version at 42 U.S.C.A. §§402[b][1], [e][1], 416[d] [West 1974 & Supp. 1979]).

127. S. Rep. No. 404, 89th Cong., 1st Sess. 108, *reprinted in* [1965] *U.S. Code Cong. & Ad. News* 1943, 2048. The 1965 amendment relaxed the dependency text for surviving divorced mothers, divorced wives, and divorced widows. Social Security Amendments of 1965, Pub. L. No. 89–97, §308(d)(4), 79 Stat. 286 (current version at 42 U.S.C.A. §402[b], [e], [g] [West 1974 & Supp. 1979]).

128. Social Security Amendments of 1972, Pub. L. No. 92–603, §114, 86 Stat. 1348 (current version at 42 U.S.C.A. §402[b], [g] [West 1974 & Supp. 1979]); *see* H.R. Rep. No. 231, 92d Cong., 1st Sess. 54–55, *reprinted in* [1972] *U.S. Code Cong. & Ad. News* 5041.

129. *See* text accompanying notes 134–37 *infra*.
130. 42 U.S.C. §402(b)(1) (1976).
131. After his retirement, the former husband's excess earnings reduce both his benefits and those of the divorced spouse. 42 U.S.C. §402(b)-(f) (1976).
132. Ibid.
133. 42 U.S.C. §402(b)(1)(B) (1976).
134. *Id.* §402(b)(1)(B), (g)(1); *see* Matthews v. DeCastro, 429 U.S. 181 (1976), H.R. Rep. No. 213, 89th Cong., 1st Sess. 211 (1965).
135. *See* text accompanying notes 130–33 *supra*.
136. The median duration of marriages ending in divorce or annulment was 6.5 years in 1975. Bureau of the Census, U.S. Dep't of Commerce, *Statistical Abstracts of the U.S.* 80 (1978).
137. *See* notes 52–54 *supra* and accompanying text.
138. In the eight community property states, Arizona, California, Idaho, Louisiana, Nevada, New Mexico, Texas, and Washington, marriage is an economic partnership in which each spouse has some ownership interest in assets and income received by the spouses during the marriage. *See* C. Foote, R. Levy and F. Sander, *Cases and Materials on Family Law* 757–62 (1976).
139. *See* e.g., Van Loan v. Van Loan, 116 Ariz. 272, 569 P.2d 214 (1977); *In re* Marriage of Brown, 15 Cal.3d 838, 544 P.2d 561, 126 Cal. Rptr. 633 (1976); Ramsey v. Ramsey, 96 Idaho 672, 535 P.2d 53 (1977); Swope v. Mitchell, 324 So. 2d 461 (La. App. 1975); LeClert v. LeClert, 80 N.M. 235, 453 P.2d 755 (1969); Clearley v. Clearley, 544 S.W.2d 663 (Tex. 1976); Wilder v. Wilder, 85 Wash. 2d 364, 534 P.2d 1355 (1975).
140. Equitable distribution occurs in all but two of the forty-two common-law states. Under modern common law, marriage is not systematically treated as an economic partnership. Ownership follows title as it would in the absence of marriage. All common-law states, however, give a surviving spouse some ownership rights at the death of the other spouse, and thirty-seven of the forty-two states allow the divorce court to apportion the couple's assets without regard to legal title. This apportionment or "equitable distribution" generally takes into account the contributions and needs of the parties, the duration of the marriage and the circumstances of its demise. *See* Foster & Freed, *Divorce in the Fifty States: An Overview as of 1978*, 13 Fam. L.Q. 105 (1979). Since that article was written, five more states have adopted equitable distribution.
141. *See*, e.g., Fenney v. Fenney, 259 Ark. 858, 537 S.W.2d 367 (1976); *In re* Marriage of Ellis, 538 P.2d 1347 (Colo. Ct. App. 1975); Hutchins v. Hutchins, 71 Mich. App. 361, 248 N.W.2d 272 (1976); Elliot v. Elliot, —Minn.—, 274 N.W.2d 75 (1978); *In re* Marriage of Powers, 537 S.W.2d 949 (Mo. Ct. App. 1975); Howard v. Howard, 196 Neb. 351, 242 N.W.2d 884 (1976); Kruger v. Kruger, 73 N.J. 464, 375 A.2d 659 (1977); Baker v. Baker, 546 P.2d 1325 (Okla. 1975); Pinkowski v. Pinkowski, 67 Wis. 2d 176, 226 N.W.2d 518 (1975).

142. *See* cases cited note 141 *supra.*

143. Prior to 1966, there were only five reported cases: three in California, French v. French, 17 Cal. 2d 775, 112 P.2d 235 (1941); Williamson v. Williamson, 203 Cal. App. 2d 8, 21 Cal. Rptr. 164 (2d Dist. 1962); Crossan v. Crossan, 35 Cal. App. 2d 39, 94 P.2d 609 (3d Dist. 1939), and two in Texas, Kirkham v. Kirkham, 335 S.W.2d 393 (Tex. Civ. App. 1965); Berg v. Berg, 115 S.W.2d 1171 (Tex. Civ. App. 1938). Since 1966, cases have become so numerous and claims so routine that an attorney's failure to press pension claims may even result in a malpractice suit. *See,* e.g., Smith v. Lewis, 13 Cal. 3d 349, 530 P.2d 589, 118 Cal. Rptr. 621 (1975).

144. The Uniform Marriage and Divorce Act was adopted by the National Conference of Commissioners of Uniform State Laws in 1970. An amended version was approved by the American Bar Association in 1974. *See* Foster, *Divorce Reform and the Uniform Act,* 7 Fam. L.Q. 179 (1973); Levy, *Comments on the Legislative History of the Uniform Marriage and Divorce Act,* 7 Fam. L.Q. 405 (1973).

The Uniform Act, while it seems to have accelerated the adoption of no-fault divorce, did not originate it. The ground of incompatibility was adopted by New Mexico in 1933. Act of Mar. 3, 1933, ch. 54, §1, 1933 N.M. Laws 71 (current version at *N.M. Stat. Ann.* §40-4-1 [1978]). This ground was also adopted by the Virgin Islands, Act of Dec. 29, 1944, §7 (current version at *V.I. Code Ann.* tit. 16, §104 [1964]), and Oklahoma. Act of May 25, 1953, ch. 22, §1, 1953 Okla. Sess. Laws 59 (current version at *Okla. Stat. Ann.* tit. 12, §1271 [West 1961]). By 1968, nearly one-half of the states accepted as a ground for divorce some version of "living separate and apart." H. Clark, *The Law of Domestic Relations in the United States* 351 (1968). In many states such recognition had only recently occurred. Ibid.; *see,* e.g., Act of Apr. 27, 1966, ch. 254, §2, 1966 N.Y. Laws 833 (current version at N.Y. Dom. Rel. Laws §170[5]–[6] [McKinney 1977]). California, a state in which much pension litigation has occurred, adopted a no-fault law in 1969. *Cal. Civ. Code* §4506 (West 1970).

145. *See* Uniform Marriage and Divorce Act §307(a).

146. 9A Nat'l Conference of Comm'rs on Uniform Laws, Uniform Laws Ann.: Matrimonial, Family and Health Laws 93 (1979) (Commissioner's Prefatory Note, Uniform Marriage and Divorce Act [1973 version]).

147. *See* Hisquierdo v. Hisquierdo, 439 U.S. 572 (1979) (state law must defer to federal statutory scheme for allocating Railroad Retirement Act benefits).

148. *See* text accompanying notes 117–22 *supra* (discussion of divorce data).

149. *See* text accompanying notes 127–29 *supra.*

150. For extended discussion of such proposals, see Blumberg, *supra* note 84, at 264–90.

151. *See,* e.g., the report of the 1975 Social Security Advisory Council Subcommittee on the Treatment of Men and Women, *Advisory Council Report, supra* note 28, at 137–53. See also R. Campbell, *Social Security: Promise and Reality* 309–11 (1977).

152. *See*, e.g., Task Force on Women and Social Security, Senate Special Comm. on Aging, 94th Cong., 1st Sess., Women and Social Security: Adapting to a New Era—A Working Paper 24, 39–40 (Comm. Print 1975).
153. *See*, e.g., H.R. 3009, 94th Cong., 1st Sess. (1975) and H.R. 11840, 94th Cong., 2d Sess. (1976) (homemaker's coverage); V. Reno, *supra* note 45, at 23–24 (child care credit); H.R. 3247, 95th Cong., 1st Sess. (1977); S. Kaltenborn, Untitled Draft Report (Mar. 23, 1977) (for the Task Force on Sex Discrimination, 155 U.S. Dep't of Justice: Blumberg, *supra* note 84, at 284–90 (economic partnership treatment of married couples).
154. *See* Task Force on Family Law and Policy, Citizens' Advisory Council on the Status of Women, *Report of the Task Force on Family Law and Policy* (1968); Comm. on Civil and Political Rights, President's Comm'n on the Status of Women, *Report of the Committee on Civil and Political Rights* 18 (1963); Krauskopf and Thomas, *Partnership Marriage: The Solution to an Ineffective and Inequitable Law of Support*, 35 Ohio St. L.J. 558, 586–600 (1974).
155. *See* text accompanying notes 139–47 *supra*.
156. *See* note 75 *supra*.
157. *See* text accompanying notes 11–12 *supra*.
158. *See generally* Prager, *Sharing Principles and the Future of Marital Property Law*, 25 U.C.L.A. L. Rev. 1 (1977).
159. *See generally*, Kay, Book Review, 60 Calif. L. Rev. 1683 (1972).
160. *See* 42 U.S.C.A. §40, 403(a)(3)(A) (West 1974 & Supp. 1979); 42 U.S.C. §423 (d)(2)(B) (1976); 42 U.S.C. §402(b)(1)(B) (1976); 42 U.S.C. §402(e)(1)(B)(ii); S. Rep. No. 744, 90th Cong. 1st Sess., *reprinted* in [1967] U.S. Code Cong. & Ad. News 2878; H.R. Rep. No. 1030, 90th Cong. 1st Sess. (1967).

Suggested Readings for Part IV

Judith A. Baer, *The Chains of Protection: The Judicial Response to Women's Labor Legislation* (Westport, Conn.: Greenwood Press, 1978).

Nancy Cott, *Bonds of Womanhood: "Woman's Sphere" in New England, 1780–1838* (New Haven: Yale University Press, 1978).

Nancy Cott and Elizabeth H. Pleck, eds., *A Heritage of Her Own* (New York: Simon & Schuster, 1979).

Leonore Davidoff, "Mastered for Life: Servant and Wife in Victorian and Edwardian England," 7 J. Soc. Hist. 406 (1974).

Carl N. Degler, *At Odds: Women and the Family in America from the Revolution to the Present* (New York: Oxford University Press, 1980).

John Demos and Sarane Spence Boocock, eds., *Turning Points: Historical and Sociological Essays on the Family* (Chicago: University of Chicago Press, 1978).

Nancy Schrom Dye, *As Equals and as Sisters: Feminism, the Labor Movement, and the Women's Trade Union League of New York* (Columbia, Mo.: University of Missouri Press, 1980).

Barbara Leslie Epstein, *Politics of Domesticity: Women, Evangelism, and Temperance in Nineteenth-Century America* (New York: Wesleyan University Press, Columbia University Press, 1981).

Lawrence M. Friedman, *A History of American Law* (New York: Simon & Schuster, 1973), especially chapter 4, "The Law of Personal Status: Wives, Paupers and Slaves," pp. 179–191.

Mary Ann Glendon, "Marriage and the States: The Withering Away of Marriage," 62 Va. L. Rev. 663 (1976).

Mary Ann Glendon, "Modern Marriage Law and its Underlying Assumption: The New Marriage and the New Property," 13 Fam. L. Q. 441 (1980).

Linda Gordon, *Woman's Body, Woman's Right: A Social History of Birth Control in America* (New York: Grossman, 1976).

Michael Gordon, ed., *The Family in Social Historical Perspective*, 2d edition (New York: St. Martin's Press, 1978).

Tamara K. Hareven, "The History of the Family as an Interdisciplinary Field," 2 J. Interdis. Hist. 339 (1971).

Tamara K. Hareven, ed., *Transitions: The Family and the Life Course
in Historical Perspectives* (New York: Academic Press, 1978).

C. Dallet Hemphill, "Women in Court: Sex-Role Differentiation in
Salem, Massachusetts, 1636–1863," 39 Wm. & Mary Q. 164
(1982).

Leo Kanowitz, *Equal Rights: The Male Stake* (Albuquerque, N.M.:
University of New Mexico Press, 1981).

Herma Hill Kay, "Legal and Social Impediments to Dual Career
Marriages," 12 U.C.D. L. Rev. 207 (1979).

Alexander Keyssar, "Widowhood in Eighteenth-Century Massachusetts: A Problem in the History of the Family," 8 Perspec.
Am. Hist. 83 (1974).

David L. Kirp and Dorothy Robyn, "Pregnancy, Justice and the
Justices," 57 Tex. L. Rev. 947 (1979).

Herman Lantz, Martin Schultz and Mary O'Hara, "The Changing
American Family from the Preindustrial to the Industrial Period:
A Final Report," 42 Am. Soc. Rev. 406 (1977).

Barbara Laslett, "The Family as a Public and Private Institution: An
Historical Perspective," 35 J. Marr. Fam. 480 (1973).

Gerda Lerner, "The Lady and the Mill Girl: Changes in the Status
of Women in the Age of Jackson," 10 Midcontinent Am. Stud. 5
(1969).

Gerhard O.W. Mueller, "Inquiry into the State of a Divorceless
Society, Domestic Relations Law and Morals in England from
1660 to 1857," 18 U. Pitt. L. Rev. 545 (1957).

Mary Beth Norton, *Liberty's Daughters: The Revolutionary Experience
of American Women, 1750–1800* (Boston: Little, Brown & Co.,
1980).

William L. O'Neill, *Divorce in the Progressive Era* (New Haven: Yale
University Press, 1967).

Theodore K. Rabb and Robert I. Rotberg, eds., *The Family in History: Interdisciplinary Essays* (New York: Harper & Row, 1973).

Charles Rosenberg, ed., *The Family in History* (Philadelphia: University of Pennsylvania Press, 1975).

Marylynn Salmon, "Equality or Submersion? Feme Covert Status
in Early Pennsylvania," in *Women of America: A History*, ed. Carol
Ruth Berkin and Mary Beth Norton (Boston: Houghton Mifflin

Co., 1979), pp. 92–111.

Lawrence Stone, *The Family, Sex, and Marriage in England, 1500–1800* (New York: Harper & Row, 1977).

Carol Weisbrod and Pamela Heingorn, *"Reynolds v. United States:* Nineteenth-Century Forms of Marriage and the Status of Women," 10 Conn. L. Rev. 828 (1978).

. . . . .

Numerous scholarly journals are also excellent sources of reference on the role of women in family history and family law. See especially *Journal of Family History: Studies in Family Kinship and Demography*, National Council on Family Relations (Minneapolis, Minn.); *Journal of Interdisciplinary History*, MIT Press (Cambridge, Mass.); *Journal of Family Issues* (Beverly Hills, Calif.: Sage Publications); *Journal of Marriage and the Family*, National Council on Family Relations (Minneapolis, Minn.); *Family Law Quarterly*, America Bar Association, Section of Family Law, (Chicago, Ill.); and *Journal of Family Law*, University of Louisville School of Law (Louisville, Ky.).

PART V

Legal Education and the Legal Profession

The next section, Part V, addresses the role of women in legal education and the legal profession from a historical perspective. These subjects are generally given only brief attention by traditional texts on sex discrimination.[1]

The essay by D. Kelly Weisberg places the struggle of the nation's first women lawyers in its historical context. In "Barred from the Bar: Women and Legal Education in the United States, 1870–1890," Weisberg examines the regulation of access to legal education and the legal profession in nineteenth-century America. She explores the struggle for women to gain entrance to law schools and the bar and also examines the legal and social rationale expressed in case law excluding women. This rationale includes: 1) statutory interpretation of the masculine pronoun, 2) legislative intent, 3) women's common-law disabilities, especially those of married women, 4) women's mental and physical nature rendering them "unfit" for the practice of law, 5) a concern with women lawyers unjustly swaying the scales of justice, and 6) a concern with women straying from their proper sex roles.

The essay also addresses the reasons this struggle took place in this historical era. Weisberg suggests that the origins of the struggle lay in certain social forces, especially the movement for coeducation and higher education, industrialization and westward expansion, the abolitionist movement and the nascent women's rights movement.

Mortimer Schwartz, Susan Brandt and Patience Milrod, in "Clara Shortridge Foltz: Pioneer in the Law," explore the struggles of one of the first women lawyers to gain admission to law school and the bar. The authors examine as well Foltz's many legal and social

227

contributions. Despite significant opposition, Clara Foltz drafted, as well as lobbied for, legislation eliminating racial and sexual restrictions in statutory qualifications for lawyers in California. She also opened formal legal education to women in that state by compelling the admission of women to Hastings College of the Law.[2]

Foltz's career reveals numerous other achievements. These include the creation of a public defender system to ensure representation for indigents, better treatment for prisoners, and the separation of juveniles from adult prisoners in local jails. She worked for legislation to give women the vote in state elections, drafted a state suffrage amendment and secured its passage. In addition, she helped secure the passage of the nineteenth amendment guaranteeing to women the right to vote in federal elections.

Cynthia Fuchs Epstein, in "Women's Entry into Corporate Law Firms," explores, from a sociological perspective, women's role in an important legal institution, the large corporate law firm. At the time of Erwin Smigel's classic study of Wall Street lawyers in the sixties,[3] few women were employed in these corporate firms. Epstein explores changes in the recruitment of women corporate lawyers over time, in addition to changes in the characteristics of these women lawyers.

Epstein finds that law firms have significantly improved their numerical profiles. In addition, more women are employed in formerly male-dominated specializations within the firms, such as litigation. Epstein also examines the factors contributing to this increased receptivity to women. These factors include: 1) the increase in the pool of eligible women, 2) the women's movement, 3) sex discrimination suits, 4) student-faculty vigilance, and 5) changes in attitudes. She concludes by exploring the impact of these women attorneys on the law and legal institutions. Although she finds that the women's presence has not significantly altered the profession, Epstein suggests that the women may have had a "humanizing effect" on the profession.

NOTES

1. Only Herma Hill Kay, *Text, Cases and Materials on Sex-Based Discrimination*, 2d ed. (St. Paul, Minn.: West Publishing Co., 1981) devotes an entire chapter section to women in legal education and the legal profession. Other texts give little attention to this topic. See Kay, pp. 872–879.

2. See Foltz v. Hoge, 54 Cal. 28 (1879).

3. Erwin O. Smigel, *The Wall Street Lawyer: Professional Organization Man* (New York: Free Press, 1964).

BARRED FROM THE BAR:
WOMEN AND LEGAL EDUCATION IN
THE UNITED STATES, 1870–1890

D. Kelly Weisberg

One of the paramount concerns of any skilled profession is the regulation of access to the profession. As Chroust has pointed out, in colonial America any person desiring to be admitted to the legal profession had four major avenues of entry.

> He might, by his own efforts and through self-directed reading and study, acquire whatever scraps of legal information were available in books, statutes, or reports; he could work in the clerk's office of some court of record; he could serve as an apprentice or clerk in the law library of a reputable lawyer, preferably one with a law library; or he could enter one of the four Inns of Court in London and receive there the "call to the bar."[1]

Chroust's use of the masculine pronoun above is not entirely without significance. "Any" person in colonial America did have four avenues of legal education open to him, provided that that person was male. The first hundred years of American legal education were characterized by a glaring absence of women lawyers. This paper shall examine women's entry into the legal profession after the Civil War in terms of their admission to law schools and to the bar.

The struggle for women to gain entrance to the legal profession began in the late 1860s with Ada Kepley the first woman to graduate from the Union College of Law (now Northwestern) in 1870[2] and Arabella Mansfield the first woman to be admitted to the

Reprinted from *Journal of Legal Education*, vol. 28, no. 4 (1977): 485–507, with minor revisions by the author. Copyright © 1977 by Association of American Law Schools. Reprinted by permission.

Special acknowledgement is made of the assistance of Professor Egon Bittner, Brandeis University, and of Leonard Klein, Senior Reference Librarian, Harvard University Law Library, for facilitating the access to rare materials.

bar of any state (Iowa, 1869). However, the battle was by no means over; in reality it had just begun.

Scarcely two months after Arabella Mansfield was admitted to the Iowa bar, Myra Bradwell passed an examination for the Chicago bar, but the Illinois Supreme Court refused to grant her a license to practice law on the grounds of her sex. When the case was taken on a writ of error to the United States Supreme Court, she was once again unsuccessful.[3] In other landmark cases Lavinia Goodell was refused admission to the Wisconsin bar in 1875,[4] Lelia Josephine Robinson was refused admission to the bar of Massachusetts in 1881,[5] and Belva Lockwood, although admitted to the District of Columbia bar and admitted to practice before the United States Supreme Court, was still refused admission to the Virginia bar in the 1890s because of her sex.[6]

Even after the turn of the century when women were admitted to the bar of almost every state,[7] the battle continued for women's admission to law school. Columbia University first admitted women law students in 1929, Harvard University in 1950 (although women had first applied to Harvard in the 1870s),[8] the University of Notre Dame in 1969, and the last male bastion, Washington and Lee University in 1972.

In order to understand better the century of discrimination against women in terms of their access to the legal profession, it is helpful to examine the legal and social rationale utilized for the exclusion of women. Often the legal and social rationale cannot be separated, as will be seen in the court decisions of this period barring women. The legal rationale for denying women access to the profession may be seen to include the following:

THE FIGHT OVER THE MASCULINE PRONOUN OR WOMEN AS NON-PERSONS

In most states admission to the bar was controlled by statutes. These statutes provided for the admission of "persons" or "citizens," or for specifically "male" persons or citizens. The language of the statutes was framed similar to the following:

> The Superior Court may admit and cause to be sworn as attorneys such *persons* as are qualified therefor agreeably to the rules established by the judges of said court, and no other person than an

attorney so admitted shall plead at the bar of any court of this state, except in *his* own cause.⁹ (emphasis added)

or, the Wisconsin statute which specified: "No *person* shall hereafter be admitted or licensed to practice . . . except in the manner hereinafter provided . . . *he* shall be first licensed by order of. . . ."¹⁰ (emphasis added)

The battle was waged over the masculine pronoun. That is, could the court (in the *Goodell* and *Bradwell* cases, for example) decide that words importing specifically masculine gender should extend to women and thereby admit women to the legal profession? The general rule of statutory interpretation was that "every word importing the masculine gender only may extend and be applied to females as well as males."¹¹ This was precisely the point on which Mrs. Mansfield was admitted to the Iowa bar. However, the court in both *Goodell* and *Bradwell* maintained that the rule of interpretation applied "unless . . . such construction would be inconsistent with the manifest intention of the legislature."¹² This brings us to another legal argument utilized to bar women from the legal profession.

SURELY, THE LEGISLATORS NEVER CONTEMPLATED THAT!

In establishing the rules by which admission to the profession should be determined, the court was bound by two limitations, maintained Justice Bradley in the *Bradwell* decision. The first was to promote the proper administration of justice and the second, " . . . that it should not admit any persons, or class of persons, not intended by the legislature to be admitted even though not expressly excluded by statute."¹³

Supporters of this argument maintained that when the legislators first framed the statutes in the eighteenth century, they did not contemplate that women would ever be admitted to the bar. Hence, in its original enactment, the application of the statute to women was not in the minds of the legislators. This interpretation naturally led to the conclusion that the court lacked the statutory authority to admit women to the legal profession. This was the interpretation utilized in both the *Bradwell* and *Goodell* decisions and by Justice Pardee in his dissent in *In re Hall.*¹⁴

In holding to this strict interpretation of legislative intent, the courts seemed influenced by an overriding concern with the social consequences of straying from the interpretation. In both the *Goodell* and *Bradwell* decisions (maintaining this lack of legislative intent) one finds the apocalyptic adumbration of the social consequences entailed by permitting women to enter the legal profession —namely, a sweeping revolution of the social order. As Justice Ryan maintained in *Goodell*:

> If we should follow that authority in ignoring the distinction of sex, we do not perceive why it should not emasculate the constitution itself and include females in the constitutional right of male suffrage and male qualification. Such a rule would be one of judicial revolution, not of judicial construction. . . . We cannot stultify the court by holding that the legislature intended to bring about, *per ambages*, a sweeping revolution of social order, by adopting a very innocent rule of statutory construction.[15]

Similarly, in the *Bradwell* decision, Justice Lawrence when delivering the majority opinion stated the consequence, fearful beyond imagination, that:

> This step, if taken by us, would mean that in the opinion of this tribunal, every civil office in this state may be filled by women; that it is in harmony with the spirit of our constitution and laws that women should be made governors, judges and sheriffs. This we are not yet prepared to hold.[16]

YOU HAVE NOT, ERGO YOU CANNOT— COMMON-LAW DISABILITY

Another common rationale utilized to bar women from the legal profession was the argument that the impediments growing out of women's legal status at the common law prevented them from gaining access to the profession. The fact that women had never been admitted to the bar had established a common-law disability. And, supporters of this argument maintained, inasmuch as women were not known as attorneys at common law, this was sufficient reason for the court to refuse to admit them. It was argued, too, that women had other disabilities at common law which would interfere with their practice of the legal profession, such as their not being able to hold office at this time. This presented a problem because an attorney was an officer of the court. However, the most serious common-law disability which would interfere with women practicing law, or so women's opponents maintained, concerned married women's inability to contract.

IF YOU'RE MARRIED, YOU CAN'T BE A LAWYER

This legal rationale was based on the fact that married women at this time were disqualified from entering into contracts with third persons without their husband's consent. In both the *Bradwell* and *Lockwood* decisions, it was held that because of this disability at common law, married women could not be permitted to gain admission to the bar.[17]

However, in some decisions which admitted women to the bar, it was held that married women's inability to contract was not an insurmountable obstacle. In the *Kilgore* decision in Pennsylvania (admitting Mrs. Kilgore), Justice Thayer held that the essential basis of the relationship between lawyer and client was not in contract.

> But what difference does it make if she cannot be sued as upon a contract. There are other adequate remedies for neglect of duty, infidelity, or misbehavior in office, which are provided by law and to which she would undoubtedly be amenable. . . . These laws are an ample security for the client in dealing with an attorney, even if she be a married woman.[18]

It can be seen that this objection was not really the primary obstacle in the minds of opposing judges. Upon the filing of Mrs. Bradwell's printed argument, the Illinois Supreme Court held that *no* female was eligible to practice in the state of Illinois—be she married or single.

In addition to legal arguments, opponents of women's entry into the legal profession also utilized social rationale for barring women. One such rationale included the argument that woman's mental and physical nature rendered her unfit for legal practice.

INFERIOR IN MIND AND BODY

One objection to women entering the legal profession was that women did not possess a "legal mind." Women's minds were thought to be more emotional than rational and logical—the requisite qualities of the legal mind. Moreover it was argued, women simply did not have the natural aptitude to perform the duties required by the profession. Or, as one woman said: "We are also told that the successful lawyer must have a logical mind, and since the mind of woman is sadly lacking in this respect, her unfitness for the legal profession is apparent."[19]

Not only did women apparently lack the necessary mental qualities for the practice of law, but also they were thought to lack the physical stamina the profession required. The opposing forces maintained that women did not have the physical strength to follow "so arduous a calling as the law."[20] Women, it would seem, were possessed of an exceedingly delicate constitution which could not withstand the long hours of study and the conflicts of the courtroom. As Justice Ryan maintained in *Goodell:*

> There are many employments in life not unfit for female character. The profession of law is surely not one of these. The peculiar qualities of womanhood, its gentle graces, its quick sensibility, its tender susceptibility, its purity, its delicacy, its emotional impulses, its subordination of hard reason to sympathetic feeling, are surely not qualifications for forensic strife. Nature has tempered woman as little for the juridical conflicts of the court room, as for the physical conflicts of the battlefield.[21]

Nowhere are these stereotypes of woman's mental and physical nature as clearly brought into relief as in the whimsical story published in 1886 by Charles C. Moore about the first woman lawyer who came to Litchfield, Connecticut.[22] The presence of these stereotypes in the story is all the more significant because the author is in favor of (more precisely, enamoured with) the idea of women lawyers.

As Miss Mary Padelford steps off the Claremont stage, Lawyer Walter Perry remarks, "and if she possesses enough physical strength I wouldn't be surprised if she makes a success." She chooses Claremont (i.e. Litchfield) because it is 1100 feet above sea-level and "her health has never been exceedingly rugged." When Miss Padelford loses her first case in court, she (what else?) bursts into tears in the courtroom. Later, the constant study out of court "was sufficient of itself to tax her constitution to the utmost and long trials in court brought a mental and physical exhaustion her ambitious nature was hardly able to resist." After another courtroom incident she faints and falls from her chair. When the physician arrives, he diagnoses her condition as "brain fever." In a fitting finale, Lawyer Walter Perry and Miss Mary Padelford are married and enter into partnership. One might surmise that thereafter Mrs. Perry's health improved because of the physical and mental assistance of a male law partner.[23]

The belief that women's physical disabilities rendered them unfit for law practice even took the form of maintaining that women's "peculiar physiological condition" (menstruation) would inhibit their practice of law. In answer to this objection, one author remarked: "Do the thousands of women who practice medicine, leave their patients to die when they are suffering from catamenial disturbances?"[24] Interestingly, it was not only men who protested that women's physiological condition would interfere with their practice of law. One woman opponent protested:

> How would a lawyeress be able to consult with her clients, when she was attacked by the nausea of the first months of pregnancy? And afterward what a figure she would make in court, when, the months of her interesting situation being advanced, her curved lines become crushed with an anterior round line? And if the pains should come upon her in the heat of argument! That would indeed be fine! Would she invite her colleagues to serve her as midwives? And in childbirth, farewell to business! Poor clients! I assure you that I laugh to myself thinking of the ridiculous figure that a woman lawyer would make.[25]

It was suggested on the death of one of the first women lawyers, Lavinia Goodell, that perhaps the "hard usage and severe mental application incidental to a legal professional career"[26] had contributed to her early demise. In answer to this, supporters of women entering the legal profession maintained: "Miss Goodell was forty-one years of age. Henry Armitt Brown, the noted lawyer of Philadelphia, died recently at thirty-two. We would like to suggest the query whether men are able to endure the hard usage. . . ."[27]

JUSTICE WOULD SUFFER

Another argument proffered against women entering the legal profession concerned the fear that the interests of justice would suffer. The female sex, opponents maintained, was reputedly garrulous and wanting in discretion.[28] Consequently, the interests of clients could not be entrusted to women's hands. This latter opinion is clearly expressed in a rather misogynic British law journal article of this period, "Prudes for Proctors":

> The fact that women are admitted to practise in the United States is sufficient to prevent the matter being passed off as a joke; but it must be remembered that, in the States, the principle that the client must be protected from the solicitor by the Courts, has almost entirely given place to the principle that the client can very well look after himself. In England the question has to be considered, whether the interests of clients can safely be entrusted to a woman's hands.[29]

This concern about the interests of justice also took the form that the introduction of women into the field of advocacy would check the fighting instincts of lawyers. Moreover, it was thought that judgment would no longer be impartial if women lawyers were present in the courtroom. This belief was expressed as: "There are some lawyers who go so far as to say that given a woman plaintiff and a woman attorney and the defense might just as well lie down if the case be before a jury."[30]

Strains of this belief can be seen in the following anecdote. A woman lawyer asked her client why he came to her for legal assistance. The client, who had been tried and convicted of a crime and awarded a new trial by an appellate court, replied: "Well, ma'am, I reckon I've had justice. What I need now is mercy, and I figger them jurors will feel mightly sorry for me if all I have is a woman to defend me."[31]

MOTHERS AS LAWYERS?—ROLE CONFLICTS

However, the primary social rationale utilized to bar women from the legal profession centered on woman's traditional role in the family. The professional role of the lawyer was seen to be in direct conflict with the traditional roles of woman as wife and mother. In both the *Bradwell* and *Goodell* decisions, the judges delivered a lengthy discourse on woman's "sphere." The proper sphere for woman, they maintained, citing by way of authority the law of nature and the law of the Creator, was in the home. The decisions are worth quoting at length. As Justice Bradley stated in *Bradwell:*

> . . . the civil law, as well as nature itself, has always recognized a wide difference in the respective spheres and destinies of man and woman. Man is, or should be, woman's protector and defender. The natural and proper timidity and delicacy which belongs to the fe-

male sex evidently unfits it for many of the occupations of civil life. The constitution of the family organization, which is found in the divine ordinance, as well as in the nature of things indicates the domestic sphere as that which properly belongs to the domain and functions of womanhood . . . The paramount destiny and mission of woman are to fulfill the noble and benign offices of wife and mother. This is the law of the Creator. . . .[32]

Similarly, Justice Ryan in *Goodell* maintained:

The law of nature destines and qualifies the female sex for the bearing and nurture of the children of our race and for the custody of the homes of the world and their maintenance in love and honor. And all life-long callings of women, inconsistent with these radical and sacred duties of their sex, as is the profession of the law, are departures from the order of nature; and when voluntary, treason against it. . . .[33]

Woman's traditional role conflicted with the professional role of lawyer in terms of the divergent sets of priorities of the role sets. The socially approved role for woman as wife and mother had duties associated with it which were expected to be woman's first and primary obligation, superseding any other claim. For the lawyer, obviously, his occupation was intended to be his first priority. Or, as Justice Ryan had asserted in *Goodell:* "The profession enters largely into the well being of society; and to be honorably filled and safely to society, exacts the devotion of life."[34] For woman, quite clearly, only her husband and children were supposed to exact the devotion of her life.

The requisite personality attributes of the lawyer, moreover, were seen as incompatible with those necessary for the role of wife and mother. The lawyer was supposed to be aggressive—a skilled combatant in the juridical conflicts of the courtroom. Woman was seen as nurturant, gentle, tender. In short, she possessed personality attributes required for the fulfillment of the role of wife and mother. It was readily apparent that the two role configurations have mutually exclusive sets of attributes.

But what of the unmarried woman? If opponents were concerned with married women straying from their duties, should not the unmarried woman, then, be able to practice law? For the single woman who was not engaged in fulfilling the role of "her destiny," the law was still not to be considered as a possible occupation. The court in *Goodell* had this to say:

> The cruel chances of life sometimes baffle both sexes, and may leave women free from the peculiar duties of their sex. These may need employment. . . . But it is public policy to provide for the sex, not for its superfluous members; and not to tempt women from the proper duties of their sex by opening to them duties peculiar to ours. There are many employments in life not unfit for female character. The profession of the law is surely not one of these.[35]

The single woman, thus, was free to enter some other occupation to provide for herself. The legal profession, women's opponents stoutly maintained, should remain forever barred both to her and to her married sisters.

THE FIRST WOMEN LAWYERS

The next issue which shall be dealt with here concerns the nation's first women lawyers. Recent articles on women and the law tend to celebrate in passing the nation's first woman to graduate from law school, or the first woman to practice in the United States Supreme Court, or the first woman to be admitted to the bar of particular states. However, in their overriding concern with the position of women lawyers today, authors have neglected to take the historical question one step further. Who were the nation's first women lawyers? What can be discovered about them and about their chapter in the history of American legal education? (Data for this section were based on two "who's who" type articles on women lawyers published in 1886 and 1890, in addition to several obituaries of the nation's first women lawyers).[36]

In 1870 approximately four women were attending the nation's law schools (although not all four would be permitted to graduate). The same year witnessed a total student population of 1,611 in thirty-one law schools.[37] (However, the total number of law students was undoubtedly somewhat greater because it was common in this period to pass the bar through private reading and office apprenticeships without ever having attended a law school.) By 1890 the number of women lawyers and law students in the United States had grown to approximately 135. In that same time period, the total law student population in the United States had risen to approximately 7,000.

What can be determined about these first women lawyers? After 1870 when law schools slowly began admitting and graduating women (Union College 1870; Michigan 1871; Washington University, St. Louis, 1871; Howard University 1872; Iowa State 1873; National University, Washington, 1873), the majority of these women attended law school in preparation for the bar, occasionally after having studied for a year or two in a law office. Before that time, the handful of women who were admitted to the bar (or more accurately, who sought admission to the bar), such as Mrs. Belle Mansfield, Mrs. Ada Kepley, Mrs. J. Ellen Foster, Miss Alta Hulette and Mrs. Myra Bradwell, gained their instruction either at home (Mrs. Foster said she read Blackstone while rocking her babies)[38] or in law offices. An interesting fact now comes to light: many of the first women to gain entrance to the legal profession were married women for whom the opportunities of law study and later, law practice, were availed to them by their lawyer-husbands. In 1890 approximately one-third of the total number of women lawyers were married women and more than half this number were married to lawyers.

Many of these lawyer-husbands helped their wives in their struggle to be admitted to the bar. Many of the first women lawyers received instruction in their husband's law offices; and, some lawyer-husbands, such as P.A.L. Smith, worked to get legislation passed which would open the profession to women. As Mr. Smith wrote refuting the argument that admitting women to the profession would interfere with women's domestic affairs:

> This is all bosh—for in the first place she may not have any domestic affairs to look after; and in the second place, she herself is the best judge as to whether it pays her better or suits her better to look after other business and pay some one to keep an eye on domestic affairs. One or two little domestic affairs are not expected to occupy all of a smart woman's attention, and in the meantime why shouldn't she be allowed to practice law if she wants to. My wife has studied hard, prepared herself for the bar, and is fully competent to stand the legal exam required of men and I see no reason convincing to me why she should not practice. She has studied at my request and anything I can do to secure her admission to the bar will be done.[39]

After admission to the bar many of these women were further facilitated in their entrance to the legal profession by going into practice with their lawyer-husbands. In fact, Robinson reports that in 1890 there were twenty husband-wife law partnerships in the United States.[40]

It is likely, too, that single women were aided by influential male lawyer relatives. Many single women who sought admission to the bar came from families with notable members in the legal profession. One woman's father (the first woman to be admitted to the bar in Utah in 1871) was Attorney General of the Utah Territory. Another woman who graduated from the University of Michigan in 1888 had a father who was a circuit judge in the Hawaiian Islands. And, of Frederika Perry, it was said "She belonged to the Strong family which has furnished a great deal of the legal talent of the United States."[41] Other women's fathers were famous judges—Bessie Bradwell's father, for one, and Mary McHenry's father who was renowned in both California and Louisiana. Other single women had fathers who were practicing lawyers and often, after these women were admitted to the bar, they entered into partnerships with their family members.

Surprisingly, in such families one finds family combinations of women seeking entrance to the bar—mothers and daughters or sister pairs. Myra Bradwell and her daughter Bessie both sought admission and Kate Pier and her mother graduated together from the University of Wisconsin in 1887. Among the sister pairs are included the Spaulding sisters from the University of Wisconsin and the Cronise sisters who were admitted together to the state courts in Ohio in 1873. The Pier mother and daughter eventually joined Mr. Pier in a partnership and the Cronise sisters also formed a partnership until one of them married and left the profession. It may be surmised that originating from families with such concentrations of legal talent eased the way into the legal profession for many of these women.

Of the women lawyers who entered into active practice, what was the nature of their practice? Many who "actively" entered the profession, it would appear, ended up doing the office work and occupying a back seat to male lawyers. In the case of Mrs. Mary Haddock (in partnership with her husband), she "devoted herself principally to office work and briefing cases," and for Mrs. LeValley "her share of the work has been principally in the office." Tabitha Holton, in partnership with one of several lawyer-brothers, "devoted herself chiefly to office work," and Miss Jessie Wright after her marriage "assisted her husband in some of his work," similar to Mrs. Frank Helmer (Bessie Bradwell) who from time to time "aids her (lawyer) husband in his business."[42]

Staying in the office was not only the fate of women lawyers in partnership with husbands or brothers. It seems this was also the fate of other early women lawyers as well. Of Miss Emma Gillet it was said, "her work has been principally in the office line—the drawing of papers, taking testimony in equity causes and probate business, together with a large amount of notarial and some financial work." Similarly, Mrs. Eliza Chambers gave her attention to such matters as equity, pensions and land claims.

The preponderance of "office work" done by women lawyers may well have been understandable in view of public prejudice. Many women lawyers may have been anxious to escape criticism and censure from the public and from other members of the legal profession and for these reasons chose to remain inconspicuous. Yet surprisingly enough, one finds a handful of these first women lawyers fearlessly engaging in criminal work. Mrs. Addie Billins in partnership with her husband was involved in several criminal cases and Mrs. Martha Strickland was active in criminal prosecutions as the assistant prosecuting attorney in Detroit. Mrs. Laura De Force Gordon had a substantial criminal practice (and represented a client in *People* v. *Sproule*, termed in 1900 "the most remarkable trial in California criminal jurisprudence"). Kate Kane wrote that in criminal law she had either prosecuted or defended every crime known to modern times except treason and piracy. And, Mrs. Marilla Ricker's interest in the defense of criminals earned her the name of "prisoner's friend."

Later in the history of women in the legal profession, it appears that the profession was quite willing to allow women to take over this specialty, if one can go by the remarks of Clarence Darrow. In an address to a group of women lawyers in Chicago, Darrow stated: "And there is another field [after divorce] you can have solely for your own. You won't make a living at it, but it's worth while and you'll have no competition. That is the free defense of criminals."[43]

WHERE TO PRACTICE?

Where did these first women lawyers practice in light of public prejudice? For married women with lawyer-husbands, as we have already seen, many did not have to face this difficult decision because they entered into practice with their husbands (although occasionally they confronted another difficulty as in the states of

Massachusetts and New York where married women were not able legally to form partnerships). However, for single women the answer to where to practice was oftentimes more problematic. In some instances these women were advised to open a practice in their home town and presumably thereby diminish public criticism. Often however, if they wished to practice at all, many women had little choice but to move to a state where it was permitted by law. The case of Mary Hall is illustrative of this. Before applying for admission in her home state of Connecticut, she seriously considered going to a state where women were already admitted to the bar "dreading the noise and criticism to which a pioneer in such a matter is always subject."[44] Miss Lemma Barkeloo furnishes another example. After being refused admission to law school in her native state of New York, she left her home and went to Missouri where she was admitted to Washington University. In her obituary was the following story by the Honorable Albert Todd: "At the close of the last session of the law school, she called at my office to consult me about opening an office here. She said her parents lived in Brooklyn, New York. I advised her to open her office at home, where she would have the support of her friends. She said she had thought of that. . . ."[45] In the end, however, Miss Barkeloo decided to stay in the "West," because "the western people were generous and liberal in their sentiments and she would be better sustained here than in the East."[46]

An interesting discovery that emerged from this research is that the West afforded better opportunities for women lawyers than the East. In fact, Robinson goes so far as to say that "It is undoubtedly owing to the Western spirit of liberality that women have ever been recognized at the bar in this country at all."[47] The first women lawyers were found predominantly in four states: Illinois, Iowa, Michigan and Wisconsin. (It is in these states where law schools first admitted women students.)

Two husband and wife teams (Alice Jordan Blake and her husband and Sara Kilgore Wertman and her husband) moved as far west as Washington, although it can only be surmised that the diminution of prejudice against women lawyers was a contributory reason for their move. The most noteworthy case of the western mobility of the woman lawyer was Lelia Robinson Sawtelle. After seeking admission to the Massachusetts bar, she left for the Washington Territory where she "established herself in practice with the expectation of remaining permanently."[48] The opportunities there which were unavailable in the East can be seen: "There she gained a valuable experience in court work (which she scarcely attempted in Boston) in trying and arguing cases before mixed juries of men and women in a new and progressive territory."[49] (It is important to note, of course, that the opportunities in the West not only attracted women lawyers, but attracted male lawyers as well. They also flocked to the West as it opened up.[50])

Lest it be thought that all the women who gained entrance to the legal profession in this epoch eventually practiced, suffice it to say that approximately one-fifth of the total number of women lawyers never practiced at all. Some women studied without the intention of practicing. Others married and became entrapped by domestic duties. In some instances, as with Rebecca May and Mary McHenry, women's husbands refused to let them enter active practice after their marriage.

Some women drifted into other fields because, it may be surmised, there they encountered less prejudice. Of these women some went into education. Belle Mansfield (the first woman to be admitted to the bar of any state) took a chair in history at De Pauw University. Catherine Waugh (before becoming the famed suffragist) was a professor of commercial law. Some women entered the literary field. One woman became a legal editor for West Publishing Company in 1886. Another woman became an author of legal texts (Marietta Shay, author of *Students' Guide to Common Law Pleading*). Bessie Bradwell Helmer compiled the last ten volumes of Bradwell's Appellate Court Reports, while her famous mother (*Bradwell v. Illinois*) became editor of "The Chicago Legal News." Catherine V. Waite became the editor of "The Chicago Legal Times."

It appears that many of these first women lawyers were well-to-do women, as can be deduced both from their mobility and from the concentration of legal talent in their families. Also, many of these women were extremely vocal. In addition to those women who expressed their opinions by virtue of their positions on periodicals, many women lawyers were involved in the social movement of temperance or in politics, as was Belva Lockwood, the first woman to run for President of the United States. (Mrs. Lockwood quite rightfully argued that although women could not vote, there was no reason they could not be voted for!)[51]

HISTORICAL CONTEXT

The century of struggle for women to gain admission to the legal profession can only be understood by placing it in its historical context—with its roots in the struggle for women's rights in the United States. Only then can the question be answered as to why this struggle of women lawyers took place at this particular time in American history.

At the beginning of the nineteenth century women were not given access to higher education because of their sex. While they were permitted to attend elementary schools since the early days of American history, their admission into secondary schools and universities took much longer. It was considered a waste of money to educate women—not only because women's minds were thought to be inferior to men's, but also because women's function was to bear and raise children and an education was deemed superfluous for this task.

Before 1814, education for women was limited to the "well-to-do"[52] and consisted of such pursuits as embroidery, painting, French, singing and playing the harpsichord. However, one event significantly altered this—the discovery of the first power-driven loom in Waltham, Massachusetts, which launched the first large-scale industry in the United States. During the period of industrial development and westward expansion following the Louisiana Purchase, women not only entered the textile mills in vast numbers but also were in increasing demand as teachers for the rapidly growing population. Consequently, "the need to equip them for the new duties being laid upon them was harder to deny."[53]

The battle for broader opportunities and rights for women really revolved around the issue of education, maintains Atkins.[54] Such early American feminists as Mary Wollstonecraft, Hannah Crocker, Emma Willard and Frances Wright all stressed the importance of education for women. The first publicly endowed institution for the education of women opened in 1821 and by the end of the 1830s seminaries and colleges for women were beginning to be established. Oberlin, in 1833, was the first institution of higher education to admit all students regardless of race or sex (although women here took a shortened literary course in accordance with the belief that their minds could not assimilate the same fare as men's and the belief that their education better prepared them for intelligent motherhood).[55] In 1837 with the founding of Mt. Holyoke, the concept finally took hold that women needed an improved education for more than carrying out their housewifely duties. Later developments in the nineteenth century saw the opening of Vassar (1865), Smith and Wellesley (1875) and the Harvard Annex (Radcliffe) in 1879.

The struggle for co-education for women proceeded hand-in-hand with the struggle for such equal rights for women as custodial rights for their children, owning property, the right to work at a job and the right to control their own earnings. The roots of these various struggles (and of the fight for suffrage which often overshadows them) can be found in the anti-slavery movement: it was the slavery issue that provided the spark which ignited the feminist movement. Before the 1840s feminism was an unorganized social movement. However, after that period women began organizing in several major American cities to form anti-slavery societies. As Flexner describes:

> It was in the abolitionist movement that women first learned to organize, to hold public meetings, to conduct petition campaigns. As abolitionists they first won the right to speak in public and began to evolve a philosophy of their place in society and of their basic rights. For a quarter of a century the two movements, to free the slave and to liberate the woman, nourished and strengthened one another.[56]

Thus, it was the abolitionist movement which first brought women out of the home and encouraged them to speak out for their rights—one of which was co-education. Once women gained ground in co-education in colleges and universities, it undoubtedly seemed the logical next step to continue the fight for co-education in law schools.

Interestingly, the fight for women's rights netted better results in the western United States than in the East. This also explains the reason why many women lawyers migrated westward. The Wyoming Territory was the first to grant full suffrage rights to women in 1869. And, in addition to giving women state control of their property and protecting them from discrimination as teachers, Wyoming also permitted the first women to sit on juries.[57] The western state of Utah, then the Utah Territory, followed Wyoming in 1870 by granting women the vote. (However, the Edmunds-Tucker Act illegalizing plural marriage passed by Congress in 1887 also revoked women's suffrage in Utah and Utah women did not regain the vote until 1896.) The realities of frontier life and the shortage of labor there resulted in women undertaking considerable responsibilities in daily activities. This gave little credence to the idea that women were inferior and should lead sheltered and protected lives.

SUFFRAGISTS?

The obvious question which comes to mind is: how many of these first women lawyers were active in the women's rights movement in the late nineteenth century? One might hypothesize that the majority of the first women to gain entrance to the legal profession would have been staunch women rightists. Perhaps, even, many were early suffragists? Yet, an examination of the biographical materials on the first women lawyers and a cross-tabulation of several sources on the suffrage movement reveal that only a few of these women evidenced their support of women's rights by being ardent suffragists. The names of women lawyers in this period which have come to light in the suffrage movement include: Mary Ahrens, Emily Buckhout Baker, Phoebe Cousins, Clara Foltz, Belva Lockwood, Catherine Waugh McCulloch and Marilla Ricker.[58]

The number of suffragist-lawyers may have been somewhat greater based on the fact that several additional women lawyers are found in the temperance movement in this era. It is known that many women's rights supporters came to the suffrage movement through temperance.[59] Among the women lawyers whose names are found in the temperance movement were: Ada Kepley, J. Ellen Foster and Ada Bittenbender. However, it can not be stated conclusively whether these particular women were women's right supporters.

What of the links between the women's rights movement in the United States and the first women lawyers? The apex of American feminism occurred in the period 1890–1920. A survey of several volumes of the *Women Lawyers' Journal* after its inception in 1911 reveals that many women lawyers in this *later* period actively participated in the suffrage movement. In fact, in these later years, the link between the women's rights movement and women lawyers is very clear. In this period, the *Women Lawyers' Journal* carried frequent articles on suffragists, on the formation of suffrage clubs, on the progress of equal suffrage, and on women lawyers who were appointed to positions in suffrage associations. In addition, many members of the Women's Lawyers Club (which published the *Women Lawyers' Journal*) were prominent suffragists. It was not uncommon to find in the *Journal* a comment such as the following: "It is expected that the women lawyers of the country will respond to the call for marchers in the suffrage parade in Washington on March 3, the day previous to the inauguration of President Wilson."[60]

However, of the women lawyers in the earlier period of 1870 to 1890, it can more likely be assumed that the majority of these women were not radical feminists. A few of the first women lawyers may have been "quiet" feminists, such as Mrs. Anne Saveny who practiced for the benefit of women, or the Cronise sisters who apprenticed several women law students in their office. By and large, however, it appears that the overwhelming majority of these first women lawyers were individualists—individualists who were content to earn their law degrees and then to disappear from public life. Rarely do we find these first women lawyers speaking out publicly for women's issues, demanding the vote or greater rights for women or seeking legislation to further woman's cause.[61]

Rather, what appears to be the case is that these first women lawyers benefited from the concurrent struggle of the women's rights movement for co-education. As opportunities for higher education for women opened up, so naturally did opportunities in the nation's law schools. These first women lawyers were undoubtedly influenced by the feminist struggles of their day and benefited therefrom. However, the vast majority of these women failed to see woman's cause as a legitimate social issue and only viewed it insofar as it helped their cause of gaining access to the legal profession.

PARALLELS TODAY

What parallels and similarities can be noted between the first women lawyers in the United States and women lawyers today?

First, it appears that a high proportion of women in the legal profession today, similar to the women lawyers of 1870–1890, tend to have lawyers in their family who are influential in their decision to study law. Barnes discovered in a study at the University of Virginia that the reason most often cited by women law students for studying law was that a member of their family was an attorney.[62]

It also appears that a large number of married women lawyers today are married to lawyers, as was also found among the nation's first women lawyers. Glancy, in a study of Harvard women law school graduates, reports that of the married women in the sample, 63% were married to lawyers.[63] She noted: "the husbands of the women lawyers tended to be more enthusiastic or approving of their lawyer-wives' legal careers than the wives of the men in the sample."[64] The significance of this finding seems to lie in the influence of a lawyer-husband. Although it was not determined in these cases whether the women's interest in law preceded her marriage or whether her marriage to a lawyer fostered her interest in law, the support of lawyer-husbands seemed to be an important motivating factor to these women in their pursuit of legal studies and a legal career. This finding of the importance of supportive husbands of professional women has also been reported in other studies—as with women doctors. Lopata has found: "Whatever the girl's hopes may be, however, it is her husband, if she marries, who ultimately determines the possibility of continuing in her profession while being a wife and mother."[65] Bernard has noted from the sociological literature on the professional woman what she terms the "law of husband cooperation." She explains: ". . . studies show that integrating a domestic and a professional role depends on the cooperation of one's husband. Without it, all else is impossible. The road is just too rough. And if there is opposition, the game is up . . ."[66]

In the nineteenth century whether the woman lawyer eventually practiced often depended on the support she received from her husband. If support was given, the woman generally went into practice—often into practice with her husband. However, if support was not forthcoming, she was more likely to remain in the home after marriage, confined to domestic duties. It would be interesting if after 100 years the same were true today: whether the married woman lawyer successfully integrates a professional and domestic career may depend on the degree of support she receives from her husband.

Another similarity is that women lawyers today, similar to the first women lawyers, tend to see fewer clients than their male counterparts. While women lawyers practicing in the late 1890s tended to maintain low visibility by remaining in the office doing office work, this phenomenon of low visibility in terms of client relations seems to hold true even of women today. According to both White and Glancy, modern women lawyers tend to interact with fewer clients than do male lawyers.[67] In addition, many women lawyers currently maintain low visibility by going into government-related work and by avoiding high visibility specialties such as criminal litigation. It is likely that by seeking low visibility, women lawyers hope to minimize discrimination and client prejudice toward them.

This characteristic of women lawyers is also true of the professional woman generally. It is a phenomenon Epstein has called "being unobtrusive." She has noted that women in the professions try to be unobtrusive and to avoid attention by accepting work which keeps them in invisible positions.

> This unobtrusiveness is a reflection of women's position within the informal structure of the profession. Women are sensitive to men's desire to be left to their own company . . . By bowing to pressure to make themselves unobtrusive . . . women are accepting common definitions about the inappropriateness of their presence in the field in which they have chosen to work. . . .[68]

Perhaps one reason for professional women and for women lawyers, specifically, to seek a low profile may lie in the conflicting behavioral expectations they face today, similar to those found in the nineteenth century. As Armstrong has noted: "A well-dressed, acquainted and endowed woman applicant arouses immediate suspicion although this is just what firms pray for in a man."[69] The qualities most admired in men—confidence, ambition, self-assurance, assertiveness, aggressiveness, competitiveness—are looked upon with disfavor in women because they conflict with the traditional image of the sex. Yet, paradoxically, these qualities historically have been and still are the qualities which are viewed as prerequisites for the successful lawyer.

WOMEN, BLACKS, JEWS AND IMMIGRANTS

It is important to note that women, historically, have not been the only target of discrimination by the legal profession. Similar exclusionary practices existed throughout the history of American legal education against Blacks, Jews and immigrants. Much of the discrimination against the latter two groups occurred in the period 1900–1922 when hostility on the part of leading academicians and practicing lawyers was directed at night schools because of the ethnic composition of their student body.[70]

It would appear that the multiplication of law schools which occurred during the peak years of immigration from 1905 to 1914, as documented by Auerbach, bore a striking similarity to the period of Jacksonian democracy, described by Stevens.[71] Both periods were marked by pressures upon the legal profession from those who demanded a freely swinging door to the profession. During the Jacksonian period, the surge of feeling which exalted the common man held that all male citizens had the inherent right to practice law. Similarly, for immigrants after the turn of the twentieth century, access to the legal profession became an index of American democracy. Both periods witnessed vigorous debates over the qualifications for admission to the bar.

In the first two decades of this century, the plea among members of the legal profession for higher standards was actually thinly concealed anti-Semitism and xenophobia. As Auerbach writes:

> Cries of overcrowding swelled the chorus of complaints about commercialization and declining ethics. The culprits were the 'unlearned, unlettered and utterly untrained young lawyers with no esprit de corps and little regard for the traditions of the profession.' In translation this meant immigrants and Jews. . . .[72]

Anti-Semitism in the legal profession goes back even further in American legal history. George T. Strong in his diary in 1874 supported the idea of a test for admission to Columbia Law School by writing: ". . . either a college diploma, or an examination including Latin. This will keep out the little scrubs (German Jews mostly) whom the School now promotes from the grocery-counters . . . to be 'gentlemen of the Bar.' "[73]

As might be expected in the history of American legal education, we also find considerable discrimination against Black law students and lawyers. Such discrimination was especially pronounced in the South where in the mid-sixties, Mississippi had three Black lawyers to serve a Black population of 800,000, Alabama had only 20 Black lawyers and Georgia had 34.[74] In 1969 there were only 22 first-year Black students at 17 predominantly white Southern law schools. Many Southern law schools until recently, "have been white law schools where blacks were simply not admitted."[75] Thus, it appears that women have shared the dubious historical honor of being targets of discrimination by the legal profession with such other minority groups as Jews, Blacks and immigrants.

DISCRIMINATION TODAY

What of discrimination and the position of women in the legal profession today? This question has received much attention.[76] Women are applying to law schools in greater numbers than ever before. From 1969 to 1973, the overall number of applicants to law schools tripled, while in the same period the number of female applicants increased 14 times.[77]

Women comprised 16% of all students entering law school in 1972,[78] and 27% in 1980.[79] Although this figure constitutes a dramatic rise from previous years, the figure is low when one realizes that 51% of the population is female. As of 1980, only one law school, Northeastern University, has achieved population parity.[80]

The participation of women lawyers in the legal profession has risen slowly since 1910. In that year women constituted 1.0% of the profession. A half century later in 1960, they constituted only 3.5%.[81] More recent statistics reveal that women constitute 9% of the legal profession.[82]

In terms of job placement, a 1972 Association of American Law Schools (AALS) questionnaire revealed that significant discrimination against women lawyers still exists. Forty percent of the respondent schools said that they had received complaints of discrimination from female students being interviewed by law firms.[83]

In addition, research reveals that women face continued discrimination in various legal specializations. Weisberg's study of women on law's faculties[84] reports that women tend to be underrepresented on law school faculties and tend to cluster at lower levels than their male counterparts. Epstein's research on women corporate attorneys notes that only 2% of all partners are women and a significant number of large law firms still have no women partners.[85] And, although one woman has been appointed to the United States Supreme Court, women continue to be underrepresented in the judiciary.[86]

That discrimination still exists in the legal profession is scarcely a point in need of belaboring here. Women were absent in the first hundred years of legal education in America. In the second hundred years they made slow progress: one hundred years after Ada Kepley became the first woman to graduate from law school, the last male bastion of legal education finally permitted women to enter the first-year class. It can only be hoped that women will occupy a more prominent position in the legal profession in the century to come.

NOTES

1. A. Chroust, The Rise of the Legal Profession in America 173 (1965).

2. Several women attended some of the nation's law schools for brief periods prior to this date; however, Ada Kepley was the first woman both to attend and graduate from a school of law. Paradoxically, Mrs. Kepley was barred from the bar of Illinois upon first application by the adverse decision in Bradwell v. Illinois, 55 Ill. 535 (1869).

3. Bradwell v. Illinois, 83 U.S. (16 Wall.) 130 (1873).

4. In re Goodell, 39 Wis. 232 (1875).

5. Ex parte Robinson, 131 Mass. 376 (1881).

6. In re Lockwood, 154 U.S. 116 (1894). Virginia and Georgia still did not admit women to the bar in 1914. Cottle, "The Prejudice Against Women Lawyers: How Can It Be Overcome?" 21 Case and Comment 371, 372 (1914).

7. By 1900, 34 states admitted women to the legal profession. Pettus, "The Legal Education of Women," 61 Alb. L.J. 325, 330 (1900).

8. When M. Frederika Perry and Ellen Martin applied to the Harvard Law School in the 1870s, the reason given for denying their applications was that "it was not considered practicable to admit young men and young women to the Law Library at the same time, and it was not considered fair to admit to the Law School without giving the privileges of the Library." Martin, "Admission of Women to the Bar," 1 Chic. L.T. 76, 83 (1886). The story of the admission of women to Columbia Law School may be found in J. Goebel, Jr., A History of the School of Law, Columbia University 290 (1955). In 1924 the Columbia faculty unanimously resolved that "such a concession would be inexpedient and contrary to the best

interests of the Law School." *Id.* Yale Law School has a similar chapter in the history of women in legal education. Although Yale was one of the first law schools to admit a woman, the school later changed its policy. Alice Jordan entered Yale Law School in the fall of 1885 after studying at University of Michigan and after being admitted to the Michigan bar. She received a degree from Yale shortly thereafter. However, as of 1890, the law school had reconsidered this decision and the catalogue specified: "It is to be understood that the courses of instruction above described are open to persons of the male sex only, except where both sexes are specifically included." Dean Wayland of the Law School wrote in private correspondence, "the marked paragraph on page 25 is intended to prevent a repetition of the Jordan incident." Robinson, "Women Lawyers in the United States," 2 Green Bag 13 (1890).

9. Conn. Gen. Stat., ch. 3, §29 (1875).
10. Wis. Stat., ch. 189, §§1, 2 (1861).
11. 39 Wis. at 233.
12. *Id.* at 241.
13. 83 U.S. (16 Wall.) at 132.
14. 50 Conn. 131, 138–39 (1882) (Pardee, J., dissenting).
15. 39 Wis. at 242–43.
16. 55 Ill. at 540.
17. Kanowitz points out that vestiges of this common-law disability remain. L. Kanowitz, Sex Roles and Society: Cases and Materials 199 (1973).
18. Quoted in "Women as Advocates," 18 Am. L. Rev. 478, 479 (1884).
19. Cottle, *supra* note 6, at 371.
20. *Id.*
21. 39 Wis. at 245.
22. It may be hypothesized, although it is nowhere stated, that the occasion which prompted this story was the successful application of Mary Hall to the Connecticut bar in 1882.
23. Moore, "The Woman Lawyer," 26 Green Bag 525 (1914). This story first appeared in the Hartford Daily Times, May 17, 1886.
24. Frank, "The Woman Lawyer," 3 Chic.L.T. 382, 411 (1899).
25. Quoted in Throop, "Woman and the Legal Profession," 30 Alb.L.J. 464, 466 (1884).
26. Robinson, *supra* note 8, at 24.
27. *Id.*
28. Frank, *supra* note 24, at 401.
29. "Prudes for Proctors," 14 L.J. 746 (1879).
30. "A Woman Lawyer's Chances," 21 Case and Comment 380 (1914).
31. Quoted in Drew, "Women and the Law," 47 Women's L.J. 20 (1961).
32. 83 U.S. (16 Wall.) at 141–42.
33. 39 Wis. at 245.
34. *Id.* at 244–45.

35. *Id.* at 245.

36. Martin, *supra* note 8; Robinson, *supra* note 8; "Mary A. Ahrens: Lawyer and Philanthropist," 21 Case and Comment 430 (1914); "Death of Miss Lemma Barkeloo," 2 Chic.L.N. 409 (1870); "Lelia Robinson Sawtelle Dead," 24 Chic.L.N. 421 (1891).

37. L. Friedman, A History of American Law 526, 527 (1973).

38. Robinson, *supra* note 8, at 21.

39. *Id.* at 181. Miss Robinson commented on Mr. Smith's remarks: "who would not be willing to stand up in a horse car when this new nineteenth century gallantry is given us in exchange for the superficial kind." *Id.* It is interesting to note that some lawyers' wives studied law either at the request of their husbands (Annie Smith, Corinne Douglass), or, as in the case of Myra Bradwell, in order to assist their husbands. See DeCrow, Sexist Justice 30 (1974).

40. Quoted in Frank, *supra* note 24, at 409, from personal correspondence with Lelia Robinson.

41. Martin, *supra* note 8, at 82.

42. Robinson, *supra* note 8, at 10.

43. Quoted in Drew, *supra* note 31, at 21. In an interesting cultural comparison it appears that French women lawyers were similarly 'bestowed' this specialty by the legal profession. As Lilly wrote: "The woman lawyer is everywhere in the criminal courts in Paris. . . . The men lawyers voted this field of the law entirely to her, and most enthusiastically does she fill it. With my American commercialism, I could not help speculating as to whether or not the men would have so gallantly accorded this distinctive place in the law courts to the women had there been any money in this particular field." Lilly, "The French Women Lawyers," 21 Case and Comment 431 (1914).

44. Robinson, *supra* note 8, at 28.

45. "Death of Miss Lemma Barkeloo," *supra* note 36.

46. *Id.*

47. Robinson, *supra* note 8, at 13.

48. "Lelia Robinson Sawtelle Dead," *supra* note 36.

49. *Id.*

50. See Friedman, *supra* note 37, at 557 for a discussion of the attraction of the frontier for Eastern lawyers.

51. For a discussion of this presidential race (which Mrs. Lockwood claimed "did more to awaken American women to their political powers than anything that happened in the nineteenth century"), see Abernathy, "Belva A. Lockwood: A First Lady," 33 Phi Delta Delta 8 (1954).

52. E. Flexner, Century of Struggle: The Women's Rights Movement in the United States 23 (1973).

53. *Id.* at 24.

54. Atkins, The Hidden History of the Female: The Early Feminist Movement in the United States 3 (n.d.).

55. Flexner, *supra* note 52, at 30.

56. *Id.* at 41.

57. Flexner, *supra* note 52, at 161, maintains that the jury issue in Wyoming caused a greater storm than suffrage. For a discussion of the first women jurors, see Robinson, "Women Jurors," 1 Chic. L.T. 22 (1886).

58. Data verifying the role of these women in the suffrage movement may be found for Mary Ahrens in her obituary, *supra* note 36; for Phoebe Cousins in Raye-Smith, "A Light that Failed," 2 Women's L.J. 45 (1914); for Clara Foltz in Johnson, The Bar Association of San Francisco: The First Hundred Years (1973); for Belva Lockwood in Abernathy, *supra* note 51; for Catherine McCulloch in A. Kraditor, The Ideas of the Woman Suffrage Movement 229 (1965); and for Marilla Ricker in Flexner, *supra* note 52, at 165.

59. S. Firestone, The Dialectic of Sex: The Case for Feminist Revolution 488 (1970).

60. 2 Women's L.J. 59 (1913).

61. Women such as Myra Bradwell seem to have been the exception rather than the rule among these first women lawyers. Mrs. Bradwell urged the Illinois state legislature to pass a law she helped draft which established married women's rights to their earnings. She also won passage of a law guaranteeing a widow a share in her husband's estate. DeCrow, *supra* note 39, at 31.

62. Barnes, "Women and Entrance to the Legal Profession," 23 J.Leg. Ed. 276, 289 (1971).

63. Glancy, "Women in Law: The Dependable Ones," Harv.L.S.Bull. 23 (1970).

64. *Id.*

65. Lopata, "Marriage and Medicine," in A. Theodore, The Professional Woman 54 (1971).

66. J. Bernard, The Future of Motherhood 162 (1974).

67. White, "Women in the Law," 65 Mich.L.Rev. 1051, 1093 (1967); Glancy, *supra* note 63.

68. C. Epstein, Woman's Place: Options and Limits in Professional Careers 192 (1970).

69. Armstrong, "Women in the Law," Harv. L.S. Record, Dec. 6 and 13, 1951, at 2.

70. See Auerbach, "Enmity and Amity: Law Teachers and Practitioners 1900–1922," 5 Persp. Am. Hist. 551 (1971).

71. Stevens, "Two Cheers for 1870: The American Law School," 5 Persp. Am. Hist. 417 (1971).

72. Auerbach, *supra* note 70, at 584.

73. Quoted in Friedman, *supra* note 37, at 553.

74. "Making the Legal System Work: How Black Students Become Lawyers in the South," 22 Carnegie Q. 1, 3 (1974).

75. *Id.* at 3.

76. Some of the most comprehensive articles include: Barnes, "Women and Entrance to the Legal Profession," *supra* note 62; Bysiewicz, "Women

Penetrating the Law," 9 Trial 27 (1973); Ginsburg, "Treatment of Women by the Law: Awakening Consciousness in the Law Schools," 5 Val. U. L. Rev. 480 (1971); Read and Petersen, "Sex Discrimination in Law School Placement," 18 Wayne L. Rev. 639 (1972); White, "Women in the Law," *supra* note 67.

77. Bysiewicz, *supra* note 76, at 27.

78. *Id.*

79. Based on the author's analysis of data in American Bar Association, "Law Schools and Bar Admission Requirements, A Review of Legal Education in the United States, 1980–81."

80. *Id.*

81. Epstein, "Encountering the Male Establishment," in Theodore, *supra* note 65.

82. U.S. Department of Labor Report, 1977, p. 9.

83. Bysiewicz, *supra* note 76, at 27.

84. Weisberg, "Women in Law School Teaching: Problems and Progress," 30 J.Legal Ed. 226 (1979); Weisberg, "Consultant Report, Women on Law Faculties Study," submitted to the American Bar Association, May 1980.

85. Epstein, "The Partnership Push," *Savvy*, March 1980, at 29; Epstein, "Women's Entry into Corporate Law Firms," *infra* in this collection.

86. See generally, Cook, "Women Judges: The End of Tokenism," in W. Lepperle and L. Crites, Women in the Courts 84 (1978); Ness, "A Sexist Selection Process Keeps Qualified Women off the Bench," Washington Post, March 26, 1978, C8; Sassower, "Women and the Judiciary: Undoing 'The Law of the Creator,'" 57 Judicature 282 (1974); Tolchin, "The Exclusion of Women from the Judicial Process," 2 Signs 877 (1977).

CLARA SHORTRIDGE FOLTZ:
PIONEER IN THE LAW

Mortimer D. Schwartz, Susan L. Brandt, and
Patience Milrod

Clara Shortridge Foltz watched the district attorney as he presented his closing argument to the San Francisco jury. He concluded wth an attempt to discredit her as attorney for the defendant:

> She is a WOMAN, she cannot be expected to reason; God Almighty decreed her limitations . . . this young woman will lead you by her sympathetic presentation of this case to violate your oaths and let a guilty man go free.[1]

Foltz was angry, but having listened to similar accusations in other courtrooms, she was not surprised.[2] Rising to address the court, she demolished both the legal and *ad hominem* arguments of the prosecutor and won her case.[3]

She was California's first woman attorney.[4] Facing opposition from both sexes, she fought for entrance to the state bar and, later, for fair treatment within it. She opened the profession to future generations of California women, and throughout her long and successful practice she used a lawyer's expertise to work for legal reform and women's rights. In this article we will chronicle Foltz's struggle to gain admission to law school and the bar in the late 1870s. We will also note the most important of her legal and social contributions, for which credit is long overdue her.[5]

EARLY YEARS

Foltz was a fighter by nature. Raised in the Midwest, she boasted, "I am descended from the heroic stock of Daniel Boone and never shrank from contest nor knew a fear. I inherit no drop of craven blood."[6] She had come to San Jose, California, with her husband and five small children[7] in 1874.[8] Two years later, she divorced Jeremiah Foltz[9] and faced the responsibility of supporting her young family. She was twenty-seven years old at that time[10] and already well-known within her community. She had been the impetus behind the paid city fire department,[11] and she was an active suffragist[12] and a "brilliant and logical" speaker on sexual equality.[13] While her work experience had been along traditional lines,[14] she had developed a fascination with the law in her childhood,[15] and she decided to try a legal career. She later observed, "I had no thought of the hardships to be encountered, the humiliation, and the thousand torments to be suffered!"[16]

Bolstered by her parents' and brothers' encouragement,[17] she asked a prominent local attorney whether she could read law with him. The response was discouraging:

> My dear young friend,
> Excuse my delay in answering your letter asking permission to enter my law office as a student. My high regard for your parents, and for you, who seem to have no right understanding of what you say you want to undertake, forbid encouraging you in so foolish a pursuit,—wherein you would invite nothing but ridicule if not contempt.
> A woman's place is at home, unless it is as a teacher. If you would like a position in our public schools I will be glad to recommend you, for I think you are well-qualified.
>
> Very respectfully,
> Francis Spencer[18]

Disappointed, she "silently went about preparing to do battle against all comers who would deny to women any right or privilege that men enjoyed."[19] She finally secured a place to study in a neighborhood law office[20] and began preparing for her career. She continued to lecture to maintain a source of income.[21]

THE WOMAN LAWYER'S BILL

Foltz realized, however, that her years spent reading law would serve no purpose as long as women were excluded from the California bar. To remedy the situation she wrote an amendment to section 275 of the Code of Civil Procedure, which set out qualifications for lawyers in California. The proposed amendment deleted the words "any white male citizen" and substituted "any citizen or person," so that the new section read:

> Any citizen or person resident of this state who has bona fide declared his or her intention to become a citizen in the manner required by law, of the age of twenty-one years, of good moral character, and who possesses the necessary qualifications of learning and ability, is entitled to admission as attorney and counselor in all the Courts of this state.[22]

In February of 1876, she persuaded a state senator[23] to present it to the legislature.[24]

The amendment, Senate Bill 66, became popularly known as the Woman Lawyer's Bill. There was little public concern over the deletion of the racial restriction; the debate focused on the elimination of the code's sex qualification. As Foltz reported:

> The bill met with a storm of opposition such as had never been witnessed upon the floor of a California Senate. Narrow-gauge statesmen grew as red as turkey gobblers mouthing their ignorance against the bill, and staid old grangers who had never seen the inside of a courthouse seemed to have been given the gift of tongues and they delivered themselves of maiden speeches pregnant with eloquent nonsense.[25]

Yet Senate Bill 66 passed the senate handily by a vote of 22–11[26] and moved to the assembly a few days later. There, the term "eloquent nonsense" seems no exaggeration, according to the account of the assembly debate in the *Sacramento Union*, February 26, 1878. One opponent of the bill[27] spoke of the omnipotent power which had defined the walks of life from which women should not be drawn. Another[28] kindly allowed that "the sphere of women was infinitely more important than that of men, and that sphere was home." Still another[29] lamented the embarrassing situations which might arise in court, when a woman attorney would have to listen to or elicit indelicate evidence. In her later years, Foltz would echo a suffragist comment: "Men are the sentimentalists . . . they become so tearfully emotional that it all spills out over 'home and mother' every time you offer a suffrage argument."[30]

The amendment also had some supporters among the assemblymen. One[31] spoke twice in its favor, stating that he saw no reason to deny a woman the right to earn her living in this manner. He pointed out that the eastern states allowed the practice, and that certainly no woman would have to take advantage of the bill. Another assemblyman[32] cited the contributions of women in the medical profession.[33]

A vote was called and the bill was defeated 33–30.[34] A quick-thinking proponent thereafter changed his aye to no and moved to reconsider the vote the following day;[35] his motion passed 39–33.[36] Foltz had been conspicuously absent during the assembly debate and vote, having been called to Oregon to address that state's Woman Suffrage Association.[37] Fortunately, she returned in time to lobby that evening for the reconsideration vote, coaxing and entreating on behalf of her amendment. She later stated, "I would have reasoned had they been reasonable men."[38] The bill was passed in the morning by a majority of two.[39]

But the fight was not over. The legislature was in the last day of its session and, as midnight approached, the governor had not yet signed the Woman Lawyer's Bill. The bill's opponents were trying to convince him that the duty of a law career should not be thrust upon the women of California. The fate of Senate Bill 66 was uncertain.

As Foltz later reported, she was among those milling outside the closed doors to the governor's chambers. When a politician emerged and stated,[40] "That Woman Lawyer's Bill's dead and buried," she decided to speak to Governor Irwin herself: "Finding that I could not convince the Sergeant-at-Arms that, his orders to the contrary, I must and I would see the Governor about the Woman Lawyer's Bill, I stooped to conquer, and slid through the door and landed in the middle of the big room with hat awry and hair disheveled."[41]

The governor sat at a large table in the center of the room, surrounded by legislators. Foltz came through the crowd and politely asked him to sign Senate Bill 66. "The governor continued to lift up bill after bill in that huge stack of discarded ones and finally, aided by a clerk, the bill was fished out and laid all but dead before him." He then signed it, just before the clock struck twelve.[42]

Foltz returned to San Jose to complete her course of reading for the bar, and subsequently took the examination for admission to the 20th District Court Bar.[43] She passed it with "highly colored compliments"[44] and took her professional oaths in early September, 1878,[45] the first woman admitted to the California bar pursuant to the code amendment which she had drafted and promoted.

THE HASTINGS LAWSUIT

Recalling her feelings upon entering into the practice of law,[46] Foltz remarked: "I had many secret misgivings as to my ability to cope with men who had a thousand years advantage over me." Nevertheless, within a few months she had a growing practice in San Jose and was a successful advocate in even her earliest cases. Never one to be guilty of false modesty, she remembered one of her first triumphs:

> I kept my wits fairly well, though I trembled, and certainly was dreadfully scared lest I should fail to serve my trusting client as capably as a man lawyer might have done. No one, not even the astute experienced Registrar himself—as he told me later—regarded me as a novice in his department—so intelligently and effectively did I guard the interests of my client by the skillful manner in which I handled the contestant and his witnesses.[47]

Foltz believed, however, that a formal legal education would enable her to serve her clients with greater skill and confidence. She applied for admission to Hastings College of the Law in San Francisco.[48]

The Hastings law school had been established as a department of the University of California, pursuant to a generous grant from Judge S. Clinton Hastings, who was also the college's first dean. A board of directors and Dean Hastings determined the law college's policies, including admissions standards. Those standards, however, did not include any reference to the candidate's sex, perhaps because the board of directors had never considered the possibility that a woman would be so audacious as to try to enroll in a law school. The admissions qualifications simply required that an applicant be over the age of twenty-one years, of good moral character, and a citizen and resident of California.[49] Foltz met all these requirements.

She paid the ten dollar tuition fee and started classes on January 9, 1879. When she returned to school the following day, she was met at the door by a janitor: "Miss, this is a law school. I'm ordered not to let you come in here."[50] Undaunted, she obtained from founder Judge Hastings a note directing the janitor to admit her.

The judge advised her that his was a conditional admission only, subject to approval by the board of directors of the college. Armed with this ticket, Foltz returned to school to find that resistance to a woman law student was not confined to the school administrators:

> The first day I had a bad cold and was forced to cough. To my astonishment every young man in the class was seized with a violent fit of coughing. You would have thought the whooping cough was a raging epidemic among the little fellows. If I turned over a leaf in my note book every student in the class did likewise. If I moved my chair—hitch went every chair in the room. I don't know what ever became of the members of that class. They must have been an inferior lot, for certain it is, I have never seen nor heard tell of one of them from that day to this.[51]

Her tenure as a law student was short-lived. On January 11, two days after she had started classes, Foltz was notified that the Board of Directors of Hastings College of the Law had decided to deny her application for admission at their meeting the previous day. The minutes of that meeting noted,[52] "The following resolution was adopted, Resolved that women be not admitted to the Hastings College of the Law. Carried unanimously."

Foltz was not the only woman whom the board's actions affected. At the same meeting, the directors rejected the application of Laura de Force Gordon, an able journalist and active women's rights advocate, who had founded and edited newspapers in Stockton and Oakland.[53] She had also helped to achieve passage of the Woman Lawyer's Bill and was now intent on pursuing a legal career.[54]

The two women decided to challenge the college's admission policy. Gordon applied to the California Supreme Court for a writ of mandamus to compel the board of directors to admit the women, and on February 10, Foltz made the same application to Judge R.F. Morrison of the Fourth District Court in San Francisco. The supreme court returned Gordon's petition to the district court for consolidation with Foltz's suit.[55]

At its February 13 meeting in 1879, the Hastings board of directors resolved that T.B. Bishop and Delos Lake should represent it in "the case of Clara S. Foltz v. J.P. Hoge et al Directors of Hastings College of the Law."[56] Both men were members of the board of directors, and Lake was a former supreme court justice. W.W. Cope, another board member and ex-supreme court justice, later joined the ranks of respondents' counsel.[57]

In her petition, Foltz maintained that she had been wrongfully excluded from Hastings College of the Law, since she met all University of California requirements for admission.[58] Judge Morrison granted the alternative writ, requiring that the board admit her "upon the same terms and conditions as other citizens of the State of California"[59] or show cause why not.

The respondents claimed in their answer that the board of directors reserved to itself complete discretion to exclude from the college any and all persons whose presence there it believed would be "useless to such persons themselves, or detrimental to said college, or likely to impair or interfere with the proper discipline and instruction of the students. . . ."[60] The board averred that it acquired this discretion in its role as sole manager and executor of a trust created by Judge Hastings upon the passage of the act establishing Hastings College of the Law and the founder's payment of $100,000 into the state treasury.[61] The board maintained that the law college was therefore administered independently of the University of California and was in fact associated with it only for the purpose of dispensing degrees.[62] Judge Morrison heard the oral arguments on February 24, 1879. By all accounts, the case had aroused much interest: the courtroom was full, "the younger and more gallant members of the profession being present in large numbers."[63] Newspaper reports, more concerned with the novelty of the petitioners' claims than with the legal arguments, focused on the dress and demeanor of the two applicants. The *San Francisco Chronicle* headlined its report of the case "Two Lady Lawyers Who Demand Admission to the Hastings Law College—How They Dress." The writer commented on every detail of their dress and jewelry and noted that Foltz's "profuse hair was done in braids, which fell backward from the crown of her head like an Alpine glacier lit by a setting sun." Laura de Force Gordon's appearance was given equal scrutiny, the journalist remarking that she "had curls enough to supply half the thin-haired ladies of San Francisco with respectable switches."[64]

Judge Morrison instructed the attorneys, "Proceed, gentlemen." Upon noting Foltz's look of astonishment and confusion, he immediately corrected his slip.[65] She did proceed, presenting her case "with both force and polish," as the *Daily Alta California* reported it the next day.[66]

She cited the 1868 act which created the University of California to show that the legislature had contemplated affiliation of medical and law colleges with the university and had intended that those departments be governed by the same admission standards as the rest of the university.[67] She then cited the act of 1878 creating the Hastings law college and pointed out that it required no special qualifications for admission to law study.[68] Nor did it indicate that the board of directors had any discretion to make rules governing the law college which were inconsistent with the rules governing the university as a whole. She concluded that the law college was a department of the University of California, bound by its rules and without authority to exclude her on the basis of her sex.[69] By Foltz's own account, "I closed my argument conscious that I had won my case. I could not then nor at any time since understand how [the counsel for respondents] could take up the time of the court in urging their foolish objections to my petition for a peremptory writ."[70]

Opposing counsel first urged that the law school was not subject to the laws governing the university as a whole because it was created and managed as a special trust. Furthermore, they maintained that no court could review the decisions of the board of directors and that therefore no writ could issue. Mr. Lake then left legal argument behind. According to the *Chronicle*, "He repeated the usual objections to the enlargement of woman's sphere. He complimented the grace and beauty of the applicant, and said that lady lawyers were dangerous to justice inasmuch as an impartial jury would be impossible when a lovely woman pleaded the case of the criminal."[71] The respondents also quoted at length from a Wisconsin decision denying a woman admission to that state's bar.[72] In that decision, Judge Ryan had declared his fervent opposition of the idea of women practicing law:

> The law of nature destines and qualifies the female sex for the bearing and nurture of the children of our race and for the custody of the homes of the world and their maintenance in love and honor. And all life-long callings of women, inconsistent with these radical and sacred duties of their sex, as is the profession of the law, are

departures from the order of nature; and when voluntary, treason against it. . . . Reverence for all womanhood would suffer in the public spectacle of woman so instructed and so engaged.[73]

Foltz replied to these assertions of the board of directors, "commiserating them if they thought a broader education would make a woman less womanly."[74] She objected to the arguments regarding "woman's sphere" and remarked that she had expected counsel to focus on the legal aspects of the case.[75]

On March 5, 1879, Judge Morrison delivered a judgment in favor of Foltz and Gordon.[76] An interview the same day with the founder, Judge Hastings, indicated that in his view the law was solidly behind the women applicants.[77] He did not favor an appeal of the district court decision, though on this point he and the directors disagreed.[78]

The board of directors pursued an appeal of Judge Morrison's decision, perhaps in the hope that if Foltz's determination would not give out, her money would. During the months that the supreme court appeal was pending, she studied for and passed the exam for admission to the state supreme court bar, though she was not formally admitted until December of 1879.[79] She represented herself before the court, facing substantially the same arguments advanced by the directors in the district court, and won her case.[80] In later years, Fotlz recalled the case as "the greatest in my more than half century before the bar."[81]

Soon after the supreme court's decision in November 1879, she took her place among the law students at Hastings, where she remained for two years, "until my increasing practice and increasing family made further attendance difficult."[82]

LEGAL REFORMS

Foltz had begun her career as a lawyer specializing in probate and divorce cases.[83] She soon found, however, that her reputation as a humane and sympathetic counselor brought many indigent clients into her office: "I kept myself continually impoverished by what my friends declared was unwise generosity."[84] She slowly acquired a criminal practice, which exposed her to the inequities of criminal justice administration in California. She became an energetic advocate of penal reform, responsible for several major pieces of legislation still in effect today.

Probably the most significant of Foltz's legislative achievements was the creation of the public defender system,[85] which ensured adequate legal representation for the indigent accused criminal. She began to promote this concept while in her early thirties, soon after her admission to the bar. At that time, any impoverished criminal defendant had to rely on court-appointed counsel for his defense, and this practice imposed a hardship on both defendant and attorney. The attorney had no guarantee of payment and received no compensation from the state. Furthermore, the court-appointed attorneys were not usually those with thriving practices who could afford to support a few *pro bono* cases with their other earnings.[86] Rather, they were generally young lawyers "from the kindergartens of the profession . . . anxious to learn the practice"[87] or lawyers too unsuccessful to maintain practices of their own. Because these attorneys had few financial resources, investigations on behalf of the defendants were often perfunctory. In many cases, a defendant's conviction became almost a matter of course.[88] Moreover, the defendant, though indigent, had a legal obligation to pay for the attorney's services and was liable to have his property seized in payment.[89]

On the other hand, public prosecutors were usually skilled and experienced and were well paid.[90] In many jurisdictions the prosecutors were offered a bonus for each conviction.[91] In addition, they had access to the manpower and investigative skills of law enforcement organizations.[92] Foltz believed that unless an accused had comparable representation, which could be furnished by a public defender, his constitutional presumption of innocence was worthless.[93]

In the 1890s she began working in earnest for adoption of the public defender concept. She wrote a model bill, which set out the qualifications, salary, duties, and term of office of a county officer who would "defend, without expense to them, all persons who are not financially able to employ counsel and who are charged with the commission of any contempt, misdemeanor, felony or other offense."[94] She wrote articles in legal periodicals explaining and advocating the idea.[95] When she was forty-four, she represented the California bar at the 1893 Congress of Jurisprudence and Law Reform, held in conjunction with the Chicago World Columbian Exposition, and there worked to convert others to her position.[96]

She personally introduced her model bill, which became known as the "Foltz Defender Bill," in thirty-two states, where it "caused a great sensation."[97] The California legislature finally adopted Foltz's public defender plan in 1921, after much legislative wrangling.[98]

One of the chief factors which spurred her interest in the public defender idea was the extensive abuse of justice she saw in most district attorneys' offices. In an article published in the *Criminal Law Magazine and Reporter*[99] she cataloged the prosecutors' prejudicial methods, which, she claimed, spawned "an evil brood of appeals that choke the courts, irritate the public mind and waste the public funds."[100] Foltz wrote that as a rule, district attorneys were overzealous in their pursuit of convictions, often sacrificing truth and objectivity to win a case. She attributed this excessive zeal to a system which rewarded successful prosecutions with public acclaim and, often, money bonuses, but which subjected the losing prosecutor to public criticism. Furthermore, the district attorneys themselves held attitudes which interfered with the proper execution of their duties. Some came to believe that the accused was always guilty, even though the statistics disproved this notion.[101] Others looked upon every conviction as a personal triumph rather than a public service. Many were anxious to "uphold a friendly police in its frequent blunders."[102] In 1910, at the age of sixty-one, Foltz was offered an opportunity to improve the situation which she had criticized: she was appointed deputy district attorney in Los Angeles and served as the first woman to hold that post.[103]

Foltz was also responsible for numerous penal reforms on both state[104] and local levels. In San Francisco, she agitated to abolish the iron cages in which prisoners were confined in the courtrooms during their trials. She argued that such confinement before judge and jury violated the constitutional presumption of a defendant's innocence, and she succeeded in convincing the San Francisco Board of Supervisors that the cages should be removed.[105] She also worked for better treatment for prisoners in San Francisco jails, obtaining segregation of the juvenile inmates from the adult prisoners and appointment of a matron in the county jail.[106]

At the state level, Foltz drafted and procured passage of the act creating a parole system for California prisoners.[107] This law, adopted in 1893, provided that any prisoner, other than one convicted of first or second degree murder, might be paroled after serving at least one year of his or her term.[108] Like many other penal reformers of her time, she also advocated adoption of the indeterminate sentence as a tool to rehabilitate the convicted criminal.[109]

FEMINIST ACTIVITIES

Foltz's interests as attorney and feminist often overlapped: "I was bent on correcting things generally where women were concerned."[110] She became particularly involved in the suffrage movement, maintaining that women had a constitutional right to vote.[111] She was determined to secure legislative action which would recognize this right.

In 1880, not long after her admission to the bar, she wrote and lobbied energetically for a bill to give women the vote in state school elections. The bill failed, but her efforts to have it enacted established her as a "leader of woman suffrage on the Pacific Coast."[112] The following year, at the age of thirty-one, she was elected president of the California Woman Suffrage Association.[113] Her activism, at a time when women were expected to be retiring and demure, made her an easy target for the satirist press. The San Francisco Saturday magazine *Wasp* ran the following "report" on a Suffrage Association meeting in 1881. Entitled "The Sexless Impracticables," it began:

> On Tuesday last the antique hens of the Incorporate California State Woman's Suffrage Association gathered one another together at Charter Oak Hall for business. Mrs. Clara Foltz presided like a little man. She has a fine baritone voice and a pleasant pug nose, and wore a single red rose in the hip pocket of her trousers. The first business of importance was the election of officers for the ensuing week—seventeen in number.[114]

Over the next thirty years, Foltz continued to work for suffrage in California, making slow progress. She found herself in demand throughout the state as a speaker on the issue,[115] but her flourishing law practice, now in Los Angeles,[116] prevented her from accepting most invitations. She regretted that her busy schedule limited her opportunities to promote suffrage, since she believed that

> I can win the cause in this state whenever I get the money sufficient to pay my way a winter's season at the Capitol and at the

same time take care of the interests that are in my office and meet the heavy demands of my home affairs.[117]

Finally, in 1909 or 1910, she reclaimed her active suffragist role. She became president of the Los Angeles Votes For Women Club, one of the largest and most vocal groups of its kind, and once again became an active personality in the suffrage cause.[118] Her brand of suffragism, however, often brought her into conflict with her contemporaries. She strongly disagreed with the tactics of the "pink tea brigade,"[119] the "rich women who have taken possession of the cause and have got into the bandwagon . . . a few women who are known only as Mrs. Col . . . or Mrs. Gen . . . or Mrs. U.S. Senator . . . and so on ad nauseum."[120] In a letter to a friend, she accused the California suffrage leaders of being disorganized and incapable of successfully promoting the suffrage cause:

> In closing, dear, let me say that I am not disgruntled. I simply say, and I reiterate it and emphasize it, that the women at the head of the suffrage question are incompetent; that the suffrage cause cannot be won until leaders of ability are chosen. . . .[121]

In 1911, when she was sixty-two, she drafted a suffrage amendment which stated simply, "Women citizens of this state who comply with elections laws and are twenty-one years old shall be entitled to vote at all elections."[122] In November of that year, the California electorate approved a similar amendment, after a campaign in which Foltz was an energetic participant.[123] On the day of its passage, she stood for hours receiving the congratulations of supporters and well-wishers.[124]

Foltz also worked for passage of the nineteenth amendment, which guaranteed all American women the right to vote in federal elections. Many of her views on national suffrage tactics were expressed in the *New American Woman*, a monthly magazine which she edited and published in Los Angeles from 1916 to 1918.[125] She strongly disagreed with those whose advocacy of suffragism diverted energy from the United States effort in World War I. In 1917, she wrote:

> Enthusiasm in the suffrage cause takes a fall when Congresswoman [Jeannette] Rankin states to a half dozen reporters who sought to know her position on various great and vital problems of

the hour, which vex the President and Congress of the United States, that she "had determined to devote her time exclusively to the cause of woman suffrage."[126]

Foltz also used the *New American Woman* as a forum to encourage women to participate in the movement for equal rights. Emphasizing the importance of women in political life, she wrote an article entitled "What We Stand For" for the magazine's opening issue. In it she urged, "Women must have a voice in the nation's affairs; they must acknowledge no political or other limitation; they must prepare to think intelligently upon great matters of state, and cease to regard themselves as a second-rate power. . . ."[127]

She herself was enthusiastically involved in politics throughout her life.[128] She ran for governor of California in 1930, when she was eighty-one years old, and polled 3,570 votes in the Republican primary.[129] Running on a women's rights platform, she wrote a friend during the campaign, "This being a candidate for governor is no small job. . . . Of course, I have no illusions as to the outcome of this last courageous effort of mine—I simply must go right on demonstrating our great *cause*."[130]

Foltz believed that all women should know the law, whether or not they intended to practice before the bar.[131] In the *New American Woman* she wrote a column entitled "Law of the Case," in which she explained simple legal principles to her readers.[132] She often included bits of advice to young women contemplating legal careers:

> If any of my young lady friends want to study law and some anti tells you nobody will marry you if you do, don't you believe it. It isn't so. You will be all the better for knowing something of the law, and infinitely more in demand by any young man worth having.[133]

Foltz encouraged the entrance of more women into the legal profession. She taught law to women students in her offices and established women lawyers' clubs in San Francisco and Los Angeles.[134] In the *New American Woman* she published a monthly autobiographical serial called "The Struggles and Triumphs of a Woman Lawyer," in which she described some of her successful battles with the (male) legal establishment.[135] Committed to expanding women's legal rights, she was responsible for California laws allowing qualified women to act as administrators, executors, and notaries public.[136]

Yet Foltz's progessive legal and feminist activities subjected her to much ostracism, and often ridicule, from the very women who benefited from her labors. Remembering the slights she had received, Foltz wrote, "I hesitate to lift from oblivion the memory of the hurts and wounds which women inflicted upon me . . . women who could not understand WHY a woman lawyer, WHY bills for the enlargement of their privileges . . . who even refused friendly recognition of my efforts."[137]

Much of the general public also criticized Foltz for attempting to expand woman's domestic role. The popular attitude was expressed by the Wisconsin Supreme Court in an opinion denying women admission to that state's bar:

> This is the first application for admission of a female to the bar of this court. And it is just a matter for congratulation that it is made in favor of a lady whose character raises no personal objection: something perhaps not always to be looked for in women who forsake the ways of their sex for the ways of ours.[138]

The press occasionally echoed this disapproval of Foltz[139] and women lawyers in general, especially in the earliest days of her legal career. During the Hastings lawsuit, a *Chronicle* journalist decried the impropriety of men and women sharing the legal class-room:

> The friction of studious silk with contemplative broadcloth was not to be thought of. It was a wild imagining. . . . The legal carpenter might be instructed to erect a gilt-edged and golden-railed balcony, a gallery with gilt and pearl-inlaid lattice in the style of Turkish harems, a pagoda with minarets, or a simple Oregon pine platform in one corner with plush furniture, sheet-iron door, and the legend "All hope (of marriage) abandon ye who enter here."[140]

The San Francisco *Wasp* printed a two-page cartoon of the "debutante" women attorneys, in which a clear caricature of Foltz danced across a stage to the tune of "Hastings' Music."[141]

Despite her reputation as a vocal feminist, many of Foltz's views on woman's role were quite traditional. While she insisted on equality for the sexes in the professional sphere, she believed that there were many jobs for which women were unsuited, especially those calling for physical labor. During World War I, when to further the war effort many women took over jobs requiring heavy work, Foltz wrote that "the tasks that are now performed by women in war-stricken Europe are not naturally theirs and when the war is over they will gladly surrender them to men."[142] She believed that woman was of such value as a moral teacher and homemaker that it was man's duty to support and protect her.[143]

Editorializing in the *San Diego Bee*, a daily newspaper which she founded, edited, and published from 1887 to 1890,[144] Foltz revealed clearly her view of woman as teacher: "Men cannot succeed without the aid of women, nor can women be more truly working for the advancement of their own sex than when seeking to uplift, dignify, and purify men. Women compel men to think. Their mission is to ennoble the race. . . ."[145]

She encouraged women not to overlook their natural domestic role.[146] Extolling the duties of motherhood, she bitterly regretted that her busy career had kept her away from her children so much of the time in their early years. She felt that in practicing law and lobbying for women's rights she had sacrificed "all of the pleasure of my young motherhood . . . having lost more for myself than I have gained for all women."[147]

CONCLUSION

Foltz believed that she should receive credit for her struggles and achievements as California's first woman lawyer: "What I have sacrificed and what I have accomplished must be told."[148] She began to write her own account of her life[149] and made reference to the scrapbooks which would aid her future biographers. Unfortunately, the comprehensive biography she envisioned is impossible, because her autobiography-in-progress and personal papers were destroyed after her death.[150]

Looking back on her extraordinary life, Clara Foltz wrote:

> Everything in retrospect seems weird, phantasmal, and unreal. I peer back across the misty years into that era of prejudice and limitation, when a woman lawyer was a joke . . . but the story of my triumphs will eventually disclose that though the battle has been long and hard-fought it was worth while.[151]

NOTES

1. Foltz, *Struggles and Triumphs of a Woman Lawyer*, NEW AM. WOMAN, Jan. 1918, at 4, 10 [hereinafter cited as *Struggles*].
2. *Id*. at 15–16.
3. *Id.*, Feb. 1918, at 9. For the entire argument in this case, see *id.* Jan. 1918, at 4.
4. C. GILB, 1 NOTABLE AMERICAN WOMEN 641 (E. James ed. 1971) [hereinafter cited as NOTABLE AMERICAN WOMEN].
5. Although we have done extensive research into Foltz's life and accomplishments, we have found little written about her. Her contributions have been incompletely cataloged in a few biographical encyclopedias, but her pioneering achievements have been overlooked in most California histories.
6. *Struggles, supra* note 1, Jan. 1918, at 4, 10.
7. Clara Virginia, Samuel Courtland, David Milton, Bertha May, Trella Evelyn. NOTABLE AMERICAN WOMEN, *supra* note 4, at 642.
8. S.F. Evening Post, Aug. 12, 1882, at 2, col. 1.
9. In a conversation with Theresa Viscoli, a personal acquaintance of Foltz in the 1930s, we learned that Foltz divorced her husband. Telephone interview with Theresa Viscoli, Aug. 11, 1975. This report is borne out by an article in the San Francisco Evening Post. S.F. Evening Post, Aug. 12, 1882, at 2, col. 1. Nevertheless, Foltz herself in her writings and correspondence always referred to herself as a widow.
10. Foltz was born on July 16, 1849 to Elias and Talitha Shortridge in Lafayette, Indiana. NATIONAL CYCLOPEDIA OF AMERICAN BIOGRAPHY 308 (Current Vol. C 1930) [hereinafter cited as NATIONAL CYCLOPEDIA]. According to her Los Angeles death certificate, she died on September 2, 1934.
11. *Struggles, supra* note 1, May 1916, at 16.
12. San Jose Pioneer, Nov. 8, 1879, at 3, col. 1.
13. *Id.*, October 6, 1877, at 3, col. 2. Some attributed Foltz's oratorical style to the influence of her lawyer-minister father, who had stumped the state of Indiana campaigning for Abraham Lincoln. N.Y. Times, Sept. 3, 1934, at 13, col. 3.
14. At the age of fifteen, Foltz (then Shortridge) took a job as a teacher near Keithsburg, Illinois. She left this job, however, to elope with Jeremiah Foltz. NOTABLE AMERICAN WOMEN, *supra* note 4, at 642. Soon after, she and her husband moved to Portland, Oregon, where they lived for about a year before moving to San Jose, California. In Portland, she was a dressmaker, according to the recollections of newspaperman Wills Drury in a letter recommending her for a notary public commission in 1891. Letter from Wills Drury to H. H. Markham, April 10, 1891, on file in California State Archives, Sacramento, California.
15. *Struggles, supra* note 1, Apr. 1916, at 10–11.

16. *Id.*, June 1916, at 5.

17. The Shortridge family had also moved to San Jose, where Foltz's brother Charles later published and edited the San Jose Mercury newspaper. R. DAVIS, CALIFORNIA WOMEN: A GUIDE TO THEIR POLITICS 151 (1967).

18. *Struggles, supra* note 1, June 1916, at 5.

19. *Id.*

20. She obtained a place in the offices of C.C. Stephens of San Jose. 1 THE BAY OF SAN FRANCISCO 670 (1892). Law schools were not to become major training grounds for lawyers until almost two decades later. At this time, would-be attorneys studied in the offices of those already admitted to practice until they themselves could pass the bar examinations.

21. 2 APPLETON'S CYCLOPEDIA OF AMERICAN BIOGRAPHY 493 (J. Wilson & J. Fiske eds. 1898).

22. Cal. Stat. 1878, ch. 600, §§ 1–3 at 99.

23. Barney Murphy, Democrat, Santa Clara.

24. 3 HISTORY OF WOMAN SUFFRAGE 757–58 (E.C. Stanton, S.B. Anthony & M.J. Gage eds. 1969).

25. *Struggles, supra* note 1, Aug. 1916, at 11.

26. Sacramento Union, Jan. 11, 1878, at 1, col. 5.

27. William F. Anderson, Democrat, San Francisco.

28. W.M. DeWitt, Democrat, Yolo.

29. Byron Waters, Democrat, San Bernardino.

30. *Struggles, supra* note 1, July 1916, at 14, *quoting* Dr. Anna Howard Shaw, a prominent minister and suffragist.

31. Grove Johnson, Republican, Sacramento.

32. R.W. Murphy, Republican, San Francisco.

33. At this time women had been practicing medicine in California for over twenty years; the California Board of Medical Examiners began issuing licenses to physicians under the Medical Practice of 1867. Cal. Stat. 1867, ch. 68, §§ 1–14, at 792. Women were among the first certified. H. HARRIS, CALIFORNIA'S MEDICAL STORY 209 (1932).

34. Sacramento Union, Mar. 30, 1878, at 8, col. 2–3.

35. "On the day succeeding that on which a final vote on any bill or resolution has been taken, said vote may be reconsidered on the motion of any member, *provided,* notice of intention to move such reconsideration shall have been given on the day on which such final vote was taken, *by a member voting with the majority.*" LEGISLATURE OF THE STATE OF CALIFORNIA, JOURNAL OF THE ASSEMBLY, 22d Sess., 1877–78, at 150. (Standing Rule 60) (emphasis added).

36. Sacramento Union, Jan. 11, 1878, at 1, col. 4.

37. HISTORY OF THE BENCH AND BAR OF CALIFORNIA 831 (O. Shuck ed. 1901).

38. *Struggles, supra* note 1, Aug. 1916, at 11.

39. Sacramento Union, Jan. 11, 1878, at 1, col. 4.

40. *Struggles, supra* note 1, Sept. 1916, at 10.

41. *Id.*
42. *Id.*
43. *Id.*, Oct. 1916, at 11. According to the California Code of Civil Procedure in effect at that time, an attorney could be admitted to practice in all courts of the state by showing proof of good moral character and passing an oral examination in open court before the justices of the supreme court. An attorney could gain admission to practice before a particular district or county court by showing proof of good moral character and passing an oral exam in that court. Cal. Stat. 1861, ch. 1, §§ 275–77 at 64 (repealed 1931).
44. *Struggles, supra* note 1, Oct. 1916, at 11.
45. 1 THE BAY OF SAN FRANCISCO 670 (1892).
46. *Struggles, supra* note 1, Feb. 1917, at 10, 11.
47. *Id.*, June 1917, at 12, 13.
48. Foltz applied to Hastings College of the Law in October, 1878. *Minutes of the Meetings of the Board of Directors of Hastings College of the Law,* Oct. 18, 1878, in 1 Record, Hastings College of Law 31 (on file at Hastings College of the Law) [hereinafter cited as *Hastings Directors' Minutes*].
49. *See* Transcript on Appeal at 2, Foltz v. Hoge, 54 Cal. 28 (1879).
50. *Struggles, supra* note 1, July 1917, at 18.
51. *Id.*, Nov. 1916, at 12.
52. *Hastings Directors' Minutes,* Jan. 10, 1879, *supra* note 48, at 31–32.
53. 2 NATIONAL CYCLOPEDIA, *supra* note 10, at 235.
54. *Id.*
55. 3 HISTORY OF WOMAN SUFFRAGE 757–58 (E.C. Stanton, S.B. Anthony & M.J. Gage eds. 1969).
56. *Hastings Directors' Minutes,* Feb. 13, 1879, *supra* note 48, at 32.
57. *See id.*
58. Transcript on Appeal at 3, Foltz v. Hoge, 54 Cal. 28 (1879).
59. *Id.* at 6.
60. *Id.* at 10. Foltz later wrote that the reason given her to justify excluding women from the college was that "The rustle of the ladies' garments would distract the attention of the young gentlemen." Foltz "was hardly able to appreciate their argument as a legal proposition." *Struggles, supra* note 1, Nov. 1916, at 12.
61. Transcript on Appeal at 7, Foltz v. Hoge, 54 Cal. 28 (1879).
62. S.F. Chronicle, Feb. 25, 1879, at 1, col. 1.
63. *Id.*
64. *Id.*
65. *Struggles, supra* note 1, Aug. 1917, at 22.
66. Daily Alta California, Feb. 25, 1879, at 1, col. 5.
67. An Act to Create and Organize the University of California, Cal. Stat. 1868, ch. 244, § 8, at 250–51.
68. An Act to Create Hastings College of the Law in the University of the State of California, Cal. Stat. 1878, ch. 351, §§ 1–15, at 533.
69. S.F. Chronicle, Feb. 25, 1879, at 1, col. 1.

70. *Struggles, supra* note 1, Aug. 1917, at 22.
71. S.F. Chronicle, Feb. 25, 1879, at 1, col. 1.
72. *Id.*
73. *Matter of Goodell*, 39 Wis. 232, 245–46 (1875).
74. Daily Alta California, Feb. 25, 1879, at 1, col. 2.
75. *Id.*
76. Transcript on Appeal at 12, Foltz v. Hoge, 54 Cal. 28 (1879).
77. S.F. Chronicle, Mar. 6, 1879, at 3, col. 2.
78. *Id.*
79. *See* NOTABLE AMERICAN WOMEN, *supra* note 4, at 643; S.F. Evening Post, Aug. 12, 1882, at 2, col. 1.
80. Foltz v. Hoge, 54 Cal. 28 (1879).
81. Estcourt, *Ladies of Law: Victors Over Custom*, S.F. Chronicle, July 2, 1939, § S, at 5, col. 1.
82. *Id.*
83. *See* Woman's Herald of Industry, Oct. 1882, at 4, col. 4. In this advertisement, Foltz described herself as "Clara S. Foltz, Attorney and Counselor at Law . . . Probate and Divorce Matters a Specialty." The Rules of Professional Conduct, which forbid advertising by attorneys, were not adopted by the California Supreme Court until May 24, 1928, forty-six years after this advertisement. *See* CAL. R. PROFESSIONAL CONDUCT 2–101.
84. *Struggles, supra* note 1, May 1918, at 9.
85. Cal. Stat. 1921, ch. 245, §§ 1–8, at 354.
86. *See* Sacramento Bee, Feb. 15, 1879, at 2, col. 2.
87. Foltz, *Public Defenders—Rights of Persons Accused of Crime—Abuses Now Existing*, 48 ALBANY L.J. 248, 249 (1893) [hereinafter cited as Foltz, *Rights of Persons Accused*].
88. *See* Foltz, *Public Defenders*, 31 AM. L. REV. 393, 399 (1897) [hereinafter cited as Foltz, *Public Defenders*].
89. Foltz, *Rights of Persons Accused, supra* note 86, at 249.
90. *Id.* at 248.
91. Foltz, *Public Defenders, supra* note 87, at 396.
92. Foltz, *Rights of Persons Accused, supra* note 86, at 248.
93. *See* Foltz, *Rights of Persons Accused, supra* note 86, at 248.
94. Cal. Stat. 1921, ch. 245, § 5, at 354.
95. *See, e.g.*, Foltz, *Rights of Persons Accused, supra* note 86, at 248; Foltz, *Public Defenders, supra* note 87, at 393; Foltz, *Public Defenders*, 25 CHICAGO LEGAL NEWS 431 (1893). Foltz wrote several of the articles in New York between 1896 and 1898, while whe was practicing in that state.
96. R. DAVIS, CALIFORNIA WOMEN: A GUIDE TO THEIR POLITICS 151 (1967).
97. 13 W. COAST MAGAZINE, 43, 44 (1912).
98. Cal. Stat. 1921, ch. 245, § 5, at 354.
99. Foltz, *Duties of District Attorneys in Prosecutions*, 18 CRIM. L. MAGAZINE 415 (1896).
100. *Id.* at 417.

101. Foltz, *Public Defenders, supra* note 87, at 402.
102. Foltz, *Duties of District Attorneys in Prosecutions,* 18 CRIM. L. MAGA-ZINE 415 (1896).
103. S.F. Call, Jan. 3, 1911, at 2, col. 2.
104. In recognition of her activity and expertise in the area of penal reform, Foltz was appointed to the California State Board of Charities and Corrections at the age of sixty. She was the first woman to serve on the board, where she was active for two years. NOTABLE AMERICAN WOMEN, *supra* note 4, at 643.
105. Foltz, *Struggles, supra* note 1, June 1918, at 9, 10.
106. NOTABLE AMERICAN WOMEN, *supra* note 4, at 643.
107. S.F. Call, Mar. 13, 1910, at 27, col. 4.
108. Cal. Stat. 1893, ch. 153, §1, at 183. The statute restricted parole to defendants who had had no prior felony convictions and who had not otherwise served time in a penal institution. *Id.*
109. Foltz, *What We Stand For,* NEW AM. WOMAN, Feb. 1916, at 3.
110. *Struggles, supra* note 1, Jan. 1917, at 26.
111. S.F. Call, Jan. 3, 1911, at 2, col. 2.
112. NATIONAL CYCLOPEDIA, *supra* note 10, at 308.
113. NOTABLE AMERICAN WOMEN, *supra* note 4, at 642.
114. 7 SAN FRANCISCO WASP, Sept. 16, 1881, at 183.
115. Letter from Clara Foltz to Clara Colby, June 26, 1908, at 4, on file in the Huntington Library, San Marino, California.
116. She moved her practice to Los Angeles in 1906. NOTABLE AMERICAN WOMEN, *supra* note 4, at 642.
117. Letter from Clara Foltz to Clara Colby, Apr. 8, 1909, at 4, on file in the Huntington Library, San Marino, California.
118. NOTABLE AMERICAN WOMEN, *supra* note 4, at 642.
119. S.F. Call, Jan. 3, 1911, at 2, col. 2.
120. Letter from Clara Foltz to Clara Colby, June 26, 1908, at 4, on file in the Huntington Library, San Marino, California.
121. *Id.* at 6.
122. S.F. Call, Jan. 3, 1911, at 2, col. 2.
123. 13 W. COAST MAGAZINE 43, 44 (1912).
124. *Id.*
125. NATIONAL CYCLOPEDIA, *supra* note 10, at 308.
126. Foltz, *Votes for Women Not an Issue,* NEW AM. WOMAN, May 1917, at 14.
127. Foltz, *What We Stand For,* NEW AM. WOMAN, Feb. 1916, at 3.
128. She campaigned across California for the Republican party in 1880, 1882, and 1884. In 1886, she supported a Democrat, Washington Bartlett, when his Republican opponent for governor, John F. Swift, expressed the opinion that a woman had no right to be a lawyer. Bartlett won, and he appointed Foltz to a State Normal School trusteeship, the only state office then open to women. S.F. Call, Nov. 5, 1911, at 45, col. 4. With her active support, her brother Samuel M. Shortridge ran for the

United States Senate, winning a seat which he occupied from 1921 to 1932, *Id.*

129. *Statement of the Vote at Primary Election Held on August 4, 1930,* at 4, in CALIFORNIA SECRETARY OF STATE, STATEMENT OF THE VOTE 1929–1939.

130. Letter from Clara Foltz to Alice Park, Mar. 20, 1930, at 1, on file in the Huntington Library, San Marino, California.

131. Foltz, *Law of the Case,* NEW AM. WOMAN, Feb. 1916, at 10.

132. *Id.* The periodical also included a section called "Law Briefs," which was a collection of one-line legal aphorisms such as: "A city or town cannot pass an ordinance punishing people for getting on and off moving trains;" and "A wife is liable on a note to which her husband attached her name by her authority." Foltz, *Law Briefs,* NEW AM. WOMAN, Mar. 1916, at 12.

133. *Struggles, supra* note 1, July 1916, at 14.

134. NOTABLE AMERICAN WOMEN, *supra* note 4, at 642.

135. *Struggles, supra* note 1, Apr. 1916, at 10.

136. NATIONAL CYCLOPEDIA, *supra* note 10, at 308.

137. *Struggles, supra* note 1, June 1917, at 12.

138. Matter of Goodell, 39 Wis. 232, 240–41 (1875).

139. Foltz felt, however, that the "gentlemen of the press" generally treated her very well. *Struggles, supra* note 1, June 1917, at 12.

140. S.F. Chronicle, Mar. 6, 1879, at 7, col. 2.

141. 6 SAN FRANCISCO WASP, Feb. 19, 1881, at 120–21.

142. Foltz, *Certain Kinds of Labor For Women Wrong and Unnatural,* NEW AM. WOMAN, Dec. 1916, at 19.

143. *Id.* Yet Foltz supported herself very well. Along with her legal practice, she developed extensive business interests. In 1905 she organized a women's department for the United Bank and Trust Company in San Francisco and began to publish a monthly magazine, *Oil Fields and Furnaces,* in the same city. She headed Foltz Oil Producers Syndicate from 1921 to 1922. This venture came to an end in August of 1922 when State Corporations Commissioner E. M. Daugherty suspended sales of shares in the corporation, for reasons he did not disclose. The San Francisco Examiner speculated that Foltz's venture may not have complied with the corporations commission regulation that 80% of money invested in oil drilling companies must be spent on development. S.F. Examiner, Aug. 12, 1922, at 3, col. 1. Foltz also apparently operated a Los Angeles real estate agency, the American Woman's Little Farms Company. *See* NEW AM. WOMAN, June 1916, at back cover (advertisement).

144. NOTABLE AMERICAN WOMEN, *supra* note 4, at 642.

145. San Diego Bee, May 16, 1887, at 2, col. 1. She continued: "and no better field for the exercise of her influence can be found than is offered in the publication of a daily paper." *Id.* Many early issues of the *Bee* were filled with diatribes against a shady Mexican land sale scheme, over which her newspaper fought a bitter journalistic duel with its chief rival, the *San Diego Union.* Foltz frequently editorialized on the themes of women's

rights and sexual politics: "[W]hen a wronged sister applied to her for the privilege of obtaining a hearing before the public, she readily consented to throw open the columns of the Bee for that purpose." *Id.*, July 17, 1887, at 2, col. 1.

146. *Id.*, May 25, 1887, at 2, col. 1.
147. *Struggles, supra* note 1, Mar. 1918, at 9.
148. Letter from Clara Foltz to Clara Colby, June 26, 1908, at 2, on file in the Huntington Library, San Marino, California.
149. Letter from Clara Colby to Alice Park, Dec. 18, 1923, at 1, on file in the Huntington Library, San Marino, California.
150. Theresa Viscoli asserted that after Foltz's death, Virginia Foltz Gatron, the only surviving child, sold all of her mother's furniture and destroyed her papers. Viscoli said, "Virginia was never a saver." Telephone interview with Theresa Viscoli, Aug. 11, 1975.
151. *Struggles, supra* note 1, Mar. 1918, at 9.

WOMEN'S ENTRY INTO CORPORATE LAW FIRMS

Cynthia Fuchs Epstein

Law and lawyers have excited sociological interest in recent years. Studies and books have explored how the legal community operates, how lawyers tend to be selected into the various strata of the bar, and how joining a given legal environment affects the lawyer.[1] The questions raised and answered have been instructive. However, more questions remain to be answered. Inquiry into one of the most powerful sectors of legal institutions, the large corporate firms, was explored by Smigel in his now classic work *The Wall Street Lawyer*[2] in 1964. But important changes have occurred since that time, particularly the growth of the firms and the changing composition of their recruits. In particular, Wall Street opened its doors to women lawyers who were virtually excluded from its ranks until the late 1960s.[3]

Women in the legal profession have come a long way. From 2.5 percent of all lawyers in the 1960s,[4] their numbers increased to 12 percent today.[5] An even more radical jump occurred in the law student population—from 4.5 percent in 1967[6] to 33.5 percent in 1980.[7] The number of women lawyers in corporate firms has also risen dramatically. Smigel reported counting only eighteen women in Wall Street firms when he conducted his research in 1956.[8] Ten years ago, forty women lawyers were scattered throughout the wood-paneled offices of New York's largest and most prestigious law firms.[9] Today in a remarkable change, there are close to six hundred women in the three dozen select firms of Wall Street—an increase from 1 to 19 percent.[10]

Based on a paper presented at the American Sociological Association, Boston, Massachusetts, August 1979, and Cynthia Fuchs Epstein, *Women In Law* (New York, Basic Books, 1981). The critical reading of Professors Ruth Bader Ginsburg and Martin Ginsburg of Columbia Law School, as well as the research assistance of Mary Murphree, Judith Thomas, Simonetti Samuels, Susan Wolf and Marlene Warshawsky, is acknowledged with appreciation.

THE WALL STREET BAR: A PROFILE

The Wall Street bar is a collection of about three dozen high-powered law firms clustered, as Paul Hoffman describes, around either the "canyons of Manhattan's financial district" or "along the flower beds of Park Avenue."[11] Their clients are large corporations, commercial banks and investment houses, and a small number of wealthy individuals. The firms derive much of their power from their ability to "make" law in this country by working on precedent-setting cases. Wall Street lawyers are by and large unknown to the public and travel a career path from law school graduation to partnership in the firm where they started practice. They periodically come to visibility, not only for making legal precedent, but also for contributing legal talent to high levels of government service. Sometimes, the firms become visible for recruiting "big names" from the highest ranks of politics and government, as in the notable case of Richard Nixon's recruitment by Mudge, Rose, Guthrie, and Alexander, after his first unsuccessful bid for the presidency.

A significant proportion of the members of the establishment bar come from the social elite of the East Coast.[12] Social background is only the first step in the social sifting process that determines the membership of these firms. Merit is important, probably more these days than in the past. Merit is defined on the basis of high grade point average, and membership on law review at a few major law schools (notably Harvard, Yale and Columbia, although there is a more diverse representation of schools in the large firms now than previously). Nowhere is the "old boy" network so characteristic of the formal and informal structure of an occupation as in the "establishment bar." And nowhere is tradition more important and the impact of background status so pertinent to recruitment.

Overlapping the blue-chip bar is a "Jewish" establishment bar, which grew after World War II in reaction to the prejudice against Jewish attorneys. These firms today, although still referred to as "Jewish firms," are characterized by a more diverse social and religious membership, and rival the large WASP firms in size, resources, and power. The stereotypes of Wall Street firms as "Protestant" versus "Jewish" have the character of all stereotypes, composed of germs of truth and a certain amount of falsehood. However, the belief in these differences makes their consequences real, a self-fulfilling prophecy that makes the firms distinctive with regard to recruitment and operation.

PROFILE OF WOMEN LAWYERS ON WALL STREET

From virtual invisibility, women entered Wall Street corporate firms in significant numbers in the 1970s. In a short period of time, Wall Street became a preferred place to seek and find employment.[13]

Women attorneys are found in corporate firms among the ranks of both partners and associates. Partners are employed at the top of the corporate hierarchy and share the firm's profits. The younger lawyers, and new recruits, are employed as associates. Some of the associates, after a seven-to-ten-year apprenticeship, are asked to join the ranks of partners.

In the largest New York City firms (thirty-two firms containing more than ninety-five attorneys each), women represent 12 percent of the legal staff.[14] In 1977, these firms had a total of 4,815 attorneys; of these, approximately 587 were women. Smigel's study of Wall Street firms in 1964 found only one woman partner. When this author surveyed the same New York firms in 1971, there had been an increase to three. However, by 1979, of the 1,520 partners distributed among the large firms, twenty-nine were women. In 1979 this author's survey showed an increase to thirty-four and to forty-one by summer 1980. At the same time (1980), of 3,987 partners in the top fifty law firms nationally, eighty-five are women. This is a large increase in numbers, yet even today only about 2 percent of all partners are women. More significantly, a quarter of the large firms in New York (including some of the giants such as Sullivan and Cromwell, with 206 lawyers) have *no* women partners. Fourteen of the large firms have one woman partner; seven firms have two, and two firms have three.[15]

Of the thirty-four women partners in 1979, only three achieved partnership before 1970; another ten joined them between 1971 and 1975. Another twenty-one were promoted between 1976 and 1979 and another seven were named between the fall and spring of 1980.

Lower in the occupational hierarchy, women have also occupied the position of associates. Smigel reported a total of eighteen women working in a small sample of firms in 1964. However, he did not specify the location of these women in the hierarchy. Several years later, in 1971, this author found these same firms had an average of four associates. By 1977, the same sample revealed seventeen female associates. In the larger sample of thirty-two firms, there were 3,142 associates in 1977; of these 587 (19 percent) were women.

Many firms reporting no women associates in 1971 currently employ between ten and twenty. Some firms employ as many as forty and fifty. This represents a rapid change in the recruitment of women. More importantly, the inclusion of women at the highest corporate level of partner represents a major alteration in the status of women attorneys on Wall Street. The recruitment of women partners reflects a long-term commitment to their participation as true peers at the highest level.

The numerical profile of women in Wall Street firms is reflected by similar patterns in the top corporate firms in Washington, D.C.[16] For example, in the firm of Wilmer and Pickering, of 108 lawyers in 1977, there were sixteen female associates and one woman partner. Although women had been employed at the more austere and WASP firm of Covington and Burling since at least the 1940s, the first woman partner was not named until the mid-1970s. By 1970, Covington had eight female associates, about 5 percent of the firm. Covington has since "improved"[17] and had thirty woman associates and two women partners among its 185 lawyers by the mid-1970s.

Other large firms across the country reflect similar numerical profiles. The firm of Fulbright and Jaworski[18] in Texas in 1979 had 123 partners and 138 associates. One woman is a partner (in the Washington, D.C. office) and twenty-eight women are associates. The 102-lawyer firm of King and Spalding of Atlanta admitted a woman to partnership rank for the first time in their 100-year history in 1980.

The social profile of the women corporate lawyers is similar in many respects to their male counterparts. Exhibiting a pattern noted by Smigel for male Wall Street lawyers, data gathered by the author reveal that eighteen of the thirty-four women partners attended Harvard, Columbia and Yale law schools. Another five attended the top rank, if not equally prestigious, New York University Law School. Most of the other women partners attended other elite national law schools. Their undergraduate education reveals a similar pattern. Sixteen of the women partners obtained their undergraduate degrees from "Seven Sisters" schools on the East Coast. Another nine women partners acquired their undergraduate degree from prestigious state universities.[19]

Another factor characterizing women in large corporate law firms is their area of legal specialization. In earlier decades women who were able to enter Wall Street firms frequently encountered discrimination regarding types of practice open to them. It was virtually unknown for women to perform litigation or practice corporate law. Many women were funneled into trusts and estates work and family law areas considered suitable for women.

Today women in the largest corporate law firms have access to a range of legal specialties. Some women make it a point not to accept stereotypically feminine assignments. Some women still are employed in trusts and estates work, but now by choice. This continues to be an attractive specialty for women because of its family orientation, predictable hours and fewer crisis situations demanding night and weekend work.

Significantly, more women are now working in litigation.[20] In one large firm, an associate reported that a majority of the new women hired request this assignment. One woman lawyer had even attained the rank of partner specializing in litigation, a rank nonexistent for women until recently. Perhaps another explanation for the increasing numbers of women in corporate litigation is a change in the way women lawyers characterize themselves today. Many lawyers interviewed characterized themselves as "big talkers," "dramatic types," and aggressively sought the recognition and drama of the courtroom. This contrasts sharply with women lawyers interviewed in the 1960s. This earlier group of women shied away from courtroom combat as being inconsistent with their own personalities.

Not only is the corporate establishment characterized by a difference in women's specialization, but also by more complete integration into the Wall Street firms. In the course of conducting the firm's business and performing the same tasks as male associates and partners, women are being treated in the same fashion as men.

Clients' perceptions of women corporate attorneys also reflect this change in women's status. The clients of these large firms are typically large corporations or businesses and have established long-term relationships with the law firms. The rank of the firm often affects the client's acceptance of a woman lawyer. Women lawyers representing firms with a good reputation tend not to have their expertise called into question. Once the woman has been hired by the large firm, she typically acquires the authority synonomous with the firm's name. She is not just a lawyer, but a "Sullivan and Cromwell" or a "Cravath" lawyer. Thus, the entry of women into traditional specialties in corporate firms seems to have been determined by their *firms'* sex-typing practices, and not merely by the sex-typed attitudes of clients.

This is not to say that all differences have been eliminated. Some lawyers report continued differentiation between men's work and women's work. Some women litigators report that they appear in court less often than men of equal rank. Of course, few attorneys in large firms appear in court, and only a small number of corporate cases go to trial. Nonetheless, significantly fewer litigators are women.

Many women still perform backroom tasks and have less client contact. One woman attorney in a large firm complained that she had been the firm's leading brief writer and theoretician for years. Although she had the firm's recognition and became a partner in the early 1970s, she still rarely saw clients. Her income was also lower than men of her rank. Another woman in a Washington, D.C. firm complained that women were "cubbyholed there, doing dribs and drabs of cases," in specific slots reserved for women—in trusts and estates, tax, and food-and-drug law.

THE PROCESS OF PROMOTION AND INCOME

Will women's greater numbers and greater visibility insure their permanent place as partners on Wall Street? The general view in the firms, by onlookers in law schools and among feminist attorneys, has been: "Let's wait and see what happens when it becomes time to promote women to partnership." We have already noted that women constitute only 2 percent of partners in the large corporate Wall Street firms. The question arises, what are the chances for other women in these firms, especially the women most recently hired, to attain partnership on Wall Street. In New York, there are more associates compared to partners than there are in other cities. In New York the associate-to-partner ratio is two-to-one, five-to-two, or three-to-one (Cravath).[21] In large firms in other cities, the ratio is closer to one-to-one. A survey by the Columbia Law School[22] showed that 50 percent of the graduates who joined major firms outside New York City stayed on to become partners. In New York City only 20 percent did so. However, for most women associates it is too soon to tell. Most women partners are between thirty-five and forty-two years old. Today the average age of women in the large firms is younger; most are recent recruits and therefore associates.

Promotion in Wall Street firms is not unlike the tenure system in academia. For periods of six to ten years, young lawyers serve as associates waiting for a final appraisal, at which time either they are promoted to partnership or asked to leave the firm. Only a few who are denied full membership stay as "permanent associates." In the past these have been minorities, ethnic group members, or women. Until recently, women have accepted these low status positions as the best they could hope for in corporate law firms.

Whereas once women did not expect to attain partnership, now many consider it a real possibility. Like their male peers, they calculate their chances and hope to maximize the possibility by meeting not only the formal, but the informal requirements.

One informal requirement is working overtime on nights and weekends. Since stakes are high on Wall Street and partnership assures both an income well into six figures and lifelong tenure, young lawyers typically invest considerable time and energy proving themselves before partnership decisions are made. Stories abound of the "old days," when it was typical for young lawyers to work every night and weekend for months on end. Interviews with women even a decade ago revealed the dilemmas they faced about working the same long hours as male associates. Most of these earlier women attorneys were excluded from the prestigious specialties such as litigation with its intense pressure to work "round-the-clock"—the characteristic marking the chosen few. Women were assigned to other specialties which were not as taxing in terms of time demands, because it was believed that women would not work the long hours which the men did. Simultaneously, women were condemned for their lack of ambition in not working long hours. This circuitous logic rationalized the decision not to promote women to partnership.

Another factor important in promotion to partnership is the ability to bring business to the firm. Business-getters or "rainmakers" as they are termed, have always received special consideration. Bringing business to the firm is a problem for women and they have not done well at it. Nor do they have high hopes for improvement. Women lack the male business networks and are less well placed to become "rainmakers." Most women recognize their limitations as business-getters and try to establish themselves as "talents" who can better serve existing clients.[23]

The recent increase in firm size has created a qualitatively different context for social relationships in the firms, a context which has consequences for partnership. Intimacy, visibility, the merging of informal and formal networks—all have undergone change. Partnerships can not be the same "brotherhood" as before, simply because of the unwieldy size of the group. Therefore, there is less necessity that every new partner "fit in" as before, which might work to the advantage of women.

Yet there also appears to be a tightening of the hierarchy, with greater polarization, more gradations between partners and associates. Advancement now may have a different meaning. For women and minority associates, there is a greater chance of becoming a partner. However, many women feel that a new partnership rank may be created for them—perhaps a junior partnership bringing a proportionately smaller share of profits. The position may also have less power and influence. This suspicion is primarily held by older women attorneys who feel this new partnership rank will be created for women as firms feel pressed to promote women associates. Although this is a step upward, it does not mean that women have "made it" in relation to men who are rising in the hierarchy. Nevertheless, partnership is still much sought after and women interviewed did not question the conditions of partnership which they might be offered.

The young women lawyers on Wall Street had not yet received negative messages about compensation differentials. They viewed the opportunity structure as open in this regard. A number of women hoped and expected to become partners, and were organizing their lives to qualify for advancement. Unlike their elder sisters and predecessors in the firms, they were working the same hours as men, aligning their personal relations to optimize their careers. As a group, they were adopting attitudes strikingly similar to their male colleagues' toward money, success, and achievement. Many did not begin law practice with these attitudes. Like their male peers, women in the 1970s were motivated to enter law through their intense participation in political and social movements. Concurrently, however, the mainstream of the women's movement was making it more legitimate for women to enunciate interest in goals of money, power, and success. Although more radical feminists, as well as traditionalists, opposed the assumption of "male values," for the first time women found support for ambition and success at the workplace. Ideological lines drawn in the early 1970s between women who felt it was legitimate and appropriate to work toward high rewards as opposed to those who believed it was morally wrong and ideologically incorrect, still exist. The latter group differs from those in generations past who believed it unfeminine for women to seek success in "male" terms. Rather, these women believe that women should avoid the corruption of the "rat race."

To some extent, women with these different ideological views have clustered in certain areas of practice. Those who believe in mainstream definitions of success in personal and material terms find themselves in large firms. Those who disclaim material success have tended to join legal services, feminist law practice, "movement law" and private practice.

This is, however, a broad classification with many exceptions. Ideology may have motivated some women, but professional practice also alters ideology. Motivations for originally entering a legal career do not necessarily correlate with the type of practice a woman chooses. Rather, the decision is often linked to economic needs, opportunity, the type of law school attended, performance at law school and personal networks. (It does not seem to be associated with either marital status or parental status.)

Some women merely sought employment in large firms because friends said they should try there, or they felt it was prestigious to be asked to join. Some sought employment there because the *best* jobs in legal resources or government practice were limited. Others elected to earn high salaries to repay law school loans before going into other areas of practice.

One striking element was the extent to which women who had entered such firms with no clear set of ambitions quickly internalized the goals of success and revised their ambitions. Accordingly, women who had not expected to become partners now considered they might achieve partnership. In contrast to earlier generations, they thought their chances were better, and followed a direct route toward the goal.

CHANGES AFFECTING RECEPTIVITY TO WOMEN

Several factors may explain the changes affecting the receptivity of large corporate firms to women. The most obvious change is the increase in the pool of eligible women. Increasing numbers of women attended law schools in the late 1960s and 1970s. For example, the law school population of women jumped from 4.5 percent in 1967 to 33.5 percent in 1980.[24] These women, by and large, performed as well or better academically than men. Thus, there was an increase in the number of qualified women for the firms to choose. In addition, the women's movement had changed the sense of legitimacy regarding women's right to work in careers which were formerly dominated by men. Thus, many men became more sensitive to and convinced of women's serious commitment to highly demanding work at the same time that women were asserting their right to sex-blind evaluation. Still another factor influencing firm's receptivity to women was legal change.

A. Legal Change

The fear of lawsuits also affected discrimination in corporate firms. Women themselves initiated legal action against some firms. Suits were brought against several major Wall Street firms in the late 1960s and 1970s. The spearhead of these challenges was Title VII,[25] the employment discrimination legislation of the Civil Rights Act of 1964, which made it unlawful for employers to discriminate in hiring practices. Law students and women lawyers used this legislation to their advantage.

Discrimination claims were brought against Sullivan and Cromwell, Rogers and Wells (the name of the firm was then Royall,

Koegel, and Wells) and ten firms with the New York City Human Rights Commission on behalf of all New York women law students, by Columbia's Dean Harriet Rabb, professors George Cooper and Howard J. Rubin, and the students of Columbia's Employment Rights Project, a clinical program concentrating on Title VII litigation.[26] The case undertaken against Sullivan and Cromwell, one of a number of select firms which recruited at New York University and Columbia Law School, was a landmark. In the fall of 1969 when the firm interviewed on campus, the women students pooled experiences and surmised that this firm, as well as others, was giving short shrift to women. The women complained to the Placement Office which supported them and telephoned members of the firm, including the hiring committee. The firm consented to conduct several interviews with women. After encountering disparaging remarks in the interviews, the women began collecting evidence of a pervasive pattern of discrimination by this and other major New York law firms.

The complaint against Sullivan and Cromwell was amended to challenge not only recruitment practices but also the firm's system of promotion. The case followed an interesting and ironic course. Sullivan and Cromwell hired Ephraim London, a former civil rights lawyer. The case was assigned to Justice Constance Baker Motley, a black, and the only woman among thirty-two judges in the federal bench in New York, whose name had been selected *at random*. The firm asked Justice Motley to excuse herself on the basis of her sex: since she was a woman, they argued, she could not decide the case on the issues. They also cited her civil rights background as grounds for their request. The justice refused. The firm moved for a writ of mandamus to remove her. An appeals court denied their request.

Complaints were also filed against other New York firms. These lawsuits were largely successful. In important settlements, they guaranteed the recruitment of women to the firms as well as women's advancement and promotion. (The settlement with Sullivan and Cromwell even included a provision not to hold firm-sponsored events in clubs which barred women.[27])

Legal challenges were maintained in other parts of the country as well. In Texas, the third largest law firm in the country, Fulbright and Jaworski, settled a sex discrimination suit brought two years earlier in 1979.[28] The complaint charged that the firm did not hire its first female attorney until 1956, and then only for a particular assignment, to wit, "collections," miscellaneous small matters firms take on to accommodate clients, which male associates did not wish to handle. This first female associate (the complaint further specified), was "instructed to do her own typing and was on at least one occasion requested to assist the typing pool . . ."[29] The story of two other women associates revealed a similar reaction to work of low regard.[30]

The battles continue. The 102-lawyer firm of King and Spalding[31] of Atlanta faced a sex discrimination suit recently for never admitting a woman to partnership in their 100-year history. In July 1980 the firm named its first woman partner.

B. Student-Faculty Vigilance

Another factor contributing to increased receptivity to women in large firms was student and faculty vigilance. The passage of Title VII helped create a change in *norms* which affected the recruitment process. Pressures on law school placement offices by students and faculty forced others to be alert to the injustices of past practices, such as selective interviewing. In the late 1960s, in addition to legal challenges, women students also began reporting discrimination or sexism from hiring partners to their law school placement offices.

Initial attempts were not always successful. A partner at a large New York firm who attended Boalt Hall School of Law at Berkeley in the late sixties (as one of ten women in a class of 250), recounted that the school permitted recruiters to interview who baldly stated, "We don't hire women." She complained to the dean who retorted, "Do you really want to hurt your male colleagues' job chances? If we bar firms who don't hire women they'll lose out on job opportunities." The next year, however, enrollment of women increased and twenty students went to the dean to complain. She described the result:

> The school wrote all firms recruiting on campus asking for their hiring practices toward women and minorities. One firm had written that they had no policy either for or against women. The school asked that he not be sent but he came anyway. The students then engaged him in an all day debate in the school cafeteria. He wanted

to interview—to have something to show his firm for the day. But we wouldn't let him. We kept changing shifts—men joined us too—to debate his prejudice against women. At the end of the day, he said, "O.K., we've had this little charade. Now when can I interview?" He was absolutely unrepentant. At this point the Dean said no, he couldn't interview at all and wrote a letter to the man's firm explaining why he had not been allowed to interview. The whole matter of firms not hiring women got cleared up at Berkeley in that one year.[32]

In some instances, women students sued their placement offices. In one such action, the federal Equal Employment Opportunities Commission found sex bias in the placement practices and in 1972 ordered the University of Chicago Law School to assist women in obtaining jobs with law firms which recruited on campus.[33]

In other instances the law school administration, as well as placement personnel, was sensitized by women students and acted informally to challenge discriminatory practices. Thus, for example, Dean Albert M. Sachs and Alfred Daniels of the Harvard Law School went to Cincinnati in 1976 to explore reasons why the seven firms in that city employed only one black and seventeen women among 253 lawyers.[34]

With this incentive, many firms moved swiftly to correct the tone and behavior of their representatives at interviews. Women who had previously complained of inappropriate questions or demeanor (such as being asked about contraceptive practices, congratulated for good looks, or otherwise not treated as serious candidates) in employment interviews at Harvard, Yale, Columbia, or Berkeley, were finally being accepted into the offending firms after they entered formal complaints with their law school administration. Although firms' reputations regarding the treatment of women still vary, with the threat of sex discrimination suits (or recent settlements), all are now conscious of the "woman question."

OTHER FACTORS AFFECTING RECEPTIVITY TO WOMEN

Two additional factors contributed to greater receptivity toward women in the large corporate law firms. The first was a change in the concomitant growth in the *size* of these firms. The second was a receptivity to women varying according to the *type* of firm.

The integration of women into large firms was facilitated by the tremendous recent increase in the size of these firms, an increase which occurred concomitantly with the other changes discussed above. Recent years have witnessed an enormous growth in the size of the major law firms. The top twenty law firms studied in 1964 by Smigel contained from fifty to one hundred lawyers. Three of these firms have grown recently from 30 to 120 percent. Some firms have doubled in size. Other firms not included in that study have made similarly radical jumps in size. Some of these firms have become larger than those included in Smigel's sample.

As the Wall Street firms grew in size and numbers, the percent of women employed there increased as well. The increase in the number of total places available, as well as the increasing numbers of women law graduates to fill these places, were important factors facilitating receptivity toward women.

Another factor was a differential integration by type of firm. On Wall Street and in other large firms, women started flocking in, as total numbers for the firms indicate. But here too, one finds clustering. That is, some firms today have many women; some have few; some have no women partners and others have several. Some firms integrate women more fully than others. The reason may be attributed to the fact that firms have different traditions, different profiles and different patterns of "courtship" of new recruits. These differences may be noted in the firms referred to as "Jewish firms."

Roosevelt's "New Deal" had given many Jewish lawyers opportunities to work in government and make valuable contacts—which made them attractive to Wall Street firms. Some Jewish men began their own firms. In short, the path to large law firms was smoother for Jews and Catholics in the 1940s and 1950s. These men finally had an opportunity to become partners in the WASP firms in the 1960s.[35] These Jewish and Catholic males tended to be assimilated into establishment culture, and became hardly distinguishable in appearance, tastes, educational background and behavior from Protestant men. Statistics indicate a slightly greater receptivity to women by the "Jewish" firms in contrast to the old line Protestant firms. This receptivity may be measured by the number of women partners.

Two New York City "Jewish firms" (Stroock, Stroock and

Lavan; and Proskauer, Rose, Goetz, and Mendelsohn) seem to have been most open to promoting women partners. Stroock and Proskauer had four women partners by spring of 1980. Kaye Scholer, before its reorganization, had three women partners, as did one WASP firm, Rogers and Wells, the highest numbers to be found in any large firms in New York City. Of the six firms with two women partners, two are Jewish firms. In sum, the seven "Jewish" firms have seventeen women partners while the twenty-five old line firms have twenty-four women partners. All Jewish firms have at least one woman partner, nine non-Jewish firms have no women partners.

Yet while the Jewish firms have more women partners, they have so few more that it is difficult to ascertain if this reflects real differences in attitudes. Women and men in these firms claim the firms are more receptive to women. Some outsiders are more skeptical. It could be argued, however, that although the difference in number of women partners in Jewish firms is slight compared to some of the established Protestant firms, this increase may signify that these firms have gone beyond tokenism.

These Jewish firms may also be more hospitable to women lawyers in terms of attitudes as well as promotion. Although women at some of the WASP firms claim the Jewish firms are "sweat shops" for women as well as men (because, as the rationale states, they are "newer," less assured of their income, more eager for new clients, and consequently demand a higher number of hours of work from their associates), there are indicators of hospitable elements which account for women's participation. For example, some of the women in the Jewish firms claim they are "warmer" and therefore more resonant to women's interpersonal styles. Another factor is the background of Jewish men. One explanation is that Jewish firms would be more receptive to women since fewer Jewish men than WASP men have the history of single sex schooling from preparatory school through college. Jewish men also spent less time at sports which focus on the all-male environments of "Protestant only" athletic clubs.[36]

Murphree[37] suggests that the rapid growth of the Jewish firms may account for greater receptivity to women as well. And, of course, there has been a greater commitment of lawyers in the Jewish firms to social justice issues because of their own past experiences with discrimination. It is probable that these differences between Jewish and Protestant firms may disappear as Wall Street firms tend to recruit from a similar pool of men and women, and because of the firms' gradual move toward shared values.

CHANGES IN ATTITUDE

Aside from greater receptivity in hiring and promotion, an important question is whether women lawyers face continued resistance by their male colleagues after they are hired. Most of the young women lawyers interviewed in the past few years reported that such resistance, at least on Wall Street, has disappeared. A few, however, did report negative comments by men in their firms. One woman told us:

> I was having a discussion with one of the partners of my firm about hiring the women—they are really good about it. You know, as I said, half of the people they hired last year were women and half of the people they will hire next year will be women. So I mean they are certainly not discriminating but some of the older partners are saying, "God damn it, why are we having all these stupid women." But the other partners were educating them. They were saying, "well, by the way, do you know the percentage of women now in the law schools?" One senior man said, "I don't know, ten percent." "No you are wrong, *it is 45 percent and if we don't interview women, we are not going to get the best people.*"[*] "So the senior man said, "then we should take less qualified men." The younger men's response was in effect, "go sit in a corner." And so it was. The firm has become really good about women. I don't think they were one of the forerunners but *once it became apparent that there were a lot of women out there in the market of jobs,* they hopped on the wagon and they hired a lot of women.

We found in our earlier study that perceptions of discrimination did not always reflect the prevailing situation. Many women had either not faced discrimination in job experiences or, because of their low expectations, characteristic of an earlier era, they did not feel they should be obtaining something which they would not have otherwise received. This still holds true for some women, even in the Wall Street firms. And for this reason, or because these women's personalities lead them not to perceive discriminatory

---

*Both these estimates are incorrect, but indicate what some people perceive to be true.

attitudes (another behavior characteristic of the earlier group), they do not report any discrimination.

However, far fewer women lawyers today are blind to prejudice. In fact, women attorneys who fought for women's rights as students in the late 1960s and early 1970s have been on guard against male chauvinism for some time. Some women in Wall Street practice today were instrumental in changing the norms as students or subsequently in women lawyers' caucuses in legal associations.

Nonetheless, accounts of discrimination on Wall Street, or interpretation of the behavior of senior men as discriminatory against women, came more often from some of the younger *men* interviewed than from the women themselves. For example, one young man noted that the large numbers of women recruited for summer jobs during law school were hired because it enabled the law firms to appear favorably in the statistical count of women.[38]

PRIVATE LIVES AND WORK COMMITMENT

Once women lawyers are hired at large law firms, they face some of the same work situations as their male counterparts. Long days, overtime and intense pressure are common. The hours of work demanded by Wall Street practice are both legendary and real. Not only do some specialties require round-the-clock activity during certain periods but working long hours is viewed as a sign of commitment. There are, however, differences as well.

Because primary responsibility for children still rests with the mother, whether to have children or not was a frequent topic of discussion among the women in the big firms, as among the men in our sample who were married to lawyers. Many respondents felt that having children could only be justified by having enough money to maintain a large residence with full-time help and/or older family members to assist.

While many young women were single-minded about their careers, even though married or in long-term relationships with men, some were more troubled. One respondent who was married and had two small children when she joined the firm reported:

> There are some women lawyers who are almost on the male track. They have adopted male values, are less concerned about integrating their lives in a way that I am, and with them I feel uncomfortable to a certain extent about being open about my problems in coping with home and work.

Women in large firms live with issues raised by the women's movement and the publicity attached to their former exclusion. While they are aware of the rationales given for their previous exclusion and critical of the injustice, most seem eager to demonstrate that traditional prescriptions do not apply to them personally. For example, women generally are reluctant to ask for special privileges for fear they will be thought less serious then men. To some extent, commitment to the firm has become their first priority. As suggested before, some women consider not having children because of anticipated pressures and because they wish to alleviate others' "fears" that they will abandon "lawyering" for full-time motherhood.

Some who *do* have children contrive to demonstrate that children will not undermine career commitment. After having a baby, one Wall Street woman, for whom partnership was important, constantly asked for travel assignments and additional work to reveal that her child offered no competition to her attention to the firm.

Yet many young married women are discovering conflicts. They report that when they put their "all" into their careers, they feel they are failing at motherhood or being wives.

Some women in these firms view the commitment demanded as too costly. For the women on the success track (and for more of the men), there is an ongoing dialogue about the costs versus the benefits of success in the large firms. For example, one woman complained:

> The firm takes up so much of your life, there's so little left over that what I have left over belongs to my husband and my children and my few good friends that I have left. I have lost a lot of friends because I work all the time.

In essence, the success-minded women are behaving as if by complying with the rules set for men they can win the same rewards. Yet there is still uncertainty about what their chances will be as individuals, or even what their futures hold because they are women. One woman lawyer looked at it this way:

> When I come up (for partnership) there will be ten of us coming up almost at the same time, and I'll bet you anything that it won't be like ten lawyers coming up, it will be ten *women*. And I don't know what the impact will be.

But it is a game where the women are calculating, as are the men:

> They look before and they look behind. There are some coming up before you and others coming up behind you, and then you come up in the middle. This year, two came up for partnership, this past year, three. But the classes are now 12. When I was hired they told me they were hiring only two; in fact they hired four because there was so much work to do. Now they are hiring 12 and 13 and 14 in a class.

While the women are waiting and assessing their chances in the large firms, there are certain factors operating in their favor. One such factor is that many enjoy their work. From our findings, the women on Wall Street, having entered a world previously closed to them, find they like being there, feel they will do well, and have intentions of competing for its prizes. Some women, like some men, find Wall Street incompatible with their personalities and their values. Yet it seems firmly established that sex roles need not interfere with work roles on Wall Street and to the extent that they do, it is a matter of old prejudices regarding what men and women ought to be doing, and what kinds of conceptions they should have about their lives. Regardless, former prejudices are narrowed.

In some respects, the influx of women into the large firms is an example of dramatic social change. It seems reasonable to interpret its "peaceful" nature as a culmination of legal and political acts. These were accompanied by reinterpretation of social norms which specified appropriate behavior and standards for "gentlemen." This was a cherished self-image. When it was no longer proper to give voice to prejudices against women, men on Wall Street reconsidered. The establishment was forced to alter its behavior to adapt to new standards. It has done so without an extreme cost to the way of life and business.

The presence of women has not really altered modes of doing business. Nor has there been any real introduction of "women's values." Women practice law and conduct business much the same way men have. Yet, some women claim that their presence has a humanizing effect on the firms. Some women say they "lighten up the place." Others say they are more humanistic, that aesthetic concerns surface in informal interaction, and that their potential needs for a work schedule which recognizes time for their family, has made men recognize that they need these things too. Some male colleagues complain that women lawyers are more businesslike and driven by work than they are. Because men expect women to be more humane, they bristle at the forthright, serious intensity many young women lawyers exhibit.

The next few years will regularize women's presence on Wall Street and indeed, in the entire profession. How women will act, "under normal circumstances" has yet to be seen. However, several things are certain. Women have shown competence and commitment, two attributes which have always been in question. This is true in all spheres of law, even those most stereotyped as the special domain of men. Surely, the underpinning of a formerly staunch set of prejudices has collapsed.

NOTES

1. J. Carlin, *Lawyers on Their Own: A Study of Individual Practioners in Chicago* (New Jersey: Rutgers University Press, 1962); J. Ladinsky, "Careers of Lawyers, Law Practice and Legal Institution," *American Sociological Review* 28 (1963): 47; Ladinsky, "The Impact of Social Backgrounds of Lawyers on Law Practice and the Law," *J. Legal Education* 16 (1963): 127; Joel F. Handler, *The Lawyer and His Community: The Practicing Bar in a Middle-Sized City* (University of Wisconsin Press, 1967); Hubert J. O'Gorman, *Lawyers and Matrimonial Cases: A Study of Informal Pressures in Private Professional Practice* (New York: Free Press, 1963); Jerome Auerbach, *Unequal Justice: Lawyers & Social Change in Modern America* (New York: Oxford University Press, 1976); and Mark J. Green, *The Other Government: The Unseen Power of Washington Lawyers* (New York: Grossman, 1975).

2. Erwin O. Smigel, *The Wall Street Lawyer: Professional Organization Man* (New York: Free Press, 1964).

3. The author's first study of women lawyers was conducted in the mid-sixties and reported in a doctoral dissertation. See Cynthia Fuchs Epstein, "Women and Professional Careers: The Case of the Woman Lawyer" (unpublished Ph.D. dissertation, Department of Sociology, Columbia University, 1968).

4. U.S. Department of Labor Report, 1977, p. 9.

5. Cynthia Fuchs Epstein, *Women in Law* (New York: Basic Books, 1981), Table 1.1, p. 4.

6. "A Review of Legal Education in the United States," (Section of Legal Education and Admissions to the Bar, 1967, American Bar Association).

7. "A Review of Legal Education," Fall 1980.

8. Smigel, *Wall Street Lawyer*, p. 18.

9. Cynthia Fuchs Epstein, *Women in Law*, p. 180.

10. Ibid.

11. Paul Hoffman, *Lions in the Street* (New York: Signet, 1973).

12. A sizeable percent of partners in these large firms are located in *The Social Register*. Smigel, *Wall Street Lawyer*, p. 18.

13. According to Ostroff, the *small* law partnerships are where women law students are not going. Ron Ostroff, "Make Way for Women," *National Law Journal* 1 (February 5, 1979): 1, 10. A recent study of New York City women lawyers shows that 16 percent practice in corporate firms. See Frances Della Cava and Madeline Engle, "Women Lawyers in New York City: Social Characteristics and Social Problems," paper presented to the Department of Sociology, Lehman College, CUNY, 1978.

14. The following figures are based on 1977 self-reported data collected by Columbia University Law School Placement Office from the 139 firms which recruit at that law school. This includes all thirty-two large New York City firms with more than ninety-five members each.

15. Epstein, *Women in Law*, p. 179. The author surveyed all thirty-two firms in 1979 and 1980 to obtain the most current data on women partners. The New York firms of Kaye, Scholer, Fienman, Hays and Handler; and Stroock, Stroock and Lavan each have three female partners. Two large firms (over a hundred attorneys) outside New York City, one in San Francisco and one in Chicago, each have four female partners as of January 1979. See Ostroff, "Make Way for Women," p. 1, 10.

16. Joseph Goulden, *The Superlawyers: The Small and Powerful World of the Great Washington Law Firms* (New York: Weybright and Talley, 1972).

17. This firm held its weekly luncheons at the Metropolitan Club which excluded women. When a woman associate complained, the partners replied that no alternative luncheon site could be found to accommodate so many people. The firm's practices became the subject of a news item entitled, "Oink, oink." (*Washingtonian*, September 1973).
One male associate reveals how complicated the "woman question" is by his comment: "It's an open question whether the partnerships are a bunch of Chauvinist pigs, but at least many of the women think so. Others think that they simply treated women as lousy as they treated everybody else." Cited in Green, *The Other Government*, p. 34.

18. Fulbright and Jaworski, the nation's third largest law firm, recently negotiated a settlement in a sex discrimination suit. See Steven Brill, "Fulbright and Jaworski Settles Sex Discrimination Suit," *The American Lawyer*, September 1979, pp. 3, 4, and text accompanying footnotes 20–23. Senior partner Leon Jaworski was a former American Bar Association President and Watergate Special Prosecutor.

19. See Epstein, "The Partnership Push," *Savvy*, March, 1980.

20. The change in women's specialization is also affected by the change in the role of litigation in the Wall Street practice. More and more large firms which formerly shunned litigation because it was thought to be

unprofitable or slightly undignified, began to build strong litigation departments. See Tom Goldstein, "A Dramatic Rise in Lawsuits and Costs Concerns Bar," *New York Times*, May 18, 1977, p. 1 B9. In fact, litigation departments are the fastest growing sections of many of these firms. Lawyers and legal scholars ascribe this unprecedented rise in litigation to two factors—an increased litigiousness among citizens and increased government involvement in regulating corporate and individual behavior.

21. Cited by Goldstein, p. 1. Goldstein names Cravath as an example of a New York firm with a three-to-one ratio and Morgan, Lewis and Bockius in Philadelphia and Sidley and Austin in Chicago as examples of firms with a ratio of one-to-one.

22. All 1977 figures are based on 1977 self-report data collected by the Columbia University Law School Placement Office. See note 14 *supra*. See also Epstein, "Partnership Push," p. 30; Lindsay Van Gelder, "Harriet Rabb, Scourge of Corporate Male Chauvinism," *New York Magazine*, June 26, 1978, pp. 38–40.

23. It is generally assumed that no woman is likely to bring in business. Some places are more anxious for business than others. One senior partner in a large midtown firm told the author that all that really mattered in his firm in considering a partner was how much money that potential partner would feed into the till. It was simply a financial calculation, he said.

24. See notes 6 and 7 *supra*.

25. 42 U.S.C. §1981 (1964).

26. See Van Gelder, "Scourge of Male Chauvinism."

27. Cited in Arnold Lubash, "Top Law Firm Bans Sex Discrimination," *New York Times*, May 8, 1977.

28. Ibid.

29. Ibid.

30. See Brill, "Fulbright and Jaworski," pp. 3, 4. Of Houston's "Big Three" firms, Fulbright and Jaworski, Baker and Botts, and Vincon and Elkins, only Fulbright and Jaworski currently has a woman partner.

31. See "Atlanta Law Firm Accused of Sex Discrimination," *New York Times*, March 26, 1980, sec. 2, p. B7. Senior partners of the firm are former Attorney General Griffin B. Bell and Charles H. Kirbo.

32. Based on interview data.

33. In their complaint, women students alleged that the firms only granted perfunctory interviews to women and that recruitment committee members said such things in interviews as "there are a couple of senior partners who won't stand for it (hiring women)." Cited in *Chicago Tribune*, June 12, 1972; *Chicago Daily News*, July 11, 1972.

34. Brill, "Fulbright and Jaworski," pp. 3–4.

35. Auerbach, *Unequal Justice*.

36. However, Jewish male attorneys are today also gravitating to the squash courts and gymnasiums. At one firm, a woman partner revealed that while there is a firm softball team the men who play on it are casual

(which is to say, not very good) players. Therefore, women players are welcome and do not pose a threat to the diminishment of fun in a "serious" sport situation.

37. Mary Murphree, "Work Rationalization and Secretarial Stress: The Case of Wall Street Legal Secretaries" (unpublished Ph.D. dissertation, Department of Sociology, Columbia University, 1980), p. 6.

38. Certainly the Martindale-Hubbell legal directory which does not include summer associates in its listing—reports far fewer (50 percent fewer) women than the self-report data on the number of women given by the firms on their resumes to Columbia Law School. This large discrepancy may be due partially to lag in updating the directory. Based on an analysis of data in *Martindale-Hubbell Law Directory*, vol. 4, Missouri-New York (Summit, N.J., 1977).

Suggested Readings for Part V

Bette Bardeen, "The Legal Profession: A New Target for Title VII?" 55 Cal. St. B. J. 360 (1980).

Janette Barnes, "Women and Entrance into the Legal Profession," 23 J. Legal Ed. 276 (1971).

Beverly B. Cook, "Women Judges: The End of Tokenism," in *Women in the Courts,* ed. Winifred L. Hepperle and Laura Crites (Williamsburg Va.: National Center for State Court, 1978).

Cynthia F. Epstein, *Women in Law* (New York: Basic Books, 1981).

Donna Fossum, "Women Law Professors," 1980 ABF Res. J. 903 (1980).

James F. Gilsinan and Lynn Obernyer, "Women Attorneys and the Judiciary," 52 Denver L. J. 881 (1975).

Ruth Bader Ginsburg, "Treatment of Women by the Law: Awakening Consciousness in the Law Schools," 5 Val. U. L. Rev. 480 (1971).

Barbara Harris, *Beyond the Sphere: Women and the Professions in American History* (Westport, Conn.: Greenwood Press, 1978).

Rosabeth Moss Kanter, "Reflections on Women and the Legal Profession: A Sociological Perspective," 1 Harv. Women's L.J. 1 (1978).

Joan D. Klein, "Women Judges Join Together," 19 Judges J. 4 (1980).

Susan Ness and Frederica Wechsler, "Women Judges—Why So Few?" 73 Graduate Women 10 (Nov/Dec 1979).

Rose Pearson and Albie Sachs, "Barristers and Gentlemen: A Critical Look at Sexism in the Legal Profession," 43 Mod. L. Rev. 400 (1980).

Margaret Poloma and T. Neal Garland, "The Married Professional Woman: A Study in the Tolerance of Domestication," 33 J. Marr. Fam. 531 (1971).

Albie Sachs and Joan Hoff Wilson, *Sexism and the Law* (New York: Free Press, 1978), especially chapter 4, "Britain: Barristers and Gentlemen," and chapter 5, "United States: Portia's Plight."

Helene E. Schwartz, *Lawyering* (New York: Farrar, Strauss & Giroux, 1976).

D. Kelly Weisberg, "Women in Law School Teaching: Problems and Progress," 30 J. Legal Ed. 226 (1979).

Contributors

GRACE GANZ BLUMBERG is Professor of Law at the University of California, Los Angeles, School of Law. She has written articles on social security, tax policy, employment discrimination and cohabitation without marriage. She is currently preparing a casebook and several articles on the subject of marital property.

SUSAN L. BRANDT earned her law degree from the University of California at Davis. She is presently in private practice in Glen Ellen, California.

CYNTHIA FUCHS EPSTEIN is Professor of Sociology at Queens College and the Graduate Center of the City University of New York. She is author of *Woman's Place: Options and Limits in Professional Careers* (Berkeley, Calif.: University of California Press, 1970); *The Other Half: Roads to Women's Equality* (Englewood Cliffs, N.J.: Prentice-Hall, 1971) (coedited with William J. Goode); *Access to Power: Cross National Studies of Women and Elites* (Winchester, Mass.: Allen & Unwin, 1981) (coedited with Rose Laub Coser); and *Women in Law* (New York: Basic Books, 1981), as well as numerous articles on women in government, business and the professions.

NANCY S. ERICKSON is Professor of Law at the Ohio State University College of Law. The author of several articles in legal journals on the subject of sex-based discrimination, she is also founder of the Society for the Study of Women in Legal History. She is currently preparing a book on the subject of *Muller* v. *Oregon* and an article on paternalism in laws affecting women.

MICHAEL S. HINDUS is a lawyer and legal historian. He is currently an attorney in San Francisco and also teaches American legal history at Stanford University Law School. Among his books are *Prison and Plantation: Crime, Justice, and Authority in Massachusetts and South Carolina, 1767–1878,* (Chapel Hill, N.C.: University of North Carolina Press, 1980), and *The Files of the Massachusetts Superior Court, 1859–1959: An Analysis and a Plan For Action* (Boston: G. K. Hall, 1980).

RUTH KITTEL has taught history at the University of California, the University of Washington, and Mills College. She is currently employed in the Systemwide Administration of the University of California and is the author of "Women under the Law in Medieval England: 1066–1485" in B. Kanner, ed., *The Women of England: From Anglo-Saxon Times to the Present*

(Hamden, Conn.: Shoe String Press, 1979).

PATIENCE MILROD recently earned her law degree from the University of California at Davis. At present, she is employed by Fresno County Legal Services, Fresno, California.

THEODORE JOHN RIVERS is a historian and the author of numerous publications on such topics as the legal status of freewomen in the Lex Alamannorum and seigneurial obligations in different legal codes. At present he is working on two books: a translation and commentary on the Lex Salica and Lex Ribuaria, as well as a volume on legal philosophy.

MORTIMER D. SCHWARTZ is Professor of Law and Associate Dean for Law Library, University of California, Davis, School of Law. He has authored articles on children's rights in the United States, and rights of privacy, edited a book on state laws on the employment of women, and published a bibliography, *Environmental Law* (Detroit, Mich.: Gale Research Company, 1977). He is currently engaged in research on Sir Francis Bacon.

ELEANOR SEARLE is Professor of History at the California Institute of Technology. Her books include: *Lordship and Community: Battle Abbey and its Banlieu, 1066–1538* (Toronto: Pontifical Institute of Medieval Studies, 1974), and an edition of a twelfth-century legal casebook, *The Chronicle of Battle Abbey* (New York: Oxford University Press, 1980). She is the author of several articles on medieval social and economic history. Her current research focuses on the operation of customary law in the eleventh and twelfth centuries, particularly as an instrument for the redistribution of wealth.

LINDA E. SPETH is currently Director, Utah State University Press. Her thesis "Women's Sphere: The Role and Status of White Women in Eighteenth Century Virginia, 1735–1775" has been accepted for publication by the Institute for Research in History and Haworth Press.

SUSAN TREGGIARI is Professor of Classical Studies at the University of Ottawa and President of the Association of Ancient Historians. Her publications include *Roman Freedmen During the Late Republic* (Oxford: Clarendon Press, 1969), and articles on the lower classes and slaves, particularly their work and family life. She is currently engaged in research on Roman marriage in the classical period of Roman society (from about 200 B.C. to A.D. 235).

D. KELLY WEISBERG is Assistant Professor, Hastings College of the Law, University of California, San Francisco. A lawyer and sociologist, she is the author of articles on women and the law and family law. Her current research focuses on sexual child abuse.

LYNNE E. WITHEY is an administrator with the University of California

Systemwide Administration and is a lecturer in women's history at the University of California at Berkeley. Her recently published book, *Dearest Friend: A Life of Abigail Adams* (New York: Free Press, 1981), was awarded Best Book in the Humanities by the Scholarly and Professional Book Division of the Association of American Publishers.

INDEX

Abduction of Anglo-Saxon
widows, 36
Abjuration of realm in medieval
England, 109
Abolitionist movement and feminism, 247
Abortion, cases on, 177
Adequacy vs. equity in social security, 190–191
Adultery
and divorce in Massachusetts
colonial, 122
nineteenth-century, 137
South Carolina's view of,
nineteenth-century, 142–144
Aethelberht (Anglo-Saxon king),
code of, 36, 37–38
Alimony without divorce,
nineteenth-century, 140–142
adultery, exclusion of, 142–143
for cruelty and desertion, 142
property, importance of, 144–146
as woman's remedy, 143
Anglo-Saxon England, widows in.
See Widows: Anglo-Saxon England
Annulment
English, 119
South Carolina's view,
nineteenth-century, 143
Anthony, Susan B., 81, 82
Anti-Semitism in legal profession,
252
Anti-slavery movement and feminism, 247
Appeal, medieval meaning of, 111
Associates in corporate law firms,
289
women as, 286
Attorneys, women. *See* Legal edu-

cation and profession, women
in
Auerbach, Jerome, 252, 302

Bakery workers, maximum hours
for, 156
Barkeloo, Lemma, 244
Barker, Christine Ross, 173
Bastardy in medieval England, 56–
57
Battle, trial by, alternatives to, 101–
102
Beard, Mary, 1
Bernard, Jessie, 250
Bigamy in colonial Massachusetts,
124–125
Bigelow, Chief Justice, 139, 149
Blacks, discrimination against, in
legal profession, 252–253
Blackstone, Sir William, quoted, 70
Blackwell, Alice Stone, 169, 171,
172, 173–174
Blinding/castration for medieval
rapists, 103
Bracton, 103, 106
Bradley, Justice, quoted, 233, 238–
239
Bradwell, Bessie, 242
Bradwell, Myra, 84, 232
Bradwell v. Illinois, 232, 233, 234,
235, 238–239, 245, 254, 255
Brandeis, Louis D., 158–160
"Brandeis brief," 159–160, 163
Brewer, Justice, opinion by, 163
press response, 164–168
suffragist, 169, 171–172, 174
Business-getters in law firms, 290

California, first woman attorney
in. *See* Foltz, Clara Shortridge

313